PRODUCED AND ABANDONED.

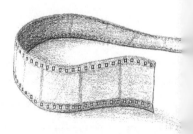

PRODUCED AND ABANDONED

THE BEST FILMS YOU'VE NEVER SEEN

reviews by members of
The National Society of Film Critics

Edited by MICHAEL SRAGOW

Mercury House, Incorporated
San Francisco

Published in the United States by
Mercury House
San Francisco

Distributed to the trade by
Consortium Book Sales & Distribution, Inc.
St. Paul, Minnesota

Library of Congress Cataloging-in-Publication Data

Produced and abandoned: the best films you've never seen / the National
   Society of Film Critics ; edited by Michael Sragow.
      p. cm.
   ISBN 0–916515–84–2 : $9.95
   1. Motion pictures — Reviews. I. Sragow, Michael. II. National Society
of Film Critics.
PN1995.P766   1990
791.43'75 — dc20
                                                                90–5853
                                                                   CIP

CONTENTS

ACKNOWLEDGMENTS

Compiling, pruning, and arranging this collection required the support of the entire National Society of Film Critics, including former chairman Dave Kehr and executive director Elisabeth Weis. The group's current chairman is Peter Rainer, who first proposed the idea for the anthology ten years ago. Special thanks go to Jay Carr for coming up with the first half of the title. Kevin Casey and Susan Braun of the *San Francisco Examiner* provided selfless assistance in all practical matters, while Josh Kornbluth proved as skillful at the dialogue of brainstorming as he is at comic monologues. Peter Moore used his encyclopedic knowledge to check the video references. Under a flurry of complicated deadlines, production coordinator Zipporah Collins performed precision editing and back-reading. And Glenda Hobbs, arts editor of the *Examiner* when this project got off the ground, supported my work on the book and helped shape and refine the material after she left the newspaper. In this, as in all other things, she has proven to me that Blake was right—exuberance *is* beauty, and vice versa.

INTRODUCTION

Especially in the last two decades, many of the most exciting English-speaking filmmakers have given birth to movies that were then abandoned by the studios and the mass audience. What made these films hard to market and thus hard for moviegoers to find and adopt is precisely what makes them special: twists in the storylines, unexpected shadings in the characters, iconoclastic attitudes, and a degree of artistry that can't be communicated in broad-stroke advertising campaigns.

The National Society of Film Critics is a group of forty-two writers from major general-interest publications. From its founding in 1966 through 1971, the membership wrote mostly for New York–based national magazines. From 1972 on, the group has grown to include writers for daily, weekly, monthly, and quarterly publications across the country, from mainstream newspapers like the *Los Angeles Times* and *Washington Post* to alternative weeklies like the *Chicago Reader* and the *Boston Phoenix*.

The group's purpose is to encourage the best in movie art, primarily through annual awards. In the '60s, it tended to salute those foreign films that were shaking up world cinema: the first four best film winners were Michelangelo Antonioni's *Blow-Up*, Ingmar Bergman's *Persona*, Bergman's *Shame*, and Costa-Gavras's *Z*. The first American best film winner was Robert Altman's *M*A*S*H*, in 1970; the next was Altman's *Nashville*, in 1975. But from '75 on, as the wave of landmark foreign offerings ebbed, more American films surged into the winner's circle, ranging from Alan J. Pakula's widely popular *All the President's Men* (1976) to Gus Van Sant's art-house hit *Drugstore Cowboy* (1989). In the last dozen years, a few foreign films, such as Bertrand Blier's *Get Out Your Handkerchiefs*, Paolo and Vittorio Taviani's *The Night of the Shooting Stars*, and Akira Kurosawa's *Ran*, have taken the best film award. But more often, the prize has gone to American movies like Jonathan Demme's *Melvin and Howard* and John Huston's *The Dead*.

These recent American choices are every bit as inspired and audacious as the American movies that won fifteen or twenty years ago. But unlike M★A★S★H or Nashville, Melvin and Howard and The Dead, in their initial releases, drew, at best, only loyal art-house devotees. The National Society of Film Critics hopes to rouse interest in such neglected movies with this eclectic collection of reviews written when the films still had a chance to snag the theatrical audiences they deserve.

Before the '80s, when films like The Late Show (1977) disappeared from movie screens without making a dent in the culture or at the box office, these abandoned films languished until college film societies or intrepid repertory programmers "rediscovered" them, or until cults grew up around their showings on late-night television. Now, in the age of the VCR, public fascination with forgotten films has ballooned. Movies that were flops or also-rans, or that fell out of circulation, have the potential to reach immense new audiences via cable and cassette. This unprecedented form of movie afterlife has forced the few remaining revival theaters to be more enterprising. Even major studios and independent distribution companies have grown more conscious of the viewership for critically acclaimed movies of earlier eras. Witness the successful reissues, in 1988 and '89 alone, of The Manchurian Candidate, Murmur of the Heart, and The Entertainer. (The latter two had reputations that outstripped their box-office performance when they were originally shown in American movie theaters.)

What venturesome audiences are finding, of course, is that many commercial failures are funnier, sexier, and more dashing—as well as more penetrating and provocative—than their money-making counterparts. That's partly because they often showcase blockbuster directors working at a feverish artistic pitch. Roger Spottiswoode had his first big sensation with the affable Turner & Hooch. But he demonstrated a subtler comic touch in the Robin Williams–Kurt Russell high-school football elegy, The Best of Times, and more robust character and action in his superb political movie, Under Fire.

Often the selections in this volume celebrate Hollywood's "A-list" directors in their most personal moods. Brian De Palma, following the success of Carrie, took the parapsychological horror thriller to the level of a Jacobean revenge drama in The Fury. Following the exhilaratingly uninhibited Dressed to Kill, he came up with Blow Out, a critique of his own brand of pop thrillers—and a prescient warning against the media manipulation that dominated America in the '80s. After the calculated smash success of The Untouchables, he returned to a project he had wanted to make since the '60s — *Casualties of War,* his controversial and wrenching depiction of a Vietnam atrocity.

The men and women who made the movies in this book dared to break their own profitable strides. When Robert Towne, the legendary screenwriter behind *The Last Detail, Shampoo,* and *Chinatown,* turned to writing–directing with *Personal Best,* his predominantly visual movie poetry surprised (and in some cases dumbfounded) fans of his highly verbal, slangy storytelling. With *Shoot the Moon,* Alan Parker veered, temporarily, from his career of big-screen bombast (*Midnight Express, Fame*) to frank, intimate drama, crafting an achingly empathic movie from a script by Bo Goldman (who also wrote *Melvin and Howard*).

What unites these and the other films honored in this book is their unpredictability, in the way they work as both art and entertainment and in the way they cut through preconceptions and established formulas.

These "best films you've never seen" were picked by individuals, not by committee. The members of the National Society of Film Critics were asked to submit strongly argued reviews of movies they had championed, even if that meant going out on a limb. Stephen Schiff didn't offer just *The Chant of Jimmie Blacksmith* and *Diner* (which is

Sean Penn gives a bravura performance and Michael J. Fox an intense, impressively contained one as the ethical opposites in *Casualties of War.* (Photo copyright © Columbia Pictures. All rights reserved. Courtesy RCA/Columbia Pictures Home Video.)

included as a critical success story—a movie that suffered studio indifference but gained an ever-growing audience partly because of unanimous acclaim). He also goes to bat for David Cronenberg's vehemently grotesque *The Brood*. Often, the writers contradict other critics' points of view. David Denby states his preference for *River's Edge* over *Blue Velvet* (which won the NSFC best film award for 1986). Richard Schickel esteems *Smash Palace* more than *Shoot the Moon*.

These critical exclamations are part of what is fun and vitalizing about the book. *Produced and Abandoned* recreates the dialogue that going to the movies used to provoke before sequels and retreads conquered America.

The release dates for the films included in this volume range from 1970 to 1990. That's partly because these years reflect the careers of the National Society's current members. But it's also because Hollywood went through whirligig changes in those years, changes that made the production and distribution of offbeat movies problematic.

When many of the best new movies clicked with youthful and "countercultural" audiences, their success didn't just baffle studio executives—it exasperated them. Old-fashioned bucks and ballyhoo couldn't sell *Paint Your Wagon* or *Half a Sixpence*, while movies like *Midnight Cowboy* and *They Shoot Horses, Don't They?* seemed to sell themselves. One 20th Century Fox employee commented, "The day it opens, everyone knows that *Tora! Tora! Tora!* is a dog; on the opening day for *M*A*S*H*, the lines are around the block."

Starting with the rise of the with-it collegiate audience that supported *Blow-Up* in 1966 and *Bonnie and Clyde* and *The Graduate* in 1967, producers and studios became unusually open to fresh approaches and subject matter. Directors like Sam Peckinpah (*The Wild Bunch*, 1969), Arthur Penn (who followed *Bonnie and Clyde* with *Alice's Restaurant*, 1969), and Robert Altman (*M*A*S*H*, 1970) succeeded in bringing to the screen new images of America and new modes of image-creating. These filmmakers challenged the cultural status quo as well as traditional notions of how movies should look and move. The crowds of what was often referred to as "the film generation" came to movies such as these to argue and commune. High school and college students and cognoscenti everywhere felt they had to see the latest films, if only to learn what the commotion was all about.

But even in the late '60s and early '70s—artistic boom years for American movies—independent-minded filmmakers were often at the mercy of national moods and marketing "experts." Peckinpah's *The*

In *Personal Best,* the attraction between Olympic pentathletes Mariel Hemingway (left) and Patrice Donnelly arouses tumultuous emotions in each of them.
(Photo © 1982 The Geffen Film Company. All rights reserved.)

Ballad of Cable Hogue was dumped into theaters without fanfare, though
The Wild Bunch, released just one year before, had made money and
churned up national debate. At the same time, young aficionados who
had interpreted *The Wild Bunch* as a statement about the violence of
Vietnam were put off by the sentiments of *Cable Hogue,* which reaches
an emotional pinnacle when the hero raises an American flag over his
waterhole.

The era from the late '60s to the mid '70s may have been overexcit-
able and overpoliticized, but to many of us who were writing about
films then, or coming of age as moviegoers, it remains the time when
movies seemed to matter most. One reason for its demise was the
country's move toward quietism and conservatism, but there were other
reasons, too. As bankers, tycoons, lawyers, and agents increased their
control over Hollywood, they geared the industry toward big-star
packages and extravaganzas — anything that looked likely to become a
mega-hit. Even in the early '70s, when hot directors at their peaks made

movies that were smaller and quirkier than their hits had been, like Altman's *The Long Goodbye* and Francis Ford Coppola's *The Conversation,* these films didn't stand a chance.

As the country slogged through the '80s, Hollywood forgot how to promote any movie that wasn't an exploitation flick, a special effects jamboree, or a roller-coaster ride. Even some highly publicized movies that seemed destined to be blockbusters, like Philip Kaufman's *The Right Stuff,* never took off. Their distinctive and courageous qualities often worked against them. Audiences couldn't tell from the ad campaign that *The Right Stuff* punches home a freewheeling and satirical treatment of the astronauts. Instead, the movie's publicity was tied to John Glenn's presidential candidacy.

English-language movies from other lands (Australia, Canada, Ireland, and England) also suffered from the rigidity of the American marketplace. Unless these films boasted international stars, they were usually buried by Hollywood's commercial juggernaut. The NSFC has sometimes tried to right the balance; in its 1987 ballot, for example, John Boorman's *Hope and Glory* won best director, screenplay, and cinematography awards.

The hope behind this book is to resurrect vital, often trailblazing, neglected movies. Almost all the films reviewed here are available on videocassette; the few exceptions are occasionally televised or screened in revival houses. This volume will fulfill its purpose if it directs readers to some of the best movies on the video shelf. Perhaps it will do more — stimulate readers to support local revival theaters and to seek out good movies *before* they can be labeled "abandoned" — before they become orphans.

—Michael Sragow
San Francisco
1990

ONLY IN AMERICA

I t's fitting that two movies in this collection are based on writing by Tom Wolfe — Lamont Johnson's *The Last American Hero* and Philip Kaufman's *The Right Stuff* (see "Beyond Media Politics"). When Wolfe burst into print in the '60s, he helped form a popular concept of America as a gigantic, messy, open smorgasbord. He chronicled all the new "styles of life" and "statuspheres" that had emerged in America's post–World War II affluence. He crisscrossed the continent and seemed to cover every nutball fad before it bounced from West to East or vice versa. He could see colossal free-form Las Vegas road signs not as visual pollution but as funky signs of life. He was never put off by fast-moving mass fashions. Unlike the heroes of *Easy Rider*, who "went looking for America. And couldn't find it anywhere," Wolfe went looking for America and found it everywhere.

So did the filmmakers who blew away Hollywood's '50s blandness. In the '60s, '70s, and '80s they brought a heterogeneous America to the screen. They found American dreams in the stock-car racing subculture of Junior Johnson in *The Last American Hero* and the hot-rod-racing world of Shirley Muldowney in *Heart Like a Wheel*, in debt-ridden

Melvin Dummar's bond with Howard Hughes (*Melvin and Howard*), in San Quentin convict Rick Cluchey's formation of a prison theater company (*Weeds*), and in the role-playing shenanigans of CB enthusiasts (*Citizens Band,* a.k.a. *Handle with Care*). They found American nightmares in the dead-end pursuit of small-time boxing (*Fat City*), in the hedonistic self-destruction of country music stardom (*Payday*), and in the '30s one-two punch of the Dust Bowl and the Depression (*Bound for Glory*).

They also found the comic potential in L.A.'s all-night drugstores and boxlike suburbs (*All Night Long*), and in unexplored pockets of quirkiness from America's past—like the "Gower Gulch" Hollywood studios that cranked out quickie westerns in the '30s (*Hearts of the West*), or the nocturnal hangouts of '50s Baltimore "diner guys" (*Diner*). This last film is included partly as an emblem of hope for neglected films. *Diner* never got the movie audience it warranted; despite unanimous critical acclaim, it received only one Oscar nomination. But its cult following was strong and vocal. Positive word-of-mouth kept growing through television showings and cassette rentals, until *Diner* entered the mass audience's consciousness and became a break-out kind of American art movie—a cult-buster.

ALL NIGHT LONG

Michael Sragow

Directed by Jean-Claude Tramont. Written by W. D. Richter. Starring Gene Hackman, Barbra Streisand, Diane Ladd, Dennis Quaid, and Kevin Dobson. **MCA Home Video.**

All Night Long is that rarity this season: a consistently witty and intelligent entertainment. Even rarer, it's a middle-class comedy blessed with grace, wisdom and integrity. Set in *echt* suburban Los Angeles, the movie's plot sounds like an episode of *Soap*: George Dupler (Gene Hackman), an executive for a drugstore chain with the constipated name Ultra-Save, is demoted to night manager for tossing a chair

Jean-Claude Tramont (kneeling left) directs Gene Hackman (sitting, right) in *All Night Long,* the offbeat comedy that brought Hackman out of a brief retirement and gave him a chance to show off the comedic gifts he first demonstrated in *Young Frankenstein.* (Photo courtesy of Jean-Claude Tramont.)

through his boss' window. Eventually, he leaves this job to become an inventor; around the same time, he leaves his wife to become the lover of his fourth cousin by marriage, Cheryl Gibbons (Barbra Streisand), who's not only married but has also been the lover of Dupler's only child, a lout named Freddie (Dennis Quaid).

What director Jean-Claude Tramont and writer W. D. Richter have fashioned from sitcom settings and demotic jokes is akin to those fantastic sculptures wrought out of twisted coat hangers or industrial wreckage. The movie is actually an ode to American nonconformity: imagine *A Thousand Clowns,* without the phony rhetoric and schmaltz, married to an offbeat romance like *Made for Each Other. All Night Long* has a visual luster and tenderness all its own, partly because of the two stars' low-key sexiness. Coming off years of desultory work, Streisand and Hackman soar like phoenixes.

If Hackman weren't a star already, this performance would make him one. He uses all his proven gifts of sensitivity, humor and simmering violence, as well as a romantic dreaminess he's never had the opportunity to demonstrate. As George Dupler, Hackman turns a man in midlife crisis into a conquering hero. Keeping his balance as an actor while Dupler's existence turns topsy-turvy, he makes this schmo *manful*.

Hackman has the uncanny knack of letting his entire body and soul go slack; in his early scenes, wearily resigned to life with his nervous, status-conscious wife (Diane Ladd) and animalistic son, he's a vivid illustration of spiritual myopia. He makes bewildered gestures with his fingers that rival Chaplin's (his muffled giggles resemble Chaplin's, too). But when Dupler's anger bubbles, he's never just a clown dangling at the end of his rope. Popping pills in the drugstore and playing with a gun, he keeps his dangerous edge. When he falls in love, his posture straightens out and his face brightens. It's as if Dupler were coming into focus.

Cheryl is always on the lookout for a fling, but as embodied by Streisand, she's more than Dupler's floozy. She's his muse, the one who hurtles him past the plastic roadblocks of suburban mores and back to his true feelings. The delicacy Streisand brings to the role may momentarily confound fans who've come to love her brass-band stridency, yet it's her best performance since 1973's *The Way We Were*. Even at the start, when Cheryl appears to be an overpampered seductress, Streisand imbues her with a breathy, soft avidity that recalls Marilyn Monroe.

Cheryl Gibbons is one of the most appealing female characters to reach the screen in recent years: impetuous but not loony, aggressive without being a ball-buster. When she runs away from her baby-macho fireman-husband (Kevin Dobson), she seems nakedly vulnerable. Taking up with Dupler, she doesn't declare a feminist manifesto. She simply realizes that she must change her life.

W. D. Richter, who also wrote *Slither* and *Invasion of the Body Snatchers,* has a keen ear for the way Americans talk when they don't think they're being overheard. He's a master at malapropisms, Freudian slip-ups and killer clichés. Dennis Quaid says that a cousin died of a "brain hemorrhoid"; as Cheryl pressures Dupler to join her on the "H_2O bed," he says, "I don't mind pleasure . . . pressure"; summoning up all her sensitivity to cheer on Dupler when he's most depressed, Cheryl says, "There was a man who cried because he had no shoes, until he met a man who had no feet." Richter makes this tired language click with comic effect. But the laughs aren't superficial: gradually, Cheryl's most shopworn expressions take on meaning.

This quality of feeling is a tribute to director Tramont's skill at suffusing the most slapstick situations with emotional reality and punch. He's an impeccable craftsman: much of this film is like a lucky collaboration between Paul Mazursky and Max Ophuls. Tramont's camera movements and choreography enhance the characterizations, and he always gives you something to savor: an eccentric shopper mumbling about teeth being his main asset, or the rows of lookalike Koreans painting lookalike pictures of Mount St. Helens outside Dupler's loft.

In its own modest fashion, *All Night Long* calls for national renewal, not by conquering new frontiers with the old cowboy mythology but by tapping our native art and know-how. By the end of the film, Dupler has made his first invention: a "positive reflection" mirror that lets people see themselves as others see them (left is right and right is left) — a refreshingly concrete metaphor for the character's progress. Even the color scheme reinforces Tramont's emphasis on new frontiers of art and ingenuity. Green, the hue of spring and rejuvenation, is here synthetic and sickly, dominating the whole Ultra-Save corporation. As Tramont sees it, the color of life is magenta. Cheryl almost always dresses in shades of lavender. When she and George first make love, plum-colored neon sneaks through the Venetian blinds. At moments like that, the film becomes a rhapsody in purple.

Peter Jamison has designed an L.A. that's almost an annex of the Midwest; I don't recall seeing a palm tree in the entire movie. And cinematographer Philip Lathrop has shot the daytime scenes in such sharp light that the boxlike houses stick out like pop-up toys. Such settings as the dry concrete waterway in the Gibbons' back yard look unreal because we're not used to observing them quite so dead-on. The pronounced forms conspire with the color to create a domestic fairy-tale atmosphere.

As in an operatic fairy tale, the music provides emotional cues: the soundtrack dreck at the beginning could be drugstore Muzak. Then, when Cheryl enters the picture, gentler or jazzier tunes take over, including "La Violetera" (purple again) from Chaplin's *City Lights*.

This movie keeps tiny surprises pinging in the brain; it is so fluid and subtle that audiences may not realize till the end that it has put into question traditional work ethics and family life. *All Night Long* is a fairy tale for tough-minded grown-ups.

Rolling Stone, April 2, 1981

BOUND FOR GLORY

★

Judith Crist

Directed by Hal Ashby. Written by Robert Getchell from
the book by Woody Guthrie. Starring David Carradine,
Melinda Dillon, Ronny Cox, and Randy Quaid. **MGM/
UA Home Video.**

David Carradine, whose brilliant stage career fizzled in the Kung-fu
stereotype, makes a stunning comeback in a remarkable work, *Bound for
Glory,* a two and a half hour film biography of the early manhood of
Woody Guthrie, the great folk singer, composer and author. The film,
obviously a labor of love as well as of fine talents, is not only an
extraordinarily detailed portrait of an artist's coming of age and consciousness-raising but also a deeply moving and accurate portrait of the
Depression years in Texas and in California, that promised land that
proved so cruel for the migrant farm workers. Above all, it is the story of
a decent man deeply involved with his fellows, a caring man who could
direct his gifts to the common cause.

Carradine, a lanky, lean abstraction of his father, John, his features
closer to the ruggedness of a young Warren Oates than the easier
handsomeness of his brother Keith, portrays Guthrie at 24 as a loving
but footloose young husband in the Texas dustbowl town of Pampas
where the Depression had, by 1936, depleted the population and the
spirit. Odd jobs as a sign painter and hoedown fiddler barely feed his
wife and two small daughters, and finally he takes to the road for
California, with a promise to send for his family. By foot, by thumb and
by rail he meets the hoboes and migrants who are heading west, only to
be stopped at the California border. It is the grapes-of-wrath world of
Okies, Georgians, Texans, midwesterners who dream of lush lands,
lured by fruit-company handbills that bring thousands and employ
handfuls at 4-cents-a-bushel wages. He finds romance as well as a
social conscience along the way. Befriended by a radio entertainer who
comes to the migrant camps to provide music and union propaganda,
he starts his professional career on a local L.A. radio station. He is able
to send for his wife and children, but his deep involvement with the
labor movement, his refusal to knuckle under to sponsors and his

admitted inability to "sit still" break up his home. At the peak of success — a Cocoanut Grove engagement and radio network spot are his for the conforming — he walks off, heading for New York, because "the worst thing that can happen is to cut yourself loose from the folks."

Carradine's performance is sweet and sure, spiced by the willfulness of a dedicated man. Melinda Dillon is deeply touching as the wife who cannot put her survival worries aside; Gail Strickland is beautifully dignified and vulnerable as the wealthy widow aware of an abortive relationship; Ronny Cox, as the entertainer who can separate his meal-ticket and his principles as Guthrie cannot, and Randy Quaid, as a migrant worker slow to enlightenment, stand out in an excellent supporting cast.

Hal Ashby, in a change of pace from his admirable *Harold and Maude, The Last Detail* and *Shampoo,* directs the film with an eye always to the interplay of his hero and the "folks," bringing a legend to throbbing life, with Haskell Wexler's cinematography, muted to shades of times remembered, providing a recall of the social grit and spiritual awakenings of a misted past.

Playgirl, February 1977

DINER

Stephen Schiff

Directed and written by Barry Levinson. Starring Steve Guttenberg, Mickey Rourke, Kevin Bacon, Daniel Stern, Ellen Barkin, and Timothy Daly. **MGM/UA Home Video.**

The movies have savaged our memories of the '50s. Whatever that buttoned-down, black-and-white era really meant has long since dissolved in a quagmire of finny cars, roller-skating waitresses, and leather jackets. Who can still separate the real cruising culture from the quaintly amusing one in *American Graffiti,* or the real greasers from *Grease?* I mean, did anyone in the '50s actually talk like the Fonz? To people under 30, the age of Eisenhower and hula hoops has become a dress-up fantasy; wearing the once-dreaded leathers and DAs, kids imitate not the hooliganism that terrorized suburbia but a kind of innocence — the innocence the sexual revolution demolished. And to people in their 30s and 40s, the '50s have become an impenetrable fog. In fact, I had despaired of ever seeing the decade afresh until I watched a tender, breathtakingly honest new comedy called *Diner* — which turned out to be the most wonderful surprise I've had at the movies in ages.

Diner doesn't have any stars, and the title isn't going to be a big draw (when you hear it, visions of Linda Lavin and Carroll O'Connor — together at last! — dance darkly in your head). I'm afraid the prospect of a movie about six young men on the threshold of manhood in 1959 will put people off; it sounds like a dozen movies you've already seen. I felt put off just hearing about it: Barry Levinson, who wrote and directed it, has never directed before, and his other screenplays and teleplays, mostly co-written with Valerie Curtin, include two of Mel Brooks's groggiest movies (*Silent Movie* and *High Anxiety*) as well as the banal and overbearing . . . *And Justice for All* and the ersatz-Saroyan fantasy *Inside Moves.* Even before releasing it, MGM had decided *Diner* was a loser; the film previewed poorly and was unceremoniously shunted back and forth among the company's divisions until critics got a look at it and began murmuring its praises. It's a terrific movie — a gentle, lyrical, magically funny portrait of the games young men play to keep from growing up, and of the oddly childish society that encourages them. The film is loose, anecdotal, and friendly; for the seductive wiles of plot, it substitutes luminous observations and nimble acting. And, incredibly, there's not a single predictable sequence or cliché in it. *Diner* is a little miracle: who would have guessed that someone could still make a completely original movie about the '50s?

In *American Graffiti, Animal House,* and their offspring, the film-makers were intent on getting the stereotypes right. And because the stereotypes had not yet been redeemed from memory, the movies became voyages of comic discovery. But now that those nostalgic fripperies have gotten in the way, it's bracing to watch how easily Levinson cuts through them. Like Fellini in *I vitelloni,* he's made a warm-hearted memoir of real people in real places, and you sense that he's delivering his recollections whole. Maybe that's how he's come up with the sort of '50s memorabilia no one else has given us. Instead of big shiny Cadillacs that muscle through the streets like Mafia dons, Levinson remembers modest Nashes and Studebakers. He remembers what a TV-and-appliance store looked like back then, with the clunky wooden cabinets and the customers suspicious of color ("The Ponderosa looked faked," one gripes). He recalls Troy Donahue and *The Seventh Seal* and odd, telling bits of slang—when a woman is especially attractive, for instance, the guys say she's "death." Set in Baltimore during the last week of the decade, the movie has a woolly, brown-and-gray texture that somehow encapsulates the '50s: the look of cloth coats and cracking vinyl, the feel of thick, breakable records, the smudgy drabness of a Dutch Masters Cigar billboard. The characters are pals, some Jewish and some Catholic, who've known one another forever. Some are toying with grad school; some are just working on their drinking. And now that they find themselves in that limbo between childhood and adulthood, they're desperate to make it last. Their daily lives are mere prelude to their nightly get-togethers at the Fells Point Diner, where they stay up till dawn, joking and jiving, betting and speculating; nothing they do during the day is as vital as their nocturnal analysis of it. They're an encounter group before there were encounter groups; they're a comedy team; they're a crew of ivory-tower philosophers, classifying and reclassifying their world. Is Mathis as good as Sinatra? Does evolution make sense? And, most important, what are women all about?

That, of course, is the big mystery. *Diner* takes place on the eve of the sexual revolution, and though the movie isn't hard on its characters, we can see they're living in a Dark Age. Women are a foreign country—and *know* it. And the men are at once obsessed with and confounded by them. The boys at the diner march bravely out into the world of femininity like gladiators, and there they are nearly overwhelmed. They don't know what to talk about, they do crazy things, they apply elaborate systems of measurement to their sexual progress, they are charming and ruthless by turns. And the women stare at them in bewilderment, wondering why men have to be so cruel, so secretive, so "sick." Afterward, the boys hightail it back to the diner, puffing and wheezing, to compare scars and recount adventures. Women make them feel like children, but when they're with their buddies, they're great wits, bon vivants, experts. If the smart, self-destructive Fenwick (Kevin Bacon) gets a girl to agree to a second date, that's a battle won. If suave Boogie (Mickey Rourke) can convince Carol Heathrow to go to bed with him, that's D-Day.

The movie takes place the week before the marriage of Eddie (Steve Guttenberg), a football fiend with a chirpy little grin. Having seen

Guttenberg in *The Boys from Brazil* and *Can't Stop the Music,* I thought I could never bear the sight of him again. But in *Diner,* he's wonderful; he's easy-going and scared beneath his earnestness, and you sympathize with him. He and the wisecracking moocher Modell (beautifully played by the young comic Paul Reiser) have a great, ornery relationship; they irritate each other and forgive each other, and you can believe they've been doing it as long as they can remember. Eddie, who knows even less about women than the other guys, is afraid he'll miss out on things when he's married. And even his best friend, Billy (Timothy Daly), a mature, reserved sort working on his MBA, can't quell his fears. To Billy, "The whole thing with girls is painful, and it seems like it keeps getting more painful." But Eddie is determined that he and his wife will not be strangers. That's why he'll marry her only if she passes the football-trivia exam he's devised — and it's a doozy. In one poignant scene, Eddie asks his married pal, Shrevie (Daniel Stern), what conjugal life is like, and Shrevie, who doesn't much want to think about it, explains that now that he and his wife, Beth (Ellen Barkin), aren't always trying to find a place to have sex, Shrevie can't seem to hold a five-minute conversation with her. For a moment, Eddie's eyes take on a scared-bunny look. "But it's good, right?" he says. "Yeah," says Shrevie. "Hey, it's good, it's good."

Daniel Stern, who plays Shrevie, was Cyril in *Breaking Away,* and he's been in *It's My Turn* and *Stardust Memories* and *Honky-Tonk Freeway;* I like him better every time I see him. Tall and goosey and genial, he could be anybody's innocuous pal or little brother. But he also takes risks, and when he lets his face do an angry burn or fold up in anguish, he can shake you. In *Diner,* we can see that Shrevie wants to accommodate his wife, and we like her too. With her broad ethnic nose and snaggly teeth, Ellen Barkin resembles a punched-in Monica Vitti; even though her Beth is unsophisticated, she's lively and smart, and when she tags along with the guys, trying to be cool and catch their references, your heart goes out to her. So it's terribly wrenching when Shrevie lights into Beth because she hasn't filed his records in the right place. "It's just music," Beth says. "It's not that big a deal." "It is to me," roars Shrevie, who knows what's on the flip side of every hit record you can think of. "You never ask me what's on the flip side," he rants, and a moment later he's in his car, singing along to Clarence Henry's "Ain't Got No Home" and letting the words soothe him and flay him, by turns.

Diner has a great soundtrack that ranges from Chuck Berry to Jane Morgan, from Howlin' Wolf to Carl Perkins, from Elvis to Sinatra. But the music is never show-offy or intrusive; it cements the scenes together, and it lifts you into each new vignette. Although Levinson is not yet a resourceful director, he scarcely needs to be: he's given *Diner* the best comic screenplay since *Atlantic City* and the best ensemble acting in recent memory. The two work together. You can see where Levinson has let the actors improvise, encouraging them to do things they wouldn't dare elsewhere. The actors get to add their own jokes, to outdo their own characters in the banter at the diner, and sometimes when the backchat gets going, it's uncannily convincing. The fight between Shrevie and Beth, the football exam, Boogie's encounter with sexy Carol Heathrow in a movie theater, Eddie's wedding, with the Baltimore Colts marching song playing instead of "Here Comes the Bride" — these are destined to become classic scenes, and I don't remember when I've seen so many in a single movie. Even the more conventional sequences feel fresh. Since Kevin Bacon's Fenwick, a good-looking ne'er-do-well with a horrible, mangy laugh, is the product of a rotten family, we know why he pulls apart a Christmas crèche and plants himself in the manger in the midst of the Holy Family. Elsewhere, to demonstrate how brilliant and wasted Fenwick is, Levinson shows him watching the GE College Bowl and gleefully beating the egghead contestants to the right answers. On paper, this sort of thing is awfully schematic, and the treacly symbolism might have thrown the movie off balance. But Bacon's maggoty laugh and his refusal to ingratiate himself give his scenes an intense, scary edge. *Diner* can be sweet and melancholy, but it's never sentimental.

Perhaps the most representative character is Boogie, the cocky young stud who works in a beauty salon by day and goes to law school at night — mostly because law school impresses the girls. Mickey Rourke was the volatile young bomb maker in *Body Heat,* and even though he's smoother and less jumpy here, he still commands the screen. He has a soft voice with a dangerous little burr in it, and mysteriously knowing eyes, and you can see why the other characters think of him as a sort of patriarch: he rescues them, challenges them, and teaches them about women; he has the assured sexuality of a young pimp. But Boogie is bedeviled. Just as he plays larger and more perilous versions of the sexual games his cronies play, so his gambling outstrips their penny-ante football pools. When he loses a big bet, he's in hock up to his ears, and he is hounded throughout the movie by a thug who plays very rough indeed. Watching Boogie, and empathizing with him, one realizes that all the men in this movie are playing games. When they run out of football contests to bet on and flip sides to identify, they turn the life around them into games: they wager on how far Boogie will get with Carol, on whether big Earl can eat everything on the diner menu, including the fried-chicken special. Eddie's wedding becomes a game. Even a car accident can be a game.

Women aren't in on all this, of course, because the games are there to protect the men from them. Playing affirms maleness and friendship, and it hints, too, that we're watching a camaraderie of children. At the heart of *Diner* is the belief that the macho ethos dominated the '50s as it has dominated no era before or since, and that that ethos was intrinsically adolescent. Eisenhower-era brinksmanship and American boosterism — these were boyish games at heart. And in *Diner*, adult men are no more grown-up than their sons: Eddie's father contributes his share of toughies to the football quiz, and the diner is full of middle-aged gamblers escaping from the world of wives and families and home-cooked meals. *Diner* shows us how the male sensibility and the American sensibility stopped growing when they cut themselves off from women; it recognizes the '60s as a convulsive national rite of passage. And Levinson knows just how hard this America run by boys was on women. When Beth tells Boogie that marriage has eroded her sense of self, she explains, "I don't know if I'm pretty," and you ache for what she might have been. In fact, the movie's chilliest, most remote character is Billy's girlfriend, Barbara (Kathryn Dowling), a TV producer who's a prototype of the '70s career woman — and who inhabits a universe far beyond the ken of the boys in the diner.

The future hangs over this movie like a pall. You know that the world the characters fit so comfortably in is about to die, and that they won't like the one that replaces it. They'll stop seeing one another. They'll drink and get fat and get divorced. And when we catch sight of a sign at the wedding that says, "Eddie and Elyse — for the '60s and forever," it rings in our heads like a knell. Levinson doesn't address regret in this movie, but you can feel it in every frame. That's the movie's magic: that these lives can seem wasted and heroic at the same time. There's a strange and lovely interlude, albeit imperfectly developed, in which Boogie and Fenwick are driving in the countryside and catch sight of a young woman on horseback. They stop and talk to her, and we can see that she's wealthier, worldlier, and more refined than anyone they've ever met. As she rides off, Fenwick says, "You ever get the feeling that there's something going on that we don't know about?" It's a splendidly funny line, and it breaks your heart. *Diner* is a beautiful movie. It doesn't just show us how men and women were in the '50s; it shows us why they had to change.

Boston Phoenix, April 20, 1982

FAT CITY

Charles Champlin

Directed by John Huston. Written by Leonard Gardner from his novel. Starring Stacy Keach and Jeff Bridges. **RCA/Columbia Pictures Home Video.**

John Huston's career has had more episodes than *The African Queen.* He has gone from the early triumphs of *The Maltese Falcon* and *The Treasure of the Sierra Madre* to so eccentric and freaked-out a masterwork as *Beat the Devil* to the glorious *Queen* herself, and forward to so admirable if unavailing an enterprise as *Reflections in a Golden Eye* and a piece of competent hackwork like *The Kremlin Letter.*

In recent times it has been only too easy to believe that some of the acting roles, vivid but trivial, and some of the directing assignments were accepted without hope or enthusiasm, just to keep the horses groomed and the foxhounds fed in Ireland. Huston jumped, or fell or was pushed, from *The Last Run* when it became perfectly clear that the power and the artistic say-so lay with the star, George C. Scott, and not with Huston himself. A mournful day, if you happen to have enjoyed *The Maltese Falcon.*

Through it all, and despite the riding to hounds abroad, Huston has remained a prototypically early American director, with the kind of equal affection for pirates and princes that I would have expected to find in Mark Twain as well.

Out of his own early meanderings Huston knows grifters, hustlers, losers, soiled ladies, small towns, side streets, the smells of dust, sweat, fear and failure and the metallic taste of your last thin dime. That information, so to speak, and the acts of charity and valor which survive despite it, gave *The Maltese Falcon* and *The Treasure of the Sierra Madre* a particular richness, showed up a continent away in the Bogart character in *African Queen* and can be traced in the mood and feel of the best of his other works.

The good news for those who have admired Huston's truest work (or for those who couldn't care less but who like engrossing movies) is that in *Fat City* Huston has confronted a piece of material and a milieu perfectly suited to his insights and his talents. The result is his best film in years, and one of the best he has ever done: a lean, compassionate, detailed, raucous, sad, strong look at some losers and survivors on the side streets of small-city Middle America.

Leonard Gardner did the script from his own lean, hard-muscled novel about a pair of boxers in Stockton, one of whom is having a side fight with the bottle but who thinks he can make a comeback in both rings, the other who still hopes, this late in time, that boxing is a way out of having to pick walnuts or top onions for a living.

Stacy Keach is the older fighter, not bad enough to quit, not good enough to go places, caught in the limbo between and surviving on cheap wine, self-fooling lies and farm labor (rolling onto the buses in the predawn darkness, hacking and moaning).

It's a very, very fine and affecting performance. Keach creates a man who is not bright but not dumb, charming in an easy, barroom way, sympathetic even when he rages because the rage is triggered by his unavoidable glimpses of his own defeat.

Jeff Bridges is the kid, and he makes him not the brightest but attractive and nice, not a winner in or out of the ring, but not a total loser either. Losing, Gardner seems to be saying, is a relative thing. Sometimes it's worse than others. Bridges conveys a tenderness, an awareness of the need to be gentle with those who are losing even harder than you are, and a strong if passive will to survive that is an effective complement to Keach's. There is in *Fat City* a third dazzling performance by a New York actress named Susan Tyrrell as a blowsy, whining, self-dramatizing barfly who takes up with Keach after her own man (played with competence and cool dignity by the fighter Curtis Cokes) leaves for a short-term engagement in jail.

Miss Tyrrell, her voice a maudlin rasp, betrayals by all mankind worn like bruises on her pale skin, is extravagantly histrionic, but you feel that the performance is part of the character, rather than a way of impersonating the character. She gives an enormous vitality to the movie.

The characters, of course, move within a milieu — of fringe streets, shacky houses with weed-grown yards, roach-ridden hotels in which the management's instructions are hand-lettered in pencil, the agri-business orchards, the worn saloons and the coffeebars as whitely sanitary as mausoleums.

Huston and his photographer, Conrad Hall, have caught all this (and more) with a kind of undramatizing accuracy which becomes the more impressive by not drawing conspicuous attention to the camerawork. The eloquence lies in letting a particular world reveal itself.

Before he made it to Hollywood as a writer (first screen credit 40 years ago), Huston had himself been a boxer, fighting in tank arenas in middle California. What surprised him, and surprises us as watchers, is the persistence of that special subculture; the clammy-walled dressing rooms crowded under the stands in the small, smoky halls, the fighters riding buses to save money, the bookers and the managers and the rituals of the gym, rhythmical and reassuring, spartan and oddly pure in contrast to the sleazy world outside.

It is all there, not with the melodramatics of *Champion* or the cynicism of *Requiem for a Heavyweight* but with a kind of everyday casualness which tends to put a ceiling on the hopes without really cushioning the despairs by way of consolation.

Huston recruited his supporting cast within the boxing world present and immediately past, and skillfully avoided the self-consciousness which often goes with that kind of casting. Art Aragon, the golden boy now a bail bondsman, is among those most prominently on view.

Candy Clark plays Bridges' girlfriend, a small but accurately observed part which reveals how much life imitates postures from popular art. She is very good.

Kris Kristofferson did the wistful score, which catches exactly the mood of lives whose principal accompaniment is from jukeboxes (which is in no way to put down the quality of Kristofferson's music).

Ray Stark produced, with evident affection.

Fat City (a gambling term for green pastures, or being in clover) is not a big picture. It's a slice of life, looked at closely and sympathetically. Its losers lose, or break even, with a kind of innate dignity, and make only small ripples.

"Chief among its virtues, if it has any at all," Huston wryly said after the showing of *Fat City* at the Cannes Festival, "is its modesty." That's true. What is also true is that although Huston and Leonard Gardner are dealing with somber materials, their film is finally ennobling, partly because there is that will to survive running through all the despairs, and partly because high artistry is always inspiring.

Los Angeles Times, November 12, 1972

HANDLE WITH CARE

Richard Schickel

Directed by Jonathan Demme. Written by Paul Brickman. Starring Paul Le Mat, Bruce McGill, Roberts Blossom, and Candy Clark. **Paramount Home Video.**

Handle with Care is the new title of a movie that had a short, unhappy life in the drive-ins last summer under the name *Citizens Band,* was discovered by a few members of the intellectual film community, successfully played at this year's New York Film Festival, and has now been re-released. For once, the intelligentsia are right about an American genre film; this one is well worth serious consideration.

A "handle" in CB parlance is the name by which a broadcaster identifies himself on the air, and what the movie seems to be saying is that one should use some care in picking it. There is a tendency to act out, first in fantasy, then in reality, the sort of life suggested by one's handle. In effect, a CB rig offers a form of power to the powerless of our society, a way for them to make themselves heard in a world that does not pay them much heed. This is what has become of the Middle Americans who exercised such a powerful, if brief, hold on journalistic and political imaginations back in the Nixon era. They are no longer fomenting a counterrevolution; they are out there on the highways talking crazy to one another.

Handle with Care brings on a bunch of them, including a bigamous truck driver whose two wives discover his double life and join forces to, in effect, punish him with kindness; a horny youth and a seemingly

Paul Le Mat is the hero of director Jonathan Demme's CB comedy, *Handle with Care* (also known as *Citizens Band*); he plays a small-town CB fanatic and do-gooder who cracks down on CB users who violate FCC regulations. (Photo courtesy Paramount Home Video.)

respectable woman who use their rigs for mutually masturbatory conversations; a radio priest and a radio fascist who employ the air waves to peddle their doctrines. In the classic manner of exploitation pictures, the movie moves fast and speaks bluntly. It does not linger long over anyone's sense of anomie or alienation, but the panel-cartoon style is effective. It is enough to be made aware of these empty lives.

This is especially true of the family whose story forms the core of the film. There is an old man (Roberts Blossom), a senile mumbler who springs to youthful life when he is gossiping with truckers; his care-taker son (Paul Le Mat) who sets himself up as a kind of CB vigilante, policing those who abuse CB privileges; an athletic-coach brother (Bruce McGill) who hates both of them and anonymously threatens vengeance on them; a schoolteacher (Candy Clark) who has had it off with both brothers, but who turns out to be the aforementioned dirty talker and is sexually alive only when she's plugged into the Citizens Band.

There is in that tangle of confused emotions the stuff of tragedy, and the film's chief flaw is that it veers suddenly from the grim direction in which it seemed to be heading and brings all the CBers together in a reconciliatory effort to rescue the old man. The sequence is an obvious effort to regain the sympathy of the CB audience, showing them as socially useful citizens, but they—and everyone else—will have long since discerned the movie's true view of their world. The question is whether the rest of the world will care enough about this milieu to become good buddies with a curious and very original movie.

Time, November 7, 1977

HEART LIKE A WHEEL

Jay Carr

Directed by Jonathan Kaplan. Written by Ken Friedman. Starring Bonnie Bedelia, Beau Bridges, Leo Rossi, Hoyt Axton, and Anthony Edwards. **CBS/Fox Home Video.**

Heart Like a Wheel is quite simply one of the best American films about a woman. It's a biography of drag-racer Shirley Muldowney, who won the National Hot Rod Association world championship three times, but it's no simple-minded celebration. Director Jonathan Kaplan and writer Ken Friedman double the film's strength by keeping the lid on the complex tangle of strong feelings that result from Muldowney's single-minded pursuit of supremacy in a macho world. The film's style, wisely, is laconic, but it resonates powerfully beneath its spare B-movie surfaces. It's got an unforced, beguiling blue-collar texture. It's got a clear fix on the trade-offs in Muldowney's life. Best of all, it's got Bonnie Bedelia, who uses body language and facial expressions to convey what words can't—and shouldn't try to—in her world.

The credits roll against a flashback to Muldowney as a child bouncing over a two-lane blacktop in an old Caddy with her father, a country singer named Tex Roque, who's played with disarming gusto and generosity by Hoyt Axton. When she begins to get carsick, he sits her on his lap and lets her take the wheel. That does it. After the car hits a bump, bounces above the road, and keeps thumping along, they're both laughing. In the film she's perpetually trying to recapture that kind of control and feel cradled by a generous man. It doesn't come. She stubbornly perseveres, and begins outperforming men, but, the film makes clear by implication, they'll make her pay for it.

In her teens, she marries Jack Muldowney (Leo Rossi), a sweet but timid mechanic in her home town, Schenectady. She beats his dragstrip rival after he chokes, and when the limo pulls away from the curb of the church after their marriage, she's the one behind the wheel. When at a race she's allowed to sit behind the wheel of a smart hot-rod, Muldowney eyes her anxiously. He's losing her to a car, and doesn't like it, but doesn't know what to do about it. The film doesn't deal in cheap, convenient climaxes. One of its strengths is its ability to convey powerful things taking place over periods of time. Jack Muldowney tries to help Shirley; he's a good mechanic. But their marriage erodes. When he sees he's losing her to a full-time racing career, he smashes her car, she bops him with a flashlight, and the marriage is over.

She takes up with Beau Bridges' impulsive puppy-dog of a philandering driver named Connie Kalitta. There's love between them as well as professional reciprocity. When a security guard grabs her injured wrist, forcing her to the ground in pain, he goes berserk, punching out everybody in sight, and is suspended. He works off his suspension as her crew chief, joining her now adolescent son (affectingly played by Anthony Edwards), but her monogamous values can't tolerate his womanizing. They split, setting the stage for a climactic race between the two.

Bridges' wayward charm is skillfully played against Bedelia's gradual hardening. Her face grows increasingly mask-like, her hair more lacquered-looking. She retreats farther and farther inside herself because she realizes that's the only way she'll get what she wants. Her predicament is captured in a stunning moment following an accident. She staggers in flames from her burning car, and as firemen spray her with foam we see one terrified eye staring out from the goggled helmet encasing her head. It's as if her eye was screaming. With jolting suddenness we realize how trapped she is, by the fire and by a life that necessitates her tunnel vision. At the end, it seems she's being forced by the fragile male egos that surround her to choose between career and them, with a strong likelihood that her son will remain the only man in her life. Talk about being lonely at the top. For all its modesty of gesture, *Heart Like a Wheel* is a knockout.

The Boston Globe, March 9, 1984

HEARTS OF THE WEST

David Ansen

Directed by Howard Zieff. Written by Rob Thompson. Starring Jeff Bridges, Alan Arkin, Andy Griffith, Blythe Danner, and Donald Pleasence. **MGM/UA Home Video.**

"Wounds suffered in tropical climes can all too swiftly become nasty infections," announces the injured young man to the motley Hollywood crew who have rescued him from the desert. "Who talks like that?" wonders the sophisticated script girl, Miss Trout. Lewis Tater, the affable hayseed hero of *Hearts of the West,* talks like that, for his head is clogged with Zane Grey adventure fantasies. More than anything, Lewis wants to be "a writer of Western prose," and he heads for the Wild West from his Iowa home in search of raw material. The time, however, is the early Thirties and the only gunslingers he finds are a pack of scratchy character actors who make a buck tumbling from horses in the shoestring productions of a hack Jewish director named Kessler. From the moment Lewis Tater's romantic dreams collide with raunchy Hollywood reality, *Hearts of the West* had me in its rambling, amiable spell. It's the most *likeable* American movie since *Alice Doesn't Live Here Anymore,* a "good time" comedy with a vivid gallery of cranky, eccentric, thoroughly engrossing characters and a plot as pleasantly wayward as a long, sunny drive down the back roads of the past.

As played by Jeff Bridges, Tater is a disarming, gullible rube, but just eager and energetic enough to someday succeed. There aren't many actors who can portray corn-fed innocence without coyness or cliché, but Bridges sails effortlessly through the part. He's always been easy to underrate because his acting doesn't look like work—he slides into a character, body first, no apparent sweat. Lewis Tater doesn't have the depth he gave Junior Jackson in *The Last American Hero* (his best performance) but he isn't meant to. Tater is conceived nostalgically — he's as much a figure of small-town American mythology as the adventure heroes he longs to emulate. Bridges gives this innocent abroad flesh, blood and irresistible charm.

The best scenes in the film involve the world of movie-making. Here director Howard (*Slither*) Zieff and young writer Rob Thompson seem most at home; when they concoct a running subplot involving two shysters who are chasing Tater down (he's unwittingly absconded with their money) it seems inserted from a routine caper movie. But when we're in the presence of the volatile, overbearing Kessler (Alan Arkin) and his bedraggled crew of bit players, *Hearts of the West* is the sort of movie you want to go on forever. Arkin — explosive, pushy, hilarious — hasn't been this good since *Catch-22,* and in the smaller role as his assistant, Alex Rocco is just as fine. Together they kvetch, harangue and milk their reluctant players into action, while the actors, led by Howard Pike (Andy Griffith), hold out for better terms — a fall from a cliff gets you more than a stand-up death, while a leap from a second-story roof onto a horse — as novice stuntman Tater painfully learns — is worth a whole lot more. Zieff captures the frantic milieu of "quickie" filmmaking — the comradeship, the competition, the extra's envy of the stars who "get to ride up in the Buick where all the money is" — in short, sharp, wonderfully funny scenes. And in Andy Griffith's beautifully underplayed Howard Pike he creates a figure who evokes the bitter vagaries of a Hollywood career. Pike, once a writer himself, takes Tater under his wing, breaks him into acting and gives him dubious financial and literary advice. Eventually he betrays his protégé, and here his motivations are a bit skimpy, but Griffith puts just enough suggestion of latent cruelty into the character to fill in the script's blank spaces.

Hearts of the West could have stayed within the slapstick world of pratfalling stuntmen and irate directors but wisely, and surprisingly, it keeps gently shifting gears — a dash of romance provided by the savvy Blythe Danner as Miss Trout; an eccentric cameo from Donald Pleasence as a rich German émigré producer; the bitter revelation that Lewis's father figure is a heel; and a rousing Art-meets-Life finale. What it lacks in thematic coherence is more than made up for in its profusion of rich, seriocomic vignettes. There are no big, show-stopping scenes here; Zieff doesn't push his farce or force the pathos. It's a movie that creeps up on you, a slow thaw in front of a warm fire.

There are gags that misfire, plot twists too arbitrary, but if anything, its biggest errors are those of omission — there are a half a dozen characters you want more of. *Hearts of the West* leaves you a little hungry, but it's nice for a change. How many movies have you seen lately that you didn't want to end?

The Real Paper, November 21, 1975

THE LAST AMERICAN HERO

★

Bruce Williamson

Directed by Lamont Johnson. Written by William Roberts from an article by Tom Wolfe. Starring Jeff Bridges, Valerie Perrine, Geraldine Fitzgerald, Gary Busey, and Art Lund. **Key Video (division of CBS/Fox Video).**

The career of automobile racing driver Junior Johnson — now in his 40s and retired from active competition on the stock-car circuit — is freely but vibrantly fictionalized in *The Last American Hero.* Adapted by William Roberts from Tom Wolfe's whiz-bang prose in an *Esquire* article about Junior, the movie calls him Junior Jackson and takes a sympathetic approach to this "wild-assed mountain boy" who is determined to remain a loner, to burn up the track without selling himself body and soul to the establishment manipulators whose sponsored, factory-built cars dominate the racing world. How Junior wins his trophies at the expense of his impossible dreams about freedom and rugged independence is *Hero*'s underlying theme — which hardly amounts to a startling new perception of the American experience. But director Lamont Johnson has a lot going for him in addition to lively footage of demolition derbies and stock-car races. Jeff Bridges as Junior has never been better at giving his down-home shtick a sense of inner-directed urgency and conviction, and he sets the pace for earthy performances by Geraldine Fitzgerald and Art Lund (with Lund especially right as Junior's dad, a stubborn mountain man dedicated to making top-grade moonshine). Another noteworthy figure in the supporting cast is built-for-speed Valerie Perrine as a track follower who calls herself "a Georgia peach-pit," an amiable girl with very low resistance to winners. Junior's disappointment in love is part of his evolution from hillbilly rebel to superpro, and *Last American Hero* salutes him in a pop saga phrased with rough vernacular authenticity. It's no easy feat to project the innate class of a hero whose idea of a smart retort is, "If you had gas for brains, you couldn't back a piss-ant out of a pea shell."

Playboy, October 1973

POSTSCRIPT: *The company presumably misunderstood the movie so well that they opened it in towns where stock-car races were the going thing, in the mistaken belief that it was not social satire but a way to woo redneck sports enthusiasts. That was their first mistake, after which it was probably decided this picture was for dumping.* —B.W.

January 1990

MELVIN AND HOWARD

Pauline Kael

Directed by Jonathan Demme. Written by Bo Goldman. Starring Paul Le Mat, Mary Steenburgen, Jason Robards, and Pamela Reed. **MCA Home Video.**

Jean Renoir instinctively understood what he had in common with characters very different from himself, and when his people are at their most ludicrous—when they are self-pitying or infuriatingly contentious—he puts us inside their skins, so we're laughing at ourselves. Asked to explain how it was that he didn't separate his characters into the good ones and the bad ones, Renoir's answer was always "Because

Paul Le Mat, as Melvin Dummar, gives a ride to a beat-up old biker, played by Jason Robards, who turns out to be Howard Hughes in *Melvin and Howard*. (Photo copyright © by Universal Pictures, a Division of Universal City Studios, Inc. Courtesy of MCA Publishing Rights, a Division of MCA Inc.)

everyone has his reasons," and in his best films we don't need those reasons explained — we intuit them. The young American director Jonathan Demme has some of this same gift, and his lyrical comedy *Melvin and Howard,* which opened the New York Film Festival on September 26th, is an almost flawless act of sympathetic imagination. Demme and the writer Bo Goldman have entered into the soul of American blue-collar suckerdom and brought us close enough to see that the people on the screen are us. Demme and Goldman have taken for their hero a chucklehead who is hooked on TV game shows and for their heroine his wife, who when she's off on her own and needs to work turns go-go dancer. And they have made us understand how it was that when something big — something legendary — touched these lives, nobody could believe it.

The lawyers and judges and jurors who were involved in the 1976–78 legal proceedings over the Howard Hughes will known as the Mormon will looked at Melvin Dummar, raked over his life, and couldn't believe that Hughes (who died in April, 1976) would have included Dummar among his beneficiaries. If you've seen Melvin Dummar on television, you may have observed that he's very touching—he looks like a more fair-haired Andy Kaufman as Latka Gravas in the TV series "Taxi," and he has that square, engaging naïveté that is so thoroughgoing it seems like a put-on. Dummar does, in fact, have links to TV: he is the representative debt-ridden American for whom game shows were created. He won a prize on "Truth or Consequences" but was unsuccessful on "The Dating Game"; he once appeared on "Let's Make a Deal" wearing a string of oranges around his neck and a hat shaped like an orange, and another time in the same hat but with a duck on top with a sign that said "Quacking up for a deal." Actually, Dummar was on "Let's Make a Deal" four times within a period of five years (which is probably a record); in the hearings on the will, an attorney said that this was a violation of federal law, and it was used against him to indicate that since "theatrics and lying" were a way of life for him, he could have faked the will and invented the story that he gave to account for the bequest—the story of how one night around Christmas of 1967 or early January of 1968 he had found Hughes in the desert and given him a ride. Even Dummar's dreams were turned against him: an attorney grilling his second wife in order to discredit him asked, "Mrs. Dummar, didn't your husband once write a song which he entitled 'A Dream Becomes Reality,' with this as one of the lines—'A beggar becomes a king'?" And, of course, the attorney had a point: the Hughes bequest did seem just like another one of Dummar's dreams, though it probably wasn't. The new nonfiction detective story *High Stakes*, by Harold Rhoden, makes a very spiky and convincing argument for the authenticity of the Mormon will, which the whole country laughed at because of the inclusion of Melvin Dummar, who seemed like a pudgy hick. (Johnny Carson got a lot of mileage out of Melvin Dummar jokes; for a while he was the national chump.) Even the many eminent institutions that were also named as beneficiaries didn't put up much of a fight for the will. Maybe their officers couldn't believe Melvin Dummar belonged among the hallowed names. More likely, these officers, knowing that the scary, powerful Summa Corporation, which controlled Hughes' wealth, would not relinquish this fortune without a costly battle in the courts which Summa, with the Hughes resources, could prolong into infinity, decided that it was wiser simply to string along with the general attitude in the media that a will in which Melvin Dummar was a beneficiary had to be a forgery. (The will, dated March,

1968, which would have effectively dissolved the Summa Corporation, left one-quarter of Hughes' estate to medical research, one-eighth to four universities, and the remainder to be divided into sixteen parcels, among beneficiaries such as the Mormon Church, the Boy Scouts, orphans, Hughes' ex-wife, relatives, business associates, and Dummar, whose one-sixteenth would have amounted to over a hundred and fifty million dollars.)

But what if the meeting between Melvin Dummar and Howard Hughes took place just as Dummar said it did? What might have caused Hughes to remember Melvin a few months later and put him in his will? That's what *Melvin and Howard* tells us. By their own imaginative leap, Demme and Goldman make us understand what Howard Hughes might have seen in Melvin Dummar that the lawyers and reporters didn't see. Paul Le Mat (he was the disarming, spacy young hero in Demme's *Citizens Band*) is such an easygoing, non-egocentric actor that he disappears inside the role of big, beefy Melvin — a sometime milk-man, sometime worker at a magnesium plant, sometime gas-station operator, and hopeful song-writer. Driving along the California–Nevada interstate at night in his pickup truck, Melvin has a bovine boyishness about him. He keeps himself in good cheer in the desert by singing "Santa's Souped-up Sleigh"; the lyrics are his own, set to a tune he bought by mail order for seventy dollars, and when he sings — ostentatiously keeping time — you feel there's not a thing in that noggin but the words of the song. Jason Robards plays Howard Hughes, who hits a snag while racing his motorcycle in the desert and is flung into the air. He is lying in the freezing darkness when Melvin spots him — a bony old man in beat-out clothes, with a dirty beard and straggly long gray hair. When Melvin helps him into the front seat of the truck, next to him, he's doubled over in pain, and even as Melvin is wrapping him up to warm him there's a malevolent, paranoid gleam in his eyes. Melvin, who takes him for an old wino — a desert rat — is bothered by his mean expression, and in order to cheer him up (and give himself some company) he insists that the old geezer sing his song with him, or get out and walk.

Jason Robards certainly wasn't a beacon to his profession in last year's *Hurricane* or in the recent classic of nincompoopery *Raise the Titanic,* and it may be true that, as he says, he works in movies "to make it possible to work on the stage." But I doubt if he has ever been greater than he is here. This Hughes is so sure that people are only after his money that he distrusts everyone; he has bribed and corrupted so many high officers in business and government that he believes in nothing but the power of bribery. His thinking processes are gnarled, twisted; he begrudges the world the smallest civility and lives incommunicado from everyone. And here he is singing "Santa's Souped-up Sleigh" while sneering at its cornball idiocy and looking over disgustedly, in disbelief, at the pleasure that this dumb bunny next to him takes in hearing his song. In recent years, Robards' Yankee suavity has occasionally been reminiscent of Walter Huston: his Ben Bradlee in *All the President's Men* recalled Huston in *Dodsworth*, and here, when his Howard Hughes responds to Melvin's amiable prodding and begins to enjoy himself on a simple level and sings "Bye, Bye, Blackbird," he's as memorable as the famous record of Huston singing "September Song." His eyes are an old man's eyes—faded into the past, shiny and glazed by recollections—yet intense. You feel that his grungy anger has melted away, that he has been healed. He and Melvin talk about how the desert, after rain, smells of greasewood and sage, and at dawn, just as they approach the lights of Las Vegas, where Hughes gets out, they smile at each other with a fraternal understanding that's a cockeyed, spooky miracle.

In an interview in the *Times* last year, Jason Robards pointed out that Robards was Hughes' middle name and that both of them had Loomises among their relatives. "They couldn't have cast anyone else as Howard Hughes," he said. "I figured I didn't have to do any preparation for the part. It's all built in genetically." What's built in genetically may be the way Jason Robards responds to an acting challenge: the son of an actor father and an actor all his life, he goes for broke in a way that never suggests recklessness. He just casually transports himself to new dimensions (that maybe nobody else has ever been in), as if he had been breathing that air all his life. Robards isn't on the screen for long, but Hughes suffuses the movie. You know he's there without your even thinking about him; he might almost be looking down on Melvin, watching what's happening to him. And this is what the picture is about. The moviemakers have understood the position that Howard Hughes has arrived at in American mythology, and they have used the encounter in the desert to confer a moment of glory on Melvin Dummar. Eight years later, when Melvin finds himself named in the will and realizes that the old coot who said he was Howard Hughes *was* Howard Hughes, he is awed—it's like being touched by God. When reporters, neighbors, and the curious and the crazy gather at his gas station, he hides in a tree and peers out at the crowd in terror.

Most of the movie is about Melvin's life during those eight years—the life that will look so makeshift and shoddy when it's examined in a courtroom. Later in the morning after the encounter in the desert, Melvin's truck is repossessed, and his wife, Lynda (Mary Steenburgen), packs her things and takes their little daughter and goes off to live with another man, pausing only to murmur a regretful goodbye to the sleeping Melvin. They get a divorce, then remarry when she's hugely pregnant, but this marriage doesn't last long. Lynda can't stand Melvin's buying things that they never get to keep, and he can't stop kidding himself that his expensive, installment-plan purchases are somehow practical—that they're investments. So they never have anything—finally not even each other.

Mary Steenburgen was oddly tremulous in *Goin' South,* and though in *Time After Time* she was very sweet in an out-of-it way—a stoned cupcake—she didn't have the quickness or the pearly aura that she has here. Her Lynda Dummar has a soft mouth and a tantalizing slender wiggliness, and she talks directly to whomever she's talking to—she addresses them with her eyes and her mouth, and when they speak she listens, watching their faces. When she listens, she's the kind of woman a man wants to tell more to. Mary Steenburgen makes Lynda the go-go dancer so appealing that you realize she's the dream Melvin attained and then couldn't hang on to. Melvin is a hard worker, though, and he believes in family life. When Lynda leaves him, he's appalled by her exhibiting herself in strip joints; he keeps charging in and making scenes. Lynda is hurt by his attitude; she loves to dance, and she doesn't think there's anything lewd about what she's doing. In a way, she's right: Lynda could shimmy and shake forever and she still wouldn't be a hardened pro. Her movements are sexy but with a tipsy charm and purity. When her boss bawls her out because of a commotion that Melvin has just caused, she quits on the spot, whips off the flimsy costume that belongs to the boss, throws it in his face, and walks through the place naked, and she does it without making an event of it—it's her body. Melvin's second wife, Bonnie (Pamela Reed, who was Belle Starr in *The Long Riders*) isn't a romantic dream, like Lynda. She's a down-to-earth woman with a couple of kids who propositions him with a solid offer—marriage and her cousin's gas station in Utah, in a package deal. She makes the offer almost hungrily. Promising him a good marriage and a good business, she's like a sexual entrepreneur who feels she can use his untapped abilities and turn him into a success.

This is comedy without a speck of sitcom aggression: the characters are slightly loony the way we all are sometimes (and it seldom involves coming up with cappers or with straight lines that somebody else can cap). When the people on the screen do unexpected things, they're not weirdos; their eccentricity is just an offshoot of the normal, and Demme suggests that maybe these people who grew up in motor homes and trailers in Nevada and California and Utah seem eccentric because they didn't learn the "normal," accepted ways of doing things. When Lynda is broke and takes her daughter, Darcy (the lovely, serious-faced Elizabeth Cheshire), to the bus station in Reno to send her to Melvin, she's frantic. Her misery about sending the child away is all mixed up with her anxiety about the child's having something to eat on the trip, and she's in a rush to put a sandwich together. She has bought French bread and bologna, and she takes over a table and borrows a knife from the man at the lunch counter so she can cut the bread; she salvages lettuce and tomatoes from the leftovers on someone's plate, and sends Darcy back to the counter to get some mustard and then back again to get some ketchup. The unperturbed counterman (played by the real Melvin Dummar) finds nothing unusual in this, and asks, "Is everything all right?" There's no sarcasm in his tone; he seems to understand what she's going through, and he wants to be helpful. She says, "Everything's just fine, thank you very much." She has dominated everyone's attention — she has practically taken over the station — yet the goofiness isn't forced; it's almost like found humor. It's a little like a throwaway moment in a Michael Ritchie film or a slapstick fracas out of Preston Sturges, but there are more unspoken crosscurrents — and richer ones — in Demme's scenes. While you're responding to the dithering confusion Lynda is causing in the bus depot, you're absorbing the emotions between mother and child. Darcy is often very grownup around her mother, as if she knew that Lynda is a bit of a moonbeam and needs looking after. But at the depot Darcy herself is so excited she becomes part of the confusion. Later, during Melvin and Lynda's remarriage ceremony in a Las Vegas "wedding chapel," Darcy is so impressed and elated that her whole face sparkles; she's like an imp Madonna. Throughout the movie, the children — Lynda's or Bonnie's, and sometimes all of them together — are part of an ongoing subtext: they're never commented on, and they never do anything cute or make a move that doesn't seem "true."

When Jonathan Demme does a thriller like *Last Embrace,* he seems an empty-headed director with a little hand-me-down craft, but in *Melvin and Howard* he shows perhaps a finer understanding of lower-middle-class life than any other American director. This picture suggests what it might have been like if Jean Renoir had directed a Preston Sturges comedy. Demme's style is so expressive that he draws you into the lives of the characters, and you're hardly aware of the technical means by which he accomplishes this — the prodigious crane and tracking shots that he has worked out with his cinematographer, Tak Fujimoto, and the fluid, mellow colors that probably owe a lot to Toby Rafelson's production design. The comedy doesn't stick out; it's part of the fluidity. And if you respond to this movie as I did, you'll hardly be aware (until you think it over afterward) that it has no plot, in the ordinary sense. (This could handicap it, though, in movie markets; the pitfall that a picture like this presents is that there's not a hard-sell scene in it. It's a soft shimmer of a movie, and the very people whom it's about and who might love it if they gave it a chance may not be tempted to see it.) There are a couple of flaws: the sequence of Melvin taking the will to the Mormon Church in Salt Lake City is so fast and cryptic it seems almost like shorthand, and if you've forgotten the stories that filled the papers a few years ago you may not understand what's going on; and the following sequence, of Melvin hiding from the crowd, doesn't have quite the clarity or the dramatic fullness that it needs. And there is a small lapse of taste: a shot too many of the blond Mrs. Worth (Charlene Holt), one of Melvin's milk-route customers — she lifts her head heavenward and mugs silly ecstasy at the prospect of his returning the next day, for another carnal visit. The dialogue is as near perfection as script dialogue gets — it's always funny, without any cackling. Bo Goldman, who is in his late forties, shared writing credits on *One Flew Over the Cuckoo's Nest* and *The Rose,* but this is his only unshared credit. (After spending a day with the real Melvin Dummar, Goldman decided he wanted to write the script; then he stayed with Dummar for a month and "got to love him," and came to know the two wives and Dummar's friends and relatives and neighbors.) The people in the movie — the large cast includes Charles Napier, John Glover, Gloria Grahame, Dabney Coleman, Michael J. Pollard, Martine Beswick, Susan Peretz, Naida Reynolds, Herbie Faye, and Robert Wentz — all seem scrubby and rumpled and believable; you feel that if you hung around Anaheim or L.A. or Reno you'd run into them. Maybe if you had been at the Sex Kat Klub at the right time, you'd have seen the dancer next to Lynda who was strutting her stuff with a broken arm in a big plaster cast.

Melvin and Howard has the same beautiful, dippy warmth as its characters. Paul Le Mat's Melvin, who barely opens his mouth when he talks, opens it wide when he sings. His proudest moment is probably the hit he makes at the dairy's Christmas party when he grins confidently as he sings a ballad about the gripes of a milkman. (The words, like the words of "Santa's Souped-up Sleigh," are by the real Melvin Dummar.) Le Mat's Melvin often has a childlike look of bewilderment that he seems to be covering up by his beaming optimism. He's very gentle; he threatens physical violence only once — when he thinks that the assistant manager of the dairy (Jack Kehoe) is trying to rook him out of the big color TV set he has won as Milkman of the Month. Watching a game show, "Easy Street," on that set, he's like an armchair quarterback, telling the contestants which doors to choose to win the prizes. When Darcy is bored by it, he tries to justify his obsession by explaining how educational these shows are, but she isn't conned — she goes out to play.

Demme stages a segment of "Easy Street" (modelled on "Let's Make a Deal") which opens up the theme of the movie by giving us a view of game shows that transcends satire. Lynda, who has been selected as a contestant, appears in an aquamarine dress with tassels and an old-fashioned bellhop's hat, and when she does a tap dance that's as slow as a clog dance the audience starts to laugh. But she keeps going, and though she has more movement in her waving arms than in her tapping feet, she's irresistible. It's the triumph of adorable pluckiness (and the uninhibited use of her beautiful figure) over technique. The host of "Easy Street" (Robert Ridgely) combines malicious charity with provocative encouragement, and the enthusiastic applause confirms the notion that every TV audience loves someone who tries sincerely. In Ritchie's *Smile*, it was plain that the teen-age beauty contestants were not nearly as vacuous as they were made to appear (and made themselves appear), and here it's evident that Lynda the winner, jumping up and down like a darling frisky puppy, is putting on the excitement that is wanted of her. She's just like the pretty women you've seen on TV making fools of themselves, except that you know her; you know the desperation that went into choosing that tawdry dress and that's behind the eagerness to play the game — to squeal and act gaga and kiss everybody. The host personifies the game show, as if he were personally giving all the prizes. He's a pygmy metaphor for Howard Hughes. The game show is the illusion that sustains Melvin: that if you pick the right door, what's behind it is happiness.

Shortly after the probate trial on the Mormon will, the judge who had presided died of cancer; at his funeral service one of the speakers said that on his deathbed the judge told him that he hoped to meet Howard Hughes in the next world — that he had a question he wanted to ask him. The movie shows us a triumphant Melvin Dummar: he knows the answer. He also knows he'll never see the money. (Maybe Howard Hughes was the naïve one, if he thought that he could smash the monster corporation he had created.) Melvin Dummar was touched by a legend. Howard Hughes came to respect him, and so do we.

The New Yorker, October 13, 1980

PAYDAY

Charles Champlin

Directed by Daryl Duke. Written by Don Carpenter. Starring Rip Torn. **Thorn-EMI/HBO Video.**

Payday leads us, with absolutely convincing detail, along the pointed boot-prints left by an amoral, recklessly ambitious, ruthlessly charming country-western singer named Maury Dann during 36 crucial hours in his young life.

While backstage dramas are nothing new and we have been shown the sneer behind the starry grin often enough, in *A Face in the Crowd* and elsewhere, *Payday* explores the Nashville-centered world of country with an easy authenticity which makes this nothing like a repetition of what has been before.

Dann is the poor boy who has strummed his way out of the rural red-clay cotton country as fast as he could learn chords. By now he has had a couple of albums and some air play, is moving up to the better roadhouses and is within a guitar length of being ready for a guest shot with Johnny Cash or the top slot on Grand Ol' Opry. He's got the road

Rip Torn (left), as Alabama-born country star Maury Dann, tears through one more Deep South gig with his lead guitarist and best friend (played by Jeff Morris) in *Payday*. (Photo copyright © 1972 Pumice Finance Co. N.V. All rights reserved.)

manager, the chauffeur-bodyguard and the big Cad with all the built-ins. The Rolls is next.

Dann is played by Rip Torn, always an intense actor who is at his best portraying men at the limits. He here has a chance to display full-out the kind of coiled-snake hypnotic power which has given some of his earlier roles a feverish watchability. He makes a convincing down-home star and quite obviously has done his own twangy singing. (Playboy cartoonist Shel Silverstein wrote several of the original songs.)

One of my few complaints about *Payday* is in fact that there is too little of Torn performing. It was a fine opportunity to make a nonsinging star entirely plausible as the sexually electric performer Dann is supposed to be, but the movie stays backstage (or backseat, where most of the action is) more than it needs to.

We meet Dann finishing a gig at one of those smoke-filled neon oases off the highway just outside any city anywhere in the South. He

An old girlfriend played by Ahna Capri (right) is wise to country star Maury Dann (Rip Torn) as he tests the thigh of a new girl (played by Elayne Heilveil) in *Payday*. (Photo copyright © 1972 Pumice Finance Co. N.V. All rights reserved.)

sings of lost love and scans the crowd hungry-eyed, looking for a temporary new one. He finds her.

The caravan moves on, to all-night poker in a motel, to another town, picking up a new groupie (Elayne Heilveil), discarding a more senior lady (Ahna Capri), looking in on the star's whiny, pill-head mother (Clara Dunn) and his bitter ex-wife (Eleanor Fell).

There are vignettes in succession: a hunting expedition on which Dann is for once at peace with himself, a visit to a small-town deejay, a sudden, vicious fistfight with one of his sidemen over a scruffy dog, a conversation about cooking between the loyal driver (Cliff Emmich) and the groupie who has just realized the mess she's in.

The script by novelist Don Carpenter has the sight and sound exactness of fine reportage, and the direction by Daryl Duke (making his first feature) is swift and efficient, drawing no distracting attention to itself. Richard Glouner's photography preserves the look of real people in real places.

The dramatic form is familiar and the seeds of self-destruction planted by the hero come to flower in those 36 inescapable hours. And we look on, fascinated, comprehending him but saving our sympathy for everyone around him, all of whom show his heelprints as scar tissue somewhere in their lives.

One of the satisfactions of the movie is that it acknowledges that in country and western music the basic life experiences are transposed into song fairly directly. We see Dann working at it, but the process is not romanticized. It seems to arise somewhere between compulsion and ambition, as a fact of life.

San Francisco jazz-rock critic Ralph J. Gleason was executive producer of *Payday,* with Martin Fink and Don Carpenter as coproducers.

The performances are consistently superior. It is Torn's finest hour, and the support, including Michael C. Gwynne as the road manager unable to arrange the last payoff, Emmich as the chauffeur, Ahna Capri and Elayne Heilveil as the temporary loves, is impeccable.

Los Angeles Times, March 16, 1973

WEEDS

David Edelstein

Directed by John Hancock. Written by Hancock and Dorothy Tristan. Starring Nick Nolte. **HBO Video.**

Weeds is the story of Lee Umstetter (Nick Nolte), a poor slob sentenced to life in San Quentin for armed robbery and assault. When we meet Lee, he has just thrown himself from the third story of the prison's atrium and is bleeding from the mouth from internal injuries; recovering, he tries to hang himself. Finally, he goes to the library and asks for a big book, any big book. With this — *War and Peace* — he does not attempt to brain himself. He reads it, and when he's finished, he gets another big book — the complete Nietzsche. He reads that, too. At this point, even the dimmest prison-flick maven will realize that *Weeds* isn't your usual snarling con picture; it's an inspirational comedy, with — luckily — more good, straight-faced gags than messianic speeches. Lee Umstetter becomes a playwright, launches a prison theater company, gets pardoned, and attempts to dig his way out of a different jail, his own antisocial impulses. He's accompanied by a ragtag band of ex-con thespians, which means that *Weeds* is about one of the few things showbiz people actually know firsthand — what it's like to drive around the country putting on plays with a bunch of lunatics.

The movie, directed by John Hancock (*Bang the Drum Slowly*), is based on the life of ex-con Rick Cluchey and his San Quentin drama troupe, which first performed *The Cage* in New York in 1970. Perhaps more than the play, the "rap sessions" attracted attention — after the show, the actors would tell their hushed audiences (sometimes schoolkids, often from correctional institutions) their sordid histories, complete with graphic accounts of "brotherhood" in the joint. Hancock met Cluchey when he was artistic director of San Francisco's Actor's Workshop, and he wrote a script with his wife (Dorothy Tristan) that's heavy on backstage anecdotes and onstage crises. Hancock has been quoted as saying that he and Tristan began with Cluchey's life and let the realities of making theater take over the story. It was a brilliant move: the fun in the movie is watching these misfits learn what it means to convert their rage and alienation into something an audience can respond to. That they never get it quite right makes the film more interesting yet.

Weeds is oddly shaped. In the prison section, it whizzes along from year to year, feeling like flashbacks from a movie we didn't see: Lee writes the play, Lee stages the play, Lee gets a good review from a San Francisco theater critic (Rita Taggert), who then mounts a campaign to free him. Even when it settles down, Hancock isn't always in control of his material — a fatal car crash seems to belong in another movie, and so (although it works) does the brutal prison riot that ends the film, when the men return with *The Cage* to San Quentin and inadvertently whip up their old comrades.

But there's something bracing about how *Weeds* flirts with formula and then refuses to surrender to it. It goes from being an angry prison picture to a comic road movie to an opening-night nail-biter, then it veers off into violence and frustration again. The play within a play is about freedom behind bars; what's refreshing about the movie is that it cleaves to its right to be weird. Even *The Cage* itself becomes a source of ambivalence: Did Umstetter lift huge chunks of Genet's *Deathwatch,* or do great minds just think alike?

Nick Nolte has what most would call a lived-in face. It's a thick slab, like Gerard Depardieu's, and it's grown increasingly pouchy and marbled over the years; its expressiveness always takes you by surprise. At first, his Umstetter seems fatally inexpressive, a groggy blur. But then you spot the loneliness in his eyes — intelligent eyes, like those of a man trapped inside an animal. Inexpressiveness is what he's *fighting.* Nolte plays him slyly, a study in bafflement, and he's wonderful hectoring his cast after an out-of-control performance: "We're not losers, we're not gonna be losers. *So don't revert!"* The losers are winning: John Toles-Bey is a jivey hustler who learns Method acting and almost backs out — "It would mean going back to the joint in my head!"; Ernie Hudson is a violent paranoid who picks up a college girl and a couple of nights later stomps on stage drunk, ready to kill whoever slept with her; Lane Smith is a bewigged embezzler who blossoms into an efficient stage manager; Bill Forsythe is a shoplifter who likes being in prison because it organizes his life; Joe Mantegna is a mousy New York actor who has never been in jail, but fakes a bio; Mark Rolston is the company exhibitionist, who takes a curtain call with his dick hanging out.

The movie isn't specific enough about what *The Cage* turns into — at times it sounds as if Umstetter, on the road to Off-Broadway, is softening his original vision, adding a spokesman for "Life." Does Hancock think he has compromised the material, or enlarged it? And when he takes it back to San Quentin, has he made it bleaker because showbiz has treated him badly, or was the material always this inflammatory? You want more of the play, and more of Nolte's relationship with the Nob Hill theater critic who falls in love with him. You want fewer speeches like the last one, about weeds asserting their right to grow. (It's not a good metaphor, since weeds kill the grass.) *Weeds* doesn't come together, but these days, a commercial movie that leaves you wanting to know more is the rarest of jailbirds.

The distributor, De Laurentiis Entertainment Group, hasn't gone after the right kind of audience. The line in the ads — "Feel what it's like from the inside" — makes no sense, since Nolte is outside for most of the movie. And DEG handled the press all wrong, not inviting the *Voice* to a screening until the day before *Weeds* opened. I caught it at the shoddy "Movieland" on 8th Street, with an audience that wasn't prepared for a subtle comedy. But the people grew to like it, responding to its shagginess, its portrait of losers making art out of their "otherness." Making scenes on stage, the cons in *Weeds* taste freedom, and pass it on to the audience.

Village Voice, November 3, 1987

BEYOND MEDIA POLITICS

n a climactic scene from 1983's enthralling Nicaragua adventure story *Under Fire*, a mysterious French operative named Jazy (Jean-Louis Trintignant) scolds a pair of journalists (Nick Nolte and Joanna Cassidy) for faking a picture of a rebel leader to give a boost to the Sandinista revolution. "I like you people, but you are sentimental shits," says Jazy. "You fall in love with the poets, the poets fall in love with the Marxists, the Marxists fall in love with themselves. The country is destroyed with rhetoric, and in the end we are stuck with tyrants."

Although the movie is in part an exposé of the Somoza government's tyranny and gets much of its charge from revolutionary ardor, director Roger Spottiswoode and writer Ron Shelton (who penned the final drafts from an original script by Clayton Frohman) moved beyond their own muckraking romanticism. Jazy, the sinister government fixer who knows everything about both Somoza and the rebel leader Rafael (a fictional composite of several revolutionaries), offers the crucial piece of political analysis in the movie: "Somoza? He is a tyrant too, of course, a butcher. But, finally, that is not the point, you see. If we wish to survive,

Ed Harris plays John Glenn, "the pious Marine" who became the first American to orbit the earth three times, in writer-director Philip Kaufman's version of Tom Wolfe's *The Right Stuff*. (Photo © 1983 The Ladd Company. All rights reserved. Courtesy Philip Kaufman.)

we have a choice of tyrants. . . . In twenty years, we will know who's right." Then the rebels kill him.

Under Fire achieves a passionate yet skeptical perspective unusual in political movies of the '70s and '80s. Typically they lack either passion or skepticism: We get merely hysteria of the left (*Betrayed*) or of the right (*Rambo*). Films with social and political themes have the greatest and most lasting power when they go beyond their immediate purpose and tap into complex combinations of attitudes and emotions—like the love of freedom and the doubt of authority that permeate *Under Fire*.

At their best, topical movies provoke you to develop your own analyses by dramatizing contemporary history from vantage points that are more personal, if not always deeper, than the front-page headlines or the nightly news. (Fred Schepisi's *A Cry in the Dark* is a *critique* of front-page headlines and nightly news.) These films throw you into volatile situations and allow you to think and feel your own way through.

All the movies that follow share at least one bedrock virtue: They cut against conventional wisdom, whether they're about Americans in over their heads in Central America (in *Salvador* as well as *Under Fire*), the media circus that surrounds our politics (in *Blow Out*) and our heroes (in *The Right Stuff*), or the perils American soldiers faced in Vietnam— military, physical, and political (in *Go Tell the Spartans* and *Hamburger Hill*), or piercingly moral (in *Casualties of War*). They encourage the discovery of *un*conventional wisdom.

BLOW OUT

Michael Sragow

Directed and written by Brian De Palma. Starring John Travolta and Nancy Allen. **Warner Home Video.**

Of all the prominent young American filmmakers, Brian De Palma does the most straight talking about his generation. Though his explosive thrillers (*Carrie, Dressed to Kill*) have been criticized as limited and manipulative, he fully expresses the fractured mentality of an age in which everything from public morality to the family car has fallen apart.

De Palma makes movies about divided personalities, characters uncertain of their social and psychological identities, torn between impulse and reason. He plays dark games with them among the land mines of our cities, where a rape, a race riot or a revolution could be just around the corner. His material is often Grand Guignol, but the intelligence behind it is as sophisticated as Edgar Allan Poe's.

A daring writer and director, De Palma attacks his controversial themes with new frankness and confidence in *Blow Out*. This powerful political thriller is raunchy, funny, yet poetic. Its vision of a robotized United States, tranquilized by the media and caught up in the escapist politics of "patriotism," registers like a clarion call to the nation: get serious!

De Palma's hero Jack Terri (played by a never-better John Travolta), is no less than an Everyman for the aging counterculture. A onetime electronics whiz kid, he lost his innocence when he worked for the police department and inadvertently caused the death of a good cop. Putting his whole life on hold, he uses his talent to turn out sound effects for horror-movie schlock. You can see why Jack can get lost in the world of whirring reels and snaking wires; it's a sensuous environment. When he stations himself on a footbridge one night to record sounds for his new film, *Co-ed Frenzy*, his long, shiny microphone acts as a phallic divining rod, enabling him to eavesdrop on owls, amphibians and nervous lovers.

Suddenly, he's jolted out of his aural voyeurism when a car shimmies out of control and careens into a river. Jack manages to save one of the passengers, a young woman named Sally Bedina (Nancy Allen). At the hospital, he's told that the other victim was the governor of Pennsylvania, a leading presidential candidate, and Jack reluctantly agrees to keep Sally's presence quiet to protect the governor's reputation. But later, when he replays the tapes he made of the accident, he hears both the blowout of a tire — and a gunshot. The excitement of the film comes in watching this technician strip away his own insulation and commit himself to exposing the truth. He tries to use his craft to make sense of a political, existential conflict.

Jack is the perfect hero for this movie, because in *Blow Out*, the country, too, is in a holding pattern, still reeling from the tumult of the Sixties and early Seventies. The media play into the complacency of the times, initially accepting the cover-up story for the "accident."

According to *Blow Out,* our public life has become a hall of mirrors — you have to smash a lot of glass to see what's really going on.

It comes as no surprise, then, that a seedy photographer (Dennis Franz) views the film he took of the governor's death as a potential gold mine — his very own Zapruder movie. A media-hungry, capitalist society will exploit anything. Though there are villains in the film, most of the characters are neither black nor white. They're citizens of a gray country.

At the start, Travolta's character keeps a certain cynical distance from the film he's making as well as the world at large, like any self-respecting hack. But Travolta's portrayal of Jack becomes wholehearted and soulful. Not since *Saturday Night Fever* has he been so much the star. By relaxing into this character, he's found more screen depth. He never overplays his quivering sensitivity. If in his early roles he paid homage to Al Pacino and perhaps even James Dean, here he's completely his own man — that rare actor who has gusto *and* a middle range. Instead of the working-class accents and mannerisms of his other work, in *Blow Out* we hear his natural speaking voice for the first time on the big screen. It has a seductive, musical sweetness.

A soft, hesitant woman with puffy hair and a pouty face, Sally is a typical American escapist. A Korvette's makeup artist who supplements her income with sexplitation, she's as alienated as Jack. Sally won't watch the news because "it's too depressing," and she's thrilled that Jack is in the movie business. When he tells her about his past with the police, she exclaims, "That's like real life in the streets!" Her naiveté works like blinders, preventing her from seeing that she leads her own life on the social fringe. Like many other Americans, she's a good scout in search of a fearless leader. But when Jack's outrage at the cover-up inspires her to clean up her act, she's the one to take physical risks; Jack keeps his distance with a wire.

Nancy Allen was a fabulous comedienne as the appealing hooker in *Dressed to Kill.* Here she proves her range, too. As Sally Bedina, she's deeply touching, breathing out a gentle, coquettish "Hy-y-y" that pierces your heart. Sally could have been an animated cuddle doll, but Allen imbues her with poignancy and strength. Jack and Sally share a sympathetic chemistry. Though their sexual relationship is never realized, the actors convince us they're soulmates.

It's unusual for political thrillers to carry a tragic sting, but in *Blow Out,* the characters' downfalls, particularly Jack's, are determined partly by their personalities. Jack is a victim of his media obsessions — a voyeur of his own life — trying to use technology to beat technology. As the movie progresses, his feelings of impotence tighten around him like a noose; De Palma zeroes in on his acid perspiration. The killer is actually Jack's dark mirror image, a Watergate-like technocrat who depersonalizes death, dangling one of his victims like a marionette strangled in her strings.

Philadelphia — the birthplace of the nation, and of Brian De Palma — is the right location for this movie. The city has a human scale — the skyline doesn't dwarf the characters — and it combines august heritage and urban blight. Seen through cinematographer Vilmos Zsigmond's acute eyes, the city is all snuggled up with sin. It's swathed with red, white and blue for an impending Liberty Day celebration to mark the 100th anniversary of the Liberty Bell's last ringing. The colors blend into the buildings like an extra layer of clothing against the cold.

Both De Palma and Zsigmond are brilliant local colorists. Liberty Day, in fact, is a De Palma creation, recalling the gaudiest Bicentennial celebrations — those desperate attempts to give artificial respiration to the spirits of the Founding Fathers. Almost every significant event in this movie occurs with a crash of symbols. As Jack rushes to apprehend the killer throughout Liberty Day and Night, he rams right into images of a storybook America: July 4th fireworks, Norman Rockwell majorettes and even a mock-up of Nathan Hale with Patrick Henry's proclamation "Give Me Liberty or Give Me Death." The cunning camera movements — visual figure eights — trap the hero in coils of subterfuge. There are aural symbols, too. At the end, the ringing of an ersatz Liberty Bell drowns out the screams of a woman fighting for her life.

In *Dressed to Kill,* De Palma made directorial twists on Hitchcock and Buñuel. In *Blow Out,* he does variations on Antonioni's *Blow-Up* and Coppola's *The Conversation.* But the results are uniquely his own. Though *The Conversation* was a fascinating portrait of a paranoid personality caught up in a similar technocratic plot, it didn't have the breadth of De Palma's film, which in content is almost a tissue sample of an entire diseased society. *Blow-Up* got so entangled in questions of illusion and reality that it lost all moral focus: despite his ethical dilemma, photographer David Hemmings' life in swinging London looked like a whole lot of fun. In contrast, few people would envy Jack's sorry fate in frigid Philadelphia.

Technically, De Palma goes way beyond Coppola and Antonioni: using split screens, lickety-split editing and superimposed images that put Jack right into the scene of the crime, he makes the components of the cinema come off as complex genetic coding. De Palma leads us to explore the *geography* of sound—how the ear and brain experience distance and direction. These scenes are a virtuoso collaboration between actor and director: Travolta's rapt alertness draws us into De Palma's audiovisual kaleidoscope until the doomed car's tire seems to blow out in our ears. *Blow Out*'s most vivid sound and image metaphors turn moviemaking itself into a risky alternative reality. As Jack sits in a darkened editing room, struggling to sync the noise of the crash with the photography, his cinematic intelligence is transformed into *political* intelligence—his filmic instinct weds these abstract elements to give them social meaning.

De Palma's distaste for Jack's hack work is as resonant as his love for Jack's detective work. *Co-ed Frenzy* looks like a *Carrie* rip-off: a mad-killer-in-a-dorm movie that Pavlov would have loved, using murder for conditioned shocks. But De Palma goes beyond riotous parody and self-parody: queasy murders take place that echo Jack's own cut-and-slash film. *Blow Out* says that the violence in our pop mythology *is* true to the tenor of American urban life. But it also says that to accept without protest the inhumanity of murder, in the theaters or in the streets, is to live in purgatory.

Blow Out is a thrillingly complicated film, exact in its elusiveness. The random encounters between characters have been carefully planned; they show us how conspiracies derive from incompetence and accidents as well as from deviousness and evil. The movie starts out like a game of "What's wrong with this picture?" and adds another game: "What's wrong with this sound?" Then it dares to ask the most puzzling question of all: "What's wrong with this country?" By using suspense techniques at full tilt, De Palma has managed to turn national torpor into an American moviemaking triumph.

Rolling Stone, September 3, 1981

CASUALTIES OF WAR

Pauline Kael

Directed by Brian De Palma. Written by David Rabe, from
the article by Daniel Lang. Starring Michael J. Fox and Sean
Penn. **RCA/Columbia Pictures Home Video.**

Some movies — *Grand Illusion* and *Shoeshine* come to mind, and the two
Godfathers and *The Chant of Jimmie Blacksmith* and *The Night of the
Shooting Stars* — can affect us in more direct, emotional ways than simple
entertainment movies. They have more imagination, more poetry, more
intensity than the usual fare; they have large themes, and a vision. They
can leave us feeling simultaneously elated and wiped out. Overwhelmed, we may experience a helpless anger if we hear people mock
them or poke holes in them in order to dismiss them. The new
Casualties of War has this kind of purity. If you meet people who are
bored by movies you love such as *The Earrings of Madame De . . .* or *The
Unbearable Lightness of Being,* chances are you can brush it off and think
it's their loss. But this new film is the kind that makes you feel
protective. When you leave the theatre, you'll probably find that you're
not ready to talk about it. You may also find it hard to talk lightly about
anything.

    Casualties of War is based on a Vietnam incident of 1966 that was
reported in [*The New Yorker*] by the late Daniel Lang, in the issue of
October 18, 1969. (The article was reprinted as a book.) Lang gave a
calm, emotionally devastating account of a squad of five American
soldiers who were sent on a five-day reconnaissance mission; they
kidnapped a Vietnamese village girl, raped her, and then covered up
their crime by killing her. The account dealt with the kind of gangbang
rape that the Vietnam War had in common with virtually all wars,
except that the rapists here, unable in general to distinguish Vietcong
sympathizers from other Vietnamese, didn't care that the girl wasn't
Vietcong. This indifference to whether a candidate for rape is friend or
foe may not really be that much of an exception; it may be frequent in
wartime. What's unusual here may simply be that a witness forced the
case into the open and it resulted in four court-martial convictions.

Pfc. Eriksson (Michael J. Fox, right) is unable to stop Sgt. Meserve (Sean Penn) from executing an innocent Vietnamese girl in *Casualties of War*. (Photo copyright © Columbia Pictures. All rights reserved. Courtesy RCA/Columbia Pictures Home Video.)

A number of movie people hoped to make a film of the Lang article, and, though it was commercially risky, Warners bought the rights and announced that Jack Clayton would make the picture — an arrangement that fell apart. Plans involving John Schlesinger and other directors also collapsed, but the article may have been the (unofficial) taking-off point for one film that did get made: Elia Kazan's low-budget, 16-mm. *The Visitors,* of 1972, which Kazan himself financed. He used a prosecution for rape and murder as background material to explain why a couple of ex-servicemen released from Leavenworth on a technicality were out to get the former buddy who had testified against them. Eventually, in 1987, after Brian De Palma had a success with *The Untouchables,* he was able to persuade Paramount to pick up the rights to the Lang story, which he'd had in the back of his mind since 1969. A script was commissioned from the playwright David Rabe, the quondam Catholic and Vietnam vet who had written *Streamers* and other plays about the war (and had wanted to work on this material for some years), but, when De Palma was all set to film it in Thailand, Paramount pulled out. The picture finally got under way at Columbia — the first picture to be approved by the company's new president, Dawn Steel. Whatever else she does, she should be honored for that decision, because twenty years later this is still risky material.

Lang's factual narrative is based on conversations with Eriksson, the witness who testified against the other men, and on the court-martial records. (The names were changed to protect everyone's privacy.) Rabe's script follows it closely, except that Rabe dramatizes the story by creating several incidents to explain what led to the rape and what followed.

When Eriksson (Michael J. Fox), who has just arrived in Vietnam, is out in a jungle skirmish at night, a mortar explosion shifts the earth under him; he drops down, caught, his feet dangling in an enemy tunnel. De Palma photographs the scene as if it were an ant farm — he shows us aboveground and underground in the same shot. Eriksson yells for help, and in the instant that a Vietcong, who has been crawling toward the dangling legs, slashes at them with his knife, Sergeant Meserve (Sean Penn) pulls Eriksson out. A minute later, Meserve saves him again from that Vietcong, who has come out of the hole to get him.

In the morning, the soldiers enter a peaceful-looking village; they stand near the mud-and-bamboo huts and see a stream and bridges and, a little way in the distance, paddy fields where women and elderly men are working, under the shadow of harsh, steep mountains. The tiered compositions are pale, like Chinese ink paintings. Throughout the movie, everything that's beyond the understanding of the Americans seems to be visualized in layered images; this subtle landscape reaching to Heaven is the site of the random violence that leads to the rape.

Smiling and eager, Eriksson walks behind two water buffalo, helping an ancient farmer with his plowing. Brownie (Erik King), a large-spirited, joshing black soldier, who is Meserve's pal—they're both due to go home in less than a month—cautions Eriksson about his exposed position on the field and walks him back to where the Sarge is taking time out, with the other men. They're all relaxed in a clearing near this friendly village, but we become ominously aware that the villagers in the paddies are evaporating. Brownie is standing with an arm around Meserve when the pastoral scene is ruptured: bullets tear into Brownie from a V.C. across the stream. An instant later, a guerrilla who's dressed as a farmer runs toward the group and flings a grenade at them. Meserve spots him and warns Eriksson, who turns and fires his grenade launcher; by luck, he explodes the V.C.'s grenade. Then the scene is divided by a couple of split-focus effects: in one, Eriksson, in closeup, rejoices at his freak shot and is so excited that he lets the grenade-thrower slip away; in another, Eriksson is staring the wrong way while behind him a couple of women open a tunnel for a V.C., who disappears into it. Meanwhile, Meserve fires his M-16 rifle, and then, his face showing his agony, he uses his hand like a poultice on Brownie's wound. A soldier radios for medical help, and Meserve, never letting go of his friend, keeps reassuring him until he's loaded on a chopper.

In these early scenes, Meserve is skillful and resourceful. He's only twenty years old, and as Sean Penn plays him he has the reckless bravery of youth. He's genuinely heroic. But Brownie dies (as Meserve knew he would), and back at the base camp the men, who have readied themselves for a visit to a brothel, are stopped and told that the village adjoining the base has been declared off limits. It's too much for Meserve, who has been put in charge of the five-day mission to check out a mountain area for signs of Vietcong activity, and later that night he finishes briefing his men by telling them to be ready to leave an hour early, so they can detour to a village to "requisition" a girl. Eriksson half thinks the Sarge is kidding. It takes a while for him (and for us) to understand that Meserve is not the man he was; only a day has passed since his friend was killed, but he has become bitter and vindictive—a conscious trickster and sinner.

Has something in Meserve snapped? Paul Fussell writes in his new book *Wartime* that in the Second World War the American military "learned that men will inevitably go mad in battle and that no appeal to patriotism, manliness, or loyalty to the group will ultimately matter." So "in later wars things were arranged differently," he explains. "In Vietnam, it was understood that a man fulfilled his combat obligation and purchased his reprieve if he served a fixed term, 365 days, and not days in combat either but days in the theatre of war. The infantry was now treated somewhat like the Air Corps in the Second War: performance of a stated number of missions guaranteed escape." Meserve, who has led dozens of combat patrols, has reached his limit with only a few weeks to go; he turns into an outlaw with a smooth justification for anything. (The kidnapping is a matter of cool planning: the girl can be explained as a "V.C. whore" taken for interrogation.) When Meserve's five-man patrol, having set out before dawn, arrives at the village he selected in advance, he and Corporal Clark (Don Harvey) peer into one hut after another, shining a flashlight on the sleeping women until they find one to their taste—Oanh (Thuy Thu Le), a girl of eighteen or twenty.

The terrified girl clings to her family. Clark carries her out, and her mother and sister come rushing after him, pleading in words that are just jabber to the soldiers, who want to get moving before it's light. They've taken only a few steps when the mother desperately hands them the girl's scarf. It's a pitiful, ambiguous gesture. She seems to want Oanh to have the comfort of this scarf—perhaps it's new, perhaps it's the only token of love the mother can offer her daughter. Eriksson says "Oh Jesus God" when he sees the men's actions, even before the mother holds out the scarf. Then he mutters helplessly, "I'm sorry." He's sick with grief, and we in the audience may experience a surge of horror; we know we're watching something irrevocable. Clark, a crude, tall kid who suggests a young Lee Marvin, is irritated by the girl's crying and whimpering, and he stuffs the scarf into her mouth, to gag her.

The men climb high above the valleys and set up a temporary command post in an abandoned hut in the mountains; it's there that the sobbing, sniffling girl is brutalized. (Thereafter, she's referred to as "the whore" or "the bitch.") Eriksson refuses his turn to rape her, but he can't keep the others from tying her up, beating her, and violating her. He himself is assaulted when he tries to stop them from killing her. Eriksson is brave, but he's also inexperienced and unsure of himself. In the few minutes in which he's alone with the girl and could help her escape, he delays because he's afraid of being charged as a deserter. The opportunity passes, and we can see misery in his eyes. Meserve sees it, too—sees that Eriksson finds him disgusting, indecent. And he begins to play up to Eriksson's view of him: he deliberately turns himself into a jeering, macho clown, taunting Eriksson, questioning his masculinity, threatening him. Meserve starts to act out his madness; that's the rationale for Penn's theatrical, heated-up performance. He brings off the early, quiet scenes, too. When Meserve shaves after learning of Brownie's death, we see that the hopefulness has drained out of him. Suddenly he's older; the radiance is gone. Soon he's all calculation. Although he was coarse before, it was good-humored coarseness; now there's cynical, low cunning in it. Fox, in contrast, uses a minimum of showmanship. He gives such an interior performance that it may be undervalued. To play a young American in Vietnam who's instinctively thoughtful and idealistic—who's uncorrupted—is excruciatingly difficult, yet Fox never lets the character come across as a prig. The two men act in totally different styles, and the styles match up.

And whatever the soldiers say or do, there's the spectre of the dazed, battered girl ranting in an accusatory singsong. The movie is haunted by Oanh long before she's dead. The rapists think they've killed her, but she rises; in our minds, she rises again and again. On the basis of the actual soldiers' descriptions of the girl's refusal to accept death, Daniel Lang called her "a wounded apparition," and De Palma and his cinematographer, Stephen H. Burum, give us images that live up to those words—perhaps even go beyond them. Trying to escape along a railway trestle high up against the wall of a canyon, Oanh might be a Kabuki ghost. She goes past suffering into the realm of myth, which in this movie has its own music—a recurring melody played on the panflute.

The lonely music keeps reminding us of the despoiled girl, of the incomprehensible language, the tunnels, the hidden meanings, the sorrow. Eriksson can't forgive himself for his failure to save Oanh. The picture shows us how daringly far he would have had to go to prevent what happened; he would have had to be lucky as well as brave. This is basically the theme that De Palma worked with in his finest movie up until now, the political fantasy *Blow Out,* in which the protagonist, played by John Travolta, also failed to save a young woman's life. We in the audience are put in the man's position: we're made to feel the awfulness of being ineffectual. This lifelike defeat is central to the movie. (One hot day on my first trip to New York City, I walked past a group of men on a tenement stoop. One of them, in a sweaty sleeveless

T-shirt, stood shouting at a screaming, weeping little boy perhaps eighteen months old. The man must have caught a glimpse of my stricken face, because he called out, "You don't like it, lady? Then how do you like this?" And he picked up a bottle of pink soda pop from the sidewalk and poured it on the baby's head. Wailing sounds, much louder than before, followed me down the street.)

Eriksson feels he must at least reveal what happened to Oanh and where her body lies. He's a dogged innocent trying to find out what to do; he goes to the higher-ups in the Army and gets a load of doubletalk and some straight talk, too. The gist of it is that in normal (i.e., peacetime) circumstances Meserve would not have buckled like this, and they want Eriksson to keep quiet about it. But he can't deal with their reasoning; he has to stick with the rules he grew up with. He moves through one layer of realization to the next; there's always another, hidden level. The longer Eriksson is in Vietnam, the more the ground opens up beneath him. He can't even go to the latrine without seeing below the floor slats a grenade that Clark has just put there, to kill him.

De Palma has mapped out every shot, yet the picture is alive and mysterious. When Meserve rapes Oanh, the horizon seems to twist into a crooked position; everything is bent away from us. Afterward, he goes outside in the rain and confronts Eriksson, who's standing guard. Meserve's relationship to the universe has changed; the images of nature have a different texture, and when he lifts his face to the sky you may think he's swapped souls with a werewolf. Eriksson is numb and demoralized, and the rain courses down his cheeks in slow motion. De Palma has such seductive, virtuosic control of film craft that he can express convulsions in the unconscious.

In the first use of the split-focus effect, Eriksson was so happy about having hit the grenade that he lost track of the enemy. In a later use of the split effect, Eriksson tries to save Oanh from execution by creating a gigantic diversion: he shoots his gun and draws enemy fire. What he doesn't know is that Clark, who is behind him, is stabbing her. He didn't know what was going on behind him after he was rescued from the tunnel, either. This is Vietnam, where you get fooled. It's also De Palmaland. There are more dimensions than you can keep track of, as the ant-farm shot tells you. And the protagonist who maps things out to protect the girl from other men (as Travolta did) will always be surprised. The theme has such personal meaning for the director that his technique — his own mapping out of the scenes — is itself a dramatization of the theme. His art is in controlling everything, but he still can't account for everything. He plans everything and discovers something more.

De Palma keeps you aware of the whole movie as a composition. Like Godard, he bounces you in and out of the assumptions about movies that you have brought with you to the theatre. He stretches time and distance, using techniques that he developed in horror-fantasy and suspense pictures, but without the pop overtones. He shifts from realism to hallucinatory Expressionism. When the wounded Brownie is flown out by helicopter, the movement of the yellow-green river running beneath him suggests being so close up against a painting that it's pure pigment. When Eriksson is flown out, it's at an angle you've never seen before: he looks up at the rotor blades as they darken the sky. These helicopters are on drugs.

Great movies are rarely perfect movies. David Rabe wrestles with the ugly side of male bonding; he's on to American men's bluster and showoff, and his scenes certainly have drive. But his dialogue is sometimes explicit in the grungy-poetic mode of "important" American theatre. The actual Eriksson was in fact (as he is in the movie) married and a Lutheran. He was also, as Daniel Lang reported, articulate. This is Eriksson talking to Lang:

> We all figured we might be dead in the next minute, so what difference did it make what we did? But the longer I was over there, the more I became convinced that it was the other way around that counted — that *because* we might not be around much longer, we had to take extra care how we behaved.

Rabe uses these remarks but places them maladroitly (as a response to something that has just happened), and he makes them sound like the stumbling thoughts of a folksy, subliterate fellow reaching for truth:

> I mean, just because each one of us might at any second be blown away, everybody's actin' like we can do anything, man, and it don't matter what we do — but I'm thinkin' maybe it's the other way around, maybe the main thing is just the opposite. Because we might be dead in the next split second, maybe we gotta be extra careful what we do — because maybe it matters more — Jesus, maybe it matters more than we even know.

This passage is the heaviest hammering in the movie (and the poorest piece of staging), but it's also a clear indication of Rabe's method. De Palma works directly on our emotions. Rabe's dialogue sometimes sounds like the work of a professional anti-war dramatist trying to make us think. Still, there's none of the ego satisfaction of moral indignation that is put into most Vietnam films, and what De Palma does with the camera is so powerful that the few times you wince at the dialogue are almost breathers.

This movie about war and rape — De Palma's nineteenth film — is the culmination of his best work. In essence, it's feminist. I think that in his earlier movies De Palma was always involved in examining (and sometimes satirizing) victimization, but he was often accused of being a victimizer. Some moviegoers (women, especially) were offended by his thrillers; they thought there was something reprehensibly sadistic in his cleverness. He *was* clever. When people talk about their sex fantasies, their descriptions almost always sound like movies, and De Palma headed right for that linkage: he teased the audience about how susceptible it was to romantic manipulation. *Carrie* and *Dressed to Kill* are like lulling erotic reveries that keep getting broken into by scary jokes. He let you know that he was jerking you around and that it was for your amused, childish delight, but a lot of highly vocal people expressed shock. This time, De Palma touches on raw places in people's reactions to his earlier movies; he gets at the reality that may have made some moviegoers too fearful to enjoy themselves. He goes to the heart of sexual victimization, and he does so with new authority. The way he makes movies now, it's as if he were saying, "What is getting older if it isn't learning more ways that you're vulnerable?"

Cruelty is not taken lightly in this movie. In the audience, we feel alone with the sounds that come out of Oanh's throat; we're alone with the sight of the blood clotting her nose. The director has isolated us from all distractions. There are no plot subterfuges; war is the only metaphor. The soldiers hate Vietnam and the Vietnamese for their frustrations, their grievances, their fear, and they take their revenge on the girl. When Brownie is shot, Eriksson, like Meserve and the others, feels that they've come to fight for the defense of the villagers who knew about the hidden guerrillas and could have warned them. They feel betrayed. Could the villagers have warned them without being killed themselves? It's doubtful, but the soldiers are sure of it, and for most of them that's justification enough for what they do to Oanh. The movie doesn't give us the aftermath: Oanh's mother searched for her and got South Vietnamese troops to help in the search; the mother was then taken away by the Vietcong, accused of having led the troops to a V.C. munitions cache. De Palma simply concentrates on what happened and why.

Meserve and Clark and one of the other men feel like conquerors when they take Oanh with them. They act out their own war fantasy; they feel it's a soldier's right to seize women for his pleasure. Comradeship is about the only spiritual value these jungle fighters still recognize; they're fighting for each other, and they feel that a gangbang relieves their tensions and brings them closer together. When Clark slings Oanh over his shoulder and carries her out of her family's hut, he's the hero of his own comic strip. These men don't suffer from guilt—not in the way that Eriksson suffers for the few minutes of indecisiveness in which he might have saved Oanh's life. He's turned from a cheerful, forthright kid into a desolate loner.

At the end, the swelling sound of musical absolution seems to be saying that Eriksson must put his experiences in Vietnam behind him—that he has to accept that he did all he could, and go on without always blaming himself. De Palma may underestimate the passion of his images: we don't believe that Eriksson can put Oanh's death into any kind of sane perspective, because we've just felt the sting of what he lived through. He may tell himself that he did all he could, but he feels he should have been able to protect her. The doubt is there in his eyes. (I hear that baby's cries after almost fifty years.) What makes the movie so eerily affecting? Possibly it's Oanh's last moments of life—the needle-sharp presentation of her frailty and strength, and how they intertwine. When she falls to her death, the image is otherworldly, lacerating. It's the supreme violation.

The New Yorker, August 21, 1989

A CRY IN THE DARK

★

Peter Rainer

Directed by Fred Schepisi. Written by Schepisi and Robert Caswell, from a book by John Bryson. Starring Meryl Streep and Sam Neill. **Warner Home Video.**

Fred Schepisi's *A Cry in the Dark* is an unremitting, almost magisterial vision of a horrific, true-to-life incident.

In the spring of 1980, Michael Chamberlain (Sam Neill), a Seventh-day Adventist pastor, and his wife, Lindy (Meryl Streep), along with their two sons and 9-week-old daughter, Azaria, vacationed in the Australian Northern Territory at Ayers Rock, Australia's most popular tourist attraction (and a sacred aboriginal site).

One evening, at a crowded campsite in the vicinity, a dingo (a wild Australian dog similar to the coyote) was seen scampering away from the tent where Azaria slept. Inside the bloodstained tent, Azaria was gone. A massive search ensued, but neither the baby nor the dingo was ever found.

Slowly, inexorably, what appeared at first to be a personal tragedy for the Chamberlains turned into a national witch hunt, as Lindy was charged with the killing of her baby. Cleared by the first inquest, Lindy, in a trial remarkable for its dubious evidence, ultimately was convicted of murder and, though pregnant, sentenced to life imprisonment. She served 3½ years before new evidence and judicial leniency resulted in her release in September of this year.

Given the opportunities for sensationalism, Schepisi and his co-screenwriter, Robert Caswell, adapting John Bryson's 1986 book *Evil Angels*—his furious defense of the Chamberlains—have done a remarkably lucid job of depicting Australia's hysteria over this case. *A Cry in the Dark* is so devoid of pulp that it's liable to be condemned by some in much the same terms as Lindy was—as too freakishly *calm* to be believable.

But the calm is only on the surface. The film, with its true-story/human-interest/courtroom-drama trappings, may have the superficial elements of a made-for-TV movie, but it has a resonance that comes from the filmmakers' deep, abiding sympathy for the Chamberlains' flinty resolve. Schepisi's great cinematographer, Ian Baker, shot the movie in wide-screen Panavision, and the vistas suggest larger meanings: waiting-to-be-tapped sources of power.

Schepisi recreates the story not only as a family tragedy but as a national tragedy. There's a tamped-down fury to his work here, a measured rage at the spectacle of prejudices unleashed. Schepisi's anger goes beyond the reformer's; it's an expression of cosmic disgust.

And yet Schepisi and Meryl Streep make you understand how it is that Lindy Chamberlain, with her hard manners and jet-black bangs, could give the country the cold creeps. Given the film's high intelligence, a more sentimental approach would have been another form of sensationalism. Schepisi acknowledges the differentness of the Chamberlains without acceding to the popular view of their "otherness." This film implies that their Seventh-day Adventism inspired fear — and therefore hatred — in a populace all too willing to believe in secret sacrificial rites. Lindy herself becomes a human sacrifice in the public's own blood sport; she and Michael are made to embody her detractors' darkest impulses. (Michael, convicted as an accessory to the crime, was allowed to remain home with the two boys and, after her birth inside prison, his baby girl.)

Lindy's prosecution hinged in a large part on the disbelief among white Australians that a dingo — the national mascot — could carry off a baby. But the point is made in the film (as in Bryson's book) that the aborigines, several of whom tracked Azaria's disappearance, knew the truth to be otherwise. Yet the aborigines were never brought in for testimony. In *A Cry in the Dark,* religious intolerance and racism are linked. Victimization makes for strange bedfellows: Seventh-day Adventists and aborigines.

The link is also made between religious intolerance and sexuality — Lindy's. Schepisi understands, as Carl Dreyer also did in *Day of Wrath,* just how intimately imputations of witchery are bound up with sexuality. Schepisi eroticizes Lindy for us; in one of her first scenes, in bed with her husband, she has a glow, a lushness, as if the armor of public rectitude had been cast aside, gently. She has a totally unself-conscious beauty in sequences like these.

On the witness stand, or giving interviews before the incessant TV camera crews, Lindy doesn't yield up her sorrows easily; but we know they are there because we've seen her in private, unveiled. It's a matter of almost religious principle that she not reveal her vulnerability to the hordes. Still, there's a sensual edge to her defiance, and her accusers pick up on it. It's what gives her sharpness its sting.

A Cry in the Dark may the most quietly uncondescending film ever made about religious fundamentalists. Schepisi can humanize Lindy and Michael and their fellow congregationalists because he isn't repelled by their rectitude; he can locate the human being inside the dogma. (Schepisi may have a special sensitivity for religious subjects; his first film, the elating, semi-autobiographical *The Devil's Playground*, set in a Marist boys' seminary, was the work of a filmmaker who could look back on his incarceration with a fond sanity.)

It's clear in *A Cry in the Dark* that Michael and Lindy's staunchness has a lot to do with their belief in the Second Coming, when they will be reunited with Azaria. When they state for the cameras that "nothing happens in the world unless God allows it," it's a way of comforting themselves, even if the public mistakes their covenant and brands them unfeeling. Michael is surprisingly media-savvy, but he's no profiteer. He has a preacher's yen to spread the word, but he's not out to convert anybody, really. He's just using the worldly materials so promiscuously at his disposal to justify his own fearsome condition.

Like Schepisi, Meryl Streep and Sam Neill have a gift for humanizing characters traditionally ill-treated in the movies. Streep sounds preternaturally Aussie: She has truly become Our Lady of the Accents. But her latest make-over is no stunt. Her performance is an attempt to make us understand how Lindy's principled, almost drab straightforwardness was her only purchase on heroism. Streep takes her cue from Lindy; there's no special pleading in her acting, no grandstanding. She makes you accept Lindy on her own ornery, embattled terms.

Sam Neill works so subtly with Streep that, for long stretches of the film, they seem to be communicating in code. Lindy and Michael share a sense of privilege based on faith, but the film is at its most ambiguously moving when it shows us how that faith is tested. In the wake of Azaria's disappearance, the Chamberlains never renounce their beliefs, but they move through the film in a state of controlled shock. They're waiting for some sign, some clue as to why this is happening to them. We can sense in their bewildered, fortified smiles the hysteria underneath. Although they may not realize it, the truest sign of grace in their ordeal is that they stayed together. After you've seen *A Cry in the Dark*, you'll know why.

Los Angeles Herald Examiner, November 11, 1988

GO TELL THE SPARTANS

★

Richard Schickel

Directed by Ted Post. Written by Wendell Mayes. Starring
Burt Lancaster. **Vestron Video.**

This unpretentious movie about a group of American "advisers" in Viet
Nam in 1964, before the war was thoroughly Americanized, has the
virtues of its defects. It is understated, lacking in powerful dramatic
incident and high human emotion, and rather flatly written and
directed. As a result, it has about it a realistically antiheroic air that is
rare enough in any movie about any war, and a grubby brutality that
matches memories of the news film that came out of Southeast Asia in
the '60s and did so much to disgust the nation with U.S. involvement
there.

Burt Lancaster, who has been playing veteran soldiers since long
before he became a veteran actor, is in command of the American
detachment and in solid command of the best starring role he has had
in years (he was, of course, superb as the dying patriarch, a character
role in Bertolucci's sprawling *1900*). Without the slightest fuss, he gives
us a portrait of a dutybound professional whose soldierly instincts tell
him that his duty this time is madness. Revolt is beyond his character,
but disgust is not. Lancaster's presence, carrying with it the memory of
other wars (and a different sort of war movie), provides a kind of bench
mark against which we measure the distance we have traveled from our
former attitudes about the military necessity.

His problems here are an ill-equipped and ill-motivated local sol-
diery (they go into battle carrying shotguns), the corruption of the local
district leader, a high command that doesn't understand the nature of
guerrilla warfare, and a less-than-inspiring crowd of American helpers.
Among them: A sergeant whose gung-ho spirit has been burned
out in the war. A lieutenant who moronically parrots—because he
moronically believes—all the official rationales for the war, all the
official ideas of how to conduct yourself on this dark and bloody
ground. A sometime college student one suspects of having literary
ambitions—he's looking for a war, any war, merely to experience it.

These soldiers are mostly seen not as brutes, but as decent if limited men doing their best in an indecent situation.

Their job is to reoccupy and defend a former French outpost called Muc Wa, which they do successfully until there is an inexplicable change in strategy and they are forced to withdraw into ambush and massacre. The picture is good at catching the absurdity and futility of the operation, but in the long siege-and-retreat sequence, Director Post's failure to rise above simple realism becomes a problem. The scenes here should be spookier and more suspenseful, imparting a developing sense of the madness of isolation in an alien land where the native enemy has all the advantages of terrain and bred-in-the-bones knowledge of it. There are hints of an effort in this direction (Muc Wa contains a cemetery for the French troops who died trying to defend it, with an inscription about the Spartans at Thermopylae that provides the picture's title; there is a one-eyed Viet Cong sniper who appears and disappears in a ghostly fashion), but they are never really developed.

Still, *Go Tell the Spartans* is, within its limits, an earnest and honest little picture that goes against the escapist grain of movies at this moment. The gesture is probably as futile, commercially, as defending Muc Wa was militarily, but you have to applaud the bravery of the effort and issue some kind of citation to a film that, all told, celebrates unconsciously honorable conduct by individuals enlisted in a bad cause. And offers a lot of good acting in the supporting roles too.

Time, September 25, 1978

HAMBURGER HILL

Hal Hinson

Directed by John Irvin. Written by Jim Carabatsos. Starring Dylan McDermott and Courtney Vance. **Vestron Video.**

More than any of the films to come out about Vietnam, *Hamburger Hill* wants to be a memorial to our experience there — a cinematic headstone. In the opening shots, under Philip Glass's swirling, hypnotic music, the camera speeds rapidly over scenes of the Vietnamese bush, intercut with shots of the Vietnam Veterans Memorial. And as the camera moves over the names chiseled into the stone, it seems to be committing them to memory, and at the same time adding them up, measuring the magnitude, and the gravity, of what occurred.

Written by Jim Carabatsos, who served with the 1st Air Cavalry Division in 1968–69 and spent five years interviewing soldiers involved in the combat there and researching the battle, it focuses on 14 members of the 3rd squad, 1st platoon, D Company, of the 3rd Infantry Battalion, who on May 10, 1969, began what has been characterized as one of the bloodiest battles of the war.

The movie isn't just about the fight at Hill 937, which came to be known as Hamburger Hill. About a third of it takes place in the camp before the soldiers are coptered into the Ashau Valley, where the battle takes place. These early scenes, in which you get to know the characters and the basic relationships are established, don't have much life, though. They're routine Vietnam War movie scenes — standard issue.

The movie doesn't really get started until the fighting begins. The sequence leading into the actual fighting, with the Animals' "We Gotta Get Out of This Place" playing on the soundtrack as the troops are dropped off at the edge of the jungle below the hill, is an exhilarating one. And it's one of the few in which director John Irvin allows himself to poeticize the action.

When the actual fighting starts, the action is divided into days, with the date given at the start of each day and each fresh attempt to capture the hill. The battle, as it was fought for those 10 grueling days, is for Carabatsos and Irvin a microcosm for the war — and for war itself. But the filmmakers don't try to enlarge on the details, or view them metaphorically, as *Platoon* did. Their film sticks to the specifics — with the soldiers clawing their way up that hill. And to the extent that it restricts its vision to that of the soldier, and gives us the experience of that battle from his point of view, it presents (at least to someone who wasn't there) a powerful representation of the fighting.

Because the film is grounded so deeply in the soldier's war, one can forgive some of the filmmakers' more blatant attempts to make political hay. From the infantryman's point of view, how should the dissension back home be viewed? When a young private named Bienstock (Tommy Swerdlow) gets word from his girl that she won't be writing him anymore because her "friends at college think it's immoral," how should he feel about left-wing activism against the war? (His reaction — three tiny sobs — is the most eloquent moment in the film.)

But Carabatsos and Irvin can't leave it at that. When on the seventh day of the battle the squad encounters a film crew at the foot of the hill, the squad leader, Sgt. Frantz (Dylan McDermott), calls them scavengers and tells them, "You haven't earned the right to be on this hill."

This is an example of the movie's hawkish, macho posturing at its most undiluted. But a similar attitude runs less obviously throughout the film. Carabatsos wrote the screenplay for *Heartbreak Ridge* (as well as the scripts to *Heroes* and *No Mercy*), and he and his collaborators seem to feel compelled not only to show us their war, but to tell us what we're to think about it. Carabatsos may have felt he was simply trying to be faithful to his own memory of the war, and to, in his words, "serve the men I was with in Vietnam." And if he had done so, the movie might have been a fitting memorial.

The issues raised in the film, most often by the men as they rest between battles, are by now familiar, but that they continue to come up, onscreen and off, expresses once again how deeply divisive the war was. The movie opens the next chapter in the public debate on the war. And if *Platoon* nudged public sentiment to the left, then *Hamburger Hill* is an attempt to reclaim it for the right.

Hamburger Hill tries to purify the war, to view it not as it was seen in *Platoon* or *Apocalypse Now,* but as a noble struggle fought by men of honor. Though the soldiers here dance, booze it up and treat themselves to an occasional massage at the local Vietnamese brothel, they aren't toked-up heads. The division within the squad itself is different here, too. It's not a conflict born out of differing opinions about the war and their role in it; the squabbles here are more personal, resulting from insults to girlfriends or, more significantly, racial sensitivities.

Hamburger Hill gets this part of the story down particularly well. There's black-white antipathy, but there are black and white bonds as well. And when racial feelings explode, there's usually something more than racial pressure behind the explosion.

Had the filmmakers resisted the temptation to politicize their material they might have made a great war movie. They might also have thought to give us some indication of the strategic significance of the hill. As it is, they've managed to create a deeply affecting, highly accomplished film.

No matter what you think of the script, it's impossible to dismiss what's up on the screen. Irvin, an English-born filmmaker who worked on several documentaries in Vietnam in 1969, has magnificent technique, and the scenes he shoots in the grass and on the side of the hill rival the battle sequences that Kubrick shot for *Paths of Glory* and Peckinpah's work in *Cross of Iron*.

The sequence in which the men try to get their footing and fight their way up the hill that has turned entirely to mud after a torrential rainfall is like a Kafkaesque nightmare of futility. And it seems an exquisite metaphor, too, for the whole Vietnam experience, a summation — fighting uphill in mud.

Unfortunately, when the fighting stops, the movie loses a lot of its percussive energy. There are, however, some wonderful performances by a cast of previously unknown actors. For most of the movie, Courtney Vance's Doc is the squad's emotional center. (He's the unofficial spiritual leader of the blacks in the squad, too.) He and the other black members of the cast — Don James, Michael Patrick Boatman, and Don Cheadle — create a real solidarity between them, and one of the highlights of the movie is the scene in which they huddle together, pattycakin' and chanting, "It don't mean nothin'. Not a thing," over and over.

"Don't mean nothin'" is the soldiers' all-purpose catch phrase, but it's more than that; there's a worldview in it. It won't fit as a pronouncement on the movie, though. The scene at the end of the film in which Beletsky (Tim Quill) looks over the battlefield has a primal intensity. *Hamburger Hill* is a punishing work; I can't say I was sorry it was over. It's a violent movie, but it doesn't have the self-satisfied, estheticized brutality of *Full Metal Jacket*. There's a purpose to it — a sense of values. The problem is that it's tough but not tough-minded. If it had been, it might have been great. Still, there's a kind of greatness in it. It takes a piece out of you.

The Washington Post, August 28, 1987

THE RIGHT STUFF

Richard T. Jameson

Directed and written by Philip Kaufman, from the book by Tom Wolfe. Starring Ed Harris, Sam Shepard, Dennis Quaid, Scott Glenn, and Fred Ward. **Warner Home Video.**

The Right Stuff is the biggest, brightest, busiest movie of the year, exhilarating in its largeness of spirit, in the sheer physical scope of its achievement, and in the breadth and complexity of its ambitions. It's also an exasperatingly difficult film to review, for its strengths and weaknesses frequently lie side-by-each, and although the former far outweigh the latter, both must be acknowledged.

Anyone setting out to make a film from Tom Wolfe's book *The Right Stuff* faced an awesome challenge: how to take 16 years' worth of aviation history, teeming with event, detail, character, and information, and shape it into a coherent, let alone an engrossing, movie. In this, writer-director Philip Kaufman has stunningly succeeded. Against all odds, unintimidated by the shifting currents of history and changing fashions in American heroism, his *Right Stuff* rushes along a breathlessly clean narrative line for 3 hours and 13 minutes. It's a joyride with substance, the sort of experience that leaves even classy kiddie-kar entertainments like *Raiders of the Lost Ark* and *Return of the Jedi* looking trivial by comparison.

How could any confected material compare with *The Right Stuff*'s real-life adventurism? What comic-book heroes could stand up alongside guys like Chuck Yeager, Scott Crossfield, and the others assembled in the "weird mad-monk squadron" at Edwards Air Force Base, on the roof of the high desert in California? In the late '40s and early '50s, these men committed themselves to "chase the demon" that lived in the clouds, just beyond every unbroken record — the sound barrier, then Mach 2, then Mach 2.1 . . . In shuddering rocketplanes, they pushed against the envelope that contained man's fragile eco-system, and reached for the outermost speed in horizontal air travel.

There seemed to be no place for them in the Space Age that got under way in the late '50s. For the government and NASA, desperate to find the likeliest specimens to hurl against the Russians, most of these wartime aces "didn't fit the profile," so there was a frantic effort to identify or develop a new breed of test pilot more disposed to play an obedient role in the space program. From this search emerged the seven Mercury astronauts—equally valiant, perhaps equally talented, men whose ordained lot was to serve as national heroes while at the same time realizing that, for all scientific intents and purposes, they were interchangeable with laboratory monkeys.

This much is history. But Wolfe's book had demonstrated that there's history and there's "history"—the reality of humankind's aspirations and achievements versus the public record of them. Kaufman elected to undertake this theme along with that of epic heroism. His *Right Stuff*, like Wolfe's, scathingly describes how that public record, in the case of the first astronauts, was engineered by politicians locked into a Cold War mentality, managed by the governmental equivalent of a public-relations agency, and constantly written and rewritten by a journalistic corps eager to set their own seal on a legend in the making.

The triumphant irony celebrated by both book and film is that, behind the screen of glitz and rhetoric, of manufactured pseudo-event and US Grade A balderdash, something legitimately magnificent was taking place after all. The film most winningly persuades us of that magnificence through its canny exploration of character, and of characters. It conveys history with the validity and straightforward drive of a documentary. But it does so without sacrificing the excitement and emotional power that can be attained only by telling a story, a story with specific, vividly knowable people who do something else with their lives besides making history.

Put it another way: character itself is "the right stuff" that differentiates Kaufman's heroes from the manipulators of official legend who surround them. After steeping the viewer in the heady atmosphere of mythos at Edwards AFB for several reels, Kaufman ventures a radical shift in tone. The American government is portrayed as a boardroom full of bumblers crawling about in the dark on hands and knees, swapping anti-Commie epithets while looking for an electric plug that has pulled out of its socket. NASA's recruiters are personified in a Mutt 'n' Jeff team (Jeff Goldblum and Harry Shearer) declaiming in ill-informed flatspeak and generally behaving as though trapped in a protracted *Saturday Night Live* skit. Once the Mercury astronauts have been selected, Kaufman introduces a "permanent press corps" who jitter about the periphery of events like spastic marionettes while a lunatic jungle-insect noise swarms on the soundtrack.

Some of this is funny, much of it is sophomorically silly, and some of it is just too much. (Did Shearer and Goldblum, interviewing Alan Shepard on a sea-tossed aircraft carrier, really have to be photographed with flecks of vomit clinging to their collars?) No matter how deserving the targets, Kaufman the satirist, doing his utmost to invent cinematic analogues for Wolfe's sardonic shticks, often plunges into overkill.

Yet one hesitates to pontificate too absolutely on this tactic. *The Right Stuff* is a high-energy movie, held on course by the fierce tensions of counterpoint. Questions of fidelity to Wolfe aside, no solemn valorization of the Mercury space voyagers and their Earthside predecessors could possibly have soared as high as Kaufman's screwball epic does. Its satirical components speak less to hipster complacency than to crazy glee; they're as bracing, in their cut-up way, as the images of Chuck

John P. Ryan (standing, left) is the NASA man who presents the seven Mercury astronauts to the press, kicking off the media circus at the center of *The Right Stuff.* They are (left to right) Fred Ward as Gus Grissom, Dennis Quaid as Gordon Cooper, Scott Paulin as "Deke" Slayton, Ed Harris as John Glenn, Charles Frank as Scott Carpenter, Scott Glenn as Alan Shepard, and Lance Henriksen as Wally Schirra. (Photo © 1983 The Ladd Company. All rights reserved.)

Yeager tilting with the demon in the stratosphere, or John Glenn's blazing reentry after the first orbiting of Earth by an American. Finally, these giddy assaults on Establishment dignity prove crucial in defining a changed America in which the Mercury 7 had to discover a new way of being heroes. What fascinates me most about the tortuous aesthetics of Kaufman's *The Right Stuff* is the way he reaches into movie classicism for talismans of rectitude. While the film's comic fall guys are sketched in a mode endemic to the TV Age, the gestures that define and bind — and, in binding, exalt — the Edwards AFB pilots and their Mercury successors are pure movie code: code in the sense of specialized communication, and code as a measure of ethical conduct.

Kaufman, who once made a relentlessly revisionist Western (*The Great Northfield Minnesota Raid*), explicitly reaches back to the genre's unadulterated phase to strike his initial keynote. Out of the sunrise, Chuck Yeager rides on horseback through the Mojave cacti to get his first look at the X-1 rocketplane, the fire-breathing steed that may carry him through the sound barrier. As Yeager, actor-playwright Sam Shepard contributes the sort of laconic, effortlessly cinemagenic presence that irresistibly recalls Gary Cooper: this *is* the American Hero. Later in the film, after Scott Crossfield (Scott Wilson) has temporarily ascended to "the top of the pyramid" by breaking Mach 2, he silently hoists his beer in salute to Yeager, and Yeager, across the flyboys' tavern and with his back turned, lifts his own glass of whisky above his shoulder in response. He's like the good-guy gunslinger in an old horse-opera who has eyes in the back of his head to spot an enemy, or a worthy rival.

Kaufman plays this movie-archetype game throughout the film. His screenplay succeeds in drawing so many characters so vividly, despite the limited screentime each can be accorded, by building on taglines of dialogue and behavior. (Nice instance of convergence measuring the growth of the astronauts' emotional solidarity: Mr. Clean Marine John Glenn, in a moment of frustration, referring to the Russians as "those . . . *darn* Commies," the earthy Gus Grissom responding with his all-purpose "Fuckenay, bubba," and Glenn immediately agreeing, "That's *right!*") This is an efficient, effective way to write movies. It also happens to parallel the style in which *The Right Stuff*'s heroes communicate.

Another of Kaufman's signal strategies is to deploy that most venerable and intrinsically cinematic means of communication, The Look. In the hilarious scene of the Mercury astronauts' first presentation to

Sam Shepard plays the ace test pilot Chuck Yeager, and Barbara Hershey is his wife, "Glamorous" Glennis, in *The Right Stuff.* (Photo © 1983 The Ladd Company. All rights reserved.)

the press, the more irreverent members of the team steal sardonic glances at one another as John Glenn (Ed Harris) gets carried away with Boy Scout enthusiasm and just can't stop talking to the avid audience; his confreres begin to get the notion that this public-hero business might be a hell of a kick, and chime in with fulsome platitudes of their own. The scene has a more sober rhyme at the climax of the film. During an appallingly gaudy Texas barbecue presided over by Lyndon Johnson (Donald Moffat), with the superannuated Sally Rand doing a solemn fandance for the multitude, the Mercury 7 again look around at one another, sharing a private recognition in the midst of a public performance. We can't know what they're thinking; we only know that it's theirs alone.

Kaufman's editing at this point, as so often in this film, is an inextricable combination of sublimity and oversimplification. Half the cuts dictate pat responses, half of them are instinct with mystical grandeur. Here, as at other key points, Kaufman defies mere earth-bound time-and-space logic to imply that the astronauts not only share a privileged perspective on the hullabaloo at the center of which they stand — they also somehow *know* that Chuck Yeager, a thousand miles away, is setting his life on the line in his most extreme and most private confrontation with "the demon." The greatest flier of them all, who didn't fit the profile, launches himself and his plane at the empyrean. No plane can get him there. But as he runs out of ceiling and starts to fall, Yeager glimpses the starry vastness of space just beyond the last wisps of cloud. That's as fine a moment as the movies have it in them to yield. That's the right stuff.

Seattle Weekly, November 9, 1983

SALVADOR

Michael Wilmington

Directed by Oliver Stone. Written by Stone and Richard
Boyle. Starring James Woods and James Belushi. **Vestron
Video.**

Whatever may be flawed in Oliver Stone's searing, full-torque new war
movie *Salvador,* one thing about it is burningly right: It's alive. It broils,
snaps and explodes with energy. The events (condensed from two years
of battles and political upheaval in El Salvador) fly past at a murderous
clip, hurtling you along almost demonically.

Everything is inflated, seething with conflict. Killers crawl over the
landscape like scorpions on a stove. When a battle erupts, it seems a
logical climax for the crazy, tense, superheated atmosphere: mad
characters floating along on a sea of booze, sex and paranoia, watching a
country die around them.

The movie is based on the El Salvador experiences of combat
photojournalist Richard Boyle, who co-wrote the script with Stone.
Boyle depicts himself—and James Woods plays him—as a paragon of
sleazy outlaw journalism. He's a yuppie-hating con man shamelessly
using everyone around him, alternately obsequious and vitriolic, living
defiantly on the edge. When Boyle flees to El Salvador (with Jim
Belushi as his bellicose disc-jockey buddy, Dr. Rock), he seems less
shining idealist than news bum making tracks. Woods is great in this
part: It's his nerviest, tightest, gutsiest performance. His Boyle is Gonzo
personified. In fact, if any movie ever caught the whole weird, racing,
arcing mind-set of Hunter Thompson's reportage, it's this one.

Salvador is packed with historical incident and thinly disguised
characters and events. Sometimes, it's constructed like a *Z*-style agitprop melodrama. Boyle and Stone obviously want you to share their
outrage at what they see as the brutality of the death squads, the
corruption of the government, and the hypocrisy of U.S. foreign and
immigration policy. But you don't have to accept all their arguments to
be impressed by this movie. This may be the rare political thriller where
the psychology moves you as much as the history.

In a way, *Salvador* is closer to *Casablanca* than to Costa-Gavras. It's a left-wing romance on a topical subject, a tale of a cynic redeemed. It might be better, actually, if Stone and Boyle didn't pour on that redemption, trying to make Boyle some universal witness to the suffering of El Salvador.

The movie goes bad briefly when Stone lets wafer-thin clouds of sentimentality deodorize the bracing cynicism and viciousness. It's as if Stone felt he had to pay for his audacity: sing a few hymns about brave, simple fighters of the soil. It's not really in him, and he's also weak on sexual relationships. (The women in *Salvador* get idealized too — perhaps their compensation for dealing with men as wily, foul-mouthed and irresponsible as the "heroes" here.) The only female who really affects you is the one Stone hates: Valerie Wildman as a promiscuous TV reporter.

But Stone is superb at showing the grungy depths of male camaraderie. He gets the rhythms, the profanity, the whiplash irreverence of professionals strung out to the limit. He writes and stages some of the best temper tantrums ever. Like Nicholson or De Niro, Woods turns these into arias.

A decorated Vietnam combat veteran, Stone seems to feel that war is a pathological subject, painting most of these participants as near-psychopaths (which is why the rebels' romanticization rings false). As a screenwriter (*Midnight Express, Scarface*), Stone has always been best at the ambiance of corruption and at bloody, primal battles. He has an eye for savagery: losers and damned souls struggling on the spit. As a director, he shows surprising gifts: immediacy, boldness, tight ensemble work. He keeps jolting you — making crescendos of violence, crackling volts of invective — and Georges Delerue's atypically taut, dissonant score beats hotly underneath it.

Salvador can't help stir up controversy — though Stone has been more scrupulous about his facts (and fictions) than the creators of many topical thrillers. *Salvador* is violent, gutsy, brainy, occasionally annoying and hellishly exciting: a "man's movie" of a kind you rarely see. It's a film that sings and screams. No one will go away from it unprovoked or unmoved.

Los Angeles Times, April 10, 1986

UNDER FIRE

Michael Sragow

Directed by Roger Spottiswoode. Written by Ron Shelton
and Clayton Frohman. Starring Nick Nolte, Gene Hackman, and Joanna Cassidy. **Vestron Video.**

Armed with microphone and camera or merely pen and pad, war
correspondents have been the roving scouts of the Western world for
more than a century, and no movie has captured the physical and moral
dangers of their job with more heartstopping immediacy or a richer
sense of irony than *Under Fire*. Set during the Nicaraguan revolution,
Under Fire is an intricate and eerie high adventure — the action, and
there's plenty, always poses the movie's most unsettling questions.
Director Roger Spottiswoode and screenwriter Ron Shelton (who
shares credit with Clayton Frohman) plummet their stars — Gene
Hackman, Nick Nolte, and Joanna Cassidy — into one life- and con-
science-threatening situation after another, leading them into a no
man's land where good intentions are not enough to be their guide.

The political background to the movie, the final days of the Somoza
regime, contrasts with the political background in this year's earlier
(and almost equally wonderful) *The Year of Living Dangerously,* which
was set in Indonesia during the final days of Sukarno's regime. In that
movie, the challenge facing its journalist heroes was to make sense of a
land so permeated with mysticism that it enveloped even politics; for
the Westerners in the film, Indonesia was unknowable. In *Under Fire,*
the challenge facing its journalist heroes is to convey the anguish and
futility of a Third World crisis that Westerners know too well: the US-
backed Somoza government maintains its oligarchy through systematic
repression while branding the native rebels as communist dupes.

Films move so slowly from script to production to distribution that
to make a movie about a social issue and maintain currency is next to
impossible. *Under Fire* is a topical movie that hasn't lost any of its
topicality. The story unfolds in Nicaragua, but the characters are introduced to us in Chad, where they're covering what radio reporter Claire
Stryder (Joanna Cassidy) characterizes as "this strange war that features
two provincial governments, three rival liberation fronts, and at

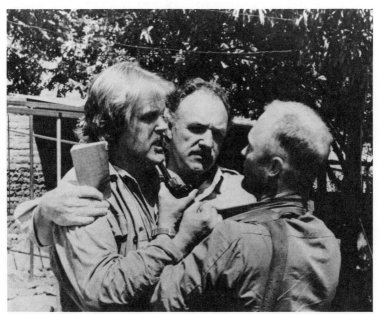

Gene Hackman (center), as war-correspondent-turned-TV-anchor Alex Grazier, breaks up a shouting and shoving match between photographer Russell
Price (Nick Nolte, left) and a brutal mercenary named Oates (played by Ed
Harris) in *Under Fire,* director Roger Spottiswoode's Nicaragua-set political
adventure story. (Photo by Bruce McBroom. © 1983 Orion Pictures Corporation. All rights reserved. Courtesy Vestron Video.)

least 12 tribal associations." As the credits roll, black soldiers in camouflage uniforms rise from the tall grass; then soldier-mounted elephants
lumber out of the shrubbery only to be met by a military helicopter,
rockets spewing as if from the fierce maw painted on its front. Whenever a repeated click is heard, the action freezes into black and white
stills—courtesy of ace photographer and war junkie Russell Price
(Nick Nolte). It's apt that Price is never visible during this sequence, for
as we learn, while taking the photographs of trouble that are his stock in
trade, he keeps himself at one remove: he is what he sees. Maybe that's
what affords Price his apparent invulnerability in battle: positioning
himself in the middle of a rebel troop truck that's about to be strafed,
standing tall with his camera, he must feel his journalistic objectivity
protects him like an invisible shield.

Price has picked up his professional standards from Alex Grazier (Gene Hackman), a *Time* magazine editor who's jousting with the networks for an anchor slot. Still handsome in his 50s, quick-witted and unflappable, Alex is every bit the old hand—he even chides Claire, his longtime lover, for editorializing about Chad by calling it "a strange war" and then "an endless story." A tragicomic figure, Alex knows his journalistic and personal limitations, yet he can't use that hard-won self-knowledge either to improve the conditions he covers or to hold on to the woman he loves. When Price asks Alex whether he's "hanging in there" with Claire, the editor replies, "Like an interim postwar government waiting for the palace to be overrun . . . by younger men." Price, of course, is the younger man. Claire, the apex of the triangle, is also the pivot of the movie. She's nearly as wised-up as Alex, but she hasn't completely succumbed to cynicism; she's nearly as adventurous as Price, but she doesn't crave thrills for their own sake. She can see through to the core of the moral quandaries. But Claire doesn't have Alex's professional distance, his self-protective reflexes, and she doesn't have Price's swaggering imperturbability. To this press gang, Nicaragua at first comes as a relief; as they say, "There's good guys, bad guys, cheap shrimp . . ."

But it's in Nicaragua that Claire and Price lose their equilibrium: maybe because the good guys are too good, the bad guys too bad, and the locations too akin to US barrios. Dennis Martinez, the Nicaragua-born pitcher for the Baltimore Orioles, is a local hero; pictures of Roman Catholic saints hang next to those of American baseball stars (in fact, some of the Sandinista rebels wear baseball caps instead of military berets). By contrast, the government of President Somoza—"Tacho" to his friends, or even to acquaintances—looks like a fat-cat country club. When he calls for a "get together" with Western journalists and VIPs, he throws a lavish party on the lawn of his compound; as a Nicaraguan nightclub singer croons American pop standards, he poses for pictures with a voluptuous Miss Panama.

The turning point for Claire and Price arrives early, as they watch the rebel-filled city of León being razed by Somoza's forces. Covering the street fighting (the Guardia is gunning down any kid with a pistol who has the bad luck to pass by), Claire and Price are led by the Sandinistas to observe the rebel takeover of a cathedral tower that has a commanding view of the city. The only Guardia survivor of the skirmish is a Chad acquaintance of Price's, an American mercenary named Oates (Ed Harris). Maintaining his journalistic noninvolvement, Price fails to warn the Sandinistas of Oates's presence; and when the mercenary shoots one of the rebels in the back, Price does what for him is unthinkable — he neglects to take a picture. What he does shoot next is the sleeping Claire after they've made love for the first time; it's these photos that tip off Alex and thus spur his departure. But Price and Claire are also getting involved in Nicaragua. After Alex leaves, the new lovers drift closer to the Sandinistas and further away from proper journalistic practice. They're tempted into foolhardy, heroic actions that endanger the lives of their friends — including Alex after his surprise return — but may just help the Sandinistas win their revolution.

Certain images of carnage in this movie — in particular that of Red Cross doctors and nurses turning into angels of fire, burning corpses in the street — have a hushed, macabre matter-of-factness. We are not engulfed by the horror; rather we, along with Claire and Price, live with it — which is more terrifying. To us, as to them, the atrocious injustice of the civil war is brought home every time a tank levels a house or the Guardia kills a civilian (Spottiswoode chillingly re-creates the 1979 roadside execution of ABC newsman Bill Stewart). But *Under Fire* is rousing, not numbing, because the moviemakers recognize that diverse emotions can take root in the most dispiriting circumstances. The film can be astonishingly humorous. Alex's wisecracking allows the movie-makers to get in their own licks at the media; the scene in which he tries to convince his superiors at *Time* that his report on the fighting in the capital city of Managua is more important than the latest travel update on the pope is a small comic masterpiece. And the Madison Avenue-ese of Somoza's PR man (Richard Masur) allows the film to satirize a State Department analysis of Somoza's "upside" and "down-side." The upside: "Somoza destroys the terrorist insurgents, rebuilds the country, shitcans the purveyors of excess, stabilizes the córdoba, and is finally beloved as the savior of Nicaragua. Our pal." The downside: "The Commies take over the world."

The film's offbeat supporting characters provide the most original comic moments. In a sly and unexpectedly touching performance, Jean-Louis Trintignant plays a CIA agent who operates as a corrupt Greek chorus, answering all the mundane questions asked by Claire and Price ("You win, I'm a spy. There, are you happy? *I* feel better") without divulging his true purpose. Ed Harris's Oates (in homage to the best bad-guy actor of them all, Warren Oates) is a lowlife worthy of Samuel Beckett. This "merc" takes his base joviality wherever he goes, joking about "spooks" in Africa and "greasers" in Nicaragua and forever

Joanna Cassidy is the radio correspondent who falls in love with the photojournalist played by Nick Nolte during the Nicaraguan revolution in *Under Fire*. (Photo courtesy Vestron Video.)

hungering for dope; with his racist naïveté intact, he adjusts to each blasted landscape. Harris calibrates his goofy volatility: he gives the sort of actor's turn we expect—and almost always get—from Gene Hackman.

In *Under Fire,* Gene Hackman is a star—and he comes through with the élan he displayed in his 1981 film *All Night Long.* It could be that playing a man close to his own middle age in that neglected comic fantasy brought him to a new, relaxed awareness. Today few actors can match his gift for projecting intelligence and torment without falling back on broad strokes: he creates instant empathy. And Hackman, Nolte, and Cassidy are inspired ensemble casting. If Hackman has a straightforward gaze, Nolte has a hooded one; if Hackman's eyes twinkle, Nolte's light up only when he has a bright idea. In Nolte's best performances—and this is one of them—he's able to convey conscious thought engaged in a tug of war with instinct. The most affecting moment in the movie is when he learns that pictures he's taken of the rebels have been used by Somoza's death squads—his political innocence, his faith in his art are shattered, and he's left with nothing. Joanna Cassidy gives the most vibrant, pugnacious performance of a working woman since Geneviève Bujold played a detective doctor five years ago in *Coma*. Lured by the romance of journalism, frightened by where it has led her, pulled every which way by her colleagues, Cassidy evinces a nervy professionalism that can't fully cushion her from the horrors.

Still photographs motivate every major plot twist. For this device to be more than gimmickry five other extraordinary performances were required—by cinematographer John Alcott, editor John Bloom, and composer Jerry Goldsmith, as well as writer Shelton and director Spottiswoode. Thanks to Alcott and Spottiswoode's salient composition, Price's photography measures up to his reputation in the film. We can see why his pictures appeal to both Somoza and the Sandinistas: because they go beyond politics to become potent, concrete statements on repression and chaos as well as emblems of courage and fortitude. The appearance, disappearance, and reappearance of Price's photos act as the building blocks of the narrative, establishing the giddy, tragic course of the story. Bloom edits them into the action smoothly and then holds the shot just long enough to freeze them into the viewer's consciousness. And the changeable visual texture—from saturated color to stark black and white and then back again—seems to have inspired Goldsmith to his most inventive score, which orchestrates Spanish guitars, Peruvian pan pipes, and synthesizers, among others, in music that is both alien and visceral, never merely exotic.

After a minor exploitation thriller (*Terror Train,* shot by Alcott) and an engagingly shaggy-dog chase picture (*The Pursuit of D. B. Cooper,* rewritten by Shelton), Spottiswoode has, with his third film, entered the ranks of major directors. Here he gently strips the characters of their illusions while putting them through tumultuous events. As a film editor, Spottiswoode worked on several Sam Peckinpah films (including *Straw Dogs*), and on Walter Hill's *Hard Times;* as a director he stages action that is less spectacular but also less coercive than either filmmaker's work. With its lucid visual flow, *Under Fire* moves between images of close conflict and images of expansion, climaxing with Claire's being carried along by a flood of humanity and ending in a square filled with triumphant revolutionaries.

Even as a political film, *Under Fire* is vastly superior to a tract like *Missing* — but I hope it won't be judged as a position paper. Spottiswoode isn't trying to stake out a definitive stance; you won't find out by watching this movie whether Cuba armed the Sandinistas. On its simplest level, all the movie says is that the US should be wary of meddling in Central America. But beyond that, the film's goal is to open viewers' minds and shake them out of categorical thinking — about journalists as well as about Third World revolutions. Fittingly, the still photographs have the last word: as the story recapitulates under the closing credits, pictures of Somoza's forces and Sandinistas become a composite portrait of a divided country crying out for nothing more than self-definition.

Boston Phoenix, October 25, 1983

THE LOST BOYS AND GIRLS

K ids! I don't know what's wrong with these kids today," sang the embattled father in *Bye Bye Birdie* on Broadway thirty years ago. "Kids! Who can understand anything they say?" This outcry has been heard with increasing frequency ever since adolescents began walking a walk, talking a talk, and dancing to a beat all their own.

As long as teenagers have been known as teenagers (the word first became standard usage in 1945), movies have tapped their energy and mirrored their explosive confusions. In the '60s and early '70s, when "youth culture" mushroomed, the most organic youth culture films (*Easy Rider, Alice's Restaurant*) offered an alternative to mainstream moviemaking much as counterculture weeklies provided an alternative to the daily press.

By the late '70s and '80s, the punk and heavy metal and drug war years, the volatility of teen street mores and the extremities of teen behavior scared away independent producers and big studios alike. Hollywood movies on the whole were more influenced than ever by the flashy images, the driving MTV rhythms, and the abbreviated attention spans demanded by media-saturated teenagers. But commercial filmmakers exploited rather than explored the young as a subject. And few talented directors even got the chance to render adolescent fantasies or realities with any degree of high fidelity.

Some exceptions follow. Four of them plug into the moods of late-'70s and '80s youth, whether through punk humor (*Repo Man*), hard-edged exposé (*River's Edge* and *Over the Edge*) or gentle, quirky courtship comedy (*Say Anything*). The other two, *Baby, It's You* and *September 30, 1955,* portray earlier generations' comings of age without knee-jerk nostalgia.

Whether their subjects are murder or class-spanning romance, whether their textures are poetic or abrasive, all these films attempt to depict teenagers without condescension or pandering—to see them eye to eye.

BABY, IT'S YOU

David Ansen

Directed and written by John Sayles. Starring Rosanna Arquette and Vincent Spano. **Paramount Home Video.**

John Sayles remembers, so vividly it can sting, about high-school joy rides and school-play auditions and the class of '67's prom night. About what it felt like to go off to a tony college hanging onto a hometown past that you're not sure whether to hide or display. In *Baby, It's You* he remembers things he couldn't have known: how it felt to be a smart, ambitious Jewish girl like Jill Rosen (Rosanna Arquette) in Trenton, N.J., a girl who wants to be an actress and keeps pinups of Paul Newman and Monica Vitti in her locker, a girl who falls for a sharkskin-suited townie called the Sheik (Vincent Spano) who gets kicked out of school just as she gets accepted to Sarah Lawrence. Jill is smart enough to know it's an inappropriate affair, and that's half the reason it turns her on. The Sheik's desperate calls to Sarah Lawrence from Miami, where he lands in a third-rate nightclub, mouthing the words to Frank Sinatra records, go increasingly unanswered. The Sheik doesn't fit into the future of a girl like Jill. And to a guy who's beginning to see he has no future, Jill becomes the only thing to pin his hopes on.

Baby, It's You may be chock full of songs like "Cherish" and "Woolly Bully," but it's not about nostalgia. It's a dark, increasingly painful look back, and one that isn't about to take sides in this romantic showdown. Sayles likes both Jill and the Sheik, but he knows them too well to place any bets on their future. The Sheik thinks he can impress Jill by taking her to the Fontainebleau in Miami Beach, but she's already been taken there, as a child, by her parents.

These are the trenchant social details that Sayles, who is attuned to every nuance of class, is so good at. He's at his best in the college scenes, recording Jill's difficult adjustment to a new set of values. On a date with an Ivy League type who's putting down "Neanderthal" guys, Jill drinks too much and starts talking about her past—only it's the Sheik's past she pretends to come from, not her own. It's a funny, painful scene: she's being loyal to her past and dishonest to herself, and she makes herself sick acting out her wildly ambivalent feelings. For scenes like this, one willingly forgives Sayles his often pedestrian visual sense and his overreliance on music to fill up the void in his images.

From the smallest role to the leads, Sayles has cast his movie brilliantly. Spano, nervy, electric and pathetic, takes just the right aim at his character. But it's Arquette who makes this movie live. This seductive 23-year-old actress—so haunting as Gary Gilmore's lover in *The Executioner's Song*—always finds the fresh note. Like Sissy Spacek or Debra Winger, she's a presence you can't keep your eyes off, for fear of missing crucial information.

Newsweek, April 11, 1983

OVER THE EDGE

David Denby

Directed by Jonathan Kaplan. Written by Tim Hunter and
Charlie Haas. Starring Michael Kramer and Matt Dillon.
Warner Home Video.

The troubled teenagers who go on a rampage in *Over the Edge* haven't
been deprived, and they're not confused, misunderstood, and hungry
for love, like James Dean or Sal Mineo three decades ago. Set in "New
Granada," a half-finished condo development in Colorado, this sensa-
tionally effective movie is about white, middle-class fourteen-year-olds
who have their parents' love, their own rooms, stereos, and color TV's,
but are going crazy from boredom, isolation, and institutionalized
rootlessness. The kids are privileged nihilists, often stoned or smashed,
growing up in a vacuum; their friendship for one another and a shared
loathing for New Granada are the only values they've got.

Too young to drive to the mountains in the distance, the kids are cut
off, sequestered in their instant "community" of flat, curved streets and
tasteful houses with vaulted ceilings in the living rooms and patios
beyond sliding glass doors. On the street, trees haven't grown in yet,
and sinister empty lots stand across the way. In this featureless paradise
the teenagers roam around with nowhere to go but a Quonset-hut rec
room. They know the "town" is a real-estate-developer's scam, and
they're utterly contemptuous of it and of their parents, who have fled
there from Denver or Chicago. Casually, without shame or fear, they
begin to vandalize the school and houses. When one of the rebellious
kids is killed by the cops, the rest explode in fiery violence.

The screenplay, which combines teen-movie conventions and hip
sociological awareness, was written by Tim Hunter and Charlie Haas,
and is largely based on what happened in the early seventies in Foster
City, a spiffy condo development built on landfill in San Francisco Bay.
Yet no one will mistake the movie for a documentary. The director,
Jonathan Kaplan, is a 33-year-old ex-student of Martin Scorsese's, and
he broke into Hollywood by making quickies for Roger Corman,
schlockmeister extraordinaire. Kaplan, whose best-known film is *White Line
Fever,* a nifty B movie starring Jan-Michael Vincent, goes all the way

Sergeant Doberman (Harry Northrup) brings in two of New Granada's alienated teens for questioning (Matt Dillon, left, as Richie, and Michael Kramer, right, as Carl) in *Over the Edge*. (Photo © 1979 Orion Pictures Corporation. All rights reserved.)

with the violent possibilities of the subject. He mixes the excesses of adolescent rage with his own exploitation-film extravagance. The movie, extremely clever and possibly incendiary in its effect, is both entertaining and disturbing. If properly promoted, it could become something of an event in the movie mythology of rebellion, a legitimate heir to *The Wild One, The Blackboard Jungle, Rebel Without a Cause,* and *The Warriors.*

So far, the movie hasn't received a decent commercial opening. Completed over two years ago, *Over the Edge* was shown regionally by its distributor, Warner's, but kept out of New York and away from the reviewers. The picture never caught on. In an interview in the November *American Film,* Jonathan Kaplan says, "In all fairness to the distributor, we delivered it at the time *Boulevard Nights* and *The Warriors* [which caused a few disturbances] were in general release. The theatre owners in the suburbs were scared. They said, 'We don't want a picture where kids are going to tear up the sixplexes.'"

Shelved, and then sold off to cable, *Over the Edge* finally played New

York for two weeks last month at the Public Theater. After sensational reviews and good crowds, the picture will be opening this Friday at the tiny, deluxe Cinema 3, in the Plaza hotel. Someone is still scared to let kids see this movie.

In some ways, *Over the Edge* is a fairly conventional tale of alienated adolescence. The hero, Carl (Michael Kramer), a rather soft, ordinary-looking boy with intelligent dark eyes, undergoes rites of initiation: He gets beaten up by a thug, spends his first night with a girl, breaks with his parents, and leads the kids in a riot. Carl will probably pass out of delinquency in a few years, but in the romantic-outlaw terms of the movie he has to say good-bye to the finkdom of being a nice boy; he has to be "bad" in order to be a man.

Carl becomes the protégé of Richie (Matt Dillon), an insolent, classically doomed movie youth. Richie woos Carl away from his parents, in particular away from his nervous, straight-arrow father, who holds the Cadillac franchise in town. Dillon, who went on to take Kristy McNichol's virginity in *Little Darlings,* has long hair and sneering lips, and wears a T-shirt cut off at the arms and above the belly. His delivery of such punk lines as "The kid who tells on another kid is a dead kid" is little more than a breathy snarl. Acting technique may come later; in 1978 he had the sensual command to play a graceful young hood on instinct alone.

Even a big-city slum neighborhood has its traditions, its places to hang out, but the elders of New Granada are so eager to protect their investments that they send the cops to hassle the kids wherever they gather. Since there's nothing to do, no place to go, hassling the cops back becomes a badge of courage, especially for a well-brought-up boy.

Trying to control their charges with pious moralizing, the teachers at the shiny new school show a "documentary" about vandalism in which a model student says, "Maybe you're mad at the school, but busting something doesn't work. I think it's childish." She's right, of course, but saying it that way doesn't settle down a kid who's angry. *Over the Edge* is worth taking seriously because it stays close to the teenagers' feelings without losing all objectivity. We can see, for instance, that Carl's father isn't a bad guy but that he's become a tense, angry martinet out of anxiety for New Granada's commercial future. Perhaps in a few years Carl will be more sympathetic to his father's worries, but at this moment he sees the man as an insensitive sellout.

Teenagers are idealistic and irrational and unfair, and the devil can get into them: Carl and the others mess up the town because they know disorder scandalizes their parents more than anything else does. "You turned your kid into what you were trying to get away from," a visitor says to the mayor. The filmmakers obviously agree with that malicious irony, but they aren't gleeful about it—they show the parents arguing with one another, stricken with guilt, trying to assess blame.

Jonathan Kaplan is a solid action director who obviously has a special rapport with teenagers. There are memorable images produced by his amused, excited youth partisanship—a boy arriving at an art-class exam stoned and looking with disbelief and dismay at a tumultuous Bosch painting; kids furiously pouring out of every door and window of a house when the cops raid a party. All along, Kaplan celebrates the kids' defiance, and at the end, when they attack all the authority figures at once—cops, teachers, parents—the movie explodes in lyrical bursts of violence and fire. This climax is morally ambiguous, to say the least. Kaplan wants to show the kids going too far, but he also wants a big bang, and our responses are divided and confused—we can hardly enjoy it when distraught parents run around in terror. *Over the Edge* is disturbing because the kids, who have some legitimate gripes, turn against the innocent and well-meaning as well as the culpable. No mistake: *Over the Edge* is an exploitation movie. But in their opportunistic way, the fellows who made it get at the social truths and middle-class nightmares more effectively than most "responsible" filmmakers would.

New York, January 18, 1982

REPO MAN

Carrie Rickey

Directed and written by Alex Cox. Starring Harry Dean Stanton and Emilio Estevez. **MCA Home Video.**

An enchanted comedy about disenchanted L.A. cultists, *Repo Man*—its title refers to the ignition cowboy who repossesses cars for creditors—is shot in that magically lit time somewhere between tequila sunset and hangover sunrise. It's a remarkable feature debut by director Alex Cox, who trails the skidmarks of an elusive '64 Chevy Malibu hauling a truckload of irradiated aliens from another planet.

Downtown Los Angeles—a non-place in the burg known as "six suburbs in search of a city"—is the site of a UFO mission (hiding under the alias of the United Fruitcake Outlet), of Diuretix' science of body over mind, of TV-reverend Larry—born-again cretin—and of the Helping Hands Acceptance Agency, a car-repossession company. The radiant '64 Chevy fulfills the prophecy of each group.

Into this cult culture blunders Otto (Emilio Estevez), a blond, brush-cut punk looking for a job and kicks. What better employment for Otto than as an auto repo man, giving him the twisted satisfaction of legally stealing cars? Estevez, talented son of actor Martin Sheen, bristles with punkster exuberance. Much of *Repo Man*'s humor comes from Estevez' understanding of Otto's perverse evolution: his sourpuss, seen-it-all experience sweetens into awestruck innocence.

Otto is initially attracted to the adrenalin high of pirating cars and returning them, for bounty, to the banks that financed them. However, guided by the ministers at Helping Hands, especially Bud (Harry Dean Stanton), Otto realizes that the repo religion worships the false god of credit. Finding the true god becomes Otto's comic and cosmic mission. It just might be in the trunk of that Malibu from another galaxy!

Like *Diva*, like the delirious and delicious *Liquid Sky*, *Repo Man* is a documentary of punkster life masquerading as a space opera: truth *is* stranger than science fiction. Otto's L.A. is a generic city: supermarkets stock cans marked, simply, "Food." When the repo men go to a liquor store, they buy generically marked "Drink" six-packs.

Robby Muller's gritty-mystical cinematography enables Cox to humorously contrast the blandness of 24-hour stores, American cars, and Los Angeles cults with piquant characters and their tasty patter.

Some examples: Skinheads in studded leather hold a Friday night confab, proposing the ultimate L.A. crime: "Let's go get sushi and not pay!" UFO worshippers, glued to the tube, offer proof that the Mayans invented TV. A hippie burnout mechanic postulates that the trouble with Los Angeles is, "The more you drive, the less intelligent you are." *Repo Man* dances across a hazy border between overwrought, paranormal comedy and overheard, normal L.A. conversation.

While acknowledging its debt to '50s teen rebel and sci-fi genres, *Repo Man* is an original because Cox puts a spin on every cliché, hilariously making a religion out of disbelief. *Repo Man* is the saltiest,

sweetest, most sublimely sleazy tickle in the Los Angeles ribs. If it
doesn't convulse you with belly laughs, then you're a stiff.

Boston Herald, July 6, 1984

RIVER'S EDGE

★

David Denby

**Directed by Tim Hunter. Written by Neal Jimenez. Star-
ring Dennis Hopper, Keanu Reeves, and Crispin Glover.
Embassy Home Entertainment/Nelson Entertainment.**

Tim Hunter's *The River's Edge* is the most disturbing movie I have seen
in the nearly nine years I have held this job. Certainly not the best, but
the most disturbing. This brilliant, messy little picture, another triumph for the independent film movement, should cause people to
argue and celebrate for years — argue over how it could have been done
better, celebrate that it was done at all. In recent years, American movies
have followed teenagers from school to shopping mall to make-out
couch, and some of these pictures have been skillful and charming. But
as far as real moral interest or complexity goes, this is the only one that
matters.

Among recent ambitious movies, David Lynch's *Blue Velvet* doesn't
get under the skin in the same way. Lynch puts demonic stuff on the
screen, but even in his most feverish moments we're aware of his grip,
his "vision." A voluptuous, insinuating look at the underside of small-
city American life, *Blue Velvet* was Lynch's cherished nightmare. *River's
Edge,* on the other hand, is everyone's nightmare, a cloud of misery
wafting out of the familiar confusions and vacancies of American
adolescence. And perhaps because they are still searching, trying to find
the sinister side of commonplace things, the director, Tim Hunter
(*Tex*), the young screenwriter, Neal Jimenez, and the cast of largely
unknown young actors don't have a perfect hold on their subject. Some

Tim Hunter (left) directs Joshua Miller (center) as a budding sociopath and Keanu Reeves as the most conscience-stricken member of a gang that keeps mum about a murder, in the fact-inspired *River's Edge*. (Photo by Jane O'Neal. © 1987 Island Pictures.)

of the movie is sheer bravado and pretty terrible. Yet the failures of *River's Edge* paradoxically make me care about it more. *Blue Velvet*, for all its flowers-of-evil bloom, quickly receded into the semi-comforting realm of "art." But this time, I'm sure, the bad dream won't fade away.

Standing on a bridge over a swollen and muddy river, a little boy slowly, deliberately drops a doll into the water. The camera, which has been looking up at him, rises over his head, crosses to the other side of the bridge, and sees what he sees upriver—a girl lying on the bank, naked, bluish-white, and a teenage boy next to her on the ground, rocking back and forth and howling at the sky. The dead girl looks like a larger version of the doll now submerged in the water. Later, in a flashback, we briefly see the crime, and we never have any reason to doubt what the teenager, John (Daniel Roebuck), says of it—that the girl didn't provoke him, didn't do much of anything, and that he killed her on a whim, because it made him feel powerful. Huge, with close-set eyes, a mean little mouth, and a hulking, shapeless body, John takes his place in the American procession of motiveless killers. We have noticed his face, with a passing shudder, on the evening news. He's scary but familiar. The movie's true horror lies elsewhere.

Casually, John boasts to his friends (girls as well as boys) that he has killed the girl, who is their friend, too. Calling his bluff, they accompany him to the river, where they poke at the cold, naked corpse, trying to make sure they aren't being kidded. They are shocked, but no one mourns; and no one denounces the killer or even *says* much of anything. The leader of the group, Layne (Crispin Glover) — as much a psychopath as John but ambitious — decides that protecting John from the cops could be a great adventure, a test of loyalty and courage. The girl is dead, isn't she? She can't be brought back, Layne reasons, so why say anything about her? Only John, who is still alive, matters. The kids' blank, unthinking amorality is so appalling, it's funny.

Though based on a 1981 incident in Northern California, the movie offers no clue as to its setting. It could be set wherever social bonds are loose and there's little to do. Hanging out together at school and around town, the kids are a bedraggled rat pack, frenetic yet depressed, worshipers of their own moth-eaten cult. Drugs, souped-up cars, crappy "Death Metal" rock — their preoccupations could be a haplessly demoralized parody of sixties culture. The little boy who drops the doll off the bridge is angry because he's too young to get into the gang — there's nothing else for him to look forward to. The mad Layne is their leader simply because he's the most determined to become a thug; he goes too far, a wildly neurotic bully whom the others can't resist (when they do, they feel they are finking out).

Like the 1979 youth-exploitation film *Over the Edge,* which Tim Hunter wrote (with Charlie Haas), *River's Edge* captures the way teens build a disastrously enclosed world. They're sure they shouldn't report the murder to the police. That would be "narcing" — ratting, telling the grown-ups, who never understand a thing. The filmmakers' point, I think, is that the kids' exclusion of adults may be tragic, but it's the source of the only emotional life they've got. *Tex* showed that Hunter is a partisan of adolescence as a state of mind and body. In his movies, the loyalties that the kids demonstrate toward one another, however dumb, are a twisted form of honor.

The one who finally breaks away and goes to the cops, Matt (Keanu Reeves), is a decent boy struggling for clarity. Like the others, Matt lives in a squalid, trailer-trash house, with harassed, overworked adults. His own father has vanished, replaced by a noisy, exasperated lout; his mom, a nurse, is worn out. All the kids have grown up in a vacuum, without any models, any authority they can respect. (At school, a teacher who is a veteran of the sixties pontificates about social responsibility, but his rap is overbearing and he's ignored.) A cranky, paranoid old biker (played, inevitably, by Dennis Hopper) is the closest thing they've got to a role model, and the guy's hold on them is based on his boast that he, too, killed his girlfriend, some twenty years earlier. The difference, he says, is that he killed her out of love. In his own myth-ridden mind, his crime of passion makes him a moral hero. Hopper's burning eyes give these pronouncements a black-comedy fanaticism.

Mere stupidity, as you may have guessed, isn't what *River's Edge* is about. Jimenez and Hunter are getting at a phenomenon that has haunted the twentieth century the way Satan haunted the Middle Ages — affectlessness, indifference, the inability to feel what we think human beings should feel. These kids aren't connected inside: The doll thrown into the water is mourned, the friend murdered by another friend is not. Why not? In part because the friendships here, however intense, are largely provisional, based on drugs, a shared mood, the jokes of a season. In their own terms, the kids are being honest.

Yet Hunter, who keeps returning to the purple-lipped, naked corpse, surely intends to suggest something momentous: Leaving a dead body

Keanu Reeves is Matt and Ione Skye is Clarissa — a couple of teenagers who try to transcend the demoralized landscape of *River's Edge*. (Photo by Jane O'Neal. © 1987 Island Pictures.)

unburied, the boys and girls casually violate a fundamental taboo of Western civilization, blithely committing a crime whose horror once resounded through the Greek myths, Homer, Sophocles. All right, this isn't ancient Greece: The rain-soaked landscapes may look godforsaken, but the ground won't rise up to accuse anyone. Still, Hunter has created a modern myth. The kids' behavior, in the end, can't be reduced to sociology. There is something uncanny about it. The rain has made a hellish, tangled bank out of the river's edge.

River's Edge sent me tumbling head over heels. Though wonderfully photographed (by Frederick Elmes), the movie is rough, with some obvious mistakes. There are boring passages of wrangling among the kids; Dennis Hopper's insane biker is a bit of mannerist, post-sixties hipsterism; and Hunter makes his points about affectlessness with too much rhetoric. Worst of all, Crispin Glover's work as Layne, which I fervently wanted to be great, risks disaster—and sometimes achieves it. Glover, whose performance as the father in *Back to the Future* was a brilliantly masochistic piece of cartoon acting, has a long pale nose and chin, and here he wears a black ski cap, with black hair flowing down to his shoulders. Pacing around crazily, he's the Wicked Witch of the Shopping Mall. His speech—industrial waste clogging a running stream—is sluttish, jeering, pathetic. Glover gets to the truth of something by wild exaggeration, yet he's not a comic, he's serious, so he seems almost nuts. The performance has already been denounced as a catastrophe. I thought it was desperate and moving. So is the whole movie.

New York, May 18, 1987

SAY ANYTHING

Roger Ebert

Directed and written by Cameron Crowe. Starring John
Cusack and Ione Skye. **CBS/Fox Video.**

She is the class brain, and so, of course, no one can see she's truly
beautiful — no one except the sort of weird kid who wants to devote his
life to kick-boxing, and who likes her because of her brains. He calls
her up and asks her out. She says no. He keeps talking. She says yes.
And after her first date, she tells her father she likes him because he is
utterly straightforward and dependable. He is a goofy teen-ager with
absolutely no career prospects, but she senses she can trust him as an
anchor.

She discusses him so openly with her father because they have made
a pact: They can say anything to one another. When her parents got
divorced, she chose to live with her father because of this trust, because
of the openness that he encourages. Her father's love for her is equalled
by his respect. And she sees him as a good man, who works long hours
running a nursing home because he wants to help people.

Honesty is at the core of *Say Anything,* but dishonesty is there, too,
and the movie is the story of how the young woman is able to weather a
terrible storm and be stronger and better afterward. This is one of the
best films of 1989 — a film that is really about something, that cares
deeply about the issues it contains — and yet it also works wonderfully
as a funny, warmhearted romantic comedy.

The young woman, Diane, is played by Ione Skye; she's a straight-A
student with a scholarship to a school in England. She is one of the
class beauties, but doesn't date much because she intimidates boys. The
boy who finally asks her out is Lloyd (John Cusack), and he dates her
not only out of hormonal urging, but because he admires her. Her
father (John Mahoney) is a caring, trusting parent who will do anything
he can to encourage his daughter — but his secret is that he has done too
much. They find that out when IRS agents come knocking on the door
with charges of criminal tax evasion.

The movie treats Diane's two relationships with equal seriousness.
This is not one of those movies where the father is a dim-witted,

middle-aged buffoon with no insights into real life, and it is also not one of those movies where the young man is obviously the hero. Everyone in this film is complicated, and has problems, and is willing to work at life and try to make it better.

The romance between Diane and Lloyd is intelligent and filled with that special curiosity that happens when two young people find each other not only attractive but interesting—when they sense they might actually be able to learn something useful from the other person. Lloyd has no career plans, no educational plans, no plans except to become a champion kick-boxer, and then, after he meets Diane, to support her because she is worthy of his dedication. In the way they trust each other and learn to depend on each other, their relationship reminded me of the equally complex teen-age love story between River Phoenix and Martha Plimpton in *Running on Empty*.

What's unique to this movie is how surefooted it is in presenting the ordinary everyday lives and rituals of kids in their late teens. The parties, the conversations, and the value systems seem real and carefully observed; these teen-agers are not simply empty-headed *Animal House* retreads; the movie pays them the compliment of seeing them as actual people with opinions and futures.

Cameron Crowe, who wrote and directed the film, develops its underlying ideas with a precise subtlety. This is not a melodrama about two kids who fall in love and a parent who gets in trouble with the IRS. It considers the story as if it were actually happening, with all the uncertainties of real life. When Diane goes in to confront a government agent, and tells him that he is harassing her father who is a good man, Crowe allows the scene to develop so that we can see more than one possibility; he even cares enough to give the IRS agent—a minor character—three dimensions.

I was also surprised to find the movie had a third act and a concluding scene that really concluded something. Today's standard movie script contains a setup, some development, and then some kind of violent or comic cataclysm that is intended to pass for a resolution. *Say Anything* follows all the threads of its story through to the end; we're interested in what happens to the characters, and so is the movie.

The performances are perfectly suited to the characters. Ione Skye—who was a model before she was an actress—successfully creates the kind of teen-age girl who is overlooked in high school because she doesn't have the surface glitz of the cheerleaders, but who emerges at the tenth class reunion as a world-class beauty. John Cusack, a unique, quirky actor with great individuality, turns in a fast-talking, intensely felt performance that is completely original; he is so good here that if you haven't seen him in *The Sure Thing* or *Eight Men Out,* you might imagine he is simply playing himself. But his performance is a complete and brilliant invention. And John Mahoney (Olympia Dukakis's sad-eyed would-be swain in *Moonstruck*) finds the right note for a father who cares, and loves, and deceives both himself and his daughter, and tries to rationalize his behavior *because* he cares and loves.

Say Anything is one of those rare movies that has something to teach us about life. It doesn't have a "lesson" or a "message," but it observes its moral choices so carefully that it helps us see our own. That such intelligence could be contained in a movie that is simultaneously so funny and so entertaining is some kind of a miracle.

Chicago Sun-Times, April 14, 1989

SEPTEMBER 30, 1955

David Ansen

Directed and written by James Bridges. Starring Richard Thomas, Deborah Benson, and Lisa Blount.

Conway, Ark. It is the day of James Dean's death, *September 30, 1955,* an apocalyptic day for Jimmy J. (Richard Thomas), who has sat wet-eyed through four viewings of *East of Eden,* willing himself into an almost mystical sense of identification with his rebellious celluloid idol. Shattered by the news, he steals some liquor, speeds down to the banks of the Arkansas River with his uncomprehending college chums and ropes them into a ceremony to honor his dead hero. Covering his body with mud (a detail picked up from a *National Geographic* article on African mourning rituals), he erects an Oscar out of wet sand, joins hands with his friends and waits breathlessly for a sign from the dead. A dog barks, and Jimmy J. shivers with the ecstasy of answered prayers.

Some of Jimmy J.'s friends think he's "sick, affected and weird." His Homecoming Queen girlfriend, Charlotte (Deborah Benson), tenders the complacent wisdom of her upper-middle-class background: he's just a "normal boy going through a phase." To the local outcast Billie Jean (Lisa Blount), who's seen *East of Eden* 22 times and also heard a dog bark from her bedroom window, Jimmy J. is a romantic soulmate who can invest life with the passionate glamour of the movies. It's one of the many accomplishments of writer-director James Bridges's ardent comedy that we see the truth in all these conflicting assessments.

September 30, 1955 explores the moment in a young man's life when art and life become hazardously entangled and caution is thrown to the winds. It does so with such a delicate mixture of satire and sentiment that our own responses are in a constant state of flux. We can be moved by Jimmy J., as he was by Jimmy Dean, even as we smile at his narcissistic role-playing and are appalled by the tragedy his irresponsibility helps bring about.

This double vision gives this small, taut film its bite. Bridges (*The Paper Chase*), a former actor who grew up in a small Arkansas town himself, has made a film with a 1970s style and sensibility that captures the feel of '50s movies. Instead of using the obligatory golden oldies to evoke instant nostalgia, he has selected Leonard Rosenman, who wrote the music for *East of Eden* and *Rebel Without a Cause,* to compose a score based on his earlier themes. While his haunting period music triggers our old moviegoing emotions, Gordon Willis's muted photography and Bridges's middle-distance framing keep us at an ironic, elegiac distance. This is the sort of low-budget, personal moviemaking that Hollywood is presumed to shy away from, and it would be a shame if it got overlooked. In its quiet, funny, morbid way, it cuts deeper into its era than *American Graffiti.* If for no other reason, it is worth seeing to watch Richard Thomas, formerly of *The Waltons,* stretch his considerable talents and to encounter a cast full of new, fresh and very convincing faces.

Newsweek, April 17, 1978

CULTURE CLASHES

O nly a handful of movies over the last twenty years have dared to confront the racial and ethnic divisiveness that ups the tension level of national and international life. In these films, people from wildly different cultures come together with disastrous results.

The Chant of Jimmie Blacksmith and *Utu,* about the history of racism Down Under, remind audiences that the chronicle of white colonialism is written in blood. *Southern Comfort*, the story of a National Guard unit lost in Cajun country, recalls the dislocations American troops suffered in the unfamiliar culture of Vietnam. *The White Dawn* turns the meeting between a remote tribe of Eskimos and marooned New England whalers into a lyrical and horrifying vision of two worlds colliding. *The Bounty,* a revisionist look at the mutiny on that ship, takes Bligh's side, seeing him as a solid seaman aghast at the spectacle of his crew "going native" in the most irresponsible way. And in *The Border,* Jack Nicholson patrols the boundaries between the United States and Mexico, Anglos and Hispanics, haves and have-nots.

This emotionally challenging, often thrilling batch of movies is related to another, equally engaging bunch some critics have labeled "stranger-in-a-strange-land films." In *E.T., Splash,* or *Witness,* an adorable alien lands in a foreign milieu, makes friends and sometimes lovers, then leaves, sadder or happier but always wiser. These movies have been extremely popular.

The culture clash movies usually bomb. They are deliberately provocative as well as exciting, and they offer hard-won truths instead of happy endings.

THE BORDER

Pauline Kael

Directed by Tony Richardson. Written by Deric Washburn, Walon Green, and David Freeman. Starring Jack Nicholson, Harvey Keitel, Valerie Perrine, Elpidia Carrillo, and Warren Oates. **MCA Home Video.**

Jack Nicholson may still have plenty of surprises in him. In the unheralded *The Border,* filmed largely on location in El Paso, Texas, by Tony Richardson, Nicholson plays a United States border patrolman whose job it is to shove Mexicans back to their side of the Rio Grande, and he gives a modulated, controlled performance, without any cutting up. Except for his brief appearance in *Reds,* this is the first real job of acting he has done in years. The film also marks a change in the work of Tony Richardson: he has a major, muckraking subject, and he works to serve the material. Over the years, he has developed a considerable body of skills, and this may be the most unobtrusively intelligent directing he has ever done for the screen. It is a solid, impressive movie.

Charlie, the patrolman, hates his work; it fills him with disgust, because most of the patrolmen are in cahoots with the American businesses that hire wetbacks, and the patrolmen make their money—their big money—by closing their eyes to vans full of workers earmarked for their business partners. It's an ugly, corrupt life—persecuting enough Mexicans to keep the government bureaus happy while functioning as slave dealers. The trade sickens Charlie, but he gets caught up in it by the social-climbing idiocies of his wife, played by Valerie Perrine. When he was an Immigration investigator in the Los Angeles area, he had felt worthless and wanted to return to the Forest Service. But his wife talked him into transferring to the Border Patrol in Texas, because she had friends there, and now she and the wives of the other slave dealers belong to a Southwestern parody of upper-middle-class society: they shop for tight, bright clothes and decorate their gaudy dream houses, and the men wear expensive boots and cowboy hats and slap each other's backs at the barbecue parties held on the patios near the swimming pools. Charlie doesn't have the stomach for this camaraderie. If the loaded vans are discovered by any stray honest patrolmen, Charlie's pals may protect themselves by jailing the passengers or getting them killed.

Back in 1933, the picture *I Cover the Waterfront* caused a great stir by showing that when the captain of a ship smuggling Chinese illegals into California ports spotted a Coast Guard vessel headed toward him, he sank his human cargo — chained to go down swiftly. With any luck, *The Border* will cause a fuss, too, because it lays out — very graphically — the essential irrationality of government policies, and the cruelty that develops out of them. Working from a script by Deric Washburn, Walon Green, and David Freeman, and with the cinematographers Ric Waite and Vilmos Zsigmond, Richardson is able to encompass so much in the wide-screen frame that he shows how the whole corrupt mess works.

Charlie is a little like the hero of Kurosawa's *Ikiru,* who knew that he couldn't do anything big to fight the bureaucracy but was determined to have one small accomplishment to leave behind. Charlie is so wasted and fed up that he tries to do one simple, decent thing — he wants to feel good about something. Among the Mexicans living in an encampment on their side of the Rio Grande and waiting to make the trip over, he spots a round-faced young madonna, who has come from a village devastated by an earthquake. Played by Elpidia Carrillo, a twenty-year-old Mexican actress who suggests a dark, adolescent Ingrid Bergman, she is clear-eyed and natural — the image of everything unspoiled, and the opposite of Charlie's giggly sexpot wife. She has a beautiful, plump babe in arms and is accompanied by her younger brother. Later, she's in a group Charlie has to round up and arrest, and when she's in the prison camp her baby is stolen from her by thieves (working in collusion with the slave dealers) who arrange for infants to be sold to childless couples. Charlie tries to help her and her brother make it over the border safely in one of the vans, but things go horribly wrong, and she is injured and the boy is shot. Charlie can't help the wounded boy, who dies, but he is determined to restore the girl's baby to her. That's all he hopes to do. He has no designs on the girl; she represents an ideal of what people can be if they are not corrupted, and his belief in that ideal is about all he has left. It gets to the point where the only thing that can give his life any meaning is to reunite the girl and her infant. In order to do it, he has to fight his buddy in the Border Patrol (played by Harvey Keitel) and the boss of the unit (Warren Oates), and he goes through hell.

Tony Richardson handles the large cast with apparent ease. Keitel is subdued and believable. Valerie Perrine, who has been giving disgraceful performances for several years, plays the dumb-tart wife to whiny perfection. And Shannon Wilcox, who plays Keitel's wife, a more confident tart, has a lifetime of teasing in her big smiles and swinging walk. There are also some very scary thugs headed by Jeff Morris.

Tony Richardson (right) directs Warren Oates in his last major role—Jack Nicholson's Border Patrol boss in the muckraking drama *The Border*. (Photo copyright © by Universal Pictures, a Division of Universal City Studios, Inc. Courtesy of MCA Publishing Rights, a Division of MCA Inc.)

Nicholson does his damnedest to make this muckracking melo-drama work. (Luckily, or maybe through shrewd calculation, he wears dark glasses in much of the picture, so we can't see if he's doing his trademark stunts with his eyeballs.) Charlie is at the center of the story: the corrupted, conscience-ridden, self-hating American wishing he could feel clean again. Maybe Nicholson hasn't regained the confidence or zest to be exciting (while staying in character) that he had in, say, *The Last Detail,* where he used his crazy-smart complicity with the audience. But probably that zest would work against the conception of Charlie, who has to be spiritually beat out. The movie might have been disastrous if anyone else had played the part. Nicholson is completely convincing as a man who has been living in dung up to his ears, and so when Charlie feels he has to do something decent before it covers his head, there's nothing sentimental about his need. It's instinctive — like a booze-soaked man's need for a drink of water.

The New Yorker, February 1, 1982

THE BOUNTY

David Denby

Directed by Roger Donaldson. Written by Robert Bolt, from a book by Richard Hough. Starring Anthony Hopkins and Mel Gibson. **Vestron Video.**

In the first (1935) movie version of *Mutiny on the Bounty,* Charles Laughton, as William Bligh, great sailor and tyrant, gives a performance of amazing power. Acting up a squall from his first appearance on the *Bounty* ("Mr. *Chris*-tian, clear this rabble from the deck!"), Laughton breaks all the sacred rules of film acting. He doesn't "internalize" anything; he's not content merely to "be" William Bligh, or to let the camera "discover" his character. On the contrary, he lunges at the role like a stage actor reaching for the balcony. Jaw thrust out, he stalks the

Bounty in a walk so theatrically rigid, he seems to be balancing himself on two wooden legs.

Laughton's Bligh is an indelible film image, but is he believable as a man? This Bligh is not only a sadist, lashing and keelhauling his men halfway around the world, he's a crook and a liar as well, a tyrant in petty matters as well as great. Can the real William Bligh have been so evil? Well, nothing diminishes art more disastrously than the truth. (Who but the most literal-minded would be interested in the actual Richard III, that earnest and able administrator?) Yet the new adventure film *The Bounty,* which restores Bligh's soul and his reputation, and presumably tells the truth, is a fascinating movie.

The screenwriter, Robert Bolt, has bypassed the fustian Nordhoff-and-Hall novel (a reworking of history) that served as the basis of the earlier film versions. Instead, Bolt adapted Richard Hough's book *Captain Bligh and Mr. Christian,* which makes liberal use of Bligh's stately, beautifully composed journals. This new "revisionist" Bligh is a fully rounded character—not a corrupt sadist but a fiercely ambitious sailor who becomes excessively harsh only when he feels his crew slipping away from him in Tahiti.

Produced by Dino De Laurentiis, *The Bounty* was directed by the Australian-born Roger Donaldson, who took over after David Lean stepped out. Donaldson, whose best-known previous work is the small domestic drama *Smash Palace,* made in New Zealand, seems an odd choice, but he turned out to be the right one. *The Bounty* is a big, spectacular movie, with the normal complement of storms, floggings, and naked Tahitian girls flinging themselves at bony Englishmen, but there isn't a melodramatic cliché in sight. Indeed, *The Bounty* is the opposite of melodrama: We can see that William Bligh and his familiar antagonist, Fletcher Christian, are both right, both wrong. *The Bounty* demythicizes without debunking; its characters emerge as fallible men with heroic dimensions.

As Bolt and Donaldson tell it, when Bligh (Anthony Hopkins) took command of the *Bounty,* in 1787, it was to make a name for himself. His task was to transport, from Tahiti to the West Indies, the breadfruit plants that the British hoped would flourish in the Caribbean and feed the slaves. The movie begins some years after the mutiny. Bligh faces a court of inquiry led by snooty officers (including Edward Fox and Laurence Olivier) who are inclined to believe he was guilty of negligence and cruelty. As Bligh defends himself, we see the voyage from his point of view: The crew, it turns out, was an undependable gang of louts, and Fletcher Christian (Mel Gibson), who was Bligh's close friend, an untested young man.

As always, Bligh and Christian represent dialectical opposites — ugliness and beauty, authority and sexuality. In 1935, Clark Gable made Christian a stolid good fellow, but when M-G-M tried again, in 1962, Marlon Brando turned the character into a lisping upper-class fop who enjoyed teasing Trevor Howard's rough-voiced, untutored Bligh. Brando's antic perversity threw the movie out of whack: It seems right that Bligh should dominate this particular bad marriage.

Anthony Hopkins, whose past movie work has been wan and over-deliberate, is a surprisingly full-voiced and powerful Bligh. He wears his hair in a clipped, Napoleonic cut that brings out the pugnacious roundness of his skull, and he lengthens his vowels, which gives an odd military music to his speech. This Bligh is highly intelligent, bluff and doughty — completely a seaman, but also a stiff and angry man whose jocularity always sounds bullying, a leader so jealous of his moral and legal right to hold sway that he must extinguish the merest spark of disrespect with a blast of scorn.

Eager for glory, Bligh endangers the lives of the crew by trying to go round stormy Cape Horn, giving up only after a month's steady battering. The voyage goes well after that — until Tahiti. As the exhausted men gape in disbelief, the natives rush out in little boats to greet them, and the way Donaldson stages and shoots the scene, the naked girls, breasts reaching upward, seem to be offering themselves as comfort and reward. In the next few months, the men give themselves up to pleasure, while Bligh, sweating in his bunk, suffers alone. This midnight anguish is mysterious — there's a suggestion of unconscious homosexuality in his pained disapproval of Christian's passion for the beautiful, silent Mauatua (Tevaite Vernette). Putting out to sea after months of play, the men can no longer stand naval discipline, and Bligh, increasingly baffled and sarcastic, becomes a self-righteous martinet.

It's good to hear Anthony Hopkins roar. When he lets it out full, his voice has a heroic timbre that no American actor can match. And yet, despite the tantrums, his Bligh is touching and pitiable — not a mes-merizing figure like the blustery Laughton, but a sympathetic man gone horribly wrong. In another fine performance, Mel Gibson, whose manner is strikingly modest for so good-looking an actor, makes Fletcher Christian callow and unsure of himself. When Christian falls in love, Gibson falls into the thick, insensible languor of a young man for whom erotic pleasure is the only thing that matters — he looks at the duty-bound, indignant Hopkins in sheer disbelief. And later, when Christian, leading the mutiny, is stricken by doubt, Gibson lets his voice go high and weepy, a dangerous gamble that works. The mutiny is both the best and the worst moment of Christian's life.

The way Roger Donaldson orchestrates the mutiny, it's not an exultant explosion of cleansing violence but a sickening, almost incoherent outburst of rage and dismay. Donaldson is not a grand-style pictorialist like David Lean. He likes to work close in, and he doesn't mind letting his shots get messy, if mess is what is called for. There are some obvious blunders—a few minor plot strands get lost; the native girls appear too pliantly fleshy and inexpressive; a couple of scenes could be juicier. But there's strength and integrity in Donaldson's evenhanded approach to the moral issues, and some of the details are superb—for instance, the way the faces of the crew, slack-jawed with amazement, are photographed through undulating thighs as the Tahitians dance and then ecstatically fornicate for the greater glory of the gods.

The Bounty isn't priggish, but it has an eighteenth-century, Tory point of view: Sensuality and indolence destroy the crew not only as members of the navy but also as men. Meanwhile Bligh and those who remain loyal to him, suffering horribly on their 3,600-mile open-boat journey, draw closer to an ideal of human conduct in their self-sacrificing concern for one another. We may not agree with the film's conservative vision, but at least it makes the case with noble eloquence. This is a somber, powerful, and satisfying movie.

New York, May 14, 1984

THE CHANT OF
JIMMIE BLACKSMITH

★

Stephen Schiff

Directed and written by Fred Schepisi, from the novel by
Thomas Keneally. Starring Tommy Lewis, Freddy
Reynolds, and Jack Thompson.

During the last five or six years, the Australians have been making
movies in a ritualistic fever. Like shamans conjuring up some lost tribal
identity, they drum up the beauties and terrors of the Australian past,
prodding and poking at them until they spill meaning. It's never really
worked. The formulas that filmmakers like Peter Weir and Gillian
Armstrong and Bruce Beresford mumble over their subjects have
always sounded rather hollow, like the attempts of European—or
Europeanized—minds to impose a pattern on random bones and
streaks of blood. In films like *My Brilliant Career, The Getting of Wisdom,*
and *Picnic at Hanging Rock,* for instance, Armstrong, Beresford, and Weir
have told us of schoolgirls straining against the fetters of the English-
style boarding school; the metaphor for an Australia struggling to break
its colonial bonds was all too pat. In *Hanging Rock* and *The Last Wave,*
Weir peered into the aboriginal soul, but there, where real mystery lay,
he found only voodoo and the gleaming grin of the noble savage. One
began to wonder whether the vaunted Australian cinema had anything
to offer besides landscape photography—the disquieting portraits of
brooding hills perpetually veiled in blue mists and the whirring of
cicadas.

The Chant of Jimmie Blacksmith, made in 1978 but arriving here only
now, is full of those strangely solemn vistas, and of cicadas and aborigines and girls in starchy white frocks. But the writer-director, Fred
Schepisi (pronounced SKEPsee), has found something new and terribly disturbing in that down-under iconography. Somehow, he has
tapped the ferocious mystery of the Australian past, and the secrets he
disgorges tumble out with an overwhelming force, because they impli-
cate us, too. Based on a novel by Thomas Keneally, which in turn is
based on a true story, *The Chant of Jimmie Blacksmith* is about a rampage.

In 1900, just before Australia is to become a federation independent of England, a young, educated half-aborigine finds he can neither enter the world of whites nor return to the spooky primitivism of the aborigine culture; suddenly, to his own astonishment, he explodes, murdering seven whites—five of them women. Schepisi tells his story without preaching and without melodrama. His images are spare and clean and imbued with a quiet, sorrowing fatalism. Things move forward calmly, at an unemphatic pace suitable to legend. The measured gait, the assurance and quietude, create an almost Brechtian distance, and yet the story Schepisi tells is so frightening that it knocks the wind out of you. I don't think I've seen anything quite as powerful since *The Deer Hunter,* and I can't recall another film that conveys so much of the passions that brew when two races share the same ground.

It's hard to imagine an American producing such a movie, because *The Chant of Jimmie Blacksmith* inhabits a realm of moral turmoil that Americans seem afraid to enter. Like 19th-century America, 19th-century Australia was a wilderness slowly being settled by immigrant whites, most of them outcasts in their native England who suddenly found themselves rulers of a vast, rich domain. Their treatment of the aborigines—slaughter, subjugation, sexual abuse—parallels our own treatment of Indians and blacks, and indeed, if colonial brutality were all that *The Chant of Jimmie Blacksmith* were about, I would have no doubts of its success in the land of *Roots* and remorse. But this movie is stronger than that. It plunges beyond the protocol of social criticism toward high tragedy. As much as we sympathize with Jimmie's plight, his killing spree is utterly appalling—a blood-revenge motivated by a series of gnat-stings. We cannot condone it, cannot even rationalize it, and were we not to experience it in this movie, we might well find it impossible to envisage. The wonder of *The Chant of Jimmie Blacksmith* is that it forces us to feel the outburst of madness and rage that occurs when two uprooted, identity-less cultures collide. We've witnessed such explosions on these shores, of course—in places like Watts, Detroit, and Miami, and in any number of personal vendettas. And yet *Jimmie Blacksmith* is probably too unsettling to be a hit here; its depiction of a black's slaughtering of innocent whites may even strike some well-meaning liberal sorts as reprehensible. That would be a shame. *The Chant of Jimmie Blacksmith* is one of the greatest pieces of political filmmaking I know, because it doesn't impose rhetorical nobility on its characters or twist their lives into social statement. Schepisi approaches politics through ritual; the ritual re-enactment of the crimes of Jimmie

Blacksmith forces us to feel the dread and regret that surrounded them. And the social statement lies in our response.

Caught between cultures, half native and half settler (his father had been white, his mother aborigine), Jimmie Blacksmith (Tommy Lewis) represents Australia itself. And though Jimmie is never less than a full-bodied character, it's clear that Schepisi wants us to view him symbolically, for he intends nothing less than a national epic. Right from the start, Schepisi makes us aware of the divisions in Jimmie's world. We see the boy undergoing his tribal initiation rites, but we also see him being tutored by the Reverend Mr. Neville (Jack Thompson), who runs a Methodist missionary school in one of the squalid "black camps" that sprawl outside the towns. And though Jimmie is accepted among the aborigines, he yearns to escape into the world of whiteness, yearns to follow Mrs. Neville's advice and marry a white girl, so that his children will be only a quarter black; in a few generations, perhaps, the blackness will be nearly eradicated from his bloodline. But when he leaves to seek his fortune, the world is not as he expects it to be. Polite, articulate, and dependable though he is, he's always mistreated and underpaid. Skilled as a fence builder, he drifts from one farm to another, always certain that his intelligence and eagerness to please will eventually win him acceptance. Actually, of course, intelligence and eagerness are the very reasons for his mistreatment. These tough white landowners have gotten where they are without education and social graces. Many of them can't read or write, and Jimmie's polish and his sycophantic smile seem a sort of rebuke to them. Schepisi sketches the farmers in such deft, economical strokes that you feel as though you were watching a great Japanese calligrapher at work. From the very poses these pale, tight-lipped actors strike in front of their little houses and rude wooden corrals, from the tense way they hold their mouths and clench the muscles around their eyes, you can feel the staunchness and fright within them, the refusal to indulge generosity or humor, lest something in the balance of things be overthrown and their hard-won dominion shattered.

The first half of the movie abounds in the sort of rich wide-screen imagery we associate with Westerns: ominous expanses of land; soft hills that disappear into a milky haze; close-ups of animals and insects, and of men working or talking against the unfeeling immensity of the backdrop. The emptiness is at once beautiful and spooky, and when Schepisi brings his camera in on Jimmie pounding at the earth with a post-hole digger, you can feel a violence in him that seems a sort of response to that emptiness. Struggling with the land, dwarfed by it, the people here change; a howl rises in them, a howl of terror and awe, not unlike the imprecation of a tribal shaman trying to impose his magic on an unfathomable universe. Schepisi introduces scenes with little portraits of the way his people respond to emptiness. When we enter the world of the whites, the scenes begin with close-ups of food and drink, of crystal decanters and china plates — the artifacts of civility and abundance that the settlers cling to. Scenes that involve the aborigines — Jimmie, his Uncle Tabidgi (Steve Dodds), or his giggly half-brother, Mort (Freddy Reynolds) — begin with shots of legs and feet: evocations of tribal dances, and later, after Jimmie's crimes, of flight. Throughout the movie, the compositions crane upward. Schepisi often places his characters near the bottom of the frame, where they struggle amid dark greens and browns, and then he lightens the colors as he ascends, finally letting them melt into a pallid sky. It's as though Schepisi were trying to locate his story in some grand cosmic scheme — as if he were keeping us mindful of the omnipresent heavens.

Tommy Lewis, who plays Jimmie, is not a very good actor. A 19-year-old half-caste, and a college student, he was discovered in an airport, and though his brightness and energy are appealing, he's a little too stolid, too opaque to move us. Lewis might sink another movie, and yet he works well here, because his remoteness intensifies the stately, Brechtian tone. And we do sympathize with him. When Jimmie takes a job as a police deputy, he's forced to join in some black-bashing and, at the behest of his white boss (played with hideous gusto by Ray Barrett), he even turns in an old friend. Here we sorrow for Jimmie, and we know he'll eventually quit in disgust. He finds a new employer, Newby, who is unusually kind and accepting, and unlike the other whites Jimmie's encountered, he's someone Jimmie can admire. To Jimmie, the Newby family is a white ideal, and brushing against that ideal electrifies him. And so, when the Newbys, too, insult him, and make it clear to him that his blackness is irredeemable, the fear and pain and rage that have been smoldering inside him ignite.

Jimmie's murderous outburst is very different from the violence we might see in a humanitarian American study of race relations, or even in a war movie or a Western; never for a moment does it seem justifiable. And yet we understand it — the depth of our understanding, in fact, is part of the horror. Schepisi stages the explosion with unflinching authority. In one shot, Jimmie rushes at the camera, and our sympathies, which have been so steadfastly with him, are thrown into confusion. Like the Newbys, we have felt for him, and now he has turned on us; as he hurtles out of the darkness, it seems that it's us he's attacking. Then Schepisi pulls the camera way back, and watching the first, irrevocable assault from afar, we are thrust into an eerie objectivity. Our identification with Jimmie shatters, but the fragments still seem to blow about in our heads like dead leaves, and just then Schepisi plunges back into the massacre, his camera whirling vertiginously — the scene may not be gory or explicit, but we can smell the blood. The way this sequence divides our loyalties is startling; it's as if *we* were committing the atrocities, and at the same time being repulsed by them. In effect, we're at war with ourselves, and when Jimmie announces later that he's declared war, we know what that war is. It's the battle that's been raging inside him and inside the divided Australia we've been watching, the battle between races and religions and aspirations, the battle for identity, and for sex and land and manhood.

Later, Uncle Tabidgi, who's been drawn into the murders, tells a jury, "You'd think it would take a good while to make up your mind to kill someone and then kill them. But take my word for it, it only takes a second." Watching the first slaughter, we can feel that dreadful loss of control, but gradually, as Jimmie roams the forests and countryside, avenging each slight he's suffered at white hands, he comes to seem a distant, almost inhuman figure. And Schepisi draws us instead toward the two men who accompany him: Mort, the full-blooded aborigine whose joyful innocence becomes a casualty of Jimmie's war, and Mac-Readie (well played by Peter Carroll), a white schoolteacher whom Jimmie takes hostage. MacReadie is perhaps too schematic a figure. Frail and liberal and a bit preachy, he emblemizes white sympathies toward the blacks. He and Mort get along beautifully, and MacReadie tells Jimmie, "You must leave Mort. . . . There's too much Christian in you. It'll bugger him up, like it's buggered you." And it's true that we can see something in Mort that Jimmie's never had, a sweetness and contentment that comes from having no ambition, no assertiveness, no self-image, perhaps no concept of time. Mort's growing sadness is what we fix on in the last part of the movie, and it sweeps us along a sort of tragic arc, away from Jimmie, whom we sense is doomed, and back to the images of earth and sky that have sustained the film. In the end, when a flock of white birds explodes from the darkness of the forest where Jimmie has hidden, you feel as though you were watching the ascent of angels, as though the movie's horrors were being released into the air. It's the sort of image that might seem too easy, too prettily symbolic in a film that had not so powerfully moved us. Coming at the end of *Jimmie Blacksmith,* it has the grandeur of a cadence.

Boston Phoenix, October 14, 1980

SOUTHERN COMFORT

★

Michael Sragow

Directed by Walter Hill. Written by Hill, David Giler, and Michael Kane. Starring Keith Carradine, Powers Boothe, Fred Ward, and Peter Coyote. **Embassy Home Entertainment/Nelson Entertainment.**

Southern Comfort, an adventure movie that dares to go beyond the beaten path, is neither a nonstop roller-coaster ride nor a simple revenge fantasy. This film, set in the Louisiana swamps, is a splendidly eerie survival drama with an austere gray beauty and a feeling of languorous danger. Director Walter Hill has created a terrifying mood piece — a blood-and-guts tale that's also a parody of the military sensibility, a metaphor for the Vietnam War and a study of gracelessness under pressure.

The whole thing takes place during a Louisiana National Guard exercise in the winter of 1973, when the guard was still full of war dodgers *and* die-hard soldiers sorry they missed out on the apocalypse. These men aren't hapless vacationers like the heroes of *Deliverance,* hoping to find some special masculine consummation in the wilderness. They're weekend soldiers playing out commando daydreams or just trying to get through their senseless maneuvers without breaking an arm or a leg. When they become embroiled in a life-or-death struggle with swamp rats, they're as ill-equipped to handle these backwater Cajuns as the regular troops were with the Viet Cong.

Hill and cinematographer Andrew Laszlo based the film's look on David Douglas Duncan's combat photos of American soldiers in Korea, their eyes barely visible under the rims of their steel helmets. Not long

Franklyn Seales, Powers Boothe, and Keith Carradine (left to right) play members of the Louisiana National Guard stranded in a bayou and attacked by a cunning, fast-moving, nearly invisible enemy in *Southern Comfort*. (Photo © 1981 Cinema Group, Inc. All rights reserved.)

into *Southern Comfort*, you begin to feel as if you're watching scenes from Vietnam relived in a twilight zone. By taking a Vietnam-like situation out of its confused political context, Hill and writers David Giler and Michael Kane clarify how such disasters and atrocities occur.

The combat begins when the guardsmen, lost in the shifting winter waters of the Atchafalaya Basin, "borrow" a few pirogues from Cajun hunters and leave behind an explanatory note, not realizing that the Cajuns are fiercely territorial and probably can't read English anyway. When the Cajuns appear as the men are paddling away in the canoes, an unreconstructed shitkicker named Stuckey (played with wild-eyed energy by Lewis Smith) gleefully fires off a salvo of blanks. The Cajuns return the fire with a real bullet — killing off the one good soldier in the Bravo Team, Squad Leader Poole (Peter Coyote). What starts out as a dumb prank turns into an excruciating, slow massacre, and a movie that begins like a satirical rendering of basic training takes us straight into the heart of darkness.

Hill and editor Freeman Davies know how to plant tiny narrative time bombs that go off at increasingly rapid intervals as the film progresses. They can establish, with as much humor as economy, that the men are carrying dummy ammunition — except for Reece (Fred Ward), a macho wild man with itchy fingers and scrambled brains who wouldn't go anywhere without live ammo. So as the film goes on, we see how every real bullet wasted affects the Bravos like an ounce of lost blood.

Hill and Davies often slow down the action so that the vivid, funereal feel of the winter bayous seeps through. The deep reds of the cypress trees fade under steely hanging moss. The spectrum is reduced to greens, browns and grays, so that your eyes cling to splashes of color as if to visual oases. The landscape is variegated, changeable: dry ground abruptly gives way to muck; cypress stubs rise from the water like muddy stalagmites. Brilliantly photographed by Andrew Laszlo, the Atchafalaya Basin becomes the physical embodiment of the characters' malaise. And Ry Cooder's subtle, understated music settles in an ominous, aural mist.

Like the Viet Cong in the jungle, the Cajuns are masters of their terrain, which they booby trap with devices that recall punji sticks. Panicked by their impotence, the soldiers seize upon the first Cajun they come upon and beat him up before they know whether or not he's guilty. For actions such as these, the guardsmen may provoke the same negative response that the Vietnam vets did at the height of the Movement, when many of the most humane, liberal Americans were callous toward their own fighting men. What's troubling about this movie is that it tests our sympathy for the poor slobs who often end up fighting wars. Some of the characters are stupid, racist animals. In its own action-movie terms, *Southern Comfort* has a rock-hard integrity. It may antagonize those who'd prefer the cracker soldiers to be either heroized or more harshly judged. And because the Cajuns are Americans, and, at first, the victims, the emotional effect of the combat is even more devastating than if they *were* Cong. We see the enemy, and it is us.

In the '40s and '50s, one of the major cinematic symbols of America was the World War II bomber crew, which inevitably contained a Jew, an Italian, an Irishman and John Wayne, all working together to save democracy and celebrate the Brotherhood of Man. The platoon in *Southern Comfort* is like a latter-day bomber crew gone berserk, with everyone at each other's throats. Instead of John Wayne, we get replacement Squad Leader Casper (Les Lannom), a *Soldier of Fortune* freak who rattles on about "maximum concealment" and "fragmentation," transforming fighting-manual jargon into a black-comic litany while his men blithely take military law into their own hands. The Bravo Team as a whole is a bubbling melting pot that occasionally, messily, erupts. Most of these men, be they black or redneck, get into a jocular locker-room frame of mind. But Hardin (Powers Boothe), an uppity, ornery "college man" who's just moved from El Paso to Baton Rouge, can't bear the idea of spending a weekend with the same rough crackers he grew up with. Boothe provides a powerful, ambivalent image of male strength.

When Hardin sardonically brags that in the Texas Guard "we had things organized—the only thing we did was watch the ball game on TV," an amiable natural aristocrat named Spencer (Keith Carradine) replies, "Our state's got us out doing real important things, like beating up on college kids and tear-gassing niggers." If anyone is a hero in this film, it's the insouciant Spencer. When the shooting starts, he doesn't take refuge in a rule book or try to live up to the masculine bluster that leads some of the men to make kamikaze charges. He simply remains himself. When he and Hardin happen onto a friendly Cajun village, Hardin is too wary to relax, but Spencer takes up the Cajun clog with a local belle. Hopping stiffly from side to side, Carradine has a humorous, decorous formality, like the young Henry Fonda's. His limberness and likability lighten up the entire movie.

Hill also gives his lesser characters enough room to make impressions in the midst of mayhem, and their faces and postures come off as pieces of sculpture. Carlos Brown, as a high-school football coach who thinks he's an avenging angel, is as big and weirdly affecting as the Incredible Hulk. Franklyn Seales, as a sensitive, middle-class black man, has the naked, despairing look of a Munch painting, while T. K. Carter's loose-limbed black street hustler brings welcome comic relief with a touch of reefer madness.

Not all of Hill's gambling pays off. At times, his men seem to make silly moves merely to propel the plot. For example, though Spencer is built up as the most intelligent character, he splits up the group and leaves them even more vulnerable to Cajun attacks. But Hill's strong, Spartan style more than compensates for such flaws. The moviemakers build the contrast between these men and the Cajuns gradually. Throughout the movie, we only glimpse the Cajun "bad guys" in frightening lightning flashes. But when Hardin and Spencer claw their way out of the bayous and into a Cajun *boucherie* — a communal celebration — the backdrop is brought to the fore, and we observe the full unity of this swamp civilization. Hogs are slaughtered and dressed for a feast, and hoop nets full of crawfish are steamed in vats. Families clog across a dance floor to plaintive but revivifying music. What we witness is a scarily alien, organic community. As Hill cuts between the Cajuns and the surviving Bravo boys, the National Guard comes into focus as a symbolic image of fragmented America today — divisive and downtrodden.

Like his previous movie, *The Long Riders* (the latest and, with Philip Kaufman's *The Great Northfield Minnesota Raid,* the finest retelling of the Jesse James saga), *Southern Comfort* shows off Walter Hill's ability to adapt traditional forms and take them to unexpected places. The movie's form dates back at least as far as 1934 with John Ford's *Lost Patrol,* in which British troops lost in the desert get picked off by Arab snipers. But *Southern Comfort* is so unusual in tone and texture that it hardly seems like a genre film at all. Not resorting to uplifting endings or ponderous verbal explanations, Hill risks the boredom of the bare-knuckled action crowd and the condescension of some intellectuals. But *Southern Comfort* could be the most daring movie of the fall season — and the most riveting.

Rolling Stone, October 29, 1981

UTU

Pauline Kael

Directed by Geoff Murphy. Written by Murphy and Keith Aberdein. Starring Anzac Wallace and Bruno Lawrence. **CBS/Fox Video.**

Geoff Murphy, the director of the New Zealand film *Utu,* has an instinct for popular entertainment. He also has a deracinated kind of hip lyricism. And they fuse quite miraculously in this epic about the relations between the Maori, the dark-skinned Polynesians who started migrating to the volcanic islands that form New Zealand around a thousand years ago, and the British, who began to migrate there in large numbers in the eighteen-thirties. By 1870, the year in which the movie is set, the British were the government (and within the next few decades confiscated millions of acres of Maori land—much of it as "punishment for rebellion"). Murphy uses the conventions of John Ford's cavalry-and-Indians Westerns, but he uses them as a form of international shorthand—to break the ice and get going, and for allusions and contrasts. His primary interest isn't in the narrative; it's in how the characters think and what they feel. By 1870, the Maori, trained and educated in mission schools, speak English and are imbued with Englishness. And they certainly know how to mock the English—playing off the Englishmen's expectations that they will behave like ignorant savages.

Te Wheke (Anzac Wallace), the troublemaker at the center of the story, is a literate, Europeanized Maori with a taste for Shakespeare. He's a uniformed scout with the British colonial forces who returns to his tribal settlement—a village friendly to the British—and finds that the huts are still smoking: the cavalry rode in and set them ablaze after casually slaughtering everyone there, leaving the bodies where they fell. In grief and rage at the death of his people, he feels the need to exact *utu*—the Maori word that means honor and includes ritualized revenge. Te Wheke's honor requires that he achieve balance through reciprocal acts—*utu* can be attained only by the shedding of blood.

By the thirteenth century, the Maori in New Zealand were having disputes over land, and warrior-cannibal tribes built fortified villages and ate or enslaved the enemies they defeated. Since the justification for the raids and killings was the need for *utu*, the members of the tribe that had been attacked would then have the same need, and the warfare was continuous—it was the normal way of life. Because of this tradition, the Maori weren't united even in resisting European encroachment on their land. Some were with the British troops, some tried to remain neutral, and by 1870 the hostile Maori were so demoralized by defeat and slaughter that they couldn't manage much more than occasional guerrilla raids. As more and more land-hungry British settlers arrived, the wars between the Maori and the British became wars of atrocities (on both sides).

Te Wheke prepares for his return to the barbaric, mystical heritage of the warrior tribes by having his face carved to symbolize his new purpose. In the Maori variant of tattooing, deep lines are cut, so that the skin in between stands out in ridges; Te Wheke, with curves and spirals covering his face, has a new aura. He's like a living version of the totemic figures that are now on exhibit in the Maori show at the Metropolitan Museum of Art. With his long, thick black hair and his mustache and elated eyes adding to the symmetrical pattern, he suggests the posters for the Broadway show *Cats*. He's a commanding presence — a Maori Che Guevara. He's also engaged in a form of make-believe — he's a travesty of an ancient warrior. When he's dressed for *utu* in his red British Army jacket, and with a military cap perched on his matted hair, it's as if all the contradictions in the society were popping out of his skin — as if he couldn't contain them anymore. He formally announces his *utu* in a rural Christian church after chopping the pastor's head off. He challenges the bewildered white and Maori parishioners by assuming the openmouthed pose of the totems and jiggling his protruding tongue at them.

Joined by a band of guerrilla recruits, Te Wheke sets out on his rampage. The code that governs *utu* does not require that the specific perpetrators of the offense be killed; any members of their tribe will do — so all Europeans are fair game. When the guerrillas attack the idyllic farmhouse of the Williamsons — Bruno Lawrence (of *Smash Palace*) and the fine actress Ilona Rodgers — they assault the two and proceed to desecrate everything European; they shoot up Mrs. Williamson's china, loot the place, and dance to the pounding of her grand piano before shoving it out the window. Picking up a volume of Shakespeare, Te Wheke entertains himself by reading a passage from *Macbeth* before setting fire to the house. It's an insane vandalization, and he knows it, but he's committed to this mad course of action because the history of his country appears to have left him with no other recourse.

At times, when you're looking at Maori, with their beautiful broad, relaxed faces, you can't tell which side they're on; then you realize that this confusion is part of the subject. They're on both sides: almost everyone in the movie wavers in his allegiance from time to time — even the young Lieutenant Scott (played with a likable mixture of callowness and élan by Kelly Johnson), who has been posted here by the British War Office, because he has been with the Boers putting down the natives in skirmishes in South Africa and has learned new, experimental counter-insurgency tactics. He turns out to be a flop, because he was born in New Zealand and becomes attached to a lovely, fleshy Maori girl; he can't give his work the wholehearted, career enthusiasm he had in South Africa. And the girl (played by an eighteen-year-old Maori student, Tania Bristowe), who is tied in with Te Wheke's band, acts the part of dusky enticer to Scott but feels closer to him than she does to her Maori friends; she gets to the point where she's marked for execution by both sides. As for Te Wheke, he runs his army as a parody of the white man's army. He and his guerrillas deck themselves out in a ragtag assortment of parts of British military uniforms and scraps of Victorian clothing they've picked up in raids on farms, and have hatchets and knives and guns tucked into their belts and boots. They have turned themselves into the Europeans' images of them as butchers and buffoons. (They're like American blacks playing Jungle Bunny.) If that's what the Europeans think they are, that's what they'll be. That's all that's left for them to be. In murdering the British, they're murdering themselves anyway. In a trancelike sequence, Te Wheke's guerrillas take over a wagon full of supplies for the militia and use it to ride in for a surprise night attack; along the road, one of the men rips open a sack of flour, plunks his face down in it, and says, "I've only been one of them for a minute, and already I hate you Maori." As the wagon rolls on, his white face is almost phosphorescent in the moonlight—he's like a phantom.

Mimicry goes on at so many levels in this horror comedy of colonialism that the viewer may be laughing, exhilarated by constant discovery, yet be a little discombobulated and scared. Murphy throws you at the start—he may want to disorient you, as Te Wheke disorients people—and he keeps you in a state of suspension. A few scenes go by before it's clear that the movie is cutting back and forth between the trial of the captured pattern-faced Te Wheke and the events that led the smooth-faced man to transform himself. At the trial, when Wiremu (Wi Kuki Kaa), a smart, fair-minded Maori who's a mercenary with the British forces, explains what has been going on to the officers, Te Wheke yawns. Wiremu, who plays chess with the racist colonel and puts a crimp in his theory of Maori inferiority by winning, has noble twin arches in his upper lip (like V. S. Naipaul)—he's smiling even when he isn't smiling. (He has some of Naipaul's gravity, too.) I doubt if any other director has treated the conventions of this colonial-epic form with Murphy's offhand audacity. He turns the form into a mirror of racism.

Murphy uses an abrupt, lurch-ahead editing that works well (except at the beginning), and there are real streaks of madness in the pursuit story. This isn't an impassioned lament, like the great Australian film *The Chant of Jimmie Blacksmith;* the lamenting quality is implicit in the material. And *Utu* doesn't have a strong protagonist; there are a whole string of leading characters—Lieutenant Scott, the young Maori girl, and others—who take over for a sequence or two and then recede, but may return. Left for dead, Bruno Lawrence's bald, bearded Williamson gets on Te Wheke's trail with the obsessiveness of a man who has lost his wife and seen the destruction of everything he has worked for. He's in the same position as Te Wheke, and has only one desire: to kill him. Slogging through the countryside carrying a quadruple-barrelled shotgun that he has put together (it's the size of a baby cannon), going for days and nights without sleep, and speaking in a dry rasp of a voice that gets lower and lower, Williamson is the only other character with the intensity of Te Wheke, who keeps firing at him but can't seem to kill him. Williamson has the same trouble killing Te Wheke. One with too much hair, the other with hair in the wrong place, they're like the pairs of adversaries in Sergio Leone's *Once Upon a Time in the West,* and we expect them to meet in a final shootout. But Murphy and his co-writer, Keith Aberdein, skewer your expectations, and you think, Of course, it's richer this way. Murphy throws you curves all through the picture: Te Wheke will suddenly be singing "Old MacDonald Had a Farm," or the soundtrack will make a satirical comment on the action, using "Marching Through Georgia," or Lieutenant Scott will casually survive being shot a few times, or Te Wheke's grimaces will remind you of Toshiro Mifune's Macbeth in *Throne of Blood.* (Anzac Wallace's performance as Te Wheke—his first acting—may owe something to his own experiences as a wild, sociopathic thief; he spent fourteen years in prison before becoming reconciled to living with other people, leading an industrial strike, and becoming a union organizer.) There are other reminders of Kurosawa, and of *Macbeth,* too, when Te Wheke stages his own version of moving Birnam wood to Dunsinane.

Te Wheke's Shakespearean flourish in the Williamsons' vandalized home may be somewhat fancy and more than somewhat trite, but Geoff Murphy has the popular touch to bring it off. This fellow, who in the late sixties was a scat singer and trumpet player in Bruno Lawrence's rock group and travelling road show, and also its visual-effects man, seems to be directing with a grin on his face. (After years of working in film, Murphy had a big hit—relative to a country of only three million people—in 1980, with *Good-bye Pork Pie,* which played around the world; that's probably what enabled him to get hold of the three million dollars it took to make *Utu*.) The score, written by John Charles, who was also with the road show, and recorded by a traditional Maori flautist and the New Zealand Symphony Orchestra, takes risks, and most of the time the risks come off gloriously. The film has sweep, yet it's singularly unpretentious—irony is turned into slapstick.

As the militia ride out to go after Te Wheke, young Lieutenant Scott asks Wiremu, "Whose side are you on?" Wiremu answers, "Same side as you, sir. I was born here, too." The fatalistic, pragmatic Wiremu knows there's no side to be on; there's no justice. It's obvious that the British will win, and just as obvious that Te Wheke is a folk hero. He's a hero even when he has become so cruel that he is more like a bug than a man, and his own followers are disgusted by him. No doubt Murphy was conscious of taking a balanced, nonjudgmental position, but you feel that the material itself—and his own instincts—dictated it. He couldn't have made this movie any other way, because it's a comedy about the characters' racial expectations of each other, which come out of the tragedy of their history—a history too grotesque for tears. In one sequence, the soldiers are tracking the guerrillas, and Te Wheke, catching their scent, sniffs the air; his dogs, also sniffing, turn their heads this way and that. Murphy's absurdism is a matter of temperament—it's part of the texture of the movie, which appears to be a reasonably accurate version of a totally crazy birth of a nation.

Probably what Murphy does that makes a viewer respond so freely is that he distances us—very slightly—and makes comedy out of the distancing. (He's a joshing, razzing director.) And because we're not asked to respond in the banal ways that action-adventure movies usually impose on us—there's no one we could conceivably root for—we're free to respond to much more. We're turned loose inside this epic, and the freedom is strange and pleasurable. Some of it has to do with the Maori, who have the placid features of Gauguin's Polynesians but appear to be completely expressive, and have such a fluent, unaffected wit that they seem to be plugged into the cosmos in a different way from the British. (In a scene out in a remote woodland area, Lieutenant Scott, talking companionably to a Maori soldier, says that Maori laugh at things that aren't funny. He gives as an example a horrible prank that some Maori played on the British—adding human meat to a barrel of pickled pork. When he finishes the story, the Maori laughs.) And some of the pleasure has to do with the quality of the light and the uncanny splendor of the New Zealand landscapes. There's a vista of an army encampment—small white tents dotting the pale-green hills—that's like a child's dream of outdoor living. Much of the film was shot in high country in wet weather, and the cinematographer, Graeme Cowley, lets us see the mountains and forests and mist-covered farms as if we just happened to look up and there they were. In New Zealand, no one is ever more than seventy miles from the sea, and maybe that helps to account for the feeling of exaltation and spirituality that hovers over this film. We know this basic story of colonialism from books and movies about other countries, but the ferocity of these skirmishes and raids is played off against an Arcadian beauty that makes your head swim.

The New Yorker, October 15, 1984

THE WHITE DAWN

Joy Gould Boyum

Directed by Philip Kaufman. Written by James Houston, Tom Rickman, and Martin Ransohoff, from Houston's novel. Starring Warren Oates, Timothy Bottoms, and Lou Gossett. **Paramount Home Video.**

Half a century ago, Robert Flaherty, an American explorer inexperienced and untrained in filmmaking, traveled to Canada's Hudson Bay territory to make a motion picture about Eskimos. The result was the classic *Nanook of the North,* a film which is generally considered to have established the documentary idiom. Today, many of the qualities which make up that idiom—the use of actual locales; of non-professional actors; of events drawn from real life with the usual disclaimer replaced by a claimer that any resemblance to persons living or dead is not at all coincidental—have more and more been adopted by the fiction film, helping to give it some of the same conviction they have given to the fact film.

The White Dawn, a fictionalized account of Eskimo life which returns us to Nanook country (or, at least, 300 miles northeast of it), perhaps

Eskimo hunter Simonie Kopapik parries and thrusts against a polar bear in *The White Dawn*, filmed on location in the Arctic. (Photo copyright © 1974 by American Film Properties. All rights reserved. Courtesy Philip Kaufman.)

goes one step further than most current films utilizing these vérité techniques. For here the documentary aspects not only serve to authenticate a drama but make for its very essence. For one thing, the story that *The White Dawn* tells—the germ of which lies in an Eskimo tale, presumably factual, concerning three shipwrecked whalers rescued by an Eskimo tribe who had never before seen Western men — is totally inseparable from its Arctic pre-20th-century world. For another, so exquisitely and so meticulously has this world on the wane been reconstructed that chief among the pleasures the film offers us is the sensation of having gained insight into a distant, primitive culture.

Through a motion picture camera put by director Philip Kaufman and cinematographer Michael Chapman to what seems here its distinctive and most special function — the capturing of things we would otherwise be unlikely to see — we find ourselves in a world washed not really white but a steely pale blue. And guided by the sensitive observations of artist-author James Houston, who lived among Eskimos for 12 years and who has, together with Tom Rickman and Martin Ransohoff, adapted his own novel to the screen, the camera makes the Eskimo way of life vivid for us. We watch the hunts and marvel at the courage it takes for a man armed only with a harpoon to kill a polar bear or at the strength needed to retrieve with nothing but human muscle the massive carcass of a walrus. We see the building of shelters: igloos in the colder months, skin tents in the warmer season. We watch the tribe's migration from winter camp to summer camp and discover how the patterns of this way of life arrange themselves according to the rhythms of a harsh and unyielding nature. And as we listen to the Eskimo language (to add to its documentary character, the film has all of its natives played by Eskimos who speak their own language, translated for us through subtitles) and observe the strange and often beautiful Eskimo customs (the winter dances, the mystical chants, the sexual games, the rituals of magic performed by the shaman), we begin to develop an extraordinary feel for the sensibility of these remarkable people whose very existence seems a testimony to man's incredible powers of endurance and his ability to adapt to his environment.

But *The White Dawn* is not merely a paean to the vitality and natural harmony of a primitive culture. It is also a saga-like adventure which shows that culture meeting another in an encounter that eventually upsets its extremely delicate balance. The three men the Eskimos rescue, after a harpooned whale has dragged their boat onto the ice, bring with them values and habits of behavior at variance with those of the Eskimos. And even when these differences seem subtle (as in wrestling, where the Western notion of fighting to the finish is only appropriate to the Eskimos as child's play; an Eskimo's adult game is a matter of a single throw), they are sufficient to disrupt the natural flow of things. Slowly, the whalers introduce elements from their own

Timothy Bottoms comes face to mask with Eskimo culture in *The White Dawn*. (Photo courtesy Paramount Home Video.)

world: gambling; the brewing of liquor from wild berries; even stealing. And the Eskimo response moves from mild amusement to irritation to a dreadful anger that precipitates the tragedy which makes for the film's conclusion.

Much of what we are given here, of course, seems to verge on cliché. On the one hand *The White Dawn* reiterates modern man's romantic view of primitive culture as a nearly ideal state of being, perfectly in tune with the earth; on the other, it restates that nowadays-commonplace conflict between the purity of primitive peoples and the corruption that seems to afflict men as they acquire civilization. But abstractly stated themes such as these are hardly equal to the terms in which they are presented, and in *The White Dawn*, atmosphere and event are so strongly felt and so effectively visualized that the familiar truths they contain gather freshness and new force.

But most impressive of all perhaps is the film's handling of character, which consistently seems to strike that perfect balance between the universal and the particular. For while the three whalers are highly distinct personalities who differ significantly in their abilities to adjust to new ways — Timothy Bottoms' young and fair Daggett is the one who adapts himself most fully, even learning the Eskimo language; Warren Oates' cunning Billy is the one most resistant to change; and Lou Gossett's powerful, black Portagee stands midway between the two — all are likable and essentially good men who bring about tragedy not so much because of their individual flaws as because of more generalized cultural differences.

Just as the whalers are sharply differentiated, so too (and perhaps more remarkably) are the Eskimos. From Sarkak (Simonie Kopapik), the courageous and generous tribe leader, to Kangiak (Joanasie Salomonie), his son and Daggett's special friend, to Nevee (Pilitak), Sarkak's wife who, according to Eskimo custom, is given to Daggett, to the mysterious shaman (Sagiaktok), each figure emerges rounded and even memorable. It helps, of course, that the performance of each of these non-professionals is superb, and much of the credit must clearly go to Philip Kaufman, a director who not only knows just where to place his camera and how long to hold it there, but who also is capable of inspiring from his actors an impressive naturalness. And because *The White Dawn*'s characters seem as genuine as they do, the very real landscape through which they move seems that much more real as does their "true story" that much more true.

The Wall Street Journal, July 29, 1974

THE
ENGLISH-LANGUAGE
GHETTO

I n his 1987 survey, *Home Movies: Tales from the Canadian Film World*, Toronto-based critic Martin Knelman calls his first section "Dancing with Hollywood." This title suggests the fancy stepping that English-speaking movie talents who aren't from the United States must do in order to grab the attention of Yankee producers and audiences. Some of the Canadian movies Knelman champions, such as *By Design* (see "Off the Beaten Laugh Track"), didn't make it in either Canada or the United States. But even those that were relatively successful in Canada, such as *I've Heard the Mermaids Singing*, a low-budget female Walter Mitty fable with a triumphantly winsome performance by Sheila McCarthy, failed to fill United States art houses. The next time Americans got a chance to see McCarthy in a movie, it was in an abysmal quick-to-video comedy, *Friends, Lovers & Lunatics*.

The most indigenous movies of English-speaking countries other than the United States face frustration on the Hollywood-dominated world market (with the peculiar exception of movies that have three-word titles beginning with "My"—England's *My Beautiful Laundrette*, Ireland's *My Left Foot*, and Australia's *My Brilliant Career*). That includes movies from the mother-tongue country, England. British directors such as Mike Leigh (*High Hopes*) and Jim O'Brien (*The Dressmaker*), who have scored popular successes on British television (Leigh with a string of BBC comedy-dramas, including "Grown Ups" and "Home Sweet Home," O'Brien with Granada's "The Jewel in the Crown"), found only specialized audiences here for their colloquial, unvarnished portrayals of common life, whether in the repressed wartime England of *The Dressmaker* or the more chaotic Thatcherite world of *High Hopes*. (*The Dressmaker* won a wider viewership on PBS's "Masterpiece Theater" than it did in movie theaters.) Director Terence Davies (*Distant Voices, Still Lives*), along with Leigh, evokes critical comparisons to Japanese director Yasujiro Ozu. But United States distributors and exhibitors fear that Leigh's and Davies's views of London and Liverpool are as alien to Americans as Ozu's depictions of Tokyo and provincial family life.

Hollywood does absorb some of the United Kingdom's liveliest talents, but it doesn't always know what to do with them. Irish writer-director Neil Jordan went from *Danny Boy* (Michael Wilmington's salute follows), *The Company of Wolves* (see "The Horrors! The Horrors!"), and the international hit *Mona Lisa* to a pair of American-financed artistic and commercial flops, *High Spirits* and *We're No Angels*.

The boundaries between the British Commonwealth and the United States are dotted with box-office land mines. Not even prolific American director Sidney Lumet, in his most successful decade (the '70s), could garner recognition for his made-in-England movie *The Offence* (1973), which showed the growing mastery of Sean Connery. Nor could a jumping soundtrack and the presence of Denzel Washington gain support for Carl Schenkel's *The Mighty Quinn*, a murder mystery that takes place in an unnamed country closely resembling Jamaica. Whether it's rendered in Caribbean patois or Scottish brogue, un-American English seems to turn off Yankee audiences as much as any foreign language. There's much talk in film circles of a "foreign-language ghetto," but these films are stuck in something even more incongruous—an English-language ghetto.

DANNY BOY

★

Michael Wilmington

Directed and written by Neil Jordan. Starring Stephen Rea.
RCA/Columbia Pictures Home Video.

There's bloody magic afoot in the Irish film *Danny Boy,* alchemy that
sets it apart from the opening frames. The colors are a bit more
scintillating than usual; the angles skewed; the camera mobile; the
atmosphere pungent and rare. The film's style might be called flam-
boyant or baroque — or damned as pretentious — but it's a genuine style,
a way of speaking. No one else speaks quite this way.

Danny Boy is set in an Ireland that seems as full of bleak, gray threat
as anything in Graham Greene. A war rages, but, inside it, good and evil
rage almost independently of the issues.

The protagonist is a jazz saxophonist (Stephen Rea) who, after hours
one night, makes love with a strange, silent convent girl, then witnesses
a double murder which shatters him. He falls into an obsessive ven-
detta, tracking down the four murderers, attempting to kill them all. As
a killer, Danny has to leach away his sensibility, his music; become a
soft-voiced, implacable zombie. The passion for murder makes him
weirdly sexual, but it also rots him away inside.

None of this is presented realistically. The camera tracks through
strange streets, a blasted dance hall named "Dreamland," interiors
abloom with smoky golds and fiery scarlets. There's an Irish lilt to
Danny's speech, and everyone's, but it's a fanged lilt, poisonously self-
conscious.

We seem to be lodged somewhere in his mind, a mind gone
psychotic. The air bends or bleeds; everything seems crazy. The cheap,
fat, voluptuous lyricism of his sax playing (Billie Holiday's "Strange
Fruit") counterpoints the horror of his pursuit. This is one film where
revenge is no holy cause. Here it diminishes and destroys; each step of
Danny's violent pilgrimage brings him closer to chaos and dissolution.

Before *Danny Boy,* writer-director Neil Jordan's primary fame was as
a prize-winning novelist and short-story writer. Yet he seems a natural
cineaste, with a special vision that could flower only on film.

Impressively, Jordan developed his style with his very first film. *Danny Boy*, his debut, was originally called *Angel*. It was made when he was 32; his only previous film experience was as documentarian and creative consultant for John Boorman's spectacular film *Excalibur*. Since then, Jordan has shot the even more magical *The Company of Wolves*, a huge critical and commercial success in Britain, but a relative flop in the United States.

Here, he is abetted by a good cast and a brilliant cinematographer. Chris Menges won the Oscar this year for *The Killing Fields* — but that film only hints at the true range of his talent. For years, he's been cameraman for Ken Loach, Britain's great cinema realist. For Loach or Stephen Frears, Menges creates aching illusions of the real; for Jordan or Bill Forsyth, his landscapes are artificial and poetically charged, dreamy and rapt.

Unlike last year's excellent *Cal, Danny Boy* mostly ignores the reality of the Irish "troubles," in search of the quicksilver soul. In this world, viciously split, built on killing, death and love are commingled. Yet, *Danny Boy* — for all its apparent sins of overreaching and Rea's sometime blandness and monotony — is a moral film and one capable of witchery, of iridescent prestidigitation.

One hesitates to call a young director "great" after only two films, but Jordan is certainly unique. His images haunt you, just as the keening tones of *Danny Boy* ravish the ear. Melodious and dirge-like, echoing with fidelity and death, they are fit emblem for this movie ballad of a land where murder threads through the fabric of life, where blood spills endlessly and tears are a ceaseless stream, where the poetry lies dark, thick and hazy like a coat of fog, rising.

Los Angeles Times, June 20, 1985

DISTANT VOICES, STILL LIVES

Armond White

Directed and written by Terence Davies. Starring Peter
Postlethwaite, Freda Dowie, Angela Walsh, and Dean
Williams. **IVE Home Video.**

Ella Fitzgerald's rendition of "Taking a Chance on Love" underscores a
remarkable sequence in *Distant Voices, Still Lives.* A group of children
watch their mother sit precariously on a window ledge as she scrubs the
grimy glass. "Please, Mommy, don't fall," one child begs. In a sudden
time shift, the mother is shown being beaten by her husband; then,
bruised and sobbing, she continues her housecleaning chores and her
movements keep time with Fitzgerald's singing.

Director-writer Terence Davies lets Fitzgerald's record fill out his
characters' unconscious. It expresses, in one sweet, melodic phrase, all
of their highest, most sincere feelings and aspirations while their
rough, risky lives mock their dreams. Davies' counterpoint gives this
stark depiction of white English working-class life true poignancy. The
unflinching revelation of pain makes a great film out of Davies' concentration on our fascination with popular music.

Distant Voices, Still Lives recalls Davies' own family history in Liverpool in the 1940s and '50s in a mosaic of vignettes and memory flashes.
He envisions dark, realistic despair and bright, pop-culture hope as the
essence of modern existence. That's not too lofty a description. Davies
realizes the way people grasp their positions in life and wrestle to
control their emotions and destinies.

Davies distills autobiography into extreme visual and musical styliza-
tion. He shuffles drama, music and different periods of his decade-long
family chronicle—not simply for contrast but for the direct, emotional
intensity of hotly remembered grief and fondly recalled joy. These
essences of family life rank with the greatest that have ever been
created—Welles' *The Magnificent Ambersons* and O'Neill's *Long Day's
Journey into Night.* He finds a common denominator in the eerie
intimacy of family life in which the structure of domestic relationships
becomes transparent and the vulnerability of the individuals is both
revealed and shared.

Women carry the songs in this powerfully metaphysical movie musical. There's a feminist basis in Davies' scrapbook-jukebox reminiscence that pays special attention to suffering under cruel patriarchy. *Distant Voices, Still Lives* is structured around the subtle, circumspect subversions practiced by oppressed groups—women, specifically, but by extension, gays, the working class, etc. "Innocuous" pop songs and conventional social rituals like public sing-alongs and moviegoing make up the special moments that are seized by the mother and sisters in Davies' recreated family to vent their usually suppressed feelings.

Fitzgerald's "Taking a Chance on Love" is one of the few professional, prerecorded singing performances used by Davies, who finds profundity in the "untrained" singing voices of his characters. This "live" singing gives a different insight from the Herbert Ross–Dennis Potter film, *Pennies from Heaven,* which only—but brilliantly—showed the imprint of pop culture on the subconscious. Davies reflects on pop culture more critically. The distance he maintains from the glossy, slick escapism of professional pop fantasy objectifies its powerful sway and marks it as placebo.

Unlike Ross and Potter, Davies is mindful of the sociological fact of pop communication. His demonstrations of this are amazing: a group of dissatisfied white housewives sing "Brown Skin Girl, Stay Home and Mind Baby (I killed nobody but me husband)"; a Catholic woman toasts her mother singing "My Yiddishe Mama." Davies shows the uses that can be made of pop from disparate cultures. Seen this way, pop music communication is an explicitly political phenomenon. But Davies never neglects the emotional basis; it comes through powerfully in the scene where Angela Walsh as the youngest sister defies her marital subjugation in a full-throated performance of "I Want to Be Around to Pick Up the Pieces (when she breaks your heart like you broke mine)." It's the most psychologically vivid, emotionally vibrant movie scene this year. Through the human effort of singing this film conveys great purity of feeling.

Davies' musical numbers are a culture and several generations away from my own experience, yet they have a raw potency like African-American storefront gospel. This is the only movie I know to capture the basic cultural function of song without swamping it in excessive production furbelows. The astringency of Davies' method—the dogged presentation of one solemn episode after another—makes this film a tough watch. Many of the greatest filmmakers have lacked a gift for buoyancy (Ozu, Dreyer, Visconti, Bresson), yet Davies accomplishes what the best movie art seeks to do. Each formally conceived sequence expresses an idea in an image: A child shown singing to herself in a doorway suspends the character — a whole life — in time; the late-night leave-taking of the family from the local pub surrounds them all with mortality; a son's pitiful view of his mother's toil and his subsequent wedding day, at which he grieves his father, summarize his inheritance. The resonance of these images and ideas ties together the terror of family life and the isolation of aesthetic experience in a way that is truthful and overwhelming.

Distant Voices, Still Lives takes place pre–rock 'n' roll, so the pop music–mass audience relationship it details is different. It's debatable that so much misery would thrive in an era of aggressive protest music but the fact remains, the majority of pop experience always comprises romantic fantasy. Davies pays tribute to pop's power while shaking up, diversifying its meanings. Two years ago Todd Haynes' *Superstar: The Karen Carpenter Story* subverted pop vapidity by dramatizing real life tragedy in absurd pop form (he used Barbie dolls as characters). Haynes' trivializing technique was deceptive — he caught the irony of Karen Carpenter's art and life with merciless cunning. Davies' sense of pop life has a little more heart yet it's too disturbing to mistake for Vincente Minnelli jollity. If he never makes another film as strong as this one, Davies ranks in the vanguard of radical pop sensibility.

City Sun, August 30, 1989

THE DRESSMAKER

Hal Hinson

Directed by Jim O'Brien. Written by John McGrath from a novel by Beryl Bainbridge. Starring Billie Whitelaw, Joan Plowright, and Jane Horrocks. **Orion Home Video.**

The Dressmaker sets a suffocating wartime mood that seeps into your bones like the English cold. At first, the picture seems almost wholly

Jane Horrocks (left) plays Rita, a naive English girl who falls in love with an American soldier during World War II; Billie Whitelaw plays her extroverted Auntie Margo in *The Dressmaker*. (Photo courtesy Capitol Entertainment.)

submerged, repressed nearly to the point of nonexistence. Then the rage that's packed under the images begins to bleed through, and everything seems charged, steeped in rancor, and the foggy light seems to mask a more radical hue. Under the gray is a layer of scarlet.

Based on a 1973 Beryl Bainbridge novel, *The Secret Glass,* the movie is a masterpiece of minimalist compression. Its centerpiece is the relationship between two sisters, Nellie and Margo (Joan Plowright and Billie Whitelaw), one a dowdy seamstress who sees herself as the custodian of tradition and moral standards, the other a bawdy exhibitionist who breaks into boisterous song while working on the assembly line in a munitions plant. Living with them in their cramped Liverpool row house is their 17-year-old niece Rita (Jane Horrocks), a scrawny lass with flaccid red curls who whimpers herself to sleep most every night, until the sisters have her crowd into bed between them.

There may not be a more horrifying movie image all year than the shot of these three women jammed together, side by side, into the same bed. Watching them, you feel like the fourth person in a world built for three. The sisters despise each other, and Rita, who was left for them to raise by her father (Peter Postlethwaite) after the death of his wife, is the object of their combat. Their fighting is close-in and dirty, the way it often is when family members struggle for power. And, as is also often the case, it is mostly covert, a part of the poisonous daily groove they've worn for themselves.

The director Jim O'Brien (who worked on "The Jewel in the Crown" for British television) and screenwriter John McGrath have created a hall of domestic horrors. Most of the film's drama takes place in rooms so tiny and stuffed with Victoriana that you wonder how the characters can breathe. The home — such as it is — is Nellie's shrine, and she putters around constantly, dusting, straightening, curating the family heirlooms. There's a streak of mania in her bustling, though; bent over her sewing table, her mouth stuffed with pins, she seems deranged, driven mad by her efforts to keep things stitched together.

Envy has played a hand in it, too. Nellie feels that her hold on the girl is threatened when Wesley (Tim Ransom), a young Yank from Mississippi, starts calling on Rita, and she goes to Margo for advice. Feeling sympathetic, Margo tells her hapless and inexperienced niece that if she loves him she has to "give." Still, though Rita would like to respond to her clumsy but ardent suitor, whenever he makes his move she finds she doesn't like it much and slaps him down.

This is as much a reflex as anything else — like a gag response to foul medicine — and Horrocks makes it both comic and pathetic. This is the young actress' first movie role and she couldn't have hit on a less flattering one — or have made more of a triumph out of it. What she does with the part seems at first nearly unimaginable — she makes us invest ourselves in this sullen girl.

Joan Plowright plays the title role in *The Dressmaker,* a woman whose crippling notions of good conduct and domesticity have dire effects on her young niece, Rita. (Photo courtesy Capitol Entertainment.)

She couldn't have debuted with a better cast of costars, either. Both Plowright and Whitelaw are among Britain's greatest actresses, and here they prove why. Plowright's performance brings out all of Nellie's acid righteousness, all the pressurized contempt for the cheap and the nasty that finally erupts in a murderous rage. She has killing standards.

Margo, on the other hand, has none at all. She's loose and vivacious and cowardly, and perhaps her greatest pleasure comes from driving her sister wild with her disregard for decorum and good taste. And Whitelaw is so uninhibited in the part that you almost flinch in the face of it.

Margo is the character we're naturally drawn to, and her spirit dominates the first half of the movie. But it's Nellie who triumphs. Toward the end, the picture takes a jolting turn toward the macabre, but it's one that we're prepared for. In the final moments, all the repressed energy, all that had been held underground, rises up. Ultimately, the scarlet leaks through.

The Washington Post, February 10, 1989

HIGH HOPES

Roger Ebert

Directed and written by Mike Leigh. Starring Philip Davis, Ruth Sheen, Edna Dore, Philip Jackson, Heather Tobias, Leslie Manville, and David Bamber. **Academy Entertainment.**

The characters in *High Hopes* exist on either side of the great divide in Margaret Thatcher's England, between the new yuppies and the die-hard socialists.

Cyril and Shirley, quasi-hippie survivors of the 1970s, live in comfortable poverty in a small flat, supported by Cyril's earnings as a motorcycle messenger. Cyril's sister, Valerie, lives in an upscale home surrounded by Modern Conveniences with her husband, Martin, who sells used cars. In their language, their values, and the way they furnish their lives, each couple serves as a stereotype for their class: Cyril and Shirley are what Tories think leftists are like, and Valerie and Martin stand for all the left hates most about Thatcherism.

Sometimes these two extremes literally live next door to each other. Cyril and Valerie's mother, a bitter, withdrawn old woman named Mrs.

Bender, lives in solitude in the last council flat on a street that has otherwise been gentrified. Her next-door neighbors are two particularly frightening examples of the emerging social class the British call Hooray Henrys (and Henriettas). Paralyzed by their affected speech and gestures, they play out a grotesque parody of upper-class life in their own converted row house, which they like to forget was recently public housing for the poor. All of these lives, and a few others, collide during the course of a few days in *High Hopes,* which was written and directed by Mike Leigh with the participation of the actors, who developed their scenes and dialogue in improvisational sessions. Leigh is a legendary figure in modern British theater, for his plays and television films that mercilessly dissect the British class system, using as their weapon the one emotion the British fear most, embarrassment.

Director Mike Leigh (front, center) poses with his *High Hopes* cross-section of '80s London: on the left, the nouveau riche Valerie (Heather Tobias), Valerie's Marxist messenger-boy brother, Cyril (Philip Davis), their mother, Mrs. Bender (Edna Dore), and Cyril's live-in mate, Shirley (Ruth Sheen); on the right (in more ways than one) the yuppie couple Rupert (David Bamber) and Laetitia (Leslie Manville). (Photo courtesy Skouras Pictures.)

Leigh has made only one other film, the brilliant *Bleak Moments*, some eighteen years ago. He cannot easily find financing for his films because, at the financing stage, they do not yet have scripts; he believes in developing the material as he goes along.

The backing for *High Hopes* came partly from Channel Four, the innovative alternative British TV channel, and with its money he has produced one of those rare films in which anger and amusement exist side by side — in which the funniest scenes are also the most painful ones.

Consider, for example, the dilemma of the old mother, Mrs. Bender, when she locks herself out of her council house. She naturally turns for help to her neighbors. But Rupert and Laetitia, who live next door, are upwardly mobile yuppies who treat the poor as a disease they hope not to catch. As the old woman stands helplessly at the foot of the steps, grasping her shopping cart, her chic neighbor supposes she must, after all, give her shelter, and says, "Hurry up, now. Chop, chop!"

Mrs. Bender calls her daughter, Valerie, who can hardly be bothered to come and help her, until she learns that her mother is actually inside the yuppie house next door. Then she's there in a flash, hoping to nose about and see what they've "done" with the place. Some of her dialogue almost draws blood, as when she looks into Rupert's leather-and-brass den and shouts, "Mum, look what they've done with your coal-hole!"

This sort of materialism and pride in possessions is far from the thoughts of Cyril and Shirley, the left-wing couple, who still sleep on a mattress on the floor and decorate their flat with posters and cacti. Lacking in ambition, they make enough from Cyril's messenger job to live on, and they smooth over the rough places with hashish. They are kind, and the movie opens with them taking a bewildered mental patient into their home; he has been wandering the streets of London, a victim of Thatcher's dismantled welfare state. (America and Britain are indeed cousins across the waters; we are reminded that the Reagan administration benevolently turned thousands of our own mentally ill out onto the streets.)

Most of the action in *High Hopes* centers around two set pieces, both involving the mother: the crisis of the lost keys, and then the mother's birthday party, which the hysterical Valerie stages as a parody of happy times. As the confused Mrs. Bender sits in bewilderment at the head of the table, her daughter shouts encouragement at her with a shrill

Shirley (Ruth Sheen) and Cyril (Philip Davis) face down the constrictions of Thatcherite England in *High Hopes*. (Photo courtesy Skouras Pictures.)

desperation. The evening ends with a bitter quarrel between the daughter and her husband, while Cyril and Shirley pack the miserable old lady away home.

High Hopes is not a movie with a simple message; it's not left-wing propaganda in which all kindness resides with the Labourites and all selfishness with the Conservatives. Leigh shows us a London that exists beyond such easy distinctions, and it is possible he is almost as angry at Cyril and Shirley — laid-back, gentle, ineffectual potheads — as at the movie's cruel upward-strivers.

Much of the movie's concern seems to center around Shirley's desire to have a child, and Cyril's desire that they should not. Their conflict is not the familiar old one of whether or not to "bring" a child into "this world." It seems to center more around the core of Cyril's laziness. He cannot be bothered. Of course, he stands for all good things and opposes all bad ones, in principle — but in practice, it's simpler to light up a joint.

High Hopes is an alive and challenging film, one that throws our own assumptions and evasions back at us. Leigh sees his characters and their lifestyles so vividly, so mercilessly, and with such a sharp satirical edge, that the movie achieves a neat trick: We start by laughing at the others, and end by feeling uncomfortable about ourselves.

Chicago Sun-Times, March 22, 1989

I'VE HEARD THE MERMAIDS SINGING

Carrie Rickey

Directed and written by Patricia Rozema. Starring Sheila McCarthy and Paule Baillargeon. **Charter Entertainment/Nelson Entertainment.**

Scatterbrained, incapable of completing a sentence or a task, carrot-topped Polly Vandersma works as an office temp though her agency despairs that this flibbertigibbet is "organizationally impaired."

Polly's account of her crushing timidity and awkwardness forms the basis of *I've Heard the Mermaids Singing,* a buoyantly confident and graceful feature debut by Toronto-born Patricia Rozema. Offbeat, comic and fresh, *Mermaids* recalls the breakthrough work of Woody Allen. Surely there hasn't been such an original, seriously funny first feature since Alex Cox's *Repo Man.*

Mermaids is told in the form of a confessional videotaped monologue in which Polly (birdlike Sheila McCarthy) records her impressions of recent events and explains why she's about to do something rash.

The surprise of Rozema's astutely observed film is how this dizzy female Walter Mitty who worries that she's a nonentity is revealed to have rare focus and depth of character. McCarthy recalls Rita Tushingham — Swinging England's challenge to static America in the '60s — but the Canadian newcomer is as unique as *Mermaids.* (Like *Eat the Peach,* which also opens today, *Mermaids* takes its title from T. S. Eliot's "The Love Song of J. Alfred Prufrock.")

A shutterbug who thinks of her candid photos as just fun, Polly recalls that her life changed when she got a job as "person Friday" to the curator at Toronto's Church Gallery, a tony establishment for serious art. Schleppy Polly, the kind of klutz who seems fated to be a rag mop for life's spills, develops a crush on her employer, a chiseled beauty named Gabrielle St-Peres (Paule Baillargeon, who resembles a languid Ingrid Bergman).

Despite Polly's crush, and despite the fact that Gabrielle already has a sultry female lover named (no kidding) Mary Joseph, *Mermaids* is a movie about aesthetic, not affectional, preferences.

Polly is a cockeyed hobbyist, whose snapshot art, like her thrilling daydreams of soaring above Toronto, gives her spiritual pleasure. The cerebral Gabrielle, who speaks of paintings in terms of their "oblique pragmatism," looks to art for intellectual rigor.

The young woman and her mature employer grow fond of each other, though their interactions have the hilarious incongruity of a friendship between the expressive Lucille Ball and the ethereal Greta Garbo.

Her kinship with the sophisticated Gabrielle changes the nature of Polly's daydreams (which, like her photos, are photographed in black-and-white, a vivid contrast to the voluptuous color of the film's realistic scenes). Still soaring, this time intellectually if not physically, she imagines herself exchanging preposterous art-worldly insights with her boss. When she learns that the curator is a closet artist who creates paintings of mystical beauty (to describe them would deprive the audience of the film's most imaginative moment), Polly steals one of the works and puts it on public view.

Now that Gabrielle has shown Polly her own work, Polly seeks reciprocity. She anonymously sends her snapshots to Gabrielle for consideration — which the curator coldly dismisses as "the trite made flesh." Crestfallen, Polly can no longer even daydream and makes a sacrificial bonfire of her daydreamy photos.

With the subtlety and radiance of Gabrielle's magic paintings, *Mermaids'* parody of the art world turns into a gentle parable of religious and artistic faith.

Newton got his breakthrough when the apple hit him on the noggin. Polly gets hers in the cathedral-like Church Gallery. Like the angel for whom she is named, Gabrielle and her strident criticism trumpet an aesthetic Judgment Day.

Only when the photographer is persuaded by the curator's lover to see that there are no absolutes does Polly realize she was worshiping a false god, artistically speaking. Without the weight of Gabrielle's disapproval to ground her, Polly—and *Mermaids*—soars.

The Philadelphia Inquirer, October 7, 1987

THE MIGHTY QUINN

Roger Ebert

Directed by Carl Schenkel. Written by Hampton Fancher, from a novel by A. H. Z. Carr. Starring Denzel Washington, James Fox, Robert Townsend, Mimi Rogers, and M. Emmet Walsh. **CBS/Fox Video.**

The Mighty Quinn is a spy thriller, a buddy movie, a musical, a comedy, and a picture that is wise about human nature. And yet with all of those qualities, it never seems to strain: This is a graceful, almost charmed, entertainment. It tells the story of a police chief on an island not unlike Jamaica, who gets caught in the middle when a wealthy developer is found murdered. Everyone seems to believe the chief's best friend, a no-account drifter named Maubee, committed the crime. Everyone but the chief and the chief's wife, who observes laconically, "Maubee is a lover, not a killer."

The film stars Denzel Washington, in one of those roles that create a movie star overnight. You might have imagined that would have happened to Washington after he starred in *Cry Freedom,* as the South African hero Steven Biko. He got an Oscar nomination for that performance, but it didn't even begin to hint at his reserves of charm, sexiness, and offbeat humor. In an effortless way that reminds me of Robert Mitchum, Michael Caine, or Sean Connery in the best of the Bond pictures, he is able to be tough and gentle at the same time, able to play a hero and yet not take himself too seriously. He plays Xavier Quinn, a local boy who once played barefoot with Maubee and got into the usual amount of trouble, but who grew up smart, went to America to be trained by the FBI, and has now returned as the police chief. The people of his district call him "The Mighty Quinn" after the Bob Dylan song, and there is something both affectionate and ironic in the nickname. He knows everybody in town, knows their habits, and is on good terms even with the island governor (Norman Beaton), a cheerfully corrupt hack who only wants to keep the lid on things.

The murder is a great embarrassment. It is likely to discourage tourism, and perhaps there are more sinister reasons for sweeping the crime under the carpet and blaming Maubee. Quinn is the only one who wants to press an investigation, and it takes him into the decadent lives of the local establishment. He encounters Elgin, the suave local fixer (played by the elegant James Fox, that British specialist in the devious and the evasive). He is powerfully attracted to Elgin's restless wife (Mimi Rogers), and has a private encounter with her that is charged with eroticism precisely because he wants to resist her seductiveness.

Most troublesome of all, he encounters a shambling, overweight, genial American who wanders around with a camera and always seems to be in the wrong place at the right time. This character, Miller, is played by M. Emmet Walsh, one of Hollywood's greatest character actors, who in this movie seems to combine the Sydney Greenstreet and Peter Lorre roles: He is comic relief at first, sinister malevolence later.

As his investigation makes its way through this moral quicksand, Quinn also weathers trouble at home. His wife, Lola (Sheryl Lee Ralph), is rehearsing with a reggae trio and is just a shade too emasculating to make a man truly comfortable around her. A local beauty (Tyra Ferrell) wants to steal Quinn away from her. An old crone (Esther Rolle), who is the island's resident witch, makes prophecies of dire outcomes. And the carefree Maubee himself (played by Robert Townsend) turns up to taunt Quinn with his innocence.

This story, rich enough to fuel one of the great and complicated old Warner Bros. plots, is enriched still further by wall-to-wall music, including a lot of reggae and even a couple of appearances by Rita Marley. And the photography by Jacques Steyn is natural and amused, allowing us to ease into the company of these people instead of confronting us with them.

Denzel Washington is at the heart of the movie, and what he accomplishes is a lesson in movie acting. He has obligatory action scenes, yes, and confrontations that are more or less routine. He handles them easily. But watch the way he and Mimi Rogers play their subtle romantic encounter. The scene develops in three beats instead of two, so that the erotic tension builds. But co-existing with his macho side is a playfulness that allows him to come up behind a woman and dance his fingers along her bare arms, and sashay off again before she knows what has happened.

If Washington is the discovery in this movie, he is only one of its many wonderful qualities. I've never heard of the director, Carl Schenkel, before, and I learn from the press releases only that he is Swiss and has directed a lot of commercials, but on the basis of this film, he's a natural. He is able in the moderate running time of 98 minutes to create a film that seems as rich and detailed as one much longer. He uses his Jamaican locations and interiors so easily that the movie seems to really inhabit its world, instead of merely being photographed in front of it. And the music helps; reggae somehow seems passionate, lilting, and comforting, all at once. *The Mighty Quinn* is one of the year's best films.

Chicago Sun-Times, February 17, 1989

THE OFFENCE

Bruce Williamson

Directed by Sidney Lumet. Written by John Hopkins. Starring Sean Connery, Trevor Howard, Ian Bannen, and Vivien Merchant.

Ever since he skyrocketed to international stardom as James Bond, Sean Connery has made an occasional stab at proving himself a serious actor. He proves it for keeps with his acutely intelligent, hypnotic work in *The Offence,* playing a psychotic English detective-sergeant who literally beats to death a prisoner accused of molesting a child. The movie's two big scenes — between Connery and Trevor Howard, as the chief inspector who comes to examine an underling, and is sickened by what he finds in the man; and between Connery and Ian Bannen, as the neurotic suspect who is killed for knowing far too much about his adversary—are grueling exercises in getting at the ugly, furtive little truths hidden behind the facades of what passes for normalcy. In still another chilling sequence at home, the detective fully reveals himself as a closet sadist who gets some kind of kick from the slow psychological crucifixion of his wife (played marvelously by Vivien Merchant, wife of playwright Harold Pinter). "Why aren't you beautiful? You're not even pretty," he rasps, blaming the poor frump who has tolerated him over the years he's been going quietly berserk while secretly savoring the cases of rape, torture, suicide, and bloody murder that have helped him bear his private disappointments and inadequacies, sexual or otherwise. Though such intimate explorations of character are precisely the job a movie camera was meant to do, *The Offence* is far from a great picture. If it were better, or just more commercial, Connery would undoubtedly be due for the Oscar nomination his performance deserves. Sidney Lumet's studied direction compounds the errors of an overwrought scenario by John Hopkins, who seldom leaves a point until he has driven it into the ground. Both deserve credit nonetheless for letting some light into those dark corners of human experience that may, on occasion, prompt precisely the wrong young men to choose a career on the police force. They also provide a solid framework in which four superlative actors whip through a series of harrowing dramatic encounters that are hell to watch, but hard to forget.

Unpublished, 1973

AUTEUR, AUTEUR!

For three decades, movie critics didn't need to look up the word *auteur,* so most never realized it had made it into *Webster's New World Dictionary.* According to the Third College Edition (1988), an *auteur* is "1. The primary creator of a film, esp. the director.   2. A film director with a distinctive personal style." And *auteurism* is "a critical theory whose adherents regard, as the creator of a film, the director, all of whose works are examined for characteristics that reflect a personal style. Also auteur theory — auteurist, n."

As the first dictionary definition indicates, use of the word has grown so loose that it's common to see articles referring to stars, writers, production designers, or cinematographers as auteurs. This evolution should amuse the initial adherents of the theory, who employed it primarily to delineate the personal visions of old-time big-studio directors such as Otto Preminger. Readers interested in the controversies surrounding the auteur theory should consult Andrew Sarris's *The American Cinema* (the auteurist bible) and Pauline Kael's anti-auteurist essay, "Circles and Squares," in *I Lost It at the Movies.*

Auteurist critics still emphasize more than other critics the formal aspects of moviemaking and the ideas, images, and themes that link a director's creations. But their new heroes tend to be the mavericks that many critics of all kinds admire (like Martin Scorsese or Bill Forsyth) rather than the studio craftsmen that auteur-theory critics alone used to champion. These days you don't have to be an auteurist to write an auteur piece. The individualistic films of moviemakers like Richard Rush (*The Stunt Man*), Carroll Ballard (*Never Cry Wolf*), Scorsese (*After Hours, The Last Temptation of Christ*), the Brothers Quay (*Street of Crocodiles*), Terry Gilliam (*The Adventures of Baron Munchausen*), Forsyth (*Comfort and Joy*), Jean-Luc Godard (*King Lear*), and John Cassavetes (*Love Streams*) demand that any critic confront the person calling the shots. "When one reads any strongly individual piece of writing," wrote George Orwell, "one has the impression of seeing a face somewhere behind the page." When one watches these movies, one has the impression of seeing a face somewhere behind the screen.

THE ADVENTURES OF BARON MUNCHAUSEN

Hal Hinson

Directed by Terry Gilliam. Written by Gilliam and Charles McKeown. Starring John Neville, Sarah Polley, Eric Idle, Uma Thurman, Oliver Reed, Bill Paterson, and Robin Williams. **RCA/Columbia Pictures Home Video.**

Terry Gilliam's *The Adventures of Baron Munchausen* is a wondrous feat of imagination. In terms of sheer inventiveness, it makes the other movies around these days look paltry and underfed. The worlds Gilliam has created here are like the ones he created in his animations for Monty Python—they have a majestic peculiarity. And you're constantly amazed by the freshness and eccentricity of what is pushed in front of your eyes.

As a director, Gilliam is a genuine novelty—a fire-and-brimstone fantasist. His assault on the senses is relentless; he never lets up, never gives us a chance to catch our breath. Visually, the film—which was shot by Fellini's longtime cinematographer Giuseppe Rotunno—is miraculously, almost perversely dense. The director gives *Munchausen* the antic personality of a cartoon, but Gilliam's fantasies aren't light. His dream universe has gravity. If it's a place where men ride through the sky on cannonballs and sail to the moon, it's also one where the flesh sags.

Munchausen is an adventure epic about a monumental liar—a tall tale about a teller of tall tales. It begins sometime in the late 18th century (on a Wednesday) with a flash of cannon fire in a German town under siege by the Turks. While the city is under attack, a band of actors is in the process of presenting a stage version of the Baron's adventures. From the back of the bomb-ravaged theater an old man—the real Baron Munchausen (John Neville)—loudly interrupts. Protesting that the playwright has gotten it all wrong, the verbose raconteur launches into

John Neville stars in Terry Gilliam's *The Adventures of Baron Munchausen,* as a globetrotter (and a moontrotter, too) with a romantic soul. (Photo © 1988 Columbia Pictures Industries, Inc. All rights reserved. Courtesy RCA/Columbia Pictures Home Video.)

his own version, explaining how, as the result of a bet with the Grand Turk, he inadvertently sparked the current war.

The picture is most transporting early on when, for example, Gilliam peels away the back of the theater to carry us inside the Turk's marbled harem. Or when, in order to escape from his enemies, the Baron patches together the undergarments of the townswomen to construct a hot-air balloon.

Its high point comes when the Baron and Sally (Sarah Polley), the young stowaway aboard his balloon, voyage to the moon in search of the adventurer's superheroic cohorts, Berthold (Eric Idle), Adolphus (Charles McKeown, who also assisted in writing the script), Albrecht (Winston Dennis) and Gustavus (Jack Purvis). Here they encounter the King of the Moon. Played by Robin Williams — in the credits he's listed as Ray D. Tutto — the King appears first as a gigantic pasty-faced head on a platter with colossal Ionic hair, spinning through space. Forever on the lam from his carnally obsessed body, the King sputters in pidgin Italian about the diversions of the flesh. "I've got a galaxy to run, I don't have time for flatulence and orgasms."

This is Williams at full bore, and truly it's a sight to behold. Flying through the stars, he's like the Wizard of Oz, but with cracked circuits. His part is only a cameo, but with it he's articulated the mind/body split for all time.

Of all the actors, though, Williams is the only one to establish any sort of performance rhythm. As Venus, Uma Thurman has a luscious entrance, rising up out of the deep in her clamshell, and Oliver Reed is a rivet-spitting simpleton as her jealous husband Vulcan. And as the Baron, Neville is physically perfect — he makes a great, larger-than-life object — and his combination of dashing charm and decrepitude gives the film a jolt of swashbuckling heart.

Somehow, though, except for Williams, the actors are never more than a detail in Gilliam's compositions. The film's true star is its design — and its whopping sense of fantasy. The picture is a sort of tract against the tyranny of reason and science, and for the director, Munchausen — who in real life was a cavalry officer in the service of Frederick the Great — is a symbol of the magical possibilities of imagination and wonder. The one true villain in the piece is a fascist bureaucrat named Jackson (Jonathan Pryce), who is so stern in his insistence on the commonplace that he has one heroic soldier (played by Sting) put to death — for being extraordinary. For the Baron, the ordinary life isn't worth living, and just as the figure of Death is about to steal away his soul because "there's no room in the world anymore for a three-legged Cyclops, cucumber trees and oceans of wine," his will to live is restored by the faith of a child—little Sally—in the phantasms of naive rapture.

As dream visions go, the one in which a moviemaker casts himself as the savior of all that is wondrous and magical is a fairly dangerous one, and if the stories of cost overruns and self-indulgence are to be believed, Gilliam may have fallen under its sway. The movie is an exhilarating one-of-a-kind achievement, but it's overbearing, too—a little too in-your-face to be as enjoyable as you might hope it to be.

This was true of Gilliam's *Brazil* as well. For all of the brilliance in that movie's first hour, its satire deteriorated into hysterical rantings. Gilliam revels in artifice and theatricality; he has an animator's obsession with mechanics, with levers and pulleys and the spinning and fitting of gears. But the impression you get from *Munchausen* is that for Gilliam, a film is perhaps too much of a contraption, too much of an object to be manipulated. In making his films, he's remaking the world completely, from the ground up, because he knows that invented worlds are the easiest to destroy. He creates his worlds in order to engulf them in flames. All his imaginings have a taste of the apocalypse in them. This is a heavy burden for any fantasy to bear, and *Munchausen* can't bear it. Legend has it that Baron Munchausen could swing his sword above his head so fast that he wouldn't get wet in the rain. Gilliam hasn't kept dry, but he's done some heavenly sword work.

The Washington Post, March 24, 1989

AFTER HOURS

Dave Kehr

Directed by Martin Scorsese. Written by Joseph Minion.
Starring Griffin Dunne, Rosanna Arquette, Linda Fioren-
tino, Teri Garr, Verna Bloom, John Heard, and Catherine
O'Hara. **Warner Home Video.**

Martin Scorsese's new film, *After Hours,* unfolds like a calculated
inversion of *Raging Bull,* his 1980 biography of prizefighter Jake La
Motta. The protagonist of *After Hours,* Paul Hackett (Griffin Dunne), is
a tiny, almost toylike man, with fragile features and a body that barely
seems able to support the weight of his clothes; the hulking La Motta
could probably have used him as a toothpick. Where *Raging Bull* covered
a period of some 20 years with its narrative wanderings up and down
the East Coast, from New York to Florida and back again, the new film
takes place in the small hours of a single night, with the action largely
confined to the few square blocks that constitute Manhattan's SoHo
district. Where La Motta's turbulent life was shaped by his ferocious
attachment to his young blond wife, Paul's night on the town is
dominated by four blonds: Marcy (Rosanna Arquette), a mysterious,
jittery woman who lures Paul from the safety of the Upper East Side
with a vague promise of unbridled sex; Julie (Teri Garr), a spacy '60s
refugee who takes Paul in when his liaison with Marcy turns unexpectedly sinister; Gail (Catherine O'Hara), the paranoid proprietor of a Mr.
Softee ice cream truck who, believing Paul responsible for a wave of
neighborhood burglaries, leads a shrieking vigilante mob against him;
and June (Verna Bloom), a gentle, earth-motherly sculptress who offers
him shelter from persecution, only to entangle him in the stickiest web
of all. And finally, where *Raging Bull* was a tragedy presented in harsh,
naturalistic terms, *After Hours* is a black, wincingly funny farce, filmed
in a wild mix of antirealist styles that range from Kafkaesque under-
statement to delirious expressionism, with a side trip through the
sketch comedy of "Saturday Night Live."

And yet, Paul Hackett and Jake La Motta have a great deal in
common: both *Raging Bull* and *After Hours* are centered on characters
who feel profoundly uncomfortable in the world, who have somehow

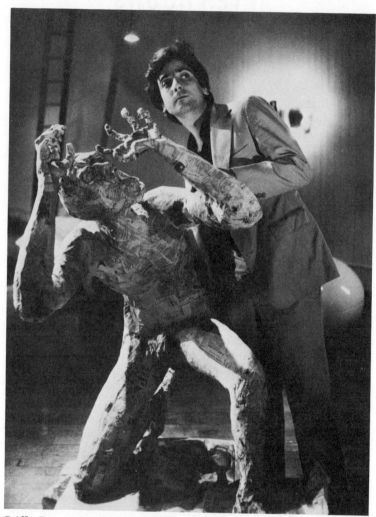

Griffin Dunne plays Paul, a midtown-Manhattan word processor whose night out in SoHo leaves him in the same shape as this papier-mâché sculpture in Martin Scorsese's *After Hours*. (Photo © 1985 The Geffen Film Company. All rights reserved.)

slipped out of sync with the rhythms of daily life. Painfully isolated individuals, they have lost the secret of easy, casual human relations that seems to be possessed by everyone around them. Unable to reach out emotionally or intellectually, Paul and Jake can connect only in physical ways—through sexuality or through violence—yet these encounters leave them guilty and ashamed. As much as they may yearn for something higher—for a spiritual connection, though the words would never occur to them—they find themselves trapped by physicality, prisoners in their own bodies. When this conflict is played out internally, as in *Raging Bull,* it becomes the stuff of self-lacerating drama; when it's projected outward, onto a world that becomes a nightmarish reflection of the central character's own conflicts, it becomes the comedy of *After Hours.* Unlike La Motta, Paul has the chance to confront his demons—the film is comedy not simply because it uses humor, but also in the classical sense of allowing the protagonist to overcome his opposition and achieve his goals. In a hilariously metaphorical final sequence, Paul is admitted to paradise, and he finds it just as light and airy as he'd always dreamed.

Scorsese keeps his distance from La Motta, approaching him externally through an objective camera technique and a narrative structure that imposes more normal, more accessible characters—Jake's wife and brother—between the audience and the eccentric hero. But in *After Hours,* Scorsese plunges us straight into Paul's consciousness with a stylistic flourish borrowed from the master of subjective filmmaking, Alfred Hitchcock: As Paul, the chief of word processing for an anonymous midtown firm, sits in his office half-listening to the whining of a new employee, Scorsese inserts a series of random, uncentered shots—desk tops, bulletin boards, passersby. These images, which represent Paul's distracted glances, interrupt what has been up until this point a perfectly traditional shot/countershot cutting pattern (the alternation of close-ups, timed to lines of dialogue, that serves to keep the focus on the interaction of the characters). Suddenly, we are sharing Paul's point of view, his very personal reactions (boredom, irritation, disengagement) to the conversation he is ostensibly taking part in. With this abrupt, strongly marked departure from realist technique, Scorsese is setting us up to accept the film's other stylistic distortions (which include speeded-up motion and unmotivated camera movements) as projections of Paul's inner state.

But it is also this sequence that, through a few quick, simple strokes, gives us the key to Paul's character. Because the random images cut off

Griffin Dunne massages the neck of Linda Fiorentino, the sensual sculptor in *After Hours*. (Photo © 1985 The Geffen Film Company. All rights reserved.)

the naturalistic flow of the shot/countershot cutting, they seem to stand in some space outside the story line. Yet, because the employee's drone continues uninterrupted on the sound track, there is something in the sequence that seems to be tugging us back to the narrative, to the "real world" established by the shot/countershot technique. Hitchcock uses this stylistic figure in *To Catch a Thief,* when Cary Grant, a reformed cat burglar, is momentarily tempted by a dazzling diamond necklace worn by Grace Kelly, and Scorsese's reworking of it retains its odd pang of guilt and shame — the embarrassment of being caught in a daydream. Scorsese lets this sense of guilty dislocation simmer for a moment, suggesting that the relationship between these nonnarrative images and the narration is also the relationship between Paul and Paul's life. Paul feels cut off from his own existence (and, from what we see of it — a sterile apartment and an impersonal office—we can understand why he'd want to be), yet he's ashamed of his noninvolvement; he wants to get back. There aren't more than a handful of filmmakers at work today who can establish an emotional condition as complex as this through purely cinematic terms; again and again in *After Hours,* Scorsese reminds us of the real power of the movies.

When Marcy comes on to Paul (he's sitting in a nearly deserted coffee shop reading a copy of *Tropic of Cancer,* when she blurts out from a nearby table that it's her favorite book too), he sees his chance to make some kind of a connection. The fact that Marcy's invitation seems to be purely sexual automatically raises him from his torpor: his reaction is involuntary, instinctual; the encounter seems safe and easy. But from the moment Marcy enters the frame, the film experiences another stylistic convulsion. Scorsese films the coffee shop conversation through a bewildering variety of lenses (again, it's a moment that would normally demand a simple shot/countershot treatment). Sometimes he uses a telephoto to isolate Paul's face in tight close-up against a blurred, indistinct background; at other moments he'll shift to a wide-angle lens that registers the background with perfect focus and clarity. The space around Paul and Marcy seems to be pulsating, changing its contours with every shot. It's as if the image track were constantly contradicting itself, and Scorsese picks up this rhythm of spiraling self-negation in the dialogue. Every statement Marcy makes is followed by another that undermines it: she likes him, she doesn't; she's coming on, she's running away. She leaves Paul her phone number, and when he calls her a couple of nights later, she invites him down to the SoHo loft she shares with an artist-friend. But by the time Paul arrives, the contradictions have escalated to the level of behavior.

Though she's just told him to come over, Marcy is gone when Paul gets there. The artist, Kiki (Linda Fiorentino), a sultry package in a black bra and slip speckled with papier-mâché, lets him in; the phone rings and it's Marcy, telling Kiki to get rid of the visitor. Kiki, though, tells him to stay, and a little while later Marcy walks in, greets him warmly, and invites him to her bedroom. Scorsese doesn't try to account for these abrupt reversals. He simply presents Marcy's actions as they appear to Paul—opaque and imponderable. Just as Paul has begun to reach out to the world, he finds the world withdrawing from him, turning into something remote and mysterious. Now that he wants to, he can't get through.

Barriers provide the film's main visual motif—the armored doors of artists' lofts, the steel security shutters that descend over bars and shop fronts, the metal gratings that cover the apartment windows through which Paul glimpses flashing scenes of sex and violence. There is even a punk bar named Berlin, where the decor consists of chain-link fencing and the bouncer who bars the door is only slightly more accommodating than an East German border guard. Paul manages to pass through several of these barriers—it's the blond women who let him in—though once he's crossed them he can't go back: the doors open only one way. Every time Paul believes he's escaped—as when he flees from Marcy's apartment to a friendly-looking saloon (though the sign over the door does say "Terminal Bar")—he finds that he's only fallen in deeper (the bartender turns out to be Marcy's boyfriend). The only characters who can pass freely through this Chinese box environment are the two burglars played by Cheech and Chong: merrily (and obliviously) cleaning out the neighborhood while the mob pursues Paul, they appear as sprightly, almost supernatural figures; eventually, they will prove to be the agents of Paul's salvation.

If *After Hours* seems to be reaching the kind of wide audience that eluded Scorsese on his last two films, *Raging Bull* and *King of Comedy*, it's probably because Scorsese has been able to tap into what has become the dominant strain in '80s comedy—the comedy of under-reaction, defined by an unflappably cool protagonist (Bill Murray, ideally) who steadfastly refuses to be provoked by the outrageous, surreal, often threatening goings-on around him. Paul's sense of detachment isn't unlike Murray's in a film like *Ghostbusters,* but Scorsese takes the idea one step further, humanizing it: he identifies its psychological roots, and then lets us see the increasing amount of effort Paul must expend on maintaining it. Paul wants to withdraw from the nightmare that's happening to him, to make himself small and inconspicuous (his most frequent lines of dialogue are "I didn't know" and "I'm sorry"), but the anger is building up inside. He's ready to turn into a raging bull himself, or at least a raging heifer. Paul's desperate detachment, his strangely hysterical reasonableness, represents another kind of barrier: you begin to feel that if only he could explode, take command of the situation, his nightmare would be over. But every time Paul lets his anger show—his violence is verbal, sarcastic, rather than physical—as he does with the first three blonds, the results are catastrophic: if he strikes out at the world, the world strikes back twice as hard at him. It was an instinctive, physical response—good old lust—

that got him into this situation. Another instinctive response — violence — isn't going to get him out.

Paul is as much a victim of his physical urges as Jake La Motta; as much as he may try to repress them, he can't entirely snuff them out — they keep getting him into trouble. This is, of course, the classic Catholic boy conundrum — why has God built these things into me if he only wants to punish me for them? — as Scorsese makes explicit when he has Paul, a Job in the SoHo wilderness, stagger down a deserted street and cry to an unseen auditor, "I just wanted to get out of my apartment, meet a nice girl . . . and now I've gotta *die* for it?" But if Catholic doctrine — the resentment of the body — is the blueprint for Scorsese's fiction, he's equally concerned with cultural doctrine, with what this resentment has done to the relations between men and women. If men must be made to bear the exclusive burden of sexual aggression, they must all become monsters; if women must somehow be placed beyond sexuality, they must all become harpies. Scorsese's four blonds — their hair color is flaunted as the traditional emblem of innocence and purity — become the objects of a mingled fear and desire, sought after because they promise some relief from the sexual burden, flown from in horror because they seem to want to appropriate the sexual prerogative for themselves. The barrier between the sexes is the ultimate line of demarcation in *After Hours;* there is only one way to cross it — the body must be cast off.

The film's concluding section consists of a riotous, virtuoso shuffling of satirical birth and death images. June, Verna Bloom's motherly sculptress, takes the by now exhausted Paul down to her dark, damp basement studio; he curls up in her lap, clutching her like a baby. When the vigilante mob arrives at her door, June decides to hide Paul by disguising him as a sculpture: covered with rapidly stiffening papier-mâché strips, his eyes peering out from a tiny hole, this thickened, immobile Paul suddenly comes to resemble the overweight La Motta at the end of *Raging Bull,* trapped inside his own physical bulk. June goes off with the mob, leaving Paul alone when Cheech and Chong arrive. Thinking he's an art object, they steal him, pulling his rigid form up into the street through a manhole cover. With Paul loaded in their van, they take off uptown, but a strategically placed pothole bumps Paul out the back door and into the street directly in front of his office building. It is dawn, and the barrier in front of the building — a magnificent golden gate — swings open magisterially to admit the new arrival. The fall having broken his plaster shell, Paul staggers to an elevator and ascends to his celestial office, where his computer, like a friendly, disembodied deity, blinks him a message of greeting—"Good morning, Paul." It is here in this lifeless land, where all sexuality has been sublimated in work and there are only words, not bodies, to deal with, that Paul finally finds freedom and peace. As if in celebration, Scorsese's camera flies off for a rushing, swooping dance around the room—a flight of angels rejoicing in the salvation of a sinner.

Chicago Reader, October 11, 1985

THE ANIMATED ART
OF THE BROTHERS QUAY

Terrence Rafferty

Devised by Stephen and Timothy Quay.

They bill themselves as the Brothers Quay, which has an archaic and faintly ridiculous ring, as if they were a vaudeville comedy act or a family of acrobats. Photographs of Timothy and Stephen Quay, who are identical twins, look like trick shots from the early days of cinema, products of the cheap camera magic that makes a single actor double and allows him, before our eyes, to talk to himself. In interviews the comments of one brother are never distinguished from those of the other: they speak as if with one voice.

The Quays, born in Philadelphia, have lived and worked together for all of their forty years, most recently in London, where since 1978 they have absorbed themselves in the absurd and intricate form of play known as puppet animation—that naively mechanistic genre of film art that preserves, a frame at a time, the memories of a childish delight in small effigies of ourselves, our wonder when at a human touch the dolls begin to move, and our vague horror as we watch their manipulated forms reflect and parody the actions of our own bodies.

Puppet animation is, as the Quays themselves admit, a freakish, marginal art: it can be as trivial as the singing, dancing raisins of American television advertising, or as ponderously symbolic as some of the Eastern European political allegories that turn up with alarming frequency on film-festival programs. But the Quays' puppets seem, like the mysterious twins who make them, to have found in their own marginality an eerier and more suggestive kind of life, a shadowy, feverish half existence in which their movements are like the choreography of dreams. These puppets have the quality, unique in the genre, of appearing to be aware of their secondhand status, conscious that they're the crude doubles of beings once or still alive. And the films — with their sinuous camera movements through rooms full of dust and clutter and dirty glass, the interiors of a playhouse decrepit from overuse — are informed by the philosophical melancholy of their creators, whose art is perhaps the product of an endless and unresolvable obsession, who make puppets perhaps because each of them has spent every day of his life looking at and talking to a moving, three-dimensional, terrifyingly exact copy of himself.

There is, of course, something fanciful about the notion that the Quays' art is a complex ritual of twinhood. It makes the Quays out to be characters in a Romantic horror story — artists haunted by their creations, men looking over their shoulders for the doubles they know (or imagine) are following them, denizens of the unsettling mirror worlds of Hoffmann and Kafka, Poe and Borges. If we see them this way, it's because the films themselves encourage us to. Just as there are dreams so intense, so cryptic, that they hold our imagination for days, even years, the Quays' short movies have the power of the truly uncanny: we sense, without knowing why, that there's something *necessary* in their mastery of this arcane craft, that they're not so much telling stories with puppets as they are searching for the human ghosts in their wood-and-cloth machines. The intimacy of the Quays' relation to their dolls is creepy. Watching these films, we feel like Hoffmann characters ourselves, enchanted into an uneasy self-consciousness by arts so overwhelming that they verge on the demonic. We seem, somehow, to have been twinned — dancers mesmerized by the strange reflections of our own movements in the mirror beyond the barre.

The metaphysical theater of the Brothers Quay — whose work until now has been visible only on British television, in European film festivals, and in a film series called *Alchemists of the Surreal,* which has toured English art cinemas since last fall — has taken its show on the road in the United States this year, on a characteristically small scale. In January the United States Film Festival in Utah showed a program of four Quay films: *Leoš Janáček: Intimate Excursions* (which runs for twenty-seven minutes), *The Cabinet of Jan Švankmajer* (fourteen minutes), *Little Songs of the Chief Officer of Hunar Louse, or This Unnameable Little Broom* (eleven minutes), and *Street of Crocodiles* (twenty minutes), their most recent film, and their first in 35mm. This same program has had a week's run at New York's Film Forum, and a slightly different selection was screened at the San Francisco Film Festival. There's talk of taking the program on tour to other cities and of showing one or more of the films on public television, but nothing is definite. Right now these films are obscure, sneaking in and out of theaters furtively, which seems oddly appropriate: they're such unlikely objects, and flash past our eyes so quickly, that they leave us dazed, unsure whether we've really seen their images or merely hallucinated them.

Even at their most straightforward, as in the Janáček film, the Quays are disorienting. The brothers, along with their longtime collaborator, the producer Keith Griffiths, have often worked in the portrait-of-the-artist genre, partly because television is always eager to supply funds for such "educational" films: they've also done a biography of the Belgian playwright Michel de Ghelderode, which was mostly documentary, and the jazzy, hilarious puppet film *Igor — The Paris Years Chez Pleyel*, about Stravinsky, with Jean Cocteau (who at one point appears in a tutu, dancing to a pianola score of *Petrushka*) and Vladimir Mayakovsky (whose body is an origami nightmare of revolutionary posters) hovering at the edges.

But the Quays' biographical films are like no one else's. In *Janáček*, as in the Stravinsky film, the artist-doll is a startlingly poignant composite — a puppet's three-dimensional body supporting a cutout photograph, slightly oversized, of the great man's head. This technique isn't simply a way of avoiding caricature. Janáček's head, monochromatic and 2-D, has the shocking gravity of many old photos: it's the visual equivalent of the ghostly scraps of the composer's diaries and correspondence that are read to us in voice-over. ("When someone speaks to me, I listen to the tonal modulations in their voice, more than to what they are actually saying. . . . I can feel or rather hear my hidden sorrow.") The tenuous relationship between head and body makes the Quays' Janáček seem, poetically, all mind, and as animated tableaux of the composer's work pass before us, we can't help feeling that we're seeing and hearing this music the way Janáček must have dreamed it.

This illusion, almost too fragile to sustain, derives its force and beauty from the rhythms of the Quays' camera, moving in mysterious concord with the stately tempos of the music itself. The camera circles the extraordinary sets—a forest of leafless trees, Janáček's bare room, a deserted gymnasium with grillwork windows, a prison, a ruined church—catching glimpses of spindly, insect-like puppet figures through the trees and the bars of windows, images as fugitive as those that appear and disappear, flickering in the mind's eye, as we listen to a piece of music. At Janáček's death all the phantoms of the composer's imagination—the frail puppets from his works, including *Diary of One Who Vanished, The Cunning Little Vixen,* and *The Makropulos Case,* among others—gather around him for a moment in the forest, which has moved, somehow, into his stark room, the trunks' dark vertical forms merging with the shadows of the windows' grills, echoing the cathedral's pillars and the prison's bars, filling the space around his fading features with a tangle of lines, like a passionately scribbled score. The delicate calligraphy of a musician's mind has never been represented more beautifully.

The Cabinet of Jan Švankmajer and *This Unnameable Little Broom* (as its impossible title is usually abbreviated) are, though brilliant, perhaps the Quays' most difficult and off-putting films. These two shorts are harder-edged and less lyrical than the Janáček film, and depend more heavily on the Eastern European puppet-film tradition: there's a hint of didacticism in them, even though we're never quite sure what we're meant to be learning. The Švankmajer film is in fact a tribute to a Czech animator whose work has influenced the Quays. It's structured as a series of little lessons in perception, taught by a puppet with an open book for hair, to a doll with a hollowed-out head, in finely detailed settings that evoke the style of encyclopedia illustration (as well as, at various points, Ernst, de Chirico, and the Mannerist painter Arcimboldo). For the viewer, the movie is a short course in the principles of animation, conducted as if the art of Švankmajer and the Quays were a lost discipline of the Renaissance, an ancient form of anatomical drawing.

This Unnameable Little Broom, which is, according to the filmmakers, a portion of "a largely disguised reduction of the *Epic of Gilgamesh,*" is a swift, savage, and largely baffling movie about a tricycle-riding monster who traps a strange winged creature in his lair. The camera whips back and forth in slashing, aggressive gestures, and the effect is stunning, but the battle is abrupt and not quite so satisfying. We have no context for what we're seeing—the film is actually a fragment, a single episode from a planned full version of *Gilgamesh*—so the whole encounter, inventively choreographed as it is, seems too starkly mythic.

But *Street of Crocodiles,* the Quays' very free adaptation of Bruno Schulz's dreamlike memoir of Poland between the wars, is a fully articulated vision. Schulz's hallucinatory prose, which renders the world as a fantastic construction whose laws seem always on the tantalizing verge of our understanding, is perfect for the Quays. Schulz writes, in the voice of his narrator's deranged father:

> Figures in a waxwork museum . . . must not be treated lightly. . . . Can you imagine the pain, the dull imprisoned suffering, hewn into the matter of that dummy which does not know why it must be what it is, why it must remain in that forcibly imposed form which is no more than a parody? . . . You give a head of canvas and oakum an expression of anger and leave it with it, with the convulsion, the tension enclosed once and for all, with a blind fury for which there is no outlet. . . .
>
> Have you heard at night the terrible howling of these wax figures, shut in the fair-booths; the pitiful chorus of those forms of wood or porcelain, banging their fists against the walls of their prisons?

The Quays, clearly, have heard these sounds. The puppet-hero of *Street of Crocodiles*—who, as we learn in a black-and-white live-action prologue, is part of an elaborate contraption locked away in a provincial museum—looks around him in something like terror when the thread connecting him to his unseen manipulator is snipped, and then, with a haunted, stricken stare, begins to explore. His environment is ominous, a decaying city inside a box, with an inscrutable system of threads and pulleys running along the ground, screws that pull free of floorboards and dance in the dust, shop windows full of blank mannequins and mechanical monkeys beating their cymbals furiously when a light shines on them, and dolls rotating shoulders whose joints are disturbingly exposed. Everything in this world seems to hint at obscure connections—the screws' threads are somehow related to the wires from which the hero has been disengaged, and also to the filaments of the light bulbs in the shops—and everything is a reflection of the weathered materials of which this abandoned puppet is made. It's no wonder he looks anxious as he wanders timidly through this labyrinth of wood and glass, no wonder the camera seems to be skulking with him, moving carefully, as if afraid of what it will find around the next corner. The Quays' *Street of Crocodiles* is a puppet film that, in its self-consciousness, transcends itself. It's about the chill of discovering, through play, what we're made of—about gazing on an aging world and seeing our own fragile anatomies reflected there.

The Atlantic, June 1987

COMFORT AND JOY

★

Terrence Rafferty

Directed and written by Bill Forsyth. Starring Bill Paterson. **MCA Home Video.**

Watching a movie by the Scottish writer and director Bill Forsyth is a little like listening to a long anecdote told by someone whose mind is far away. The narrative keeps wandering off the track, but the digressions are odd enough to keep our attention and even to surprise us into laughing—sporadically and uncertainly at first, then more steadily, until we are brought up short by the punch line we nearly forgot was coming. The end of the story is always a letdown, neither as interesting nor as funny as the circuitous route we've taken to get there. The storyteller has drawn us into his mind's peculiar terrain and allowed us to wander happily, wondering where we are, not wanting to be let off at any of the usual stops. Forsyth's movies have a dreamy, distracted air, a surface modesty, and none of the usual jokes. They mimic the style of a befuddled storyteller so uncannily that we may not catch on right away to their daring and originality: these comedies want us to laugh in the wrong places.

Forsyth's new picture, *Comfort and Joy,* is his riskiest and most ambitious work—a comedy about depression, loneliness, ice cream, and the radio. Its hero, Alan Bird (Bill Paterson), is a Glasgow radio personality known to the public as "Dicky Bird." His morning drive-time show dispenses music and cheerful patter, along with the grim necessities of time, traffic, and weather, in a smooth, easy-to-swallow mixture for shut-ins and groggy commuters. Sitting in his studio with his headset on, swiveling in his chair, surrounded by other people (engineers, newsreaders, the traffic girl) — all isolated, like him, in windowed booths — Dicky Bird gives a masterfully orchestrated performance of soothing inanities. He makes jokes about the 6 A.M. newsreader falling asleep at his console, invites his listeners to enter a contest whose prize is a day's use of the station manager's American Express card, creates characters out of the station's personnel ("Ah, here comes the lovely Ann!"). His show conjures up the illusion of a workday paradise, a family of charming creatures who converse in the trilling tones of commercial jingles — and it's an illusion that Alan Bird probably couldn't create so well if he didn't half believe in it. The comic premise of *Comfort and Joy* is that Bird's half-belief will, for a few days, be fully and sternly tested. At the beginning of the film his girlfriend of four years, the lovely (but slightly crazy) Maddy, interrupts a peaceful evening at home by announcing that she's having a couple of friends over to move out her things. She walks out of his life, leaving him stranded in an apartment suddenly barer and lonelier than Dicky Bird's studio.

Forsyth knows that you don't have to be deep to be depressed, and he dignifies his hero's personal tragedy with a few bleak, piercing scenes: Bird standing in a light snowfall watching Maddy's van pull away; wandering disconsolately through the empty apartment, pouring himself a drink, avoiding the bedroom as long as he can; dreaming of Maddy's return every time he falls asleep, and waking up, every time, alone. But Forsyth also knows that the attempt to escape depression, to change your life (once, of course, someone has already changed it for you), can be deeply funny. Alan Bird, a man who by both temperament and profession is light, amiable, and easygoing, decides to become more serious: maybe he'll do a documentary on the "real" Glasgow, the violence and industrial squalor he's glossed over every morning on the air, which he seems to be seeing for the first time, as if the city reflected his own gloomy state of mind. The basic situation here is close to that of Preston Sturges's *Sullivan's Travels,* in which a successful Hollywood director of musicals and light comedies decides to make a "worthy" picture (to be called *O Brother, Where Art Thou?*), and goes out on the road disguised as a hobo to see at first hand the lives of the poor and the dispossessed. The vehicle that Bird finds for his new seriousness is the opportunity to serve as the mediator in a territorial battle between two rival ice-cream operations—the sleek, powerful Mr. McCool and the renegade Mr. Bunny.

Once the ironies of the narrative are in place, we can laugh wherever we like, and Forsyth plays Bird's mission for maximum absurdity. "Mr. Bunny does not play by the rules," exclaims Mr. McCool (who is, it turns out, a rather elegant Italian gentleman). "Mr. Bunny is a rogue elephant." On his morning show Dicky Bird begs his listeners' indulgence while he gets "a teensy bit serious" and relays a message on the air from Mr. McCool to Mr. Bunny. His descent into the ominous nocturnal world of the Glasgow ice-cream wars cheers him with new purpose and new metaphors: "My life," he explains to his friends and his alarmed boss, "was the wrong flavor."

The flavor of *Comfort and Joy* is strange and rich, but not completely unfamiliar to those who have sampled Forsyth's humor in *That Sinking Feeling, Gregory's Girl,* and *Local Hero.* His movies are filled with people who feel that they're in the wrong place and yearn (with varying degrees of urgency) for someplace else. The Glasgow youths in *That Sinking Feeling* decide that crime—that is, pinching a load of bathroom fixtures—is the remedy for the boredom and poverty of unemployment; the teenage boys in *Gregory's Girl* lurch timidly into the world of romantic love, a couple of them desperate enough to get out on the highway and start thumbing their way to Caracas, where women, they've heard, outnumber men eight to one; *Local Hero*'s hotshot young oil executive winds up wanting to trade places with the innkeeper of the Scottish coastal village that he's been sent from Houston to buy out. After four movies, this starts to look like a theme—unobtrusive, but persistent enough to give Forsyth's pictures a distinctive rhythm, a pace unlike anything we're used to in screen comedy. It's not the lickety-split timing of farce or the accelerating gags of silent slapstick or the steady, metronomic rationing of jokes in situation comedy but the languid, daydreaming tempo of a Sunday drive.

The films are funny because Forsyth seems to be following his dreamers at just the right distance, watching them swerve and meander but keeping his own eye on the road. What amuses him is the way our fantasies foul up our relationship to the place we're in, the way they put us at odds with mundane things—the time, the traffic, the weather. He loves adolescents like Gregory, because they're so profoundly out of it, as if they didn't fully inhabit even their own bodies. For Gregory, going

Bill Paterson (left) plays Alan "Dicky" Bird, a Glasgow radio personality who's embroiled in a perilous war between ice-cream powers in Bill Forsyth's *Comfort and Joy*. (Photo copyright © by Universal Pictures, a Division of Universal City Studios, Inc. Courtesy of MCA Publishing Rights, a Division of MCA Inc.)

about the little business of life, such as getting himself off to school, is a fantastic adventure. He rolls out of bed, beats aimlessly (but vigorously) on his drum set for a minute or two, wanders downstairs with an electric toothbrush whirring in his mouth, lays it down, still running, to buzz and travel erratically across the kitchen counter as he fixes his breakfast; and then, finally out and on his way, shirttail flapping as he lopes across the highway, he somehow manages to put himself in the path of the only car for miles around. Gregory's mind is always miles away, which makes him silly but gives him a kind of comic grace. To be "not all there" is a real gift if "there" is Glasgow, or high school. Forsyth also confers this gift, for a while, on Mac, the young businessman of *Local Hero,* whose stay in the village of Ferness begins as an assignment and ends up a blissful holiday. His suits and ties give way to floppy pullovers, he stops carrying his attaché case on the beach, he lets the shaving go for a few days. He even leaves his beeper watch, which tells him that it's meeting time in Houston, on a rock, and never misses it.

Gregory's Girl is probably Forsyth's funniest movie, and *Local Hero* (which, in the end, returns the reluctant Mac to Houston) is his most satisfying, the smoothest blend of irony and reverie. *Comfort and Joy* shares those films' desultory rhythms and out-of-place humor, but, perhaps because its hero is older and apparently settled in his life, there seems to be more at stake here — real violence, real depression, an even greater yearning for escape. Forsyth is trying to stretch his delicate comic vision to its limit, and he nearly brings off something very difficult: a comedy that delights us and disturbs us at the same time. For the first time in his work Forsyth has a mixture of elements so volatile that they demand a resolution, a punch line, and he can't quite deliver a satisfactory one. Sturges, facing a similar problem in *Sullivan's Travels* but blessed with a brash, aggressive style, just went ahead and belted out a stupid one: Sullivan learns that his mindless, frothy movies are worth more to America's unfortunates than his beloved social-problem picture ever could be. *Comfort and Joy*'s gentler, fable-like resolution completes the ironic curves of the story, using the radio and Bird's lightweight charm to effect the end of the ice-cream wars. It's graceful and clever, but too simple, too self-consciously charming; it brings Forsyth perilously close to endorsing the fun-conquers-all moral of *Sullivan's Travels.*

Forsyth seems more comfortable in the film's very last scene — just a coda, really — and he tosses off a lovely riff that leaves us half believing in the value of the commercial daydream that Dicky Bird provides for his audience. Sitting at his mike on Christmas Day, with no company at the station except an engineer who brings him a tiny piece of cake, Bird spins out the illusion of a joyous Christmas party ("Don't you feel too sorry for us!") and promises his listeners a day of nothing but music and jokes — no time, no traffic, no weather reports. His radio show in this last scene takes on a beauty as unearthly and as unexpected as Glasgow's in the streetlit evenings through which Bird has chased down Mr. Bunny vans. It has the beauty, too, of an apt and resonant metaphor for the art of Bill Forsyth's comedies, these diverting, original anecdotes that are both daydreams themselves and sympathetic reports on the daydreamers. Forsyth's movies always end by telling us, from some-place far away, that the traffic on the way to wherever we'd rather be is moving slowly, but the weather is good and there's all the time in the world.

The Atlantic, November 1984

KING LEAR

Jonathan Baumbach

Directed and written by Jean-Luc Godard. Starring Peter
Sellars, Burgess Meredith, Godard, and Molly Ringwald.

And take upon 's the mystery of things
As if we were God's spies.

ACT V, SCENE iii

The advance word on the new film by Jean-Luc Godard is that it is a
thorough disaster, which turns out to mean that it runs contrary to
expectations for mainstream "art" films in the 1980s. It was only when
we expected the unlikely, when we were eager to be turned on to the
new, that Godard's films ever satisfied expectation. He is a surviving
figure of the '60s and as such is something of an embarrassment to us in
the '80s, another exemplar of apparently misspent passion. And passion
it was for those of us who loved the seemingly infinite possibilities of
film (and, by extension, literature, painting, music, life, etc.). Godard
writes in one of his early pieces in the *Cahiers du Cinéma*, "Everything
remains to be done." We no longer want to believe that; Godard still
does.

Between 1959 and 1968, Godard produced virtually all his major
work, such flawed masterpieces as *Breathless, Vivre sa Vie, Band of
Outsiders, A Married Woman, Masculin-Feminin, Alphaville,* and *Weekend.*
(Or perhaps *La Chinoise, Two or Three Things I Know about Her, Pierrot le
Fou* — you make the list.) After that there was a period of agitprop films,
in collaboration with Pierre Gorin, where Godard attempted to efface
himself as an artist. And though he returned to making commercial
films in 1981 with the admirable *Every Man for Himself* (his second first
film, as he called it), he was no longer at the center of our consciousness. He was speaking to us, or such was the general perception, from a
vanished time.

Where Ingmar Bergman and Federico Fellini still inspire reverence
(even on uninspired occasions), Jean-Luc is virtually unknown among a
new generation of filmgoers (who think Spielberg or Lucas or perhaps

Siskel and Ebert invented the medium). If he has any identity for us now, it is as the clown prince of marginal film. In our moment, playfulness is perceived as incompatible with seriousness; it seems a confession of triviality. While most of his great contemporaries seem to be consolidating their oeuvre with ready-made masterpieces, Godard appears to be still rediscovering with each new film what it is to make a film. He remains ahead of us (that's avant-garde, for God's sake), but we're too far behind to care. In the '80s, we like films that look like masterpieces so long as they don't have the off-putting surprise of being original.

King Lear was an unlikely project from the start, an occasion to raise money from Golan and Globus (the myth of how the deal was made is its own story) to make a film with Norman Mailer and Woody Allen. (Both have inconsequential cameos.) As Godard has stated in various interviews, his film is a meditation on virtue and power, or virtue versus power. Like most of his films it is less concerned with narrative than with dialectic. It is a commentary in images on its own presumed text, which has been mostly effaced. Godard's *King Lear* is in effect a filmed essay on a film that only exists as imaginary text.

The plot (or occasion) of *King Lear* is as follows: As a consequence of Chernobyl, all art and literature have apparently been lost. William Shakespeare the Fifth (Peter Sellars) is commissioned to rediscover his great ancestor's lost plays. By eavesdropping on conversations between Learo, a Mafia entrepreneur (Burgess Meredith) and his daughter Cordelia (Molly Ringwald), he begins to reassemble *King Lear*. So this is a film about reclaiming itself. Cordelia and Lear are not characters but commentaries on characters, undramatized images, totems. Sometimes they speak Shakespeare's lines, sometimes contemporary idiom. It is as if the Shakespearean voices we hear were internal monologues, inchoate feelings given poetic representation. The old man wants to be wanted for himself and not his power and money. The girl wants her father to recognize that she loves him without having the truth of it vitiated by exaggeration.

Jean-Luc himself plays a clownish character called the professor, the Shakespearean fool as filmmaker, and gives us in passing a lecture on filmmaking esthetics. I suspect that Godard's strongest identification is with Cordelia, and that her role is a metaphor for the director, who refuses to falsify to win our good will, who is unable "to heave his heart into his mouth." Here, as elsewhere, Godard is nothing if not uncompromising.

King Lear is elegantly filmed, full of images that take us by surprise (e.g., stop-action movement of a white horse), though it is also static in the manner of an essay. The film doesn't seem to end so much as trail off, as if it had run out of time or money. In the recovery (or discovery) of *King Lear,* goes the metaphor, the author loses his innocence. The film ends, as all art must, with the death of innocence. There are loose ends, private jokes — the character of Edgar, for example, seems gratuitous. If *King Lear* is not among Godard's best work (though more interesting than *Hail Mary,* which preceded it), it is nevertheless the most original new film currently available in New York. It is a willfully didactic work. It willfully insists, against our predilection to experience only the predetermined, on teaching us once again to see.

Unpublished, 1987

THE LAST TEMPTATION OF CHRIST

Owen Gleiberman

Directed by Martin Scorsese. Written by Paul Schrader, from the novel by Nikos Kazantzakis. Starring Willem Dafoe, Harvey Keitel, and Barbara Hershey. **MCA Home Video.**

The mountain is studded with skulls and gnarled trees, and there at its center is the crucified Jesus, yet the day itself has a shimmering electric beauty: the sky as blue and clear as the brightest explosion of spring, the light sunshiny, ecstatic. For a few minutes, Golgotha might be the most spectacular movie set in history — a metaphysical soundstage. As streams of blood flow down his face and chest, Jesus of Nazareth soaks up the light, gazes Heavenward, and then does something you don't expect: he smiles, broadly, releasing his fear, embracing pain and death.

His smile seems to melt right into the gold-spangled day; at last, the job on earth is done.

At its visionary best, Martin Scorsese's *The Last Temptation of Christ* has scenes of feverish intensity that hold one in thrall. It's a radiant and, I think, genuinely religious film — as impassioned a vision of the Gospels as we're likely to see on screen. It's also far from the masterpiece many of us had hoped for from Scorsese, perhaps the most gifted American director of his generation, and certainly the most rhapsodically Catholic. This two-hour-and-40-minute movie, an adaptation of Nikos Kazantzakis's celebrated (and equally controversial) 1955 novel, is the film Scorsese has wanted to make for 16 years, yet it doesn't look or feel like other long-cherished labors of love. It's loose and freewheeling and a little sloppy. Some of it falls flat, a few of the scenes are a hoot (this may be endemic to Biblical epics), and some of the movie's philosophy seems slipshod, the casualty of a weak script and a rush-rush production schedule. The film is also relentlessly bloody, something that might be more effective if you didn't feel the stuff was being ladled on for show — especially in a scene where Jesus reaches into his chest and pulls out his glimmering heart.

Still, for all its many (and obvious) flaws, *The Last Temptation of Christ* exerts a cumulative power. It's the Jesus story as a mythic psychodrama; it's about a Christ burdened with self-consciousness — a Messiah who stands back and watches himself save mankind. In Kazantzakis's novel (which got him excommunicated from the Greek Orthodox Church), the author envisioned his hero as an almost neurotic figure, a projection of the way contemporary men and women at once crave and fear the totality of religious devotion. The idea has extraordinary resonance, and there's daring in the way Kazantzakis gives his Jesus a sense of Nietzschean destiny, portraying him as a weakling who must rise up and harness the superman in himself. Yet as drama, I found the book stiff-jointed and monotonous. Kazantzakis doesn't take his conceit far enough. He himself seems torn between this revisionist, human view of Christ and a traditionally stoic, reverential treatment, and the book reads like the Bible with humanist footnotes.

Scorsese, too, doesn't push the human-Christ idea that far. After all, this *is* Jesus we're talking about. Had the character on screen strayed too much from the image of Christ as a figure of infinite compassion and strength, he would have seemed trivial — a case of innocent, liberal blasphemy. Yet the idea of a "human Jesus" does seem made for the big screen. Most Biblical epics are the purest camp, because we can never forget the distance between the famous, lacquered actors in their robes and sandals and the cosmic characters they're supposedly portraying. Watching *The Last Temptation of Christ,* that distance is sometimes an issue (in the year 33 AD, Harry Dean Stanton requires much suspension of disbelief), yet in the case of Jesus it disappears. This Christ isn't "flawed" or complex so much as he is a soulful, three-dimensional presence. And watching Willem Dafoe's beautiful performance, which is like a more tumultuous version of the usual beatific Christs, one feels closer to Jesus than one does in perhaps any other Biblical movie – closer to his righteousness and joy, to his anger, and (this is part of what's raising hackles) to his fear.

Given the controversy it's inspired, *The Last Temptation of Christ* seems startlingly conventional, an honest attempt to wipe away the hokey grandiosity of Biblical epics, and to bring the Gospels to the screen with a modern urgency and boldness.

One hesitates to point out the obvious: that the protest against this film, to the extent that it has advocated censorship, couldn't be less American; that the wrath of the protesters and, especially, their organizers (principally the Methodist minister Donald Wildmon, but also that meek and humble servant of the Lord Jerry Falwell) seems the expression of a peculiarly nasty, scolding, and intolerant temperament – a coarse cheapening of the Christian spirit; and that the scene at the heart of the controversy – a 10-second shot in which Jesus, *imagining* what his life would be like had he lived as a mere mortal, is seen discreetly making love to his imagined wife, Mary Magdalene, in bed – admits only that Jesus was subject to temptation, and hardly constitutes a violation of his divinity. Were Jesus himself to see this film, he'd surely understand the sincerity behind it, the attempt (whether successful or not) to explore how Christianity lives in the contemporary consciousness.

Unable to finance the film for years, Scorsese, coming off his 1986 hit *The Color of Money,* finally received backing from Universal, and also from Cineplex Odeon (the company whose theaters are currently the only place you can see the film). Even then, he was able to scrape together only $6.5 million – less than the budget of your average John Candy flick. Supported by a crew of actors willing to work for scale, he went to Morocco and, armed with this paltry budget, proceeded to shoot . . . a big, wide-screen, Biblical spectacular.

A part of me wishes he'd stayed truer to that budget, that he'd shot the whole thing with snaky, hand-held camerawork and improvised dialogue. *The Last Temptation of Christ* is a bit impersonal. Like most Biblical movies, it's heavy-spirited and episodic, galumphing from one famous story to the next. Yet Scorsese, even working on this broader-than-usual canvas, knows how to draw you in. Using a calmer, more sweeping version of his usual white-hot visual style, he creates a majestically primitive Palestine, and Peter Gabriel has written one of his percussion-based scores, which works magnificently here; it lends the action a dark, volcanic power.

The first part of the film presents Jesus as a reluctant Messiah who only gradually recognizes (and accepts) his divinity. At first, he regards it as a burden and a far-off mystery—a spiritual disease that torments him with self-doubt. It's as though he were feeling the eight warning signs of Messiah-hood. Dafoe's Christ speaks of how he longs to sin (to kill, to have a woman), yet doesn't out of fear. We may recognize this sentiment from other Scorsese heroes, and certainly we recognize it in ourselves. For the moment, Jesus's passion has turned inward. This young carpenter actually makes crosses used to crucify Zealots and then assists in the crucifixions, spattering himself with blood. He seems pathetic and kowtowing; he's the scourge of Nazareth—and of his strong, righteous boyhood friend, the red-haired Judas Iscariot (Harvey Keitel)—for aiding in the murder of his brothers.

What Jesus is really doing by building crosses himself is indulging in the lowest activity he can, so as not to confront his sanctity. In voice-over, he speaks of God appearing to him as a bird, of the talons digging into his back. And as we listen, Scorsese gives us hallucinatory shots of Willem Dafoe lying on a beach, as though Jesus were trying to block out the murmurings of his soul. The character seems lost, depressive, yet this hardly diminishes him. In a sense, the movie merges Jesus's super-earthly burdens with our earthly ones. The psychological effect of this couldn't be further from blasphemy. Staring down at this tormented Jesus, we see him as an organic figure who demands our fullest awe and empathy—someone whose triumph, for once, seems less than given.

Some of the scenes, such as Jesus's first big encounter with Mary Magdalene, are dramatically off-center. Still, what an image Barbara Hershey's Mary is! Her hair long and dark, her body covered in intricate tattoos, she seems to meld pride and shame into one. The script, adapted by Paul Schrader (and with an uncredited assist by Scorsese and former *Time* magazine critic Jay Cocks), substitutes modern, colloquial language for well-known Biblical dialogue, and the scene in which Jesus accepts his destiny by halting the stoning of Mary features one of the least successful examples of it. Standing before the crowd, with two stones in his hand, he says, "Who has never sinned? Whoever that is, come up here, and throw one of these!" (It sounds like a translation from Esperanto.) Sometimes, there's so little going on in the script *besides* empty, contemporary language that it's a little embarrassing. The scenes with the apostles are especially bad — I kept looking at this crew and thinking it was bowling night.

By and large, though, the updating works, not because the language is especially imaginative, but because the decision to jettison anything resembling the King's English frees Willem Dafoe as an actor. The wonderful thing about the Sermon on the Mount scene, which opens with Jesus mumbling that he's "sorry" for telling a story, is that it plays spontaneously, with Christ literally having no idea what he's going to say next. In a sense, he's discovering his skill as an actor, letting God's magic flow through him. Jesus has to become Christ-like, to grow into the role. If he sounds surprised by some of his own thoughts, you may be too, because seeing this Jesus through the eyes of the locals, he sounds just a little extreme. (What would you do if a fellow came along preaching love, and then mentioned, incidentally, that you should abandon your family to follow him?) The movie restores the challenge of Jesus's teachings, the radicalism of his demands.

At first, Dafoe looks horsey and weak, but as the movie goes on he begins to resemble the classic image of Jesus — long, golden-brown ringlets, beautiful, caressing eyes. The change is so subliminal it seems magical, because it's more than a matter of make-up; Dafoe lets a kind of virility seep into his performance. He shows us the existential dimension of Jesus's quest: that each encounter brings forth a new risk, a new compassion, and that with each one Jesus's power — his belief in his own love of humanity — becomes richer. At the same time, he comes to accept that what he's really after is a revolution — a complete disruption of the world, an overturning of man's law so as to follow God's. The scenes with Jesus healing the sick or casting out demons aren't sanctimonious. They're a little scary — raw, urgent flashes that go by violently, like something out of a fever dream. The crowd scenes are a bit too costume-epic stodgy, yet when Jesus leads his followers into the Temple to disrupt the money-changers, Dafoe shows us a Christ brimming with divine wrath. He knows how little time there is, and you understand why Jesus was doomed to fail. He was preaching to mere men. How could they begin to grasp the vastness of what he was saying?

In restaging the Biblical parables, the movie scores about half the time. The raising-Lazarus scene is powerful — a miracle presented in all its ghoulish eccentricity. Hidden under long, matted hair, Andre Gregory makes a startlingly good John the Baptist. He's ravaged, deranged, burning — as possessed with finding the Messiah as he was with finding the meaning of life in *My Dinner with Andre*. And David Bowie brings a convincing quietude to his one-scene role as Pontius Pilate. Shrewd, friendly, eminently practical, he looks at Jesus and sees nothing but another rebellious ragamuffin, and Bowie's presence is so strong that, for a moment, that's all we see too.

But some of this stuff, like the Last Supper, is simply too iconically familiar to work; you notice things like an apostle pouring the wine *on* the bread, like strawberry jam on toast. And the relationship between Jesus and Judas is weak. Kazantzakis, who went through a Marxist period, created a noble Judas who argues against Jesus's impulse to love everyone, including the Roman oppressors, but who agrees to "betray" him when Jesus explains that it's part of God's plan. Harvey Keitel, with his Little Italy whine, sounds crucially out of period here (the word "rabbi" does not fall trippingly off his tongue), and he seems not so much frustrated by Jesus's teachings as testy, annoyed. Then too, making Judas a simple good guy neuters the dramatic tension in the relationship. Had he been a complex, divided character with real doubts about Jesus, the betrayal could have provided more of a climax.

And I'm afraid the big sequence at the end is something of a disaster. Jesus, on the Cross, is greeted by a young "angel" (actually a messenger of Satan) who tries to tempt him into renouncing his divinity for a happy, earthly existence. In his fantasy, Jesus makes love to Mary Magdalene; when she's killed, he becomes husband to both Mary and Martha (Lazarus's sisters), and father to a number of children. The sequence, which lasts close to half an hour, is the film's centerpiece, yet the movie goes thud. The staging is tepid and meandering, but more than that, the essential enticement of the fantasy doesn't come across. Jesus's struggle is with the fear he feels in accepting his role as God's son; in the film at least, it's had virtually nothing to do with his dreams of an earthly life. So the whole choice seems arbitrary and hollow, something imposed on the movie.

Where *The Last Temptation of Christ* finds its dramatic power — and where it reveals itself as a personal film, linked with Scorsese's other work — is in Jesus's confrontation of the physical fact of crucifixion: his consuming apprehension of the pain. In one scene, he speaks to God about it, his head bathed in darkness, and Dafoe's voice is so frightened it can give you shudders. Jesus experiences a kind of galvanic dread. This is his unique neurosis—the feeling that his divinity is alienated from his humanity, from his body. He knows he has to die, and in this precise, grisly way, yet it's the man—not the God—who must accept the death. And that requires all the courage of any man accepting death. Dafoe makes this live for us. He never lets the struggle to embrace crucifixion seem easier than it is; it creeps up on him slowly, like the greatest of terrors, the greatest of sorrows. And Scorsese gives us the most brilliant crucifixion scene ever filmed, culminating in an over-powering close-up of Jesus's face. The extended shot is at once shocking and sublime, a nightmare that seems to melt into golden-surreal ecstasy—and, like the rest of this flawed, spellbinding movie, it haunts you for days.

Boston Phoenix, August 19, 1988

LOVE STREAMS

Dave Kehr

Directed by John Cassavetes. Written by Cassavetes and Ted Allan. Starring Cassavetes, Gena Rowlands, Diahnne Abbott, and Seymour Cassel. **MGM/UA Home Video.**

The history of film is in some ways also a history of the repression of emotion. The actors in silent films used the whole of the body as an expression of feeling: gestures were large, movements broad and rhyth-mic, the eyes and mouth were exaggerated by makeup and by the orthochromatic photography into emotional signs of a startling direct-ness. Sound films diminished the importance of the body, focusing expressiveness on the voice. And when, after the war, the first modernist films appeared—those of Bresson, Tati, Antonioni—the voice lost its primacy, too: emotion eluded words; it became concentrated in the actor's regard, in the silent exchange of looks. The refinement and repressiveness of modernism continues to define the dominant film styles — it's our generation's index of realism, just as extravagance was "real" for the filmgoers of the teens and early '20s. Pop melodramas like *Kramer vs. Kramer* fake the placid surfaces of *L'avventura;* comedies — notably *Ghostbusters* — are built on a hip detachment carried to an absurd degree.

John Cassavetes stands outside this history. His actors are full-bodied, demonstrative, and his camera doesn't back off from them: there is an emotional intensity in his films, a readiness always to go too far, that can be embarrassing, intimidating, for some audiences. And because Cassavetes couches his emotional extravagance within the traditional signs of realism — location shooting, long takes, a grainy documentary quality to the image — many audiences feel betrayed by his films: they present themselves as "real," but this isn't the reality of other movies. Cassavetes is compelled to expose, expand, to apotheosize emotion; it is no wonder then that he is consistently drawn to themes of breakdown and madness — the only way the contemporary cinema can assimilate emotions of Cassavetes's size is to characterize them as insanity.

Love Streams renews those habitual themes; it takes the essence of his 1974 *A Woman Under the Influence* — Gena Rowlands as a woman who drives her family away because she loves them too intently — and marries it to the essence of his 1970 *Husbands* — Cassavetes himself as a man who looks for emotional refuge in brief affairs. The synthesis produces a masterwork, a film that brings together the insights and innovations of an entire career and allows them to cross-breed and flower. *Love Streams* is by far the best American film of 1984; as the culmination of Cassavetes's personal aesthetic, it will probably prove to be one of the best American films, period.

One of the hallmarks of Cassavetes's style is his complete disdain for exposition. There's no setting up of the story, no introduction to the characters: typically, the films begin full blast in the middle of an already extreme situation, and several minutes pass before we can begin to decipher the action and identify the players. I used to think that Cassavetes's neglect of the narrative niceties was the sign of a far-reaching contempt for the artificial smoothness and symmetry of the classical style — a rejection of classicism in the name of a ragged naturalism. But *Love Streams* makes it clear that Cassavetes's deepest concerns have nothing to do with realism: at the innermost level, the film is as classically constructed as could be imagined, bound together by a tight system of thematic contrasts and echoing imagery. It is only the narrative surface that seems chaotic, and if the story is sometimes confusing, it is only because Cassavetes is unwilling to distance himself from his characters even for the few minutes required to introduce the expository information. Cassavetes's commitment to his two principal characters is complete: his camera never once abandons them — never goes behind their backs to offer an editorial judgment — and we must experience the events of the film as they experience them, as integral blocks of time.

Love Streams opens with Cassavetes in a violent argument with a woman; as he strides up and down, he keeps a little girl slung over his shoulder. Eventually we learn that this is Robert Harmon, a celebrated novelist, and that he is fighting over alimony with one of his ex-wives, using the girl, his daughter, as an emotional buffer. Mother and daughter leave, and Robert goes back to his current companions — half a dozen young prostitutes whom he pays, apparently, to live with him in his Los Angeles canyon home. There is a jump cut to a scene in a darkened gay bar, where Robert watches a parade of transvestites and listens to a young black singer, Susan (Diahnne Abbott), perform; intrigued, he asks after her. Another jump cut takes us to a hearing room in Chicago, where Sarah Lawson (Gena Rowlands) is settling the terms of her divorce from her husband, Jack (Seymour Cassel). Sarah strains to be reasonable, to present herself as a calm, compassionate woman, resigned to the death of her marriage. But suddenly she cracks: her mouth stretched into a desperately charming smile, her eyes burning, she demands that Jack not be allowed to see their daughter, though she had previously granted him visiting rights. The negotiations in ruins, she storms from the room. Another cut takes us back to the nightclub, where Robert has taken up a position near the bar. Susan is still performing, and we assume that the scene is picking up from before. But the dialogue tells us that four months have passed: Robert has become a regular at the club, and Susan is his new obsession — the latest in the line of women he has looked to for salvation.

These opening scenes, apparently so arbitrary and disconnected, establish Cassavetes's rhythm and method. Much of *Love Streams* is constructed around the ambiguity of the editing. Because Cassavetes refuses to mark his transitions, we have no way of knowing that what seems to be a simple case of parallel montage (the return to the transvestite bar) is actually a radical flash-forward: the unmarked edit covers a huge elision of narrative time. In a similar way, Cassavetes later takes Sarah to Europe with a single cut—suddenly, she's in a train station in Paris, struggling with a mountain of luggage, without Cassavetes making the slightest allusion to how she got there. Space, as well as time, disappears in the black hole between two shots. And the editing even devours different levels of reality: Sarah's hallucinations are also introduced with a simple cut; there are none of the traditional codings of subjectivity—no dissolves or camera movements in to the subject's face—that allow us to sort things out. When Sarah imagines her husband and daughter killed in a car wreck, the sequence is "real" for all the time it's on the screen. It's only with the cut back to Sarah's face that we find it has all been a fantasy.

The unmarked editing creates a profound instability in the film. Time, space, and reality are no longer constants; they don't exist independently, but are instead subsumed by character—by the perceptions of Robert and Sarah. But if the editing is subjective—tied to the specific experiences of the two leads—Cassavetes's visual presentation is studiously objective. Though he keeps his camera close to Robert and Sarah, he doesn't privilege their point of view over any of the other characters' in the scene; in fact, he often introduces moderating figures—minor characters who react more or less normally to the goings-on—who function as bridges between the audience and the eccentric behavior of Sarah and Robert. What Cassavetes creates with this objective/subjective friction is the sense of a terrible disparity between a world of emotions and a world of facts. Both worlds are equally real: the tragedy of Robert and Sarah, and also their glory, lies in their inability to reconcile the two realms. Their feelings—their love and their pain—are too large to be contained by the literal world, and yet they are not large enough to break it.

One hour of *Love Streams* passes before Sarah and Robert meet; another 45 minutes go by before we learn that they are brother and sister. Movies haven't often treated sibling relationships, perhaps because—short of taking them into incest—there's something fundamentally antidramatic about them: there's no real possibility for a strong resolution. But Cassavetes's indirect treatment of the subject lifts it above a literal level. The cross-cutting of the film's first section (between Sarah's failed attempts to escape her pain on a trip to Europe and Robert's boozily incompetent seduction of the wary Susan) builds a mysterious bond between the two characters; we feel that they are strongly linked—through a shared temperament, sensitivity, desperation—even though the script refuses to specify their relationship (Sarah even denies, in one of the early scenes, that she has any family). We are invited to believe that they are lovers who are fated to meet (the high romantic option) or former lovers who have separated (the grimly naturalistic solution); the revelation that they are brother and sister is at once a shock (though Cassavetes characteristically underplays its climactic value) and a deep disappointment—we have begun to feel that their only real hope lies in each other, yet this is the one relationship that can never be consummated. But disappointment soon gives way to a strange sense of awe. There is an almost mythological dimension to the relationship, as if Robert and Sarah were the last survivors of an ancient race: they must be related; the world could not have produced two people of such unworldly intensity otherwise. There is no one else in the world who could understand them, love them, or even put up with them for long. Robert and Sarah do attract other people to them (one of the film's motifs, a witty one, involves the number of service personnel—taxi drivers, porters, doctors—they seem to require, and the good grace with which these people respond to Sarah and Robert's excessive demands), but they are ultimately alone. During the brief time Sarah spends as a guest in Robert's home, he learns to focus his free-floating, always hopeful affection on her; only she, it seems, is sufficiently constant and uncompromising in her affection to genuinely forgive him. But she, divorced from her family, rejected by her husband and daughter, is beginning to learn an opposite truth: that a too-exclusive focus of affection is a terrible risk. At the end of the film, after a long, stormy night during which Sarah collapses from nervous exhaustion and Robert cares for her as if she were a child, they seem to have traded roles. Sarah packs her bags and goes off with a man she barely knows, leaving Robert alone in the house to face its sudden, and apparently permanent, emptiness.

Cassavetes's direction of dialogue is so fresh and sensitive that it's a shock to discover that *Love Streams* was fully scripted (it was cowritten by Cassavetes and Ted Allan, and actually began as a play). The dialogue throughout has the authenticity and slightly loopy spontaneity of inspired improvisation, though in fact only one scene—Sarah's fantasy of winning back her family by making them laugh—was improvised. It's only in retrospect that the superb literary qualities of the piece begin to emerge. Robert has a line—"Whenever I meet a beautiful woman, I ask her to give me her secret"—which he repeats several times in the film; it begins as the show-offy pronouncement of a professional writer trying to impress with his poetic nature (it could be the opening line of the novel Robert is planning to write), becomes a clumsy pickup line when he tries it out on Susan, and ends up as a cry for help addressed to the unconscious Sarah — the variation is elegant, accomplished, and deeply moving. And Cassavetes is just as attentive to his use of objects. The house in which much of the action takes place is Rowlands and Cassavetes's own home in Los Angeles; it seems alive in a way movie settings almost never do: everything in the house, from the pictures on the wall to the jukebox in the den to the box of kitchen matches on the stove, seems to have been chosen and set out by the characters. Cassavetes gets more expressive mileage out of cigarettes than any director since Howard Hawks in *To Have and Have Not:* the inch-long ash that hangs precariously from Robert's perpetual smoke is the perfect index of his manic recklessness; when he hugs Sarah to him at the end, his cigarette still in his mouth, its smoldering tip comes close to brushing her cheek, and the image is a sublime embodiment of both Robert's needfulness and his obliviousness, his need for constant succor and his inability to see very far beyond himself. In the fury of his tenderness, he threatens pain.

But the actors, of course, are Cassavetes's primary medium. In Rowlands's work and his own, you can see Method acting brought to a new level, extended to the point where it becomes something else: it's no longer the externalization of interior feelings, but the complete possession of the body by those feelings; the actor is almost inseparable from his expression. Which isn't to say that the performances are consistently tense and emphatic: one of the richest moments in the film — Robert's reaction to Sarah, when he finds that she's brought home a whole menagerie of pets (birds, a dog, a pair of miniature horses) — is played entirely in Cassavetes's gaze, which shifts from comic double-take to a serious concern for his sister's sanity and finally (as he too slips into her madness) to an ecstatic acceptance. It should be pointed out, though, that the scene — or any other scene in the film — would not be nearly as effective if Cassavetes were not also an accomplished visual stylist. The framing he gives to the reaction — a slightly distanced, full-figure shot, rather than the expected close-up — transforms it from an isolated show of technique into an expressive stroke fully integrated with the dramatic context.

Late in the film, Robert is sitting alone in a darkened room when he hears a noise. He looks over and sees a heavyset, bearded man — a total stranger — sitting in one of the armchairs. There is a cut back to Robert, and a cut back to the chair, which we now see to be occupied by the dog

Sarah brought home. It's an astounding sequence (the more so because it's executed so simply, as a standard shot/countershot cut), not so much for its narrative purpose (to show that Robert is now sharing Sarah's hallucinations) or for its thematic suggestion (that Robert's womanizing might have something to do with a repressed homosexuality) as its sheer, startling originality. Is there another filmmaker in the world who would even think, in the context of a straight dramatic narrative, of turning a dog into its human personification? As Cassavetes's work progresses, it becomes more and more unaccountable. He no longer seems to be working in any identifiable tradition, and his films share no concerns — either thematic or stylistic — with those of any other filmmaker I know of. He is genuinely out there on his own, making his own way in uncharted territory. At a time when American films have become almost obsessively standardized, Cassavetes is an invaluable resource — the last American individualist.

Chicago Reader, September 28, 1984

NEVER CRY WOLF

David Ansen

Directed by Carroll Ballard. Written by Curtis Hanson, Sam Hamm, and Richard Kletter, from the book by Farley Mowat. Starring Charles Martin Smith and Brian Dennehy. (Narration by Charles Martin Smith, Eugene Corr, and Christina Luescher.) **Walt Disney Home Video.**

As *The Black Stallion,* his first feature, showed, Carroll Ballard is a filmmaker of ravishing talent. Now comes *Never Cry Wolf,* which reconfirms what may be his rarest gift: the capacity to evoke a sense of wonder. There are sequences in this movie that make your jaw drop open out of genuine amazement. To put it simply, he shows you sights you've never seen before.

In *Never Cry Wolf,* based on the popular Farley Mowat book, you are plopped down in the Arctic silence with a biologist named Tyler (Charles Martin Smith), whom the Canadian government has sent on a solitary mission to study wolves. This may sound like the stuff of a dry documentary; for long stretches, in fact, there is no one on the screen but Tyler and the wolves. But Ballard, using a spare but eloquent narration, has shaped this material into an emotionally complex and utterly absorbing drama. It's no mere environmentalist film, but a meditation on survival and the story of its hero's inner rebirth.

Ballard doesn't forget sheer adventure either — starting with Tyler's hilariously perilous flight into the Arctic in the hands of a swaggering pilot (Brian Dennehy). Later, in a terrifying episode, Tyler falls through a frozen lake and is trapped underwater. No less astonishing is the sight of Tyler and a wolf negotiating their territorial boundaries. Playing by the wolf's rules, the biologist stakes out his turf by urinating on its borders, and the wolf responds in kind.

Tyler rediscovers his own sense of wonder on his journey, as he progresses from a frightened loner to a man who can run, naked and elated, amidst a herd of galloping caribou who are fleeing the wolves. Tyler is an ardent preservationist (he's a fictional version of Mowat, whose study of wolves helped overturn all the preconceptions about the species), but his point of view is set against the needs of the native Innuits (beautifully played by nonactors), who hunt the wolves for their own survival. The movie claims to have no villains, but Ballard can't resist showing up some fat-cat Americans who scheme to exploit the land, in the one sequence of black-and-white melodrama. The fact that there are no solutions gives the film an overlay of melancholy. *The Black Stallion* was a fairy-tale rhapsody; *Never Cry Wolf* is an elegy. But if it's more muted in mood, Hiro Narita's exquisite cinematography, Mark Isham's excellent score and Alan R. Splet's hypersensitive sound track make it a sensory feast.

"I didn't want to make another animal movie," confessed the craggy, 46-year-old Ballard, a painstaking perfectionist who never seems satisfied with his work, to *Newsweek*'s Sharon Walters in San Francisco. What persuaded him to make *Never Cry Wolf* was not Mowat's book but Peter Matthiessen's *The Snow Leopard,* with its account of the inner journey of a man who travels to Tibet. Hoping to capture some of that spirit in his movie, Ballard went to the Yukon. What he thought would be a six-month shoot became a three-year, $10 million project.

The wolves themselves were far easier to direct than the weather, the caribou or the hundreds of voles who "play" the mice the wolves eat. Ten adult wolves and six pups underwent four weeks of training. On the set, these Hollywood wolves exhibited the intelligence that Mowat discovered in them; one wolf, Kolchak, dutifully submitted to 57 takes of leg-lifting for the scene in which he marks off his territory. But if the movie shows wolves as a benign species integrated into the ecological system, many in the crew were terrified of them, and the wolves had to be protected from locals who wanted to shoot them.

The hardest part of making the movie, however, took place in the editing room. "That was the real killer," says Ballard. "We shot a six-hour movie, essentially. There were at least 15 different movies that were made out of that material and the one that exists now is quite different from any one of the others." Version after version of the narration was tried and rejected (the final version is credited to actor Smith, Eugene Corr and Christina Luescher, Ballard's wife; three other writers are credited with the screenplay).

For his next project, Ballard wants to do "a nonanimal, studio fantasy film" — a new, suburban-set version of *Beauty and the Beast* he's writing with his wife for Walt Disney. But the movie this maverick director, who lives in Napa Valley, would really love to make is Edward Abbey's militant wilderness-preservation novel, *The Monkey Wrench Gang*. "But you'd never get money out of the system to make that. That's too radical. You could make a film about Trotsky — you could make a film about anything — but that film? Forget it."

Newsweek, October 17, 1983

THE STUNT MAN

Kenneth Turan

Directed by Richard Rush. Written by Lawrence B. Marcus,
from the novel by Paul Brodeur. Starring Peter O'Toole,
Steve Railsback, Barbara Hershey, and Allan Goorwitz.
CBS/Fox Video.

The Stunt Man is a trompe l'oeil painting done in a fluid, cinematic
style, a movie that deceives not only the eye but the mind and the
emotions as well. As original and venturesome an American motion
picture as has come out of the industry in years, it is a joyously
dishonest piece of business in which nothing but nothing is as it seems.

Everyone is familiar with the type of film — examples range from
Invasion of the Body Snatchers to *Close Encounters of the Third Kind* — in
which the obtuse hero is totally confused by a train of events while the
smug audience, tipped off by a generous director, knows perfectly well
what is going on. Richard Rush, *The Stunt Man*'s producer/director/
adapter, takes this one step beyond. In his movie (from a 1970 novel by
Paul Brodeur, with a screenplay by Lawrence B. Marcus, who wrote the
similarly ambiguous *Petulia*) the audience, given no extra hints, is left as
baffled as the protagonist. Is this a comedy or a tragedy, a dark picture
with touches of wit or a witty film with overtones of darkness? Until
the closing sequences, it is beguilingly hard to say.

In this era of studio timidity, topped off by a summer so uncertain
that, as Rush puts it, "they're afraid to order lunch at this point," the
only thing that isn't surprising about *The Stunt Man* is the difficulty it
has had in getting released. Rush, best known for *Getting Straight,* has
been working on the project since 1970, turning down everything from
Klute to *Rocky* in the process. The Melvin Simon organization finally
agreed to finance the picture, and it has been finished for more than a
year, but despite superior sneaks in three cities and an excellent run in
Seattle, *The Stunt Man* is still without a distributor. The majors, says
Rush, "don't understand that the public would love this." The film's
current L.A. engagement is yet another attempt to prove that point.

Rush says *The Stunt Man* is a film about paranoia, about inventing
and believing in limited views of the truth, and that is as good a

It took producer-director Richard Rush (top) most of the '70s to make *The Stunt Man,* starring Peter O'Toole (middle) as Eli Cross, a visionary director, and Steve Railsback (bottom) as the Vietnam vet who hides out from the cops on Cross's movie set. (Photo courtesy Richard Rush.)

skeleton key as any. Certainly this is a film that is disconcerting right from the opening episode, which shows a scruffy young man named Cameron fleeing from the law for reason or reasons unknown. Hitch-hiking across a rickety bridge, he is first picked up and then inexplicably pushed out and nearly run over by a man driving a mint-condition vintage Duesenberg. Then the Duesenberg is suddenly gone, and more or less in its place appears a helicopter, its passenger staring through the window at Cameron with unsettling intensity.

Explanations, but only partial ones, are soon forthcoming. The man in the helicopter is the imperious film director Eli Cross (Peter O'Toole in his best role within memory), who is making some half-baked pacifist World War I epic. The man in the car was a stunt man named Burt, who died when the car went off the bridge. Realizing from his handcuffs that Cameron is a fugitive, and wanting to postpone discovery of Burt's death for the three days he needs to finish his picture, Cross convinces Cameron to become Burt, rechristened Lucky because of his "miraculous" escape. "Through that door is Wonder-land," Cross tells him at the threshold of San Diego's Hotel del Coronado, the major set for the film within a film. "Have faith, Alice. Close your eyes and enjoy."

Steve Railsback, best remembered as Charlie Manson in the TV movie *Helter Skelter,* is excellent as Cameron/Lucky; his feral, not quite to be trusted face is just what the ambiguous part demands. But this film really belongs to Peter O'Toole. His omniscient, omnipotent Eli Cross is a literal deus ex machina, always descending with celestial arrogance from either his chopper or his crane. Cross is an out-of-work Shakespearean king, a Harry Percy moonlighting as a motion picture director. His supreme confidence keeps both the film he is making and the one we are watching from falling to pieces.

Though *The Stunt Man* may appear slapdash, it is in reality a very intricately put together puzzle, overlaid with the same moviemaking jollity that François Truffaut, who at one time wanted to direct *The Stunt Man,* put into *Day for Night.* A film that plays hard to get in an age of cinematic promiscuity, *The Stunt Man* reveals its charms grudgingly, but they are easily worth the struggle.

New West, September 6, 1980

PAGE TO SCREEN

In the '80s, directors like John Huston, Jack Clayton, and Bill Forsyth challenged the critical cliché that the better a piece of fiction, the worse the movie made from it. Huston's intimate, spiritually expansive adaptation of James Joyce's greatest short story, "The Dead"; Clayton's superbly acted rendering of Brian Moore's contemporary classic, *The Lonely Passion of Judith Hearne;* and Forsyth's spookily intense version of Marilynne Robinson's literary meditation on freedom and loneliness, *Housekeeping,* succeeded in filming the unfilmable. (So did Philip Kaufman's more widely seen movie of Milan Kundera's *The Unbearable Lightness of Being,* which won the National Society of Film Critics' Best Picture citation for 1988, as *The Dead* had the year before.)

In *Dreamchild,* director Gavin Millar and screenwriter Dennis Potter (with a big assist from puppet master Jim Henson) filmed portions of *Alice's Adventures in Wonderland* and *Through the Looking Glass* with eeriness and imagination. They also dramatized the Alice fantasy's roots in the life of its creator, Lewis Carroll (behind the nom de plume, he was Oxford don Charles Dodgson). In movies like these, adaptation is more than an act of simple transference from one medium to another. It's an act of empathic creativity.

THE DEAD

Jay Carr

Directed by John Huston. Written by Tony Huston, from the short story by James Joyce. Starring Donal McCann, Anjelica Huston, Marie Kean, Donal Donnelly, and Dan O'Herlihy. **Vestron Video.**

William Blake found the world in a grain of sand. In "The Dead," James Joyce — and now John Huston — finds the universe in a Dublin dinner party and its melancholy aftermath. The late director's film of "The Dead" is more than just a heartfelt genuflection to Joyce. On the grandest, most unsentimental level, it's a poignantly exquisite leave-taking and an extraordinary piece of reconciliation on several levels. Scrupulously written by Huston's son, Tony, and starring his daughter, Anjelica, *The Dead* represents on the most obvious plane a gathering of the clan by a still-potent patriarch who directed from a video monitor while breathing oxygen through two nose tubes. But the astonishing thing about *The Dead* is the way the clan keeps expanding, until at the end it includes not just Joyce and Ireland but the whole human race. As snow falls, laying a mantle of death over Ireland and the world, Joyce's own words kick in mesmerizingly, with unifying inevitability, voiced by a rueful snob who might have been Joyce.

He's saddened by his realization of how poor a part he's played in his wife's inner life, heartsick over her revelation that she once was loved by a boy who wanted to die when she went off to a convent. Yet alongside the desolation he feels after his wife has cried herself to sleep, he also takes unforeseen comfort in the imperishable kinship of the living and the dead. No less than Joyce's words, Huston's images — especially the faces of his actors — spin a web of connections. *The Dead* is a film that couldn't have been made with knowledge alone, or even with Huston's love for Ireland and its people and its culture. It's a radiant, triumphant work in which wisdom, experience and olympian vision play just as strong a part. That they're all there is what makes *The Dead* special.

It begins on a deceptively lulling note of prosaic coziness, with guests arriving at the modest Georgian gas-lit, candle-lit Dublin house of two music-teacher sisters and their niece for a black-tie dinner following a musicale on a January evening in 1904. By design, it's the Feast of the Epiphany. Joyce always was after epiphanies, and they unobtrusively begin to build in the slightly stuffy Joyce surrogate. This is as good a place as any to say that Huston has thoroughly reclaimed Joyce from academia. What he gives us is far from the customary exegesis; it's a roomful of supremely Irish gentlefolk who know one another, anticipate each other's stances on such burning questions as opera and drink, and, in their own way, love one another. While in no way scanting Joyce's writing, Huston's *The Dead* is about warmth and bonds, decorous and heartbreakingly fragile, not literary strategems.

The proof of the authority with which the mostly Irish cast inscribes its characters comes at the end of the dinner, when the goose has been

Anjelica Huston heads the ensemble in her father John Huston's last movie, *The Dead;* she plays Gretta Conroy, whose remembrance of a youthful lover sparks a profound epiphany. (Photo by François Duhamel. Copyright © 1987 Vestron Pictures. All rights reserved. Courtesy Vestron Video.)

eaten and the wine has been drunk and the Joyce surrogate finally delivers the after-dinner speech he has been fretting over for weeks. Essentially, it's in praise of Irish hospitality and warmheartedness, and of his three kindly female relatives. The proof of the mastery with which Huston has laid everything in place is that we assent to it. In this respect, Huston exceeds Joyce's original. It wasn't until years later that Joyce admitted his fondness for the Irish society, including that of his family, that he left behind. With simplicity and unerring rightness, Huston knits the gathering together with shared warmth.

The character observation is sharp and economical. When Donal McCann's central figure, ironically named Gabriel, arrives complaining about how long his wife took dressing, her grimace speaks volumes. A moment later, they're photographed standing in an entryway, with a wall between them. It's the kind of detail that doesn't seem much at the time, but resurfaces in memory when the gulf between them is bared at the end. Ditto for Aunt Julia, whose occasionally blank stare and sweet quaver when singing Bellini pave the way for Gabriel's glum reflection that she'll probably be the next to go. Helena Carroll, the great Irish actress, is unforgettable as Aunt Julia, with one foot in the next world. Yet it's Anjelica Huston who has the film's most telling reaction shot. Her eyes fill with tears as she stands in a hallway listening to Frank Patterson's sweet, fluted, silvery tenor voice singing the same sad ballad, "The Lass of Aughrim," that her dead young lover sang years ago.

There's humor, too, but Donal Donnelly never overdoes the drunken comic relief he's assigned. He's touching, too, always caving in before his mother's disapproval, too cowed to notice that she isn't really as scornful of him as she sounds. The genteel sniping during the discussion of operatic tenors, including a newcomer named Caruso, is amusing, too, reminding us that Joyce himself was a tenor who once won a medal. But then *The Dead* is profoundly, sublimely satisfying on every human level, spiraling outward from its corner of Dublin through space and time, embracing all humankind. It is, as Huston said while filming it, about love and disappointment and lost opportunities and a man being revealed to himself. It's lacework rather than broadloom—funny and dear and ever so sad. And with the most telling use of music of any John Huston film, from its parlor waltz to its mournful solo clarinet at the end. In several senses, Huston saved his best, most intimate work until this valedictory. What a way to go!

The Boston Globe, January 15, 1988

DREAMCHILD

Jay Carr

Directed by Gavin Millar. Written by Dennis Potter. Starring Coral Browne, Ian Holm, and Peter Gallagher. **Cannon Video.**

It's only January, but I doubt if the rest of 1986 will give us a film so satisfyingly drawn from a celebrated literary source as Gavin Millar's *Dreamchild*. It not only knows, loves, honors and celebrates *Alice in Wonderland,* but expands and deepens it. *Dreamchild* reverberates with extraordinary thematic richness, brilliantly worked out in Dennis Potter's screenplay, and acted with poignant delicacy by Coral Browne as the 80-year-old Alice Hargreaves, who inspired the Alice books, and Ian Holm as Charles Dodgson, the fussy, inventive, tender-hearted, sexually repressed Oxford don who wrote them under the name of Lewis Carroll.

The film's springboard is ingenious—America as the new Wonderland, when the aging Alice comes to New York in 1932 to participate in a Dodgson centennial ceremony at Columbia University. Browne plays her as a heavily starched Victorian lady who believes that God is a gentleman and reporters are rabble, especially the ones who pounce on her as she alights from an ocean liner. They suggest the chaotic playing cards that greet Alice when she tumbles down the rabbit hole. To the complacent grande dame, speakeasy America becomes a latter-day rabbit hole, into which she plummets as she recollects in flashback the summer day in 1862 when she and her mother, father and sisters first heard Dodgson's Wonderland tale from his own mouth as they all floated upstream in a boat.

That afternoon, in which so much of Alice's subsequent life is rooted, is portrayed lovingly and sensually. In fact, this film is one of the most unobtrusively sensual in ages. I can't remember the last time polished wood was photographed so lovingly; the glimpse of a hand trailing in water is all we need to propel us into a sunny, lazy, sensual day a century ago. When Holm is emboldened to stare at Alice, she reacts as if knowing instinctively that something is wrong. She splashes water on him for staring at her. Her mother, shocked, scolds her and orders her to apologize, but Holm's Dodgson, ever ready to slip into shame for his too-intense regard of the little girl, meekly accepts his comeuppance. Then he's sent to heaven when Alice wipes off his cheek with her handkerchief and kisses him.

Touchingly and with great economy — a few lip-biting, self-negating facial expressions from Holm — *Dreamchild* conveys both the purity and the sadness of Dodgson's fixation on childhood. Like Wonderland, it's a place where a glass that reads "Drink me" may let you stay small forever, where the buttered watch at the Mad Hatter's Tea Party will always read six o'clock — tea time. It's cozy, topsy-turvy and, in Dodgson's case, a place of no exit.

Meanwhile, the film also conveys the terror of Alice's plunge into the second childhood of old age. With her husband dead and two sons killed in the war, she finds she's poured love into things that have turned to dust. Adrift in an America she doesn't understand, she imagines herself re-immersed in the Mad Hatter's Tea Party, trapped there. In it, Jim Henson's cobwebbed, arthritic, moth-eaten Mad Hatter and March Hare embody a world where everything's moving too fast, nothing holds still, and characters shout "Move down! New tea!" Confronting her own impending end, she's jolted into an appreciation of Dodgson's sublimated feelings, and into a recognition of the strange beauty of Dodgson's impossible love. Browne's face, initially rigid with fear as she awakens in a strange art deco hotel room and doesn't know what time it is, or even where she is, youthens. Scales drop away in the dawning of ethical growth as she belatedly, retroactively empathizes with Dodgson's pain.

Nor does the film stop there. It expands to include a historical dimension — contrasting, yet ultimately embracing, England and America. Though initially jarred and disoriented, this Victorian lady begins to be drawn into the crazy childworld of America. During the recording of an ad at a radio studio, a sound effects man at work provides a counterpoint to the rude, noisy, nutty world she's finding improbably charming. Amusingly, her young paid companion, Lucy (Nicola Cowper), is a surrogate Alice who hangs back as the old lady begins to be caught up in American moneymaking. Poor, repressed, conscientious, Lucy has a sense of responsibility that's a deeper, more touching version of Alice's stiff-backed propriety. Lucy's steadiness wins the heart of Jack Dolan (Peter Gallagher), the brash young reporter trying to parlay Alice's story to business success. In the end, the only thing Alice will leave behind is her catalytic uniting of Lucy and go-getting Jack, whose shared future will move forward in the new world.

Dreamchild is cherishable not only in the elaborateness and completeness with which its themes are worked out, but also in its evenhandedness. It's not the usual British fussing over the loss of empire, but a magnanimous tribute to both cautious, civilized English values and American energy. Beyond that, there's its deeply felt tribute to Carroll. As a glee club at the Columbia ceremony sings "Will you, won't you?" Alice realizes that, while Carroll couldn't join the dance of life, she still can, and does. It means inevitable loss, but it also means an enlarging of the heart, and in her belated response to Carroll's stammering passion, Alice turns her own life's final chapter into a triumph of affirmation. Is it any wonder I've been cheering the achievement of *Dreamchild* at virtually novelistic length? Wistfully, enchantingly, it brings the Alice books full circle.

The Boston Globe, January 31, 1986

HOUSEKEEPING

Jonathan Rosenbaum

Directed by Bill Forsyth. Written by Forsyth, from the novel by Marilynne Robinson. Starring Christine Lahti, Sara Walker, and Andrea Burchill. **RCA/Columbia Pictures Video.**

Two or three days and nights went by; I reckon I might say they swum by, they slid along so quiet and smooth and lovely.

THE ADVENTURES OF HUCKLEBERRY FINN

Marilynne Robinson's novel *Housekeeping* is virtually defined by its slow, swirling rhythms, but one of the first things that is apparent about Bill Forsyth's passionate, faithful film adaptation is that, as storytelling, it starts out with a hop, skip, and jump; and although an idea of leisurely pacing is sustained throughout, the movie never dawdles, stalls, or grinds to a halt. Like the magical opening of Terrence Malick's 1973 *Badlands* and the no less incandescent ending of his 1978 *Days of Heaven* — two more films in which the heroine's offscreen narration plays a musical role in the narrative structure — the story unfolds with the combined immediacy and remoteness of a fairy tale. An elliptical stream of details and events spanning three generations flows by in minutes, without imparting any feeling of haste.

For fans of Bill Forsyth, who has become something of a directorial brand name, the effect may be more than a little disconcerting. My own spotty sense of Forsyth's previous work — mainly restricted to having seen *Gregory's Girl* (1980) many years ago — hadn't led me to expect a film with this sort of ambition or depth. A lowercase filmmaker in the sense that e.e. cummings is a lowercase poet, Forsyth is a master of the small point, the sidelong glance, and the quirky off moment. Perhaps by associating *Gregory's Girl* with the behavioral charm of a François Truffaut or a Milos Forman, I was misled into assuming that the Scottish filmmaker wasn't above milking his audience with a related form of humanist hype, effective but rather facile; now I'm inclined to suspect that he may be a good deal more subtle than either.

The story is about two sisters, Ruthie (Sara Walker, the narrator) and Lucille (Andrea Burchill) Foster, who, after an early childhood in Seattle and the early departure of their father, are raised in the small town of Fingerbone — a lakeside community in the mountains of the Pacific northwest — by a succession of women. After their mother Helen (Margot Pinvidic) drops them at the family homestead before driving off a cliff and drowning in the lake, for mysterious reasons that are never discussed, they are raised first by their grandmother; then, after she dies, by two great-aunts; and finally by Helen's itinerant and eccentric younger sister Sylvie (Christine Lahti), who returns to Fingerbone to assume this job.

Although the sisters are very close and mutually isolated from the community, the weirdness of their even more isolated aunt and her impact on the town eventually drive them apart, and Lucille goes to live with her home-economics teacher. After Sylvie takes Ruth on an excursion by boat to a frost-covered valley, and they wind up staying out all night and returning home by hopping a freight car, the sheriff and various local women begin to question Sylvie's suitability as a guardian.

When a hearing is scheduled, Sylvie and Ruth burn their house down and set out for a life on the road.

This is more or less the plot of the film, although it omits a major incident in the memory of the family and the town that hovers over the entire action and setting like a gigantic phantom. The girls' grandfather — who grew up in the flat plains of the midwest, dreaming of and painting mountains — married and settled in Fingerbone, working for the railroad. Returning home one night from Spokane, his train derailed on the bridge and sank into the lake without leaving a trace; none of the 200 passengers was ever recovered. As reminders and sole witnesses of this tragedy, the elevated train tracks, mountains, and lake might be said to function in the story as characters equal in importance to the Fosters.

Two hauntingly beautiful shots of these train tracks frame the main body of the narrative, from the grandmother's death to the final departure of Ruth and Sylvie. In the first and briefer of these, the mountains, lake, and an approaching train might be considered the scene's major protagonists, although the tiny figures of the young sisters and their grandmother are also visible at the base of the embankment. In the second, only the tracks are visible, glowing luminously at night, and this semiabstract image is held on the screen for an extended length of time.

As fictional material, Robinson's novel is at times closer to reverie and landscape painting than to straight narrative, and part of Forsyth's remarkable achievement is to have captured much of this mood without impeding the narrative flow. A certain parallel to the book and film can be found in elements from *Huckleberry Finn* and its own reflections on the conditions and meaning of freedom, with orphaned Ruth standing in for Huck, Sylvie as a counterpart to Jim — her onetime marriage and her escape from it give her some of the status of an "escaped slave" — and Lucille's hankering after middle-class acceptance and respectability putting her roughly in Tom Sawyer's camp. Admittedly, these parallels are loose and approximate, but the all-male world of Mark Twain's novel and the all-female world of Robinson's account for some of the differences, while the relationship between black struggle and feminist struggle serves to elucidate others.

Film adaptations of literary works can be compared in certain ways to translations from one language to another; both require, I think, a technique that bears a resemblance to Method acting, a manner of working inside rather than outside the material. While it's often thought that the best translation of a text is literal and word-for-word, professional translators know that such a model is generally unworkable because of the idioms involved. To take a crude example, the French term *baise anglaise* means literally "English kiss," but signifies the same thing that we and the English mean by "French kiss"; a more complex example would point up the syntactical differences between French and English, such as the fact that each French noun has a masculine or feminine gender.

The syntactical differences between prose and film are a good deal more complex, and it is naive to assume that the best film adaptations of novels can provide precise equivalents to each of the elements in the originals. While one can plausibly cite Stroheim's *Greed* as a model film adaptation, the common assumption that Stroheim made it by filming Frank Norris's *McTeague* "page by page, never missing a paragraph" — as Kenneth Rexroth puts it in the Signet edition — couldn't be further from the truth. In fact, Stroheim got so far inside the spirit and texture of the original that, like any good Method actor, he was able to generate his own material out of it: almost the first fifth of the published script of *Greed,* nearly 60 pages, describes incidents invented by Stroheim that occur prior to the action at the beginning of the novel.

Forsyth's adaptation of *Housekeeping* is much closer to Stroheim's method than it is to the more literal — hence reductive — approach taken by adapters ranging from Joseph Strick to John Huston. (It is true that Tony Huston's script for *The Dead* is at least bold enough to add a character to Joyce's story; but on the whole Huston *père* followed a route of faithful reduction rather than one of empathetic embellishment.) This is not merely a matter of rearranging the exposition — so that, for instance, the account of the train plunging to the bottom of the lake occurs in detail much later in the film than in the novel, figuring as a flashback — or ending the story many years and pages before the novel does, but also of adding new details and lines of dialogue that are improvisations on elements found in the original.

The film's treatment of Helen and her suicide are characteristic of this inventiveness. While driving into downtown Fingerbone with her daughters early in the morning, she stops at a green light, pauses, and then charges ahead when it changes to red. (Forsyth frames this gag in a Tatiesque long shot, and, again like Tati, waits patiently for it to happen — a small addition, but one that deftly anticipates the quirkiness of Sylvie.) Prior to her suicide, she parks her car in a field and gets stuck in the mud. As in the novel, a group of boys offer her a hand and she

A flood may invade their home, but Aunt Sylvie (Christine Lahti, center) and her nieces (Andrea Burchill, left, and Sara Walker, right) carry on with their own odd version of normal life in Bill Forsyth's *Housekeeping*. (Photo copyright © 1986 Columbia Pictures Industries. All rights reserved. Courtesy RCA/ Columbia Pictures Home Video.)

give them her purse in return; Forsyth's embellishment is to have her insist that they put her own jacket and overcoat under a rear wheel before they push the car — another small detail that speaks volumes. When, moments later, she sails over a cliff into the lake, Forsyth's depiction of the event, restricted to the boys' viewpoint, is as elliptical as the suicide in Bresson's *Une femme douce;* we see only the bubbles rising to the lake's surface. And because the account of the train disaster occurs shortly after this, the mysteriousness of the plunge both prepares us for it and subtly suggests — as Robinson does in other ways — that Helen's suicide was probably inspired in part by her father's demise.

A slippery character in book and film alike, Sylvie projects a combined serenity and distractedness that makes her antisocial and emotionally sealed off in a friendly way, and blissfully daffy without ever losing her basic grip on reality. (One of her favorite activities is sitting alone in the dark.) It's alarming to hear that Diane Keaton was originally cast in the role, and backed out of it only at the last moment — not because she lacks the talent to play such a character, but because it is almost impossible to imagine her not doing a star turn with the part.

Although Christine Lahti, her inspired replacement, has already been criticized in some quarters for not being more of a show-off as Sylvie, it's clear that any grandstanding could shatter the delicate textures that Forsyth carefully builds around her. One of her loveliest speeches, about the train accident — "The lake must be full of people. I've heard stories all my life. You can bet there were a lot of people on the train nobody knew about" — could be crushed by anything but an offhand delivery, and Lahti makes it sweetly sing.

Indeed, Lahti seems so buried in the character's inwardness that she becomes the perfect instrument for the kind of grace notes that Forsyth's style abounds in. When Fingerbone becomes flooded and the sisters come downstairs one morning to encounter their aunt casually greeting them with a coffee cup while trudging around in several inches of muddy water, Keaton, one imagines, would likely have given the moment a Neil Simon inflection. Lahti's consummate professionalism — all the more impressive in her seamless interplay with the Vancouver nonprofessionals who play Ruthie and Lucille — is to blend her throaty Paula Prentiss voice, dopey smile, and spiky movements with the film's overall low-key temperature, resulting in some of the best naturalistic acting to be found anywhere at the moment. It is the kind of nonegotistical performance, moreover, that allows her to fit in a period context without any hint of anachronism — a virtue she already displayed as Goldie Hawn's next-door neighbor in *Swing Shift,* and which Keaton conspicuously lacked as Louise Bryant in *Reds.*

It is a sensitivity that Lahti shares with Forsyth and his largely Scottish crew in getting the early '50s just right without trumpeting the fact — although a director friend points out that the film *does* fudge Lahti's makeup in relation to the period on a few occasions. Some of the movie's finer inventions — Sylvie laughing at a hokey refrigerator ad with a smiling couple in a shop window, Lucille and Ruthie softly singing "Oh My Papa" while smoking grapevine on a leafy hillside, and an impeccably imagined red vinyl soda shop where "Sh-boom" is purring on the jukebox — come from this unobtrusive perfection, which extends to its gorgeous use of the local scenery. (The film was shot in Nelson, British Columbia, which was also used in *Roxanne.*) A period song mentioned in the novel, "Goodnight Irene," is utilized as well, but elaborated upon so effectively, in separate scenes with Helen and Sylvie, that the film intensifies its meaning.

Although the early '50s is a period we usually associate with affluence and stolidity (unless we think of *On the Road*), part of the film's mysterious beauty relates to the lives of the wandering and the home-less that we more readily associate with the '30s — the grim yet lyrical world of Nelson Algren's *Somebody in Boots,* which has more than anecdotal relevance to the world of the homeless today. (The hoboes often passed by Sylvie, Ruth, and Lucille near the lake and railroad tracks are mainly ignored by the characters and plot, but their presence is frequently felt, and remarked on twice in Ruth's narration.)

The discomfort that some spectators may feel about Sylvie, which may lead some of them to dismiss her as a "bag lady" — a comfortable, reassuring epithet for anyone unwilling to consider too closely her current, real-life counterparts — points to the degree to which non-Americans may be privy to certain insights about this country that we're too shielded to see for ourselves. After a second look at *Housekeeping,* I wouldn't call it a great film, but it comes very close to being a perfect one in everything that it sets out to do. Which is only to say that it may have taken a Scotsman to show us the contemporary importance, the depths and radiance, of Robinson's novel.

Chicago Reader, January 22, 1988

THE LONELY PASSION
OF JUDITH HEARNE

Owen Gleiberman

Directed by Jack Clayton. Written by Peter Nelson, from the novel by Brian Moore. Starring Maggie Smith, Bob Hoskins, and Wendy Hiller. **Cannon Video.**

I generally don't buy it when people come out of a film saying, "That was depressing" — as though experiencing dark emotions in a movie theater were the equivalent of having a bad day. Yet I'm not sure it's possible to watch Maggie Smith's great, lacerating performance in *The Lonely Passion of Judith Hearne* without a twinge of sympathetic despair.

It's a cleansing despair, but despair all the same; it's the feeling of seeing a life so pitiful you're compelled to say, "There but for the grace of God . . ." Judith Hearne is a terribly plain, 40ish spinster who lives in one Dublin rooming house after another and earns her meager upkeep giving piano lessons. She longs for human contact — for friends, for a husband. Deep down, though, her personality is organized to cut any such contact off. Polite, refined, dismally repressed, she's a victim and a dupe, a prisoner of her Catholicism, her lady-of-leisure airs, and her own frail nature. This woman has spent so many years not revealing herself that, amid the desperation of middle age, she discovers she has nothing to reveal.

The movie is an adaptation of Brian Moore's celebrated 1955 novel, and like the book it's at once stirring and relentless; the claustrophobic loneliness of Judith Hearne's life gets to you. Judith is aware that her prudishness and gentility shut people out, yet she can't do a thing about it; on some level, she doesn't want to. Moore's novel, which is about her unraveling, her slow, horrid realization that the God she's spent her life praying to is never going to answer, is bitterly anticlerical. In his deadpan way, Moore turns as furious an eye on Irish Catholicism as *Portnoy's Complaint* does on American-Jewish culture. The book takes its force from the understanding — the pity and terror — he lavishes on his heroine's pious repression. Judith, who attended school at a prestigious convent, has fantasies of love, even sex, yet she can't disentangle them from her idea of sin. Her soul longs for release, yet her heart and mind belong to a tea-party world of empty comfort and politesse, a world where everything is "nice." (It's through this world that the Church keeps its grip on the entire country.) And just as Portnoy had his Jewish mother, Judith has her dead Victorian aunt, the one who brought her up after she was orphaned; she's chained to this matriarchal ghost, to the piety she represents. Moore never lets you forget that though Judith's faith has grown life-denying, it couldn't exist without her own eagerness to believe. That's the agony of it. The book is about the walls of self-deception that sexually terrified people build around themselves, and about how those walls, given enough time, can become fortresses.

Moore had left Ireland and was living in Canada when he wrote *Judith Hearne* (his first novel) at 27, and there's perhaps an element of unconscious sadism in the way he uses his heroine as a receptacle for all his Catholic demons; memorable as it is, the book can give you the cold creeps. The movie, written by Peter Nelson and directed by the British-film-industry veteran Jack Clayton, is a superbly faithful adaptation, and Maggie Smith endows Judith with a sympathetic vibrance she didn't have on the page. (This may simply have to do with the way we instinctively react to the presence of actors.) The film opens with shots of the young, blonde Judith, perhaps eight years old, sitting in church, her hand held in the defiant clasp of her aunt and a mysterious tear rolling down her cheek. What's that tear? It's her response to the dramatic lushness of the Catholic ritual – her sense of Catholicism as *beautiful*. The film dissolves to a shot of the grown-up Judith, and we can see in Maggie Smith's face – weary, hollowed-out, yet with a goofy radiance – that Judith lives for the memory of that beauty, that she's entrapped by it.

The movie takes place over the few weeks in which she moves into a new rooming house and befriends the landlady's brother, James Madden (Bob Hoskins), a loud, pudgy lowlife who spent 30 years in Manhattan and now brags about the place as though he'd built it. He talks about being in the "hotel business" in Times Square (in fact, he was a doorman), and everyone in the house knows he's a blowhard and a phony. But he's come into some insurance money (a bus accident left him with a limp), and he's so eager to parlay it into a successful restaurant that he mistakes Judith's trivial refinement for a sign that she's loaded; he thinks he's found a business partner. And when he asks her out on some friendly dates, preparing to spring his financial proposition on her, she's so ecstatic that a man has finally looked her way that she mistakes his friendliness for romance. The film isn't really about the irony of this missed connection. For, of course, even if a man were to court Judith Hearne, to ask for her hand, she'd never be able to deal with it. The intimacy of adult love is beyond her. *The Lonely Passion of Judith Hearne* is about the cocoon of illusion Judith has spent her life spinning, and about what happens when it's ripped away, strand by strand, leaving the woman-child with nothing but her fears, her emptiness, and her booze.

Maggie Smith turns a face to the camera that's the image of ghostly-white vulnerability. There's always been something slightly masculine about her gawky, angular features, and she accentuates that here by keeping those features absurdly poised. The mask – an image of fixed, worldly bemusement – fools you at first, but it can't really camouflage the fear in Miss Hearne's eyes. What Smith does here could almost be a deeper, tragic version of her Oscar-winning neurotic-flake turn in *The Prime of Miss Jean Brodie*. Judith Hearne, too, is ridiculous despite herself, but she's not a lyrical eccentric, like Jean Brodie. The goofiness springs from how transparent she is when she's trying to fit in—when she's deceiving people into thinking she has a social life, or when she's telling Madden how *exciting* America must be. She's well aware, as she takes her Sunday-afternoon visit with the O'Neill family, that she's not quite wanted there; she peeks into the living room saying, "It's only me!", a ritual the O'Neill children mimic with ghastly accuracy. But she isn't sure why she's tolerated rather than liked. Maggie Smith lets you see every excruciating gradation of Judith's discomfort—the way she turns each gesture and phrase into a tiny piece of acting. Judith's entire personality is acting, because she treats her whole life as a secret (even though she has nothing to hide—well, nothing but her drinking). She even acts when she's standing before her aunt's scowling portrait.

After a while, her traumas begin to bleed through the façade, and Smith has some moments that are unbearably moving: she seems to have a direct pipeline into the character. We've all watched the cliché scene in which an alcoholic, after a period of abstinence, is suddenly driven to pour himself a drink. But I've never seen anything comparable to the moment when Judith goes for her whiskey stash to take her first nip in months. As she reaches into the bureau, her sobs come slowly, compulsively (you feel you're breathing right along with her), and when she finally sits there with her glass full, her eyes turned downward in despair, she seems more human than she has for the entire film. Drink liberates Judith, at least temporarily, of the need not to sin; it has to, since she's sinning with every sip. And it's her whole relation to the drink—fierce, compulsive, yearning— that tells you she's a far more spiritual woman than her dainty Catholicism suggests. *This* is her religion, her salvation; it's the only thing she truly has faith in.

The scenes at the rooming-house breakfast table play like loony-bin burlesque. Madden, his prim, smiling sister Mrs. Rice (Marie Kean), and the two other boarders spend the time tossing verbal spitballs at one another, and the atmosphere is comic but oppressive. The one character who seems to have escaped the Catholic blues is Bernard (Ian McNeice), the landlady's fat-slob son, whose humungous double chin makes him resemble a giant blond bullfrog; all day long, he sits at home, fed and pampered by his doting mother so that he can compose his "epic poem." This character is so obviously a lazy sot that we're surprised when he turns out to be perceptive and wily, with a seductively gentle manner. McNeice makes him a sly psychologist, a lisping, manipulative creep who's mastered the art of getting the most out of a situation. Bernard differs from the other boarders in one central respect: he isn't religious, and he suffers no guilt for it. He's banging the housemaid, a 16-year-old country lass who can't get enough of his abundant flesh, and this drives his uncle mad with jealous lust, until one night Madden bursts into her room and forces himself on her. Bob Hoskins is believably goatish in this scene, but his performance is generally the weak link in the movie. His tasteless-American-clown routine is too broadly comic, and though he has a nice, restrained moment when he tells Judith that he was never interested in her as a woman, the casting is simply off. Hoskins's ferocious dynamism overwhelms this ineffectual schemer.

Wendy Hiller, on the other hand, is splendid as Judith's feisty, domineering Aunt D'Arcy. We see her in flashback, in the years when, bedridden, she coerced Judith into taking care of her, and Hiller gets across how this proper, purse-lipped lady could have been an infantile monster beneath; she knew she was ruining her niece's life, even as she guilt-tripped her into sticking around. This is the key relationship in the movie. It's the one that explains Judith, a woman who could never quite bring herself to live without authority. In a searing scene inside her parish church, she finally rejects the Catholicism that's been her lifelong crutch (and resentment), flailing away inside the chancel — though it's the emptiest of rebellions, since she really has nothing with which to replace her faith. The filmmakers' solution is to tack an extra episode onto the book: they have James Madden reappear, so that Judith can reject him in triumph, an event that makes absolutely no sense (it renders the end of the movie an "upbeat" muddle) and wasn't necessary anyway. It's when Judith is at her most anguished and self-aware, when she's cut off from redemption, that her pain becomes ours — or, at least, a reflection of those moments when the traps we're caught in are our own.

Boston Phoenix, January 29, 1988

UNSEEN TRUTHS

Whatever the merits or demerits of Michael Moore's "docu-comedy" *Roger & Me,* about the ravaged General Motors factory town of Flint, Michigan, it fired up audiences and critics (pro and con) more than any other contemporary documentary. Moore has often said that he didn't want to make just another boring documentary that nobody goes to see.

Actually, some exciting, provocative work has been done in documentaries over the last few years, not just by media favorites like Moore and Errol Morris (*The Thin Blue Line*), but also by the seasoned pro Antony Thomas, a South African–born British-TV veteran (*Thy Kingdom Come, Thy Will Be Done*); by the team of journalist Cheryl McCall and cinematographer Martin Bell (her husband), who collaborated on *Streetwise;* and by Alan Adelson, executive director of the Jewish Heritage Project, whose movie *Lodz Ghetto,* created with codirector and editor Kathryn Taverna, grew out of a long-held preoccupation. Other documentarians managed to be just as first-person-singular as Moore but in less inflammatory ways: Ira Wohl in *Best Boy* offers a portrait of his retarded cousin, and George Stevens, Jr., in *George Stevens: A*

Filmmaker's Journey presents a son's elegy to his father. If few people went to see *these* documentaries, it wasn't because they were stock or boring. It's because documentaries don't often get the mainstream attention or the prime theaters that could help turn them into hits. One of the keys to *Roger & Me*'s success was its distribution by a major studio, Warner Bros.

BEST BOY

Stephen Schiff

Directed and written by Ira Wohl. **Today Home Entertainment.**

There are some six million mentally retarded people in this country, and few of us know quite how to think of them. They are terribly afflicted, of course, and for that we believe we should pity them. And yet pity is not really what we feel. More often, there is horror and revulsion, and also a certain curiosity — the same curiosity about human extremes that draws us to the sideshow or to the photographs of Diane Arbus. Pity is something we're more likely to bear for the families of the retarded than for the retarded themselves, for pity requires identification, and who can put himself in the shoes of someone who can't think or count to 10 or dress himself? The retarded are a breed apart: alien, inaccessible. We make attempts to comprehend, of course. We say, for instance, that a grown man has the brain of a five-year-old — never mind that his mannerisms are habitual as no five-year-old's are and that, in truth, he is neither as articulate nor as adventurous as the average five-year-old. Or we place the retarded in fictional situations and we note, with unwitting condescension, how "humanly" they behave. Romance among the retarded, for instance, has been the subject of at least two recent TV movies — which is fine, except that in neither film were the stars (actors like Shaun Cassidy or Richard "John-boy" Thomas) able to convince us that they were anything but slow-talking souls who couldn't find a thing to wear. Second-rate fiction often fails in this way: it makes up what it cannot understand. And so we get anomalies instead of real characters — anomalies like Jon Voight's paraplegic in *Coming Home,* a handicapped man so handsome and brave and smart and sexy that he made women everywhere want to rush right out and get a paraplegic of their own. Or like Amy Irving's brainy, beautiful deaf girl in *Voices,* who, when she finally spoke, uttered such a musical glossolalia that the men in the audience began to think that the deaf were generally lovely, graceful creatures with cute accents — sort of like French girls. Ron Ellis's cheap and shoddy "Board and Care," a Romeo-and-Juliet story which just won the Academy Award for best live-action short, is rather better, because its lead actors are actual victims of Down's Syndrome. They are strange, almost otherworldly, and their hushed, eerily contemplative presences lift some of the film's passages toward the sublime. Richard Goss, the male lead, is especially touching. His big, strikingly round head looks like the bud of a poppy waving on its stem, and, as he floats through the wheat fields and forests of the film's wonders-of-nature sequences, he's like some sort of plant-man from outer space, silently communing with his terrestrial brethren. His strangeness is important to the film — much more so than the star-crossed-lovers theme that coaxes our pity throughout — for that strangeness rings true. It's what allows us to see a retarded man as really different from us, different enough not to be threatening, not to arouse our guilt — different enough to seem oddly beautiful.

Ira Wohl's *Best Boy* goes a step further. It's a documentary — a great documentary — and it acknowledges not just the strangeness and beauty of its retarded hero, but the funniness. It lets us laugh at the dumb things he does, because they tickle us, because they give us the kind of fizzy, affectionate sensation we get from the fumblings of a child or a pet. *Best Boy,* which received this year's Academy Award for best documentary feature, is a rites-of-passage film, a good-natured study of a nice Jewish boy named Philly who's leaving his family in Queens to enter the world for the first time. The twist, of course, is that Philly is 52 years old and, except for a few unhappy childhood years in an institution, has never been out of the house without his parents. The filmmaker, Ira Wohl, is Philly's cousin. Just over three years ago, Wohl became concerned because Philly's mother and father, Pearl and Max, were getting old. What would happen when they died or grew too feeble to care for their helpless son? Philly didn't know how to shave, how to buy something at the store, how to catch a bus or make a phone call. Where would he go? Camera and crew in tow, Wohl and his friend,

Christine, began to take Philly on little outings to the zoo or the park, finally enrolling him in a special day school. We watch all this, and before our eyes, a small miracle takes place. This strange, hopeless boy-man, with his scrunched-up face and his paunch and his waddle, begins to blossom. He learns to draw pictures, to shave, to enjoy the companionship of his schoolmates, and, in the end, after his father dies, he moves away from his mother's home to live in a comfortable training center — where he probably resides to this day. In one joyful scene, we see him trotting away from the day school to buy an ice cream. On the way, he meets a classmate returning from a similar mission, and when the two catch sight of each other, they break into giggles, like a couple of giddy kids sharing a forbidden adventure. It's a wonderful sequence, because we know exactly what these two lost creatures are feeling. Though getting an ice cream has probably never been such a thrill for us, other things have, and, for a moment, we are thrust into a world we never thought we could inhabit — a world of a different scale, where small events acquire the heightened quality they might have in a country of miniatures: a Lilliput of the mind.

Obviously, *Best Boy* could have turned into one of those sentimental, admonitory films that you drag yourself to see because it will make you a better person; it could have been a worthy cause instead of a movie. Fortunately, Philly isn't the sort of fellow you can feel sorry for. He's too exuberant, too spunky, too well-adjusted. Tottering around the city, cheering people up with his gap-toothed grin and his squeaky, Elmer Fudd voice, he cheers us, too. Here is the secure, happy product of a close-knit family — a nice boy, his mama's pride. "I wash the dishes. I clean the sink," he muses. "Sure. Best boy." From Philly, everything has been stripped away — intelligence, knowledge, the ability to communicate — and yet something very touching remains, something we can only identify as his humanity. He is a real hero, and in the narrative structure of the movie, he works the way most great fictional characters do: his functions and desires are simplified, so that we can get a look at how they operate, and thus learn something about what it means to be human. Though Philly is a character no novelist or playwright could ever dream up, there are scenes in *Best Boy* that are as amusing and moving as anything in fiction. During an examination, for instance, a doctor gives Philly a watch and asks him if he can tell what time it is — whereupon Philly grabs it excitedly, holds it up to his ear, and blurts, "Ten o'clock!" Later, Ira takes him to see *Fiddler on the Roof* and to meet Zero Mostel after the show. Though he's unable to remember lyrics,

Philly likes to sing (he can hold a tune remarkably well), and, backstage, when Mostel comes bounding from his dressing room, he and Philly hold hands and stumble through "If I Were a Rich Man"; presently Mostel asks him how old he is, and Philly quickly replies, "16." All Philly's replies are like that—quick and breathless. He responds to most questions with an excited "Yeah!" as if to say, "I can't formulate an answer, but I'm with you." And even Philly's "yeah" seems to illuminate something about humanness: it reminds me of Gregory Bateson's assertion that most conversation is simply an attempt by one person to tell another that he's not angry.

Best Boy's quirky comic edge comes largely from its loving and hilarious portrait of the Jewish family—that great American joke, that great American treasure. Philly himself often seems a living parody of Jewish gestures and homilies. At times, when he sings, he'll suddenly turn to the camera and deliver a chorus with a Borscht-Belt razzmatazz that's wildly funny. And I loved his little conversational outbursts around the house, unwitting goofs on the schmoozing about health that goes on in so many Jewish households. Watching Pearl eat a bowl of Product 19, Philly unleashes a torrent of gobbledygook about her "noives" and her blood sugar; later, he tells his father, "Sit down, Max. Relax your bones a bit, you'll feel better," and we know he doesn't really understand what the words mean: he's just parroting advice he's heard at home for years. Pearl and Max, meanwhile, are everything we could wish for in an elderly Jewish couple. At 78, Max is stiff and taciturn, a worn-down old grandpa who can't help resenting the attention his wife has always lavished on her "baby"—at his expense. In one scene, Max takes Philly to the barber shop, and we get a glimpse of the toll that raising a retarded son has taken. Leading a 52-year-old man by the hand, he is a martyr to fatherhood; embarrassment, frustration, and guilt have become habits with him. Yet Max is not all crust. After undergoing an eye operation, he returns home to tell Pearl that he really missed her, a gesture which shocks her to tears. The operation has left Max looking gaunt and desiccated, and, as he sits in the sun, gazing into space, your heart goes out to him; he's as haunted and distant as a sea captain after a strange voyage.

Then there's Pearl, a great movie character: a worrier, a doter, and a self-dramatizer given to silent tears and quiet kvetching. Pearl is a goose-like woman whose resemblance to her retarded son becomes a sort of visual pun, and her dialogue is a stream of clichés, many of which she mangles hilariously. In one scene, we actually find her telling a severely retarded classmate of Philly's to "be good. And if you can't be good, be careful." No mother has ever watched her baby leave home with more misery and pride. Noting Philly's excitement after his first outing, she whines, "You don't wanna stay home with Mama no more?" When Ira tells her that he thinks it's time for Philly to move out, to learn to live without her now instead of waiting for her to die, she knows he's right, but the idea is hard to accept. "I never thought it would come to this," she moans dramatically. And then she sings, "What will I do/When you/Are far/From me?" Yet the separation is nearly as wrenching for us as for her, because the film has made us understand how unexpectedly companionable Philly can be, and because we ache for Pearl; we've come to know her. *Best Boy* isn't just the story of a retarded man. It's also a knowing, sweet-souled homage to that formidable creature, the Jewish mother.

For years, documentarians like Frederick Wiseman and the Maysles brothers have been wrestling with the technical and philosophical conundrums of "direct cinema" and "*cinéma vérité.*" How do you record a situation without letting the camera's presence alter it or intrude upon it? How do you avoid shaping the material and editorializing, whether by the selections you make in the editing room or by shooting what interests you instead of what is? In *Best Boy,* Ira Wohl doesn't answer these questions; he leaps right over them. This is personal cinema, the kind that independent filmmakers have been attempting for years with tiny budgets and shoddy equipment: recording family weddings, deaths of friends, walks in the country, and, all too often, rather thoroughgoing self-examinations. But *Best Boy* is a real breakthrough for the personal documentary, not simply because it is commercial and entertaining, and not simply because of the purity of Tom McDonough's photography or because of Wohl's refusal to "help" the story along with soundtrack music, "instructive" commentary, or tricky editing. Wohl is filming bits of his own life here. He is the story's prime mover and one of its main characters, and he brings to it a passion and an intimacy that are unlike anything in the world of *cinéma vérité.* To watch the film is to live in it for a while. And the intimacy transforms us. For by letting us in on the life of an American family, not as an observer but as a participant, Wohl seduces us into sharing that family's attitudes. Since the people who live with Philly don't feel sorry for him (at most, they pity only themselves), neither can we. Pearl, Max, and Ira laugh at Philly when he does stupid things, and they enjoy his generosity of spirit. In short, they treat him as a human being. And so we find ourselves loving Philly not in spite of what he is but because of it. We begin to look at him in a new way, to appreciate the peculiar virtues of his condition. There's something wondrously direct, for instance, about his gaze, and Wohl lets him peer into the camera all he wants, so that his face often bubbles up into the corner of the frame, staring out curiously at us as if to reflect our curiosity about him. (In one scene, he even leaps up and begins bobbing in front of the camera like a demented Carmen Miranda yelling, "I'm gonna dance the hotcha-cha to the movies!") His awkward gestures often appear refreshingly straightforward and expressive; he takes criticism better than most of us do; he enjoys any social contact, and he's never frightened or taken aback or ashamed. He and the other retarded people in the film (some of whom are obviously very troubled) are the only figures on screen who show no sign of pretense or affectation. They expose fraudulence in the world around them; they are true holy fools. Wohl's film lifts us to a new, paradoxical attitude toward the retarded; he exhorts us to laugh at Philly and simultaneously to see what a remarkably pleasant person his cousin really is. And laughing releases us from the hollow feeling we get when the emotions we think we *should* feel aren't there. Like so many of the greatest American comedies, *Best Boy* is quite serious—and wonderfully liberating.

Boston Phoenix, April 29, 1980

GEORGE STEVENS: A FILMMAKER'S JOURNEY

Richard T. Jameson

Directed and written by George Stevens, Jr. **Continental Video.**

The best movies tend to be those in which you can look past the ostensible action and see something else going on. This is, first of all, a visual principle: It's more fun to look when there's more to look at. One enters an illusory film-world more confidently when the filmmaker has taken the trouble to imagine foregrounds and backgrounds in addition to agreeably blocking the star personnel in the middle distance. So much the better if, beyond questions of pictorial and topographic richness, those foregrounds, backgrounds, and peripheries are populated by supporting characters who, no matter how briefly they participate in the scenario, seem to bring with them a fullness of personality and a personal history independent of the main storyline. Movies move us best when they not only serve up a memorably particular slice of life, but also acknowledge a larger spectrum of life from which that slice has been taken.

George Stevens made that kind of movie. He made it in an imposing variety of genres, and, more often than not, produced a classic: that brilliantly limned satire of social aspirations, *Alice Adams* (1935), featuring what may be Katharine Hepburn's most luminous performance; *Swing Time* (1936), arguably the finest of Astaire–Rogers musical romances; *Gunga Din* (1939), the exhilarating action-adventure that has inspired filmmakers as divergent as Steven Spielberg and Sam Peckinpah; *Penny Serenade* (1941), a devastating tearjerker; *Woman of the Year* (1942), which first paired Tracy and Hepburn; the deliriously funny wartime comedy *The More the Merrier* (1943); *I Remember Mama* (1948), a beautifully textured nostalgia piece; and the so-called "American trilogy" that brought him the greatest honor in his own time, *A Place in the Sun* (1951), *Shane* (1953), and *Giant* (1956). Now his son, American Film Institute director George Stevens, Jr., has put together a splendid tribute to his father's life and achievements, *George Stevens: A Filmmaker's Journey*, that in itself shapes up as an immensely satisfying and unexpectedly powerful movie.

Stevens' early history stands as an exemplary filmmaker's bio. Born to an actor–actress team in the pre-earthquake Bay Area, he grew up in show business. When he was 10 someone gave him a Brownie camera, and he set about sharpening an already extraordinarily expressive compositional sense for the lines and mood of a place, the convergence of story and personality in a human face.

When the movies put an end to his parents' vaudeville career, the family moved to Hollywood and young Stevens dropped out of school to seek gainful employment. He found it in films, starting out as camera assistant and all-purpose roustabout on a Western series featuring Rex the Wonder Horse. Soon he had graduated to top cameraman and apprentice gagman on Hal Roach comedies. From Laurel & Hardy and their best director, Leo McCarey, Stevens learned the value of balletic comedy patiently observed from an astutely judged camera position. Married to a penchant for comedic development based on the elaboration of character rather than mechanical gagmanship, the "slow build" became the hallmark of the emerging Stevens style for both serious and comic films.

Stevens' enthusiasm for his early on-location experiences with the Rex series was also to translate into a significant dimension of his own directorial style. Watching his films from the Hollywood-studio heyday of the '30s and '40s, one is struck time and again by how much he pushed against the habitual soundstage restrictions of the film industry. When Fred Astaire leaves his hotel in *A Damsel in Distress* (1937), he also appears (even if he didn't really) to step free of the RKO-moderne precincts of the studio. A persuasive facsimile of real sunlight slants just beyond the hotel awning, and the street and sidewalks bustle with "London" traffic going about its gregarious business, giving Astaire's ensuing dance number a real-life setting a world away from the suspended dream-state environs where Fred and Ginger had heretofore strutted their stuff. Likewise, *Gunga Din* broke with the studio-tank-and-painted-horizon traditions of, say, the Flynn–Curtiz swashbucklers to stage a vigorous, eternal-adolescent adventure story against the mountains and desert around Lone Pine, California. Fresh air still gusts through this boisterously good movie-movie decades after its contemporaries have come to seem musty and quaint.

Gunga Din marked Stevens' ascension to producer-director status and the first occasion on which he was able to assume total control of a movie. Appropriately, the sequence on its making is a glorious high point in George Stevens Jr.'s documentary. Stevens *père* took along the latter-day equivalent of that childhood Brownie, a 16mm movie camera, when he went on location, and his Kodachrome record of the feature filming is intercut with black-and-white scenes from *Gunga Din* itself. The wonderful passage involving Din and Sgt. Archibald Cutter (Sam Jaffe and Cary Grant) menaced, on a swaying rope bridge, by the fond fidelity of their elephant Annie loses none of its giddy splendor for our seeing that Grant and Jaffe were wailing and keening a mere 3 feet off the desert floor, not over a bottomless chasm. Just as Stevens *père* knew what he was going to make of the mixture of comedy, action, and fervent sentiment that so bewildered the executives watching the dailies back at RKO, so George Jr. orchestrates the interlayering of home movie and Hollywood movie, the finished soundtrack of *Gunga Din* and the voiceover commentaries of his director father (from the archives) and surviving stars Cary Grant and Douglas Fairbanks Jr., in a triumphant synthesis celebrating the joys of illusionmaking. And at the height of the British cavalry's rally to attack the Indian murder cult's stronghold, Stevens *fils* cuts to a snapshot of his exultant father gesturing from his director's chair, and looking for all the world like a big kid having the time of his life.

It's this personal reference that makes *George Stevens: A Filmmaker's Journey* so much more than an and-then-he-directed summary of a distinguished career. The film possesses a strong emotional line all its own; it's an authentically heroic account of a man of estimable talent and even greater integrity.

Like his fellow directors Frank Capra, John Ford, John Huston, and William Wyler, in the 1940s Stevens took leave from a lucrative and prestigious career to contribute his services to the war effort. He supervised the filming of the D-Day invasion and the liberation of Paris, spent Christmas 1944 not far from Bastogne, and was among the first Allied forces to witness the horror of Dachau. (His own home-movie footage, only recently discovered among his private holdings and incorporated here, constitutes the only available color-film record of that chapter in world history.)

He came home a changed man—deeper, perhaps; certainly more overtly serious, and resolved, among other things, to make no more of the comedies at which he so excelled. It is possible—indeed, I think it is necessary—to resist George Jr.'s and the Museum of Modern Art's contention that he progressed "from craftsman to artist, romantic to realist" and produced his most important work in his later years. The overdeliberate style of latter-day Stevens, the middlebrow pieties of *A Place in the Sun* and *Giant,* are not to be preferred over the exuberance and beauty of the "craftsman's" work; nor are exuberance and beauty to be dismissed as less salutary to the human condition than the earnest turgidity of much of *The Diary of Anne Frank* (1959) and *The Greatest Story Ever Told* (1965). But Stevens' sincerity and commitment remained unimpeachable—never more so than in the real-life war he waged on homegrown fascism when he led the fight against McCarthy-era terrorism in Hollywood.

That fight is stirringly recounted by Joseph L. Mankiewicz (a liberal director who became the focus of internecine politics in the Screen Directors' Guild) and others, who pay eloquent tribute to Stevens as, in

John Huston's words, "a patriotic American in the very best sense." It is the emotional climax of a life history, though not necessarily of this film of a life.

That climax is realized on another level, and involves our recognition that, ultimately, this movie is really about two George Stevenses — the father and the son who, in making this film, may have come to know him better, and to form a closer bond with him, than ever before. What's so thrilling, and so profoundly moving, is that we seem to participate in this experience while watching the film. There is a moment during the World War II segment when Stevens is seen in uniform amid the snows of that last bitter winter, opening a Christmas parcel from home. "To Dad," the handwritten card reads, and the wrapping is lifted away to reveal a child's gift of candy. George Stevens Sr. looks up into the camera and beams. That piece of film lay undiscovered in the director's files for decades. Ten years after his death, it was found by his son. Now the look passes between them forever.

Seattle Weekly, October 16, 1985

LODZ GHETTO

Julie Salamon

Directed by Alan Adelson and Kathryn Taverna. Written by Adelson from historical documents.

When the Nazis marched into the Polish city of Lodz in 1940, they were greeted warmly by many locals. The Jews, however, were herded into a decrepit part of town and sealed into a ghetto set apart from the world by barbed wire and guards. For the next four years, with decreasing success, the ghetto dwellers attempted "normalcy." They worked, they bore children, and they dreamed, even as hunger overwhelmed them and as they watched their friends and family disappear, first by the dozens, then the thousands. When it was all over, four years

Mordechai Chaim Rumkowski—a former businessman and child welfare specialist—was the man appointed by the Nazis to be "the Eldest of the Jews" and to run the Lodz Ghetto for their profit. He is the infuriating, complicated figure at the center of *Lodz Ghetto*. (Photo courtesy Alan Adelson.)

later, 800 Jews were left from a ghetto population that peaked at 200,000, when deportees from Prague were taken there.

As it turns out, we don't have to imagine what went on in the Lodz ghetto. Strongly suspecting their fate, the inhabitants left behind an extensive record: diaries, letters, official documents. Their captors, too, kept scrupulous accounts. The camera-happy Germans couldn't stop filming their own atrocities, like crazed tourists in a psychopath's Disneyland.

A crew of American filmmakers has assembled this material into a stunning documentary called, simply, *Lodz Ghetto*. Nothing could be more evocative and horrifying than these eyewitness accounts, both written and visual. A woman speaks despairingly about the ghetto children with their hungry, empty eyes: "They no longer seem like creatures with souls." Images appear showing a multiple gallows set up in the square, and men and women stepping up to the nooses for such crimes as stealing a spool of thread.

The filmmakers have chosen to tell this story as a poetic montage, with an eye to making it seem relevant, universal. To that end they have woven together historical footage with film they shot in modern-day Lodz with a Polish crew, creating an eerie link between past and present. For example, in one sequence, clearly filmed recently in color, the camera hurtles along a trolley car track toward a town square; suddenly the film looks different, black-and-white, old — but the scene hasn't changed at all.

Even more startling is a cache of color slides the filmmakers uncovered, which were taken by a German photographer. Suddenly the Nazis look very real, not safely distanced by the dreaminess of black and white. One of these shots shows a rosy Reichsfuhrer Heinrich Himmler sitting in his open BMW Cabriolet with the vanity license plate: SS1. The filmmakers run dialogue with the photo: "How are you doing here?" Himmler asks the Jewish leader, Mordechai Chaim Rumkowski.

"We work and we build a city of labor," Rumkowski replies.

"Then go on working for the sake of your brethren in the ghetto. It will do you good."

Producer and first-time film director Alan Adelson, a writer (who many years ago worked for *The Wall Street Journal*) and executive director of the Jewish Heritage Project, compiled the script and directed the actors who speak the words. Co-director and film editor Kathryn Taverna, an experienced documentarian, created some extraordinary imagery by transferring still photos into moving pictures.

The project was inspired by the publication in 1984 of *The Chronicle of the Lodz Ghetto*. That volume, edited by historian Lucjan Dobroszycki, was the record of ghetto life organized by Jewish ghetto leaders during the war. From that base, the filmmakers went all over the world, to Poland, Israel and England, where they found unofficial records, diaries and letters written in Polish, Yiddish, German and English.

These documents allow *Lodz Ghetto* to be very specific about what life was like day to day. Life day to day was awful. There is the picture of a horse-drawn wagon serving as a hearse; later, after the horses have died, people pull the wagons. There are images of a city at night and a woman's voice, berating herself for having failed to see the danger and escape. But perhaps most moving are the photographs taken in the sweatshops set up in the ghetto, where the people staring into the camera look so ordinary, so recognizable. They haven't yet become skeletons.

A brother feeds his starving little sister in *Lodz Ghetto*. (Photo courtesy Alan Adelson.)

Death was everywhere. It was so cold, "the keys freeze in the keyhole," one woman wrote. Bodies piled up because they couldn't be buried fast enough, creating "smells that are not experienced in the West," one man wrote. But hunger became the dominant theme, overwhelming even fear. To reinforce that idea, the filmmakers intersperse throughout the film the sight of bakers kneading vast tubs of dough, and shoving loaves into giant, commercial ovens. This metaphor for the importance of bread in the ghetto, and of ovens, later, isn't subtle but is powerful nevertheless.

The film's dramatic core lies in the tale of Mordechai Chaim Rumkowski, the man the Nazis ordained King of the Jews. He organized the Jewish work force, trading slave labor for food. When the workers wondered whether it was worth working if they were going to be deported anyway, Rumkowski called them "parasites" and told them the Germans were "full of admiration for our work." Long after it became evident that there was no light at the end of the tunnel, only the inferno at Auschwitz, Rumkowski continued to strike bargains with the devil — thinking he'd made a deal when the Nazis agreed to ship off 20,000 of his Jews to the gas chambers, instead of 24,000.

Most Lodz survivors spit on Rumkowski's memory. The filmmakers portray him as a gross example of self-delusion, a symbol of the impossibility of accommodating evil. He is both pathetic and disgusting, and brought to tragic life by the shrill voice of the author Jerzy Kosinski, who was born in Lodz and whose family died there.

Yet depressing as this story is — you know from the beginning how it will end — there also is gallows humor that seems nothing less than courageous. Ghetto residents refer to deportation orders as "wedding invitations." The Czech scholar Oskar Rosenfeld muses on his religion and his fate: "If God had left us in Egypt, I'd be sitting in a hotel in Cairo now, drinking Turkish coffee now."

This fall *Lodz Ghetto* will be available in book form, with photographs and material drawn from more than 10,000 pages of diaries, notebooks, poems and sketches of ghetto life that were hidden beneath floorboards or in dry walls in the ghetto that, unlike most of its residents, survived the war.

The Wall Street Journal, March 23, 1989

STREETWISE

★

Peter Rainer

Directed by Martin Bell. Produced by Cheryl McCall. Inspired by an article by McCall and photographer Mary Ellen Mark. **New World Video.**

The documentary *Streetwise* was shot using a new high-speed Kodak film and extremely sensitive radio mikes, and the result is a heightened realism that has the in-close observation and intensity of a dramatic film. We've never seen filmed-on-the-sly confrontations captured with quite this much verity before. As a result, the movie has a strange complexion — it seems to be staged. And, in a sense, it *is* staged. The nine Seattle street kids whose lives were filmed by the camera crew during a two-month shoot in 1983 play up to the camera; some of them have the instincts of improv performers, and they love to show off their down-and-dirty savvy. But the movie's steady, dispassionate gaze neutralizes the kids' antics. They can't help revealing themselves. They can't disguise how scared and unformed they are.

Streetwise has its origins in a July 1983 *Life* magazine story by photographer Mary Ellen Mark and staff writer Cheryl McCall. Titled "Streets of the Lost," it was a slick, unromanticized report from the front. Given the richness of the material, it's not surprising that McCall and Mark felt the need to go back to the streets with a camera crew and capture the subculture in a movie. Mark's husband Martin Bell, a British cinematographer with several anthropological documentaries to his credit, returned with the women to Seattle in mid-August, and much of the filming was done on Pike Street, in Seattle's Tenderloin district.

At first, the movie seems haphazard, as we slide in and out of the lives of the street kids. But they gradually become familiar to us: There's Rat, a puny, malnourished, wily 17-year-old boy who wears a Yankee cap backward; Tiny, a 14-year-old prostitute with a hard-set jaw; DeWayne, an emaciated 16-year-old whose father is serving 30 years in the federal pen for robbery and arson; Shadow, 18, who gives blood for money, goes in for heavy tattooing and hair-dying, and considers himself not a pimp but a "playboy"; Kim, 16, an adoptee who has run away from her suburban parents and become a whore; Patty and Munchkin, 17 and 18, a street couple; Shellie, 13, a runaway, sexually molested by her step-father, who moves in with Patty and Munchkin and turns tricks to pay her way; and Lulu, 19, a tough lesbian who patrols the streets with a protective swagger—she boasts about how many runaways she's sent home.

The movie is something of a crash course in how to survive on the streets. Many of the kids live in abandoned apartments and flophouses and earn their money turning tricks, pimping, selling blood, cadging spare change. They're too young for government relief. They bathe in public restrooms, wash their clothes in laundromats, forage for food in garbage dumpsters. In one of the movie's lighter moments, Rat demon-strates a technique called "dumpster diving": Call a pizza joint from a pay phone, order a few pizzas with something unpopular on it, like pineapple, stick around at the pay phone for the verifying call-back, wait an hour, and then raid the dumpster behind the restaurant for the unclaimed pies.

What's extraordinary about these kids, however, is not their street savvy. (If they were so savvy, they wouldn't keep ending up in jail or detention centers—or worse.) The amazing thing is how they still manage to come off like kids. They're a weird combo: wised-up, hard-bitten cynics who look prematurely old, and yet have the sportive childishness and goofy, aloof dreams of pre-adolescents. Wizened by malnutrition, their features are tight and pasty and their eyes are deadened. And yet, as if to compensate for their enforced maturation, they often cavort and tumble like kids who are *younger* than they are.

These children who have been mugged of their childhood don't show much remorse or anxiety; that would imply a perspective on their actions that, for the most part, they don't have. Kids like Rat and Tiny live continually in the moment, and that gives the movie a vivid, present-tense immediacy; when violence suddenly erupts on the street, it's not shocking—it's just part of the continuum we've been witnessing.

Rat talks about the parents he ran away from and how they're "a part of my past now." But he doesn't seem to have had any past—it's as remote as his future (he wants to be an Air Force pilot). Tiny, who lives with her alcoholic mother, never knew her father—for all she knows, she might have "dated" him without knowing it. When she's with her mother, there's a cuckoo quality to the pairing: We see Tiny pick out makeup with her mother from a mail-order kit, and it's a nice, homey tableau until you realize that Tiny will be using the cosmetics to doll up for her johns. Her mother, who looks like a bigger-boned duplicate of her daughter, knows Tiny is hooking but thinks it's "just a phase she's going through." The mother's massive self-delusion has carried over to the daughter: She probably no more believes her daughter is a prostitute than she believes herself to be an alcoholic. But you know where her real sympathies lie when Tiny, craving attention, asks her too many questions and the mother, in the next room with a bottle, barks out: "Don't bug me, I'm drinking." It's the most heartfelt statement we hear from Tiny's mother in the entire movie.

A moment like this captures the horror of addiction in a way that most fiction films never approach. And certainly there's more truth in the movie's view of streetwalking than in an exploitation film like *Angel*. Exploitation films have raided so many of the same subjects in this movie for so long that some people may think that *Streetwise* is more sensationalistic than it really is. They may quarrel with the way the filmmakers structure the film to lead up to the suicide of one of the kids. But, if I have one complaint about the film, it's that the filmmakers weren't unscrupulous *enough*. For the most part they don't romanticize the kids (although I could easily have done without the growly Tom Waits soundtrack, which tells us to "Take Care of All the Children"), but we don't have a wide-enough overview of what the kids are up to. Rat and some of his buddies carry guns, which they claim are only for self-defense. Is that really true? And, if it is true, for how long will it continue to be? There are a couple of scenes with social workers and doctors, but no interviews with the police, who might have given us an even more sordid (and unsympathetic) view of the life we're witnessing. There's no treatment of male prostitution.

In the *Life* piece, McCall wrote: "Boys do drugs to survive the humiliation of turning tricks, just to live with themselves." In the movie, we don't see the street kids shooting up, and, more importantly, we don't see them shooting up other kids. (If we did, we might not so easily condone their victimization.) The whole business of drug trafficking is downplayed in the movie in a way it wasn't in *Life*, and I'm not quite sure why—it couldn't have been because of legal constraints, when you consider that the movie crew managed to gain permission to film just about every nook and cranny in Seattle, including a coffin with the body of one of the kids.

Maybe one of the problems was the filmmakers' decision to let the kids themselves provide the narration. That technique gets us into their heads in a startlingly direct way, but it also closes us off from the information—the facts and figures—that this material cries out for. Documentaries have gotten such a bad name from the learning-lab horrors of our high-school days, which always seemed to be about the life cycles of the basic food groups, or from the propagandistic *March of Time* genre, that documentary filmmakers, following the lead of the recent Fred Wiseman, may have overcorrected. We never seem to find out enough about the *subjects* in modern documentaries; the difference between a richly detailed piece of impressionism and a gloss is not always clear, and *Streetwise* is no exception.

Still, it's a tribute to the film that it makes you want to know more. The movie is a real eye-opener, even though we might want our eyes opened even wider. And some of the movie's deficiencies may be inherent in the documentary form: It's possible that the full richness of this material can only be expressed in drama. *Streetwise* is the best movie I've seen on its subject, but it doesn't have the power or the depth of *Shoeshine* and *Pixote* and *The 400 Blows*. What you take away from the movie is a portrait of a spooky new underclass of child-drifters, and a couple of extraordinary scenes, like Rat's detention-cell farewell to Tiny, or DeWayne's chain-smoking father, in prison, lovingly scolding his visiting son. At its best, *Streetwise* does justice to a great tragedy: the corruption of innocence. There aren't many movies around that can make that boast.

Los Angeles Herald Examiner, May 3, 1985

THY KINGDOM COME, THY WILL BE DONE

David Edelstein

Directed and written by Antony Thomas. **Roxie Video.**

When driven to consider the religious right, papers like *The Village Voice* — secular-humanist, communistic, homosexual-friendly, in rare instances godless even (albeit never actively Satan-worshipping, except for the music section) — have a hard time mustering sympathy for the millions of decent Americans who are born again in sacramental waters, lay their shekels in the palms of men like Oral Roberts and Jim Bakker, and plaster primary and caucus states with signs for God's candidate and close personal friend, Pat Robertson.

Yet any meaningful criticism of this movement must take pains to separate its shepherds from its flock, and to distance itself from Christianity itself — which has, at the very least, a mixed record in the sociopolitical arena. The idea that politics and religion have no place in each other's company is nonsense: religion nourished the abolitionist and civil rights movements, and played a significant part in the fight to end the Vietnam War; religious convictions send young men and women to El Salvador and South Africa, in defiance of our ruling party's policies. Any religion worth its pillar of salt must address the ways private conscience and public responsibility go hand in hand. The issue here is that they're handcuffed.

That ordinary Americans, guilty of nothing more than a yearning for transcendence, have found a home and friends in the bonkers reaches of conservative politics is the grim irony of a stupendous new documentary, *Thy Kingdom Come, Thy Will Be Done.* The prevailing tone of this cautionary study — which examines a movement that claims tens of millions currently, with more being baptized every day — is lamentorybewildered: How, it asks, can such a Good Book and such Good People be perverted to such Bad Ends? In short, it is a film about Christian fundamentalism made by a horrified Christian, Antony Thomas, a man who learned from the New Testament the meaning of self-sacrifice, concern for the poor, and all the qualities that have come to be associated with godless communism. Few have put their finger as deftly on the colossal scam beneath this movement, or viewed its fruits with the right mixture of shock, irony, and sadness.

It is in many ways a film about advertising, and it unsettles in the most soothing fashion imaginable. Thomas meets the televangelists on their own slick terms: he shoots Jim Bakker's Heritage U.S.A. with a Muzak-powered awe that apes its kitschy vision; he uses soaring hymns to thrill and move us, while laying them over shots of the forsaken homeless; he lingers on the gleaming high rises of Dallas's filthy-rich First Baptist Church. To this civilized anxiety he lends his own crisp presence, brooding over the contradictions with reassuring, Old Boy steadiness. Perhaps it's that subversiveness that finally scared off Boston's WGBH, which coproduced the film (with Britain's ITV) and subsequently refused to air it. It will finally be shown on American television this spring, but a better setting is a communal one: the movie provokes shouts and cries undreamt of by its onscreen evangelists.

Wisely, Thomas grounds *Thy Kingdom Come* in the emotions of the kingdom's loyal subjects. The film begins with tales of empty lives, of drug addiction, incest, and the void that this (yes, materialistic) culture helps to engender. You can't help but empathize with these people's pain, and when they speak of hitting bottom and then, by some miracle, being lifted up by Jesus, you're grateful that something, anything, could come along and infuse their lives with purpose. Suddenly, out of nowhere, comes the babble about the literal truth of the Bible, the secular, godless, communistic humanism, etc., etc., that has warped the public school system, and it's as if they were speaking in tongues. Before our eyes they've metamorphosed into mouthpieces for Jerry Falwell and Pat Robertson, who have offered them an emotional, one-to-one relationship with God — in return for their dollars and votes.

The journey through the synthetic, hermetically sealed Main Street of Jim-and-Tammy-land — "satisfying a yearning for an America that never was, and where the only reality is the hard sell, the hard Christian sell" — seems almost benign beside the direct-mail shenanigans of Richard Viguerie, or the men who churn out high-pressure "report cards" on a candidate's "traditional values." (Somehow Star Wars and nuclear power represent Christian values.) In the last section of the film, Thomas scrutinizes Dallas's First Baptist and its pastor, Dr. W. A. Criswell, who introduced candidate Ronald Reagan at an infamous 1980 Christian-right assembly. ("I endorse you," Reagan told them.) At First Dallas, the emphasis is not on deeds: charity accounts for less than one-third of 1 percent of the church's swollen coffers; and we are told unabashedly that every congregation member will enter the kingdom of heaven, whereas Mother Teresa — unless she has had a born-again experience — will not.

The point, of course, is to make these disciples feel comfortable with their wealth — and comfortable giving it away only to evangelists and right-wing political action groups. "Fundamentalists are only prepared to accept the literal truth of some of the Bible," explains a leading New Testament scholar, dismissed from First Dallas's university after writing a paper suggesting that, according to the Gospels, the rich have an obligation to help the poor. There is an awful irony here: The evangelists prey on the need for transcendence in a materialistic, consumer-oriented culture, and then use the money they make to sustain that culture — and to reconcile these good Christians to their own materialism. Go forth, they say, and make money.

Thomas grew up with money, and in South Africa to boot. He reeks of his upbringing: meeting him recently at the United States Film Festival in Park City, Utah, I observed not a hair out of place. Thomas jokes about it, too — he's sure it's why so many fundamentalists opened up to him. "I think I have all sorts of little gestures and mannerisms and politenesses which all come out of that right-wing background," he said, "and these things helped them to feel enormously comfortable with me. It's my tribe, you see." In the Dutch Reform Church, Thomas had an "Anglo-Catholic education," with two services a day and three on Sunday — but the only blacks around were the ones who did the cleaning. Sent to an English boarding school in the '60s, he was promptly radicalized, and today lives in England.

The subject of *Thy Kingdom Come*, he said, "is something that cuts people who think like I do below the ankles because we've been arguing for years that Christianity demands political and social responsibility, and in the past, really up to the late '70s, the people I made the film about kept right out of politics, didn't touch it." Serves him right for bringing it up. He was one of the last to interview Jim and Tammy before the scandal broke, and professes an odd admiration for them: "Jim Bakker was the fastest growing phenomenon of the time, and his personality meant something to me in a way that Falwell's doesn't. Falwell is an up and down brute, with no nuance except an ability to appear like everyone's favorite uncle when the cameras are rolling and appear like a sort of SS *Oberführer* when they're not running. Have you ever seen him candid? A very frightening man — a bully, a thug. Jim

Jim and Tammy Bakker's struggle to establish a fundamentalist theme park, Heritage USA, is at the center of the first half of *Thy Kingdom Come, Thy Will Be Done*. (Photo courtesy Roxie Releasing.)

Bakker's message to his people was the opposite. It was, 'I hate religiosity. Prostitutes, sinners, those were the people Christ lived with and we must learn from them.' It was a very soft, accommodating message, quite different from the tub-thumping fundamentalists'. That fascinated me, as well as the warmth that flowed through this blue-collar audience for these people. Tammy made a speech: 'I said to God, "People accuse me of being a Jezebel with makeup," and God said to me, "Tammy, I want you to be pretty. . . ."' They held the key, they were extraordinary. They could touch buttons that nobody else could: familiarity and loneliness. The whole thing was brilliant. How much of it was instinctive and how much of it was calculated I don't know."

Perhaps the most troubling aspect of *Thy Kingdom Come* is the degree to which Americans are led — and wish to be led — by advertising. "I would have thought people get eventually inured to advertising," said Thomas, "but it doesn't seem to work that way in this country. The same old hucksterism can go on again and again and again. The same techniques, the same appeals. When I switch on television here I'm always amazed that the old snake-oil salesmen are still going on today, selling cars in ways that are so unsubtle compared to the insidious ways that Europeans like to advertise—they try to get at people's inferiority complexes, their class-consciousness. But this is good, up-front stuff and it always works: 'Give me a dollar.' Tammy Bakker is ludicrous to a British viewer—no one would give five pence to that."

Thomas thinks Americans' vulnerability is a sign of innocence. "There's something about America which is so much more generous and so much less cynical and devious. I don't think televangelists would have a cat in hell's chance in England. Not because I think the British are so wonderfully superior, it's just that there's so much cynicism there. Whereas so many of these people are . . . unprotected." And yet, I suggested, there is something in the American character that is willfully ignorant, proudly anti-intellectual.

"That's interesting," he said, at length. "I'm extrapolating a lot from the experience of these fundamentalist victims, which I see totally as innocence. But that anti-intellectualism is very strong with people like Falwell. I've just been writing a long drama series on Henry Ford, the Ford dynasty. And it's quite interesting to see how Henry's thoughts were shaped in the 1870s. All the ingredients—anti-intellectualism, ignorance—were there in that 1870 rural Michigan mindset without any connection to religion at all. It's as though there's this national characteristic and folk quality that this religion has come along and hooked onto. But the main force is secular, it's all sorts of prejudices and attitudes. And the tail of the dog is religion. It's almost apologetically tacked on there. And what an instrument—the Gospels tacked onto something like this. The Gospels, which are all about the sanctity of poverty, the degradation of wealth. You couldn't take anything more antithetical to pop on as a badge."

To Thomas, it's a pity more Christians and Christian leaders have not taken arms against the Falwells and Robertsons: "I talked to a lot of them about that very question, and they told me, 'We mustn't play their game. If we use their language and methods, we'll be no better than them.' But as what you would call in America a mainline Christian, I felt almost a jealousy when I walked into those churches like Church on the Rock and saw those crowds and felt my feet tapping. The Church has gone from 13 families, 50 people to 7000, and you can see why: That's worship. And that's surely what worship was always intended to be. But in this church tradition we're frozen in late-medieval hymns and tunes. And sitting in my poor old church up the road with 40 people there on a Sunday churning out these dreadful hymns written in the 1830s, I feel a great jealousy."

One of the most frightening aspects of these revival meetings is the enormous energy released, which Thomas agrees that the left should be competing for. "There's absolutely no reason at all why that same church shouldn't be marching against support of the contras, shouldn't be helping with a strike fund," he said. "What was so extraordinary to me was all the pain those people felt, all the things they talked about, were the things that in any other system would turn one radical: the unemployment, the fear of nuclear war, the materialism. . . . There are things I cut out, the woman stuck in a typing pool, who talked about the heartlessness of working in a large corporation. And her politics are extremely right-wing. And the woman who talks about nuclear war and says our children don't have the security of any future was going out there to support Pat Robertson, who says it is God's will that we multiply our nuclear arsenal.

"That's what's so brilliant. A lot of what they've done has been copied from the liberationists in South and Central America. Inside the homes 12 families form a little nucleus and look after each other. One household we went into was completely Christian, run by a couple who don't charge those guys anything to live there. These people are gonna vote for Pat Robertson. But you can see what they're attracted to. It's a very powerful combination that you're offering people. You're saying to that lady who works in the typing pool at IBM and lives in a trailer park that she can have a personal, emotional, one-to-one relationship to Jesus Christ. You're also saying with this book that any problem you have, anything you want to deal with, it's all in here."

Consequently, the average fundamentalist hasn't been trained to cope with complexity: "I would find when I questioned them, when I asked this question about the dichotomy between the Gospels and the Church, that their eyes glazed over, and they became very frightened and inarticulate. They said, 'I don't want to talk about politics.' It was as though I kicked something in the mechanism and they were shorting." It's almost comical, except that the people themselves are serious, their numbers are serious, and this year, they have a serious presidential candidate. "You can't laugh at them," said Thomas. "A lot of laughter went on in 1923, '24, when a guy called Adolf Hitler was bouncing around in Bavaria. We learnt our historical lesson: Don't abuse them, don't rant at them, because they love that. The American Way—

Norman Lear's crowd—do these antifundamentalist films, and you come away from them so battered by their propaganda that you're twitching—you don't know which noise is actually the most depressing."

Village Voice, March 1, 1988

LOVE IN THE DARK

T hroughout the '60s and beyond, no subject hung up more moviemakers than the War between the Sexes. It became a war of attrition. Sexual liberation helped destroy Hollywood's romantic models, and no new ones were cast to take their place. How two people should conduct a courtship, a marriage, or a "relationship" became a crucial creative question. Consciousness-raising movements forced disciples to analyze and talk about their feelings, often in terms that seemed incongruously banal. Movies that tried to appeal to "New Women" and "Sensitive Men" often incorporated their jargon in the scripts. The kinds of conversations that should have taken place in the lobby after the movie became *part* of the movie.

Still, some dauntless writers, directors, and actors broke through prevailing cant and chic. And if they didn't shatter box-office records or garner awards, they did earn passionate critical support. Bo Goldman's script for *Shoot the Moon* (directed by Alan Parker) is the most wounding account in American movies of the breakup of a modern marriage. *Personal Best,* the directorial debut of another great screenwriter, Robert Towne, treats the coming of age of a young woman (including a same-sex love affair) with the robust lyricism usually reserved for tales of heterosexual men. *Smash Palace* is a bristling New Zealand counterpart to *Shoot the Moon,* rendered by director and co-writer Roger Donaldson in a veracious style that owes a debt to Old Hollywood's ripped-from-the-headlines melodramas. So does the Los Angeles nightmare *Mike's Murder,* from writer-director James Bridges, which daringly explicates love in the age of cocaine.

Chilly Scenes of Winter (first released as *Head over Heels*), Joan Micklin Silver's beautifully acted adaptation of Ann Beattie's novel, brings romantic dementia into the world of perennially disappointed '60s burnouts. Jonathan Demme's *Something Wild* and Alan Rudolph's *Choose Me* depict people coming to terms with sexual freedom and the emotional dangers that often go with it. Demme weds screwball farce to the physical jeopardy of a violent, runaway road movie. In an even more stylized fashion, Rudolph creates a moody, volatile fantasia out of an L.A. bar and a radio talk show.

In *The Good Mother,* Diane Keaton plays a single mother who goes through a sexual awakening. She gives a fierce, tender, original performance that transcends some booby-trapped, inchoate material. From *Annie Hall* in 1977 to *Shoot the Moon* five years later and *The Good Mother* six years after that, Keaton has become the embodiment of our fractured domesticity. Early in her career, her feathery ditherings came off as nervous mannerisms. By now they've gained such resonance that they sum up the romantic chaos of the age.

Director Gillian Armstrong's *High Tide* is a welcome antidote to the you-can-have-it-all mythology that sprung up around the baby-boomers' baby boom. Armstrong asks: What does a free spirit do when she's a mother? For her heroine, the tug-of-war between family commitment and freedom will never end.

CHILLY SCENES OF WINTER

Kenneth Turan

Directed and written by Joan Micklin Silver, from the novel
by Ann Beattie. Starring John Heard, Mary Beth Hurt, and
Peter Riegert. **MGM/UA Home Video.**

"Love Hurts," a song of a few years back announced, "love scars, love
wounds and mars." Not exactly news, but as Joan Micklin Silver's *Chilly
Scenes of Winter* points out, this is the merest beginning. What this sad,
sweet, and delicately humorous film emphasizes is that falling in love
can be an act of unflinching madness, with the potential to drive those
involved far, far over the edge.

Taken from the Ann Beattie novel of the same title, *Chilly Scenes* has
had a history as tempestuous as the relationship it details. First released
in 1979 as *Head over Heels* but weighted down with that inept title plus a
confused ad campaign and uncomprehending reviews, it never had a
hope of finding its audience. Now, with its rightful name restored and
with a revised ending, *Chilly Scenes* has been given that rarest of
Hollywood breaks, a genuine second chance.

Writer-director Silver, previously responsible for *Hester Street, Between
the Lines,* and the PBS-sponsored *Bernice Bobs Her Hair,* has a style that
is insinuating in the most pleasant and positive ways. Her films start
slowly, almost tentatively, but the authenticity of the feelings expressed
and the fidelity of characterization gradually build until the stories
become involving in just the way close friends draw you tightly into
their private lives. So it is with *Chilly Scenes.*

Silver has adroitly but firmly pared away some of the people and
situations of the novel in order to concentrate on and flesh out the
book's central relationship, such as it is, between a young man named
Charles and a young woman named Laura. Charles (John Heard) is a
middle-level government bureaucrat in his late twenties, someone who
writes reports on other people's reports. When we first meet him it is a
full year after he and Laura (Mary Beth Hurt) have broken up, but he is
still so hounded by his memories that when a blind newsstand vendor
barks at him, "Whaddya got?" we immediately hear him think, in
voice-over, "I don't have Laura."

This complicity between the audience and Charles is at the heart of *Chilly Scenes'* appeal. At various times in the film Charles turns to the audience and artlessly takes us into his confidence, saying things like "Here's how I met Laura" and, before a key confrontation, "Don't worry, I'm not going to beg her." Aside from establishing an ironic point of view, this interaction creates a sympathetic bond between the audience and Charles, a bond that is necessary because he is a man totally, heedlessly in love, and that is not always a pleasant sight.

Charles met Laura, extensive flashbacks reveal, through a chance encounter at the office. As soon as he saw her he was hooked, and John Heard, who once deprecatingly described his usual screen persona as that of "a goofy, arrogant preppie," is surprisingly good at delineating the innocent, giggly silliness of that first rush of falling in love. Mary Beth Hurt, since seen to advantage as Garp's wife, Helen, in *The World According to Garp,* is also excellent as the sprightly Laura, a woman who refuses to view herself as anything other than unexceptional. Married to a hearty oaf nicknamed "Ox," Laura is separated from him at the time she meets Charles, and, though she is attracted to him, she really isn't prepared for the intensity of his passion, for his insistence, for example, after she makes them a chocolate and orange dessert concoction, that she promise never, *ever* to make it for anyone else again.

While Charles in his mania may not sound like the most lovable character, it is Heard's and the film's accomplishment that no matter how painfully preposterous his actions become, we are never other than completely sympathetic to the emotions that drive him. Whether he is responding to Janis Joplin singing "Get It While You Can" by screaming at his radio, "How can I get it, Janis, how can I get it?" or pulling out his telephone only to find a self-written note next to it reading, "Laura, 372-7307, Don't Call!" we truly feel for him. If you've never been even a bit in love this way, you've never been in love.

Joan Micklin Silver, besides telling this story with a becoming drollness, has filled the periphery of the film with wonderful character roles: Peter Riegert as Charles's best friend, Sam, the unemployed jacket salesman; Kenneth McMillan as Charles's stepfather; Mark Metcalf (one of the film's producers) as Ox; and close to half a dozen others. All are finely done, but a special word must be said about the redoubtable Gloria Grahame, a memorable good-bad girl of 1950s Hollywood, cast here as Charles's schizoid mother in the last important role she took before she died.

Chilly Scenes presents *l'affaire* Charles-Laura in its entirety, from those fervid beginnings to the reasons for the breakup to Charles's increasingly frantic attempts to get Laura back. It is in many ways the truest, most achingly accurate portrait of a modern relationship we've had on screen. It captures so much—how perfect things are when they're right, how everything reminds you of the loss when they're not, how incapable we often feel of extricating ourselves from the maelstrom—that it will make you laugh to keep from crying. Its new ending, edited down from the original, which was planned to be ambiguous but didn't play that way, does nothing to hamper this feeling. *Chilly Scenes of Winter* remains consistently wise and surprising in small but delightful ways, and it subtly underlines how unreachable, even unknowable, we all can be even to the people we care for the most.

New West, November 1982

CHOOSE ME

Sheila Benson

Directed and written by Alan Rudolph. Starring Genevieve Bujold, Keith Carradine, Lesley Ann Warren, Patrick Bauchau, and Rae Dawn Chong. **Media Home Entertainment.**

Many-layered and funny, Alan Rudolph's *Choose Me* is an L.A. flower, a neon orchid—hip, outrageous, beautiful. It's a romance—music at its heart and farce around its edges—for those afraid to be in love, a *film noir* comedy. If at times it teeters toward self-parody, it fortunately contains its own gyroscope, which keeps it spinning in blissful romantic arcs.

The paths of its five interlocking lovers cross in a sleek dream of a bar called Eve's Place, set east of the L.A. skyline and entirely in the imagination. The Eve who runs it now is not the original owner; she shot herself for love. This Eve (Lesley Ann Warren), with her long-legged showgirl's strut and heavy-lidded tragedienne's eyes, is an ex-hooker who bought the bar on an impulse, the way she does almost everything.

She's been involved with an elegant, married European (Patrick Bauchau, from *The State of Things*) of very dubious character for more than three years now, and it's getting *old*. And so, like the rest of the city, she goes for advice to the low-voiced, soothing radio sex-academician, Dr. Nancy Love (Genevieve Bujold).

Dr. Love is a bright, mysterious woman who hides behind a pseudonym and changes her address constantly. Better at everyone else's emotional problems than her own, she turns up at Eve's Place in answer to the owner's ad for a roommate. And so the two, unknowingly linked by the telephone, become roommates.

The third of *Choose Me*'s irresistible ladies is dizzy Rae Dawn Chong, she of the sweet spirit and the truly terrible poetry. She parks herself nightly at the end of the bar at Eve's to get a long look at the owner, the woman her husband—ah yes, Bauchau—has been cutting out with these three years, and perhaps to catch him too.

Finally, we have the erotic catalyst of *Choose Me* and one of writer-director Rudolph's most inspired creations, Mickey (Keith Carradine), who either never lies or doesn't know the meaning of the truth. A faintly dangerous man, he may have been a gambler/spy/mechanic/photographer or a madman, or both. He is certainly a Redi-Mix romantic: Add wine, and he instantly proposes to whatever girl he's kissing.

And so this modern variation of *La Ronde* begins to spin, commented upon and augmented by the film's throbbing, hyper-romantic songs sung by Teddy Pendergrass. As he did in *Welcome to L.A.,* Rudolph uses music almost as an unseen character — the lyrics whisper in the charac-ters' ears, leading them, mirroring their thoughts and actions.

All of *Choose Me* is full of comment — ironic, savage, hip. More than almost any other contemporary movie (except *One from the Heart,* which it faintly resembles), it uses paintings, clothing, the decoration of a house, even arrangements of flowers to augment what we know about the characters. If Lesley Ann Warren's brittle, neurotic sensuality wasn't message enough, you could look at the pleasantly murderous captions to the paintings in her house and know about her love-hate relationship with men.

As Bujold and Warren talk over tea, images of loneliness and vio-lence, looming down from the wall, form their own punctuation.

Not all the comment is earnest: Funniest of all are the movie posters in Rae Dawn Chong's loft which, laid end to end, tell the story of the movie, from *Don't Bother to Knock* to *Lady in the Dark* to *All About Eve* to *When Ladies Meet*, *The Accused* and finally, the wistful *Together Again* right over her bed.

For all their with-it trappings, some of the characters have interestingly square values. Never married, Warren explains straightfacedly to roommate Bujold that she has shied away because she wouldn't want her marriage to fail. And during those times when Carradine *was* married, apparently he throttled down to be a true-blue husband. It's these touches that may touch a chord in the movie's contemporaneous audience, who seem to be swinging back to a romantic idealism themselves.

Exquisitely cast, *Choose Me*'s actors are all absolutely fine, although Bujold's ardent Dr. Love, Carradine's haunted romantic and Warren's "prisoner of sex" stand out particularly.

Melodrama and drama fight near the film's end, but everything is redeemed by that splendid last shot, the single best comment on the chanciness of the matrimonial seas that you could hope to find.

Los Angeles Times, August 29, 1984

THE GOOD MOTHER

Hal Hinson

Directed by Leonard Nimoy. Written by Michael Bortman, from the novel by Sue Miller. Starring Diane Keaton, Asia Vieira, James Naughton, and Liam Neeson. **Touchstone Video.**

From moment to moment in *The Good Mother*, Diane Keaton is so truthful, so tantalizing and full of life that you almost forget that the character she's playing is a fraud.

Directed by Leonard Nimoy, from the Sue Miller novel, *The Good Mother* is retrograde in an up-to-the-minute way, and for that reason, it may well strike a chord. Basically it's another in a long line of '80s "Be Careful" movies. It's a cautionary tale — like *Fatal Attraction* — that tells us to keep a close watch on ourselves, that passion and openness are to be distrusted, and that if we want to preserve what is dear to us we have to play it safe.

The story is focused on Anna (Keaton), a divorced Boston mother who works in a medical lab and teaches a little piano on the side. The title comes from Anna's relationship with her 6-year-old daughter Molly, played by Asia Vieira. Tolerant, nurturing, attentive, Anna has a gift for mothering that borders on genius. The day-to-day routine of getting the kid into her clothes, fed and out the door seems a sort of higher calling for Anna, and she goes about her domestic chores joyfully, giggling happily to herself.

Though Nimoy creates an idyllic portrait of the bond between mother and daughter, at the same time he conveys a sense that something's missing — namely a man. Of late, men have been creeping more and more into Anna's thoughts. At a girlfriend's one night, she talks about how she has never been a very erotic person, especially with her emotionally reserved ex-husband Brian (James Naughton). But the desire to be a passionate, open, sexy person has always been latent inside her, and so when she meets a good-looking Irish sculptor named Leo (Liam Neeson), who wines her and dines her and holds out the promise of a full, transcendent sexual life, she falls unreservedly, heedlessly in love.

The outline of a story in which a repressed woman is transformed by the love of a virile, artistic swain will be recognizable from countless earlier films. (Though it dates back decades, let's call it the Alan Bates *Unmarried Woman* Syndrome.) The foundation for Anna's yearnings is laid at the film's beginning, in a forever-amber prelude in which she reminisces about her rebellious, lusty Aunt Babe. A radiant young redhead played by Tracy Griffith, Babe rows off into the starry New England nights at their family homestead for romantic rendezvous, gets pregnant, goes to Switzerland to have her baby, then, unsteady from drink, dives out of a rowboat and drowns. She's not so much a character as Nimoy's easy idealization of the rebellious romanticism that Anna feels is missing in herself.

Nimoy has structured his film as a series of commercials — there's a spot for the unbridled Babe and the life of passion, a spot for Anna the miracle mother, a spot for the happy coupling of Anna and Leo. And this appears to be a natural mode of thought for him. Nimoy sees things — emotions, relationships, *life* — in absolute terms, free of nuance or complexity. He doesn't so much direct his scenes as act as their account executive.

As part of the commercial for how wonderful things are between Leo and Anna, we are shown scenes demonstrating the marvelous, easy rapport that the new boyfriend, who has virtually moved in, has built with Molly. All along we are meant to feel the care and love that Leo, and especially Anna, bestow on Molly, and what's pictured here is a liberal, progressive but structured approach to child-rearing in which it is perfectly normal for Leo to sit on the bathroom floor reading aloud from children's books as Anna and Molly splash together in the tub.

At this point, though, Nimoy, who is working from Michael Bortman's script, introduces another commercial — one in which all the happiness Anna has claimed for herself is dashed on the rocks. The incident that causes the crackup is deceptively innocuous and is only reported to us, not shown. One night when Anna was working late and Leo was taking care of Molly, the girl came into the bathroom where Leo was taking his shower and, being curious as most kids are, began to ask questions about his genitalia — and then asked if she could touch him.

The repercussions from his assent — which was given with the intent of dispelling any potential hang-ups about the body and sexual matters — are devastating for Anna. Immediately her ex-husband, who heard the story one morning while shaving ("Leo lets me see it. He lets me *touch* it"), introduces a custody suit, claiming that Anna is incompetent. Most of the second half of the movie is set in court, and to be blunt, these scenes are a bust, even though Jason Robards and the wonderfully clipped Joe Morton play the attorneys. (Robards is Anna's lawyer and if I ever go into court I want a guy looking just like him standing next to me.)

There's not much suspense in these scenes, though we sort of play along and pretend not to know what's going to happen. But we might not if Keaton weren't such a marvel. In *The Good Mother* and, earlier, in *Baby Boom,* Keaton has managed to wring miracles out of material that would have stymied lesser actresses. And in both cases her work has exemplified the most exalted form of contemporary star acting. All the signature Keaton mannerisms — the hesitations and stammers and idiosyncratic, amusical phrasings, the hair business, the seductive coyness — are there in both performances, as they were whenever Bogart was on screen, or Davis or Hepburn. But added to them is a very modern sense of authenticity. Her characters may have things in common, but you sense that each has a different and unique interior life, that each one thinks differently.

The Good Mother is a movie about a woman who loses everything precious in her life because her boyfriend let her 6-year-old daughter touch It. And though there's poignancy in this, and even some plausibility, the film is too loaded with issues and positions on issues. Keaton outclasses her material. She has the kind of talent that, at times, exposes phoniness in the writing, and in some of her scenes, like the big moment speech in which she tells Leo of her passion for being a mother, her acting degenerates into hype — as if she's trying to sell an idea she can't fully believe in. (In another, when she goes to ask her grandparents, Ralph Bellamy and Teresa Wright, for money, she looks poleaxed.)

At other times — as in her scene with the court psychologist — she burrows into her emotions and sustains them until we're spent from the pain and the exhilaration. And at these moments, *The Good Mother* is very nearly cherishable, if only for that. Even shackled to banalities, Keaton has the power to amaze.

The Washington Post, November 4, 1988

HIGH TIDE

Carrie Rickey

Directed by Gillian Armstrong. Written by Laura Jones. Starring Judy Davis, Jan Adele, Claudia Karvan, and Colin Friels. **Nelson Entertainment.**

Sounds like potboiler fiction: A mother who abandoned her child encounters the girl 12 years later.

But unlike potboiler fiction, Gillian Armstrong's unforgettable *High Tide* is no schmaltz-larded tribute to mother love, no *Stella Dallas* offering on the altar of motherly self-sacrifice.

High Tide breaks taboo by probing the depths of maternal ambivalence with a fearlessness and lack of sentimentality that rank the film with such novels as Sue Miller's *The Good Mother* and Doris Lessing's *The Fifth Child.*

In *High Tide* — which conceivably could be called *The Bad Mother* — when Lilly (Judy Davis) sees young Ally (Claudia Karvan), she's too blotto to feel the proverbial tug on the heartstrings. And even when Lilly sobers up, it's hard for the itinerant pop singer to care for anyone besides herself.

The film is as much a panoramic landscape as it is a character portrait of Lilly's irresponsibility and Ally's need. Armstrong, the gifted director of *My Brilliant Career* and *Mrs. Soffel,* establishes mood much as a novelist might, using the wintry coast of Australia's New South Wales as correlations for her characters.

Lilly is restless and pounding, like the crashing waves; Ally is as still as a tidepool. Is it primal or coincidental that Ally's pastime is surfing? Though it goes against her pacific nature, she tries to battle the breakers. In this movie where the colors range from aquamarine to emerald, mother and daughter resemble each other only in their seafoam green eyes.

Though her film is moody, Armstrong has some fun with its aquatic motif. She introduces us to Lilly — singing backup to an Elvis impersonator who inexplicably croons Chuck Berry — dolled up in a spangled green dress with a tulle mermaid flounce.

She introduces us to Ally returning, surfboard in tow, to her trailer at Mermaid Caravan Park where she lives with her paternal grandma, Bet (Jan Adele). At the park, where she has encamped until her car gets fixed, the just-fired Lilly goes on a bender and requires Ally's aid to get back to the trailer. Only later, when Lilly recognizes her estranged mother-in-law, does she realize who Ally is.

The mermaid symbolism underscores the fact that Lilly is something of nature's freak, socially amphibious but not entirely at home either on land or at sea. Depending on how you interpret her erratic behavior, Lilly's a fish out of water or a woman at sea. Whether on land or sea, Lilly's typical reaction is to run away from trouble — which is why she abandoned Ally in the first place.

Davis, so memorable in *My Brilliant Career* and *A Passage to India,* is haunting as the unsympathetic Lilly, whose response to her daughter's fond expression of love is to snarl, "You don't know me." Davis creates a complex character, paralyzed by cowardice and unable to call what she feels for Ally love, as feelings of tenderness are foreign to her. Equally moving is Claudia Karvan as Ally, the simplicity and directness of whose love terrifies her indirect mother.

There have never been characters like Ally and her mom in the movies. And there has never been a film like this emotional riptide.

Despite uniformly enthusiastic reviews, *High Tide*'s distributors opened the film only in New York and Los Angeles. Coincidentally — or is it ironically? — the film enjoys a Philadelphia debut today, the same week as its videocassette release.

High Tide's stunning wide-screen cinematography so powerfully evokes the characters' sense of isolation, so subtly examines nuances of mood, that it would do the film a disservice not to see it on the big screen. To experience this panorama for the first time on cassette would be like looking at *The Last Supper* on a slide — with five of the apostles cut out so the image would fit the squarish format. Don't shortchange yourself.

The Philadelphia Inquirer, July 8, 1988

MIKE'S MURDER

Sheila Benson

Directed and written by James Bridges. Starring Debra Winger, Mark Keyloun, and Paul Winfield. **Warner Home Video.**

The world of *Mike's Murder* is not safe or nice or, possibly, even imaginable to some people. But it has a disquietingly truthful ring to it. It is very hard to "like" anything this harrowing, but it's absolutely

Mark Keyloun plays Mike, a tennis instructor with a secret life who strikes up a doomed affair with Debra Winger in *Mike's Murder*. (Photo © 1984 The Ladd Company. All rights reserved.)

possible to believe every character in this tour through the high and low extremes of the Los Angeles cocaine trade.

Writer-director James Bridges frames his chilling cautionary tale as a love story, although a story of powerful attraction might be closer to the truth. Debra Winger's faintly daffy, Brentwood-dwelling bank teller, Betty, has one day with the scruffy, casual Mike of the title (Mark Keyloun): tennis, terrific sex-in-the-afternoon, hey, let's get together again sometime. Not exactly Cathy and Heathcliff but par for the decade.

From then on over the next six months it's accidental meetings as he's hitchhiking along Sunset, more "we gotta get togethers" and more broken dates via her telephone answering machine than any pretty woman has a right to (and every woman will identify with).

Our attention is split, partly following Mike and his super bad-news buddy Pete (Darrell Larson, particularly fine) in a downward spiral following their stupidity in a high-level coke deal, and partly watching Winger watch her watch, pick up lame excuses on her answering machine and fill up her time with friends (Brooke Alderson, excellent in a cruelly written role).

It's painful stuff, even though every detail is perfectly observed. It's a world of first names only, electronic gadgets, fast freeways, faster sex and black tie elegance with coke on the side and violence under every serving plate.

Where Bridges lets us down is in giving Winger nothing to play, and in making Mike less than charismatic. He's a magnet for everyone, not only for Betty but for middle-aged photographer/voyeur Sam (Robert Crosson), and for Philip (Paul Winfield), a successful, faintly dangerous record producer who brought Mike to Los Angeles when he found him hitchhiking on an Indiana highway. To Philip, in his caftan on his Brentwood terrace, the faintly doughy, cherubic-faced Mike was a love he will never forget; to us Mike never reveals anything beyond a talent for late-night erotic phone conversations to set him apart from hundreds of boys fast-talking their way around Los Angeles.

Any movie called *Mike's Murder* in which you spend a lot of time with someone named Mike begins to feel like a stomach-clutching game of musical chairs. Each "safe" scene in this milieu increases the odds that we'll be in for the nastiest kind of bloodletting in the next scene. That sequence was apparently in the original cut of the film (made in mid-1982). Now we have only the ghastly aftermath. It proves, if that needed proving, that the mind can supply horrors far worse than any graphic camera.

Los Angeles Times, March 16, 1984

PERSONAL BEST

Michael Sragow

Directed and written by Robert Towne. Starring Mariel Hemingway, Patrice Donnelly, and Scott Glenn. **Warner Home Video.**

Personal Best is the most penetrating, heartfelt and thrilling movie yet made about an American woman's rite of passage. Academy Award-winning screenwriter Robert Towne has chosen an audacious subject for his debut as a producer-writer-director: the personal and sporting lives of two female athletes who fall in love en route to the Olympics. Towne is never tempted into porno exploitation, or a simple celebration of sports, or a glorification of the gay life. He perceives the erotic, athletic and psychological progress of his heroines with such completeness that their coming-of-age becomes a universal experience. Charges of sensationalism to the contrary, Towne imbues the film with a carnality that's radically pure: the euphoria of an adolescent's struggle for self-creation. More than anything else, the movie is about young people's yearning to transcend all limitations. Every emotional or physical hurdle the athletes face takes them closer to realizing their individuality—whatever makes them *them*. The movie gets stronger as it goes along, like the human body tautening and toughening.

This quest for identity turns the movie into a contemporary Pilgrim's Progress. Hurdler Chris Cahill, played by Mariel Hemingway, is the athletic pilgrim. When she fails to make the 1976 Olympic team in the Eugene, Oregon, trials, her father-coach tells her she has no "killer instinct"; what she really lacks, though, is self-direction. Her father's aggressive ideals thwart her development; Chris must find her own reasons for winning. The person who acts as her guide is another young woman, an experienced pentathlete named Tory (Patrice Donnelly). The movie is, in part, a vision of women helping each other mature without embracing the single-minded masculine assertiveness that dominates the competitive world.

In Tory, Chris finds a nurturing force: a lover, a mother and a friend. And though Tory is by far the more seasoned and determined athlete, she sees Chris as a superior creature with extraordinary gifts of grace, strength and speed. Before their first kiss, Tory tells Chris that she's scared—and her fear is profound. Chris arouses tumultuous sexual emotions and heightens Tory's consciousness of her physical limitations. Tory is willing to give Chris some of her own strength to help Chris realize her potential; this sacrifice is terrifying. But Chris teaches Tory something, too: that you can offer strength to another person without losing your own.

Their coach, Terry Tingloff (Scott Glenn), acts as the couple's catalyst. He's an irascible, pragmatic authority jockeying for their loyalty and affection. The beauty of Tingloff's role is that he's a total macho man consumed by fascination with women. His attempt to instill a warrior spirit in his athletes is only slightly tempered by his wells of affection. It's Tingloff who insists that Chris extend her skills beyond hurdling to become a pentathlete, which inevitably pits the lovers against each other. He teaches Chris the athletic tools and the physical toughness to take on all comers.

The world of female athletes enraptures Towne for its naked emotions as much as its seminaked bodies. Unlike stereotyped male athletes who wear a grim mask of determination whenever they enter one-on-one competition, these women are mercurial and as ardent in defeat as in victory. When Chris grows up, she realizes she can express her feelings without fear of Tingloff's bullying.

Mariel Hemingway is utterly believable as an athlete, demonstrating, by her improved confidence on the track, the gains that Chris makes in self-reliance. Starting with her art-imitating-life role as Margaux Hemingway's younger sister in Lamont Johnson's woefully underrated rape drama *Lipstick* (1976), Mariel has brought a luminous sanity to her small body of work: the TV movie *I Want to Keep My Baby* (1976) and Woody Allen's *Manhattan* (1979). She's a natural actress with a powerful center of gravity, so unaffected that she appears to be less shy about her emotions than more fully trained performers. Whimpering uncertainty has been her specialty, but, as Chris, she's volatile, too. With her great golden mane, strong jaw, feral eyes and full mouth, she's a budding lioness.

One reason for the film's startling immediacy is that Towne cast *Personal Best* with real athletes and filmed them in the most realistic settings. He guides them with such sureness that you're aware of characters rather than performers.

In her acting debut, Patrice Donnelly, a one-time world-class hurdler, holds her own with Hemingway in poignancy and vigor. Even

Mariel Hemingway (right) plays an inexperienced pentathlete and Patrice Donnelly the veteran competitor who becomes her mentor and lover in Robert Towne's *Personal Best*. (Photo © 1982 The Geffen Film Company. All rights reserved.)

in her depths of melancholy, Donnelly's Tory is heroic, not pitiable. Chris' confusion derives from ignorance, Tory's from experience. She knows that Chris can handle the pressures of their love and competition only if she serves as mentor and guardian. Donnelly is able to show the payment that this sacrifice exacts in jealousy and paranoia. Donnelly in motion is an unlikely combination of the mechanical and the lyrical. In repose, she's just as eloquent. Tides of emotion wash over her face — surging, crackling and subsiding.

Scott Glenn's Tingloff is the third crucial characterization: he clears the air of any undue mysticism or heroics. The actor displays wonderful gifts of comedy and contained emotion. Underneath the rough talk and manipulation, this coach loves his athletes. With the subtlest means — little more than a wave of the hand or a prolonged glance — Glenn is able to suggest that Tory and Tingloff once went beyond closeness to intimacy. The sexual innuendo adds tension to the story of Tory and Chris. These three never merge into a clichéd love triangle but instead convey the full range of feelings in their emotional circle.

Towne entrusts the critical role of Chris' sweet, spacey swimmer-boyfriend, Denny, to sportswriter and former Olympic marathoner Kenny Moore. Denny sums up much of what Towne loves about sport—the cleansing purity it can have at its best. It's Denny who teaches Chris that she need only compete with herself. Moore paints a perfect portrait of an athlete who, though past his prime, retains his youthful ideals with a mellow style. And Towne's directorial personality weds that character's loamy good nature to Tingloff's aggression and abandonment.

Towne bathes the film in fog, mist and perspiration; he suffuses the entire world with a sense of incipience. But none of his own sweat shows up on the screen. He accomplishes the unique and the unexpected with apparent ease. He and cinematographer Michael Chapman are master jugglers of camera angles and film speeds—photographic marksmen—capturing each contest's decisive moment, and sometimes slowing the action down just to catch the tensile grace of quivering flesh. Editors Bud Smith, Ned Humphreys and Jere Huggins (who worked with Jacqueline Cambas and Walt Mulconery) help give the images rhythm, flow and lucidity. Sequences like the climactic 800-meter race are masterly combinations of cutting, staging and camera work: the runners' rippling muscles and coalescing shadows signal the progress of the race far more expressively than any trackside announcer. As a screenwriter, Towne is known for sharp, perfectly structured scripts: *Chinatown* is essentially a detective story, *Shampoo* a comedy of manners. *Personal Best* is also rigorously constructed, but more as a piece of movie poetry. Towne makes an audience experience the film through *synesthesia*. The juxtaposition of Chris' flailing arms and legs and the rumbling sound and music is what gets across the full scrambling impact of the long jump.

Tory and Chris' affair is a celebration of fervor and prowess and the fearless giving of love. The movie itself is, in part, a panegyric to female youth. Bawdy good humor surrounds all the female athletes. Joking in parties or steam rooms, tearing into life with the unrestrained buoyancy of a rising generation, they act out their urges without hesitation or embarrassment. Towne may be the first popular artist in any art form and of either sex to picture the wild beauty of young women with the mythic gusto usually reserved for young men. The result—*Personal Best*—is one sweet explosion.

Rolling Stone, April 1, 1982

SHOOT THE MOON

Peter Rainer

Directed by Alan Parker. Written by Bo Goldman. Starring
Albert Finney, Diane Keaton, Karen Allen, Peter Weller, and
Dana Hill. **MGM/UA Home Video.**

Shoot the Moon, starring Albert Finney and Diane Keaton, has so many
emotional crosscurrents that the screen almost trembles. The movie
mainlines pure feeling from its very first shot. It's about a hellish
marriage and, at least on the surface, the plot is not that unfamiliar —
we've seen this domestic discord before in scores of soap operas and
"problem" plays. But Alan Parker, the director, and Bo Goldman, the
screenwriter, take such a fresh view of a marital breakup that it's almost
like watching this material on screen for the first time.

George Dunlap (Finney) is a successful writer who, when the movie
begins, can no longer abide his marriage. His face is sodden with
blocked emotion; he's at the end of his rope, and the rope soon snaps —
he leaves his family and moves in with his young girlfriend (Karen
Allen). In the beginning his wife, Faith (Keaton), has the blowsy, beaten
look of a woman who's trying to hold her life together and salvage her
emotions while still taking care of four rambunctious daughters, ranging in age from perhaps 5 to 13. Sherry (Dana Hill), the oldest daughter,
understands intuitively what's going on with her parents; she's hypersensitive to their torments, which she internalizes until her pain is as
great as theirs. Sherry is trying to comprehend her parents as though
they were adults who are responsible for their actions. What she is too
young to realize is how pain can contort the behavior of adults into
something childlike and irrational. George and Faith are no more in
control of their feelings than their children, and yet their children look
to them for comfort. That's the tragedy at the heart of the movie.

It's a tragedy in the most pastoral of settings. The Marin County
countryside where the Dunlaps reside, in their spacious, old house, is
startlingly verdant. The landscape is so beautiful that the unhappiness
of its inhabitants is made to seem even more shocking than it would be
in, say, an urban setting. If these people can't get sustenance from such
beauty, then what can they get sustenance from? Throughout the film,

Alan Parker isolates Faith and, particularly, George, in compositions set against the coastline and the hills. Whenever there's a downpour, the landscape seems to be weeping.

Unlike most marital breakup movies, *Shoot the Moon* doesn't ennoble suffering. Misery hasn't made George soulful—he looks wracked. Even when he's with his girlfriend, his brow is a tight band of tension. Faith has more moods, more expressions. In an early scene, when she drives in silent misery with George to a book-awards dinner, her face looks as hard as a harridan's. (From certain angles, Diane Keaton resembles Garbo in one of those fugitive shots of her outside her New York apartment.) At other times, her face in the moonlight seems frosted. When, after George has left her, Faith invites to dinner the contractor who's building a tennis court on her property, she has the luminescence of a debutante. But Faith is hopeful without having much hope: She has a chummy, tentative affair with that contractor (Peter Weller), but she doesn't really put much store in it. She knows it isn't meant to last.

George is far less practical than Faith. Even though he is the one who breaks off the marriage, he can't quite accept what that means. Without being fully aware of it, he wants back in. He keeps returning to the scene of the crime, not just to see his children but to tempt Faith. When he realizes that she has not crumpled without him—that she has, in fact, taken a lover—he's both proud of her and maddened by her independence.

George doesn't take a very romantic view of his own suffering; it turns him into a violent rampager who, at one point, breaks into his house and crashes into his eldest daughter's bedroom in an attempt to see her against her wishes. But George does harbor certain romantic-masochistic fancies about being a writer. He feels a kinship with Jack London, whose burned-down home, now a historical landmark, he visits with his girlfriend and three of his daughters. George has led a privileged life, and he knows it. His wife has devoted her life to their children, leaving him pretty much free to ruminate. As the movie develops, we become aware of how guilty George feels for that privilege. That's really why he leaves: He can't handle either the guilt or the awe he feels for what Faith has done.

I hope all this doesn't imply that *Shoot the Moon* is some sort of feminist tract. It's far too complex and unsentimental for that. Alan Parker and Bo Goldman are scrupulously fair-minded—they give all the characters their due. The Marin County of this movie is the same stomping ground that Cyra McFadden ploughed in *Serial,* but, seen through artists' eyes this time, it's barely recognizable as such. Karen Allen as smiley Sandy, George's girlfriend, whose speech is awash in pop-therapy cant (she tells George, "You're my friend"), is viewed by the filmmakers with the same even-handedness as George and Faith. And the Dunlap children are perhaps the most unsentimentalized, and therefore the most realistic, children ever seen in a movie. (Besides the extraordinary Dana Hill, there's Viveka Davis, Tracey Gold and Tina Yothers.) Except for Sherry, George's daughters are equal-opportunity ragamuffins — they give each of their parents countless chances to prove their love. They're surprisingly resilient — almost comically so. Their high-spiritedness has a slapstick energy that turns even the most brutal assaults, such as George's household rampage, into black comedy. (After the smoke clears, the youngest daughter, the red-headed Molly, asks her father if she can make him a hamburger with onions.)

Diane Keaton has often been a graceful, offhandedly funny performer but, except for moments in *Interiors* and *Reds,* she's never demonstrated as much depth as she does here. Every gesture is in character; every look has overtones. We can see in Faith not only the woman she has become but the girl she was when she married George — a little star-struck, perhaps, and eager for nurturing. Albert Finney's performance is not quite as translucent as Keaton's — we can't see as many emotional possibilities in it — but he's more than up to the role's demands. I think it's his finest performance on film. And on a smaller scale, Peter Weller's Frank matches him as the tennis-court contractor.

It's possible, I think, to view *Shoot the Moon* as a screwball comedy turned inside out. When George and Faith accidentally meet at a swank restaurant and create a scene, the episode is played for broad laughs. Alan Parker's staging here is maladroit, but the sequence works anyway; it carries us back to the pleasures of '30s screwball comedies even as the movie goes beyond those pleasures. Howard Hawks once said that he would only direct a tragedy if he saw no way to make it a comedy. Alan Parker and Bo Goldman have it both ways in *Shoot the Moon.* It's a sorrowful film, but it expresses the human comedy. Watching it, you're amazed at what love and lovelessness can do to people, how it can warp them into monsters and rag dolls and buffoons. This movie is saying the same things the screwball comedies were saying, only in a different key: It's saying that, on some

essential level, human beings are bewilderingly inadequate to the
demands of love. They can't handle it.

Los Angeles Herald Examiner, January 22, 1982

SMASH PALACE

Richard Schickel

Directed by Roger Donaldson. Written by Donaldson,
Peter Hansard, and Bruno Lawrence. Starring Lawrence,
Ann Jemison, and Greer Robson. **Vestron Video.**

Man is born to toil, and to be obsessive about his labors. Woman was
born to complain: "You never pay any attention to me." More divorce
wars seem to start with this skirmish than with anything else these days,
and the virtues of *Smash Palace* begin with the simple fact that it has
observed the phenomenon closely and painfully. Odd that we have to
look as far away as New Zealand (not exactly one of our major movie
centers) for what may be the most melodramatic but also the most
acutely motivated film yet about divorce.

The title is obviously symbolic, but it is also quite literal, the name of
the auto-salvage company run by a race-car driver, Al Shaw (Bruno
Lawrence, a strong actor who also worked on the script). His wife,
Jacqui (Anna Jemison), and his daughter, Georgie (Greer Robson, a
child of uncommon appeal), must attempt to create their small domestic civilization among the rusting reminders of the larger civilization's
discontents. When Jacqui cannot get Al to stop tinkering with his cars,
she starts tinkering with his best friend. One cannot help sympathizing
with her; it is clear that she is seeking human warmth more than sexual
heat. But, it develops, she also has a taste for revenge. Why shouldn't Al
feel some of the chill she endured all those years with him? When she
moves out she forbids him access to their daughter, and the maneuver
sends him in short, beautifully logical steps up the scale of frustration
from startled hurt to an outrage that is almost lethally self-destructive.

By the end he has kidnapped Georgie and precipitated an armed confrontation with the riot squad. Unlike the male anger that brought *Shoot the Moon* to its dissatisfying conclusion, this rage is explicated. We have watched it grow out of the relationship's contentious core, and we know whom to blame for its explosion: a wife who has tried to score one point too many. We also know whom we are rooting for, namely a man who has been driven temporarily insane.

It is possible that *Smash Palace* is either very brave or very foolish in its refusal to calculate how its moral is likely to anger feminists. But since it is a movie stamped with integrity in every frame, it seems more likely that it was made with no ideology in mind, just a desire to show how a specific marriage was put asunder. Al and Jacqui may or may not be typical, but they are poignantly particularized people without a drop of soapsuds clinging to them.

Time, May 17, 1982

SOMETHING WILD

Peter Rainer

Directed by Jonathan Demme. Written by E. Max Frye. Starring Jeff Daniels, Melanie Griffith, and Ray Liotta. **HBO Video.**

Something Wild makes you feel wonderful, like a great piece of funky pop music or a jazz riff that whisks you around corners you didn't even know were there. It begins as a comedy and turns deadly serious, but you still come out of the theater on a high, percolating. The director, Jonathan Demme, has such a sympathetic embrace of wayward American lunacy that you're grooved by how wild things are out there — how screw-loose everybody is if you give them half a chance.

Among other things, *Something Wild* is probably the first film to demonstrate that yuppies have soul — although not at first glance. Charlie Driggs (Jeff Daniels) — he's a company tax consultant — has just been promoted to vice president. We first see him in a midtown Manhattan diner where, for thrills, he sneaks out without paying the check. On the street he's stopped by a woman from the diner, Lulu (Melanie Griffith), who's on to him. Dressed in a slick black number and a drizzle of African and American Indian jewelry, wigged in a jet-black pageboy like Louise Brooks (whose most famous role was Lulu in *Pandora's Box*), she looks like a nouveau Navajo. Before Charlie has a chance to argue, he's in her ball-fringed convertible heading for a motel in Jersey.

Even after Lulu manacles Charlie to the bedpost, it's not clear what this slutty Tinkerbell is after. Lulu's affectless deadpan and little-girl voice is all-American creepy, but there's a sharp glint of sanity in her eyes. She's like the embodiment of Charlie's shaggy escapist fantasies; he's flattered by her attentions and wants to impress her with what a closet outlaw he is. ("I channelled my rebellion into the mainstream," he tells Lulu in the car, gloating with tiny self-satisfaction.)

There's no malevolence in Lulu, despite the S&M trappings and the pranks. (She calls Charlie's boss while he's shackled and puts him on the line.) She apparently knows exactly what turns Charlie on — not just sexually, but emotionally, too. She represents his filthiest fantasies, but sanitized, without the sting of true eroticism. When Lulu convinces Charlie to drive on with her to Pennsylvania and stay the night at her mother's house, we begin to recognize that Lulu is concocting a fantasy of her own. Dressed small-town conservative now, with blond hair, she introduces Charlie to her mother (Dana Preu) as her new husband and, later on, maintains the ruse at her high school's 10th reunion party. (A nice touch: Her mother, without letting on to Lulu, sees right through her.) Charlie goes along with it — he's a little freaked about what he's gotten into, but he's also digging the subterfuge. He's tickled by his new-found capacity for lying.

Until the moment that Lulu runs into an old flame at her reunion, *Something Wild* is a lark. The movie captures the giddy exhilaration of jumping into a car and hitting the road — chucking it all. Demme, and his first-time screenwriter, E. Max Frye, show us roadside America, with its slush cones and all-night convenience stores and ragtag motels, better than any moviemaker ever has. The flimsy bric-a-brac is illuminated by the illicit; this is, after all, the territory you light out to when you want to escape, have affairs, change your identity. Demme puts reggae on the sound track, and pop-funk rhythms and rock, to enhance the allurement, the strangeness, the sexiness of the terrain. (The artists range from John Cale and David Byrne to the Feelies, who also appear in the reunion scene.)

The scariness of being cut off from your home base begins to creep into the movie when Lulu's flame, a recent ex-con, takes over the picture. Ray Sinclair (Ray Liotta) looks like a '50s hood: tattooed, brush-cut, with a muscle-man T-shirt and a smiley sneer. He's so far out of Charlie's world that it doesn't even occur to Charlie to be afraid of him; it's not until Ray holds up a convenience store and busts Charlie's nose, while Lulu looks on helplessly, that the jig is up. Holed up in a motel with Lulu and a nose-bleeding Charlie, Ray can't believe this doofus has actually had a go with his girl. But Ray doesn't see in Charlie what we do. His fantasies have been fermenting so rapidly on the road that he can't just drop the whole thing and go back to his vice presidency. The terrain that promised such illicit pleasure now becomes his nightmare, and he has to find his way out of it. He begins to trail Ray and the trapped, resigned Lulu. (Audrey turns out to be her real name.) He's fired up to be a hero. All at once, his "real" life has turned counterfeit.

Demme has made slapstick comedies before, like *Crazy Mama,* and he's made revenge thrillers, like *Fighting Mad.* But he's never blended the two the way he has here. In a way, *Something Wild* is Demme's *Blue Velvet.* It has a similar scenario: A callow guy allows himself to be seduced into a hellish world dominated by a crazy. The difference is, Lynch's movie took its imagery from the abstractions of modern art; Demme works off pop culture—specifically, pop music. Lynch is interested in seeing just how far you can bring a movie image to stasis and still make it resonate; Demme gives his images a beat—a syncopation—that carries you along. The resonances sink in later. (Maybe that's why Demme's movies are always even better in the memory.)

The trio of lead performances in *Something Wild* are extraordinary. Melanie Griffith, who was so good in Brian De Palma's *Body Double,* isn't like anyone else on the screen today. Her Lulu is prematurely savvy: a tinkly-voiced bad girl with a wised-up matron's air. When she's held captive by Ray, her allurements vanish and we see the scared, hard-bitten woman underneath. Newcomer Ray Liotta (he's appeared in soaps and a few TV movies) creates the kind of powerhouse impression that major careers are based on. It's a classic debut performance—right up there with Richard Widmark in *Kiss of Death.* Charlie may not pick up on Ray's danger at first, but we sure do: This guy carries around with him the sour, impacted rage of a hoodlum who no longer connects with the straight world. All of his psychosexual webbing is with the underworld; he has a con's radar for people's soft spots, and he waits a while, for sport, before he moves in for the kill. And yet—and this is what makes Liotta's performance so original—Ray doesn't think of himself as a bad guy. He's simply going after what he thinks is rightfully his.

But it's Jeff Daniels' performance that the movie hinges on. He has to somehow convince us that the milquetoast Charlie of the opening scenes has the same potential for rage as Ray. Daniels' acting is so beautifully worked out that you never doubt what you're watching; his transition into brutality has a cockeyed inevitability. What's so frightening about *Something Wild* is that Demme uses our good-time feelings for Charlie as a set-up for the disturbances that follow. Trailing Ray and Lulu to Virginia, he's obsessed, humiliated, and it's both funny and awful to see him so murderously wound up. He's linked to Ray in a way we never thought possible, not just through his love for Lulu, but on a deeper, more primal level. Charlie isn't enhanced by violence, though, the way he might have been in a Peckinpah movie; and he doesn't work through it to sweet-tempered oblivion, the way David Lynch might have had it. Demme's humanism softens the script's territorial edge. Charlie isn't really better off for this joyride, he's just different. He has a capacity for horror now.

The black joke in *Something Wild* is that yuppies are only one step away from the abyss—just like everybody else. Their cushioned, moneyed world may seem infection-free, but only on the surface. Demme and Frye are using Charlie's yuppieness as a modern archetype, just as Ray's swagger is vintage '50s Hoodlum. The movie clashes these archetypes to get at something new in the ethos: the malice rattling inside the culture's complacency. *Something Wild* may be one of those rare American movies, like *Shoot the Moon* and *Blue Velvet* and some of Altman's work, that intuits more about what's going on in society than can possibly be known first-hand. For all its frolics, the movie is an apprehension of a coming storm.

Los Angeles Herald Examiner, November 7, 1986

THE HORRORS!
THE HORRORS!

Nothing has hurt Hollywood movies more than the death of durable genres. Westerns, light romances and swashbucklers, sophisticated, madcap comedies and splashy, heartfelt kids' movies, torn-from-the-headlines muckrakers and lowdown, crazy farces — all these were once commercial staples. Unlike most television series, genre movies weren't uniform: They allowed individual talents to do variations on popular subjects or dramatic motifs. Most producers today concentrate not on movie genres but on movie fads — the dirty-cop shoot-'em-up, the dirty-dancing musical — all made quickly and strictly according to formula.

The only genres that have prevailed are sci-fi and horror, which have grown so close over the years that at times they're as difficult to separate as Siamese twins. They've survived partly because they're usually filled with visceral shocks and special effects. But they've also followed Darwinian principles, cross-fertilizing not just with each other but with all the other genres, and bringing forth sturdy hybrids.

In *The Fury,* Brian De Palma mixes ultra-psychic bloodletting with espionage and misunderstood-kid melodrama. *Parents* and *The Step-*

father wed nightmare visions of the American family to social satire of the Eisenhower and Reagan eras, respectively; Michael Laughlin's similar *Strange Invaders,* a sci-fi replay of his horror movie, *Strange Behavior,* centers on a bizarre secret hidden beneath the surface of a small midwestern town. In the controversial *Henry: Portrait of a Serial Killer,* John McNaughton combines a clinical approach to the title character with stripped-down, sometimes quasi-documentary techniques, arriving at horror vérité.

Terrence Rafferty describes a portion of Herk Harvey's *Carnival of Souls* as "*Topper* directed by Ingmar Bergman"; Stephen Schiff invokes both Bergman and Jean Renoir in his review of David Cronenberg's *The Brood.* The critics aren't overreaching; in the last few decades, horror moviemakers have appropriated ideas that used to be the common coin of art house auteurs. It's not surprising that some of the most intelligent and aesthetic young directors have achieved artistic breakthroughs in horror films — for example, Kathryn Bigelow, in *Near Dark,* tells a vampire story as a contemporary southwestern, and Neil Jordan, in *The Company of Wolves,* brings sexual fear and desire back into fairy tales with an audacity that puts the Broadway musical *Into the Woods* to shame. They've simply realized what the masters of gruesome fantasy have always known — that a horror movie needs more than a creepy person or thing. To make our minds reel as well as our skins crawl, it needs a creepy idea.

THE BROOD

Stephen Schiff

Directed and written by David Cronenberg. Starring Samantha Eggar, Art Hindle, and Oliver Reed. **Embassy Home Entertainment/Nelson Entertainment.**

Considering the resurgence of horror in popular culture over the last few years, it's surprising how little the genre has developed. Oh, there are occasional milestones. *Rosemary's Baby* (1968) brought the horror film into the bosom of the American family, around which it had long been hovering. *Night of the Living Dead* (1968) suggested that there was art in the refusal to pull punches. And Philip Kaufman's remake of *Invasion of the Body Snatchers* (1978) showed how our comforting culture could become the perfect setting for our nightmares. Still, these are peaks among goose pimples, and for every one, there's a host of lesser creations: the exploitation hack-'em-ups, for instance; the ludicrous attempts to expand the social conscience of the genre (like last year's *Prophecy,* which prophesied that the sleep of ecological concern would produce monsters); and the Catholic Comix, in which Satan possesses a toddler or a house or the laundry room in the basement of your building, and only the proper application of crucifixes and Latinate mumblings will halt his depredations. Even these woebegone examples, however, indicate where horror films are headed. Gone are the days when horror was the province of Skull Island, when evil wafted our way from Transylvania or Mars. Nowadays, horror is born very close to home. And horror pictures are now among the most visible reflections of everything we find disquieting in our lives and culture.

Call it what you will — alienation, anomie, future shock — we've long been so dazed by the steady stream of real-life horrors that it seems rather difficult to jolt us. We have to be prodded, and forcefully at times, if we are to feel anything at all. Which is part of the reason those cultural experiences that are directed toward our emotions — religion, music, movies — have become so assaultive of late. The minions of Reverend Moon are said to whisk youngsters off to sunnier climes, there to indoctrinate them and deprive them of their rest. Werner Erhard hammers away at stubborn egos until their owners surrender to "it." Punk-rock groups name themselves things like Shrapnel and the Dead Boys and scream out their imprecations at jackhammer tempos. And, in movies, our repressed guilts and fears come howling back to haunt us the way all repressed emotions do — in dream images, in cinematic nightmares. We're hungry for feelings. Because movies can still make us feel, we turn toward them as toward some sort of purgative therapy. And in good horror movies, we're rewarded; an emotional alchemy occurs. It works like this: just before the monster (or whatever form the horrific metaphor takes) is revealed, we may tremble in fearful anticipation. But when it is finally unveiled, that fear is replaced by quite a different sensation. We stare and stare at the screen in a sort of ecstasy, transported by a vision of the unthinkable. And there lies the lure of horror movies, in that privileged moment, that oddly pleasurable catharsis that occurs when our fears are stretched beyond their limits, beyond our worst imaginings, to a realm in which the only possible response is a sort of cleansing awe.

Of course, such moments are rare and precious, and few horror movies provide them. David Cronenberg's new film, *The Brood,* is a blessed exception. For my money, this is the next horror-movie milestone, and the best work done in the genre since Kaufman's *Invasion of the Body Snatchers.* Writer-director Cronenberg is a young Canadian whose two previous films, *They Came from Within* (1975) and *Rabid* (1977), gave him a reputation for unbridled grisliness. But *The Brood* reveals him to be a superb natural filmmaker who brings to the horror movie a compassion and, yes, an innocence that somehow ennoble it. In Cronenberg's hands, horror is no longer a disreputable bastard genre but a new avenue of expression, glistening with possibility. He seems born to make horror movies, the way John Ford was born to make Westerns. And when we enter the world of *The Brood,* we find ourselves in the exhilarating position of happening upon uncharted territory. The giggly self-consciousness of a John Carpenter, of a Brian De Palma, or of the young followers of Roger Corman is nowhere in evidence; nor are we in the grip of a cool manipulator like William Friedkin (or a not-so-cool manipulator like *The Texas Chainsaw Massacre's* Tobe Hooper). Gradually we realize that Cronenberg's principal purpose is not, in fact, to scare us. *The Brood* is, above all, a personal, rather serious contemplation of marital breakdown—and the rage that accompanies it—in the era of "self-realization." Cronenberg calls it an "autobiographical horror film," and that's how it plays. The sensations of loss, regret, and separation in it are deeply felt in a way we've rarely seen in horror films—where characters and relationships are usually attached like shock absorbers, just to keep the thing bouncing properly. Cronenberg's story is a horror movie because that's the only way he can envision it. Horror is his native language; he dreams in it.

Mysteriously, *The Brood* begins like a Bergman movie, with two illuminated heads against a black background. "You are weak," one man growls to the other. "It would have been better for you to have been born a girl." The fellow opposite winces and hangs his head, but we can see that a terrible rage is boiling within him. We are in wintry Toronto, and the bizarre exchange is a psychodrama staged by Dr. Raglan (Oliver Reed) at his Somafree Institute of Psychoplasmics. Psychoplasmics is evidently the latest kicky therapy to hit town, and

Frank Carveth (Art Hindle, who played Brooke Adams's pod-boyfriend in *Invasion of the Body Snatchers*) thinks it's a bit of a crock. He has reason. His high-strung wife, Nola (Samantha Eggar), has left him and their daughter Candice (Cindy Hinds) to seek Dr. Raglan's help, and because she is in some mysterious way "gifted," Raglan deems her his star disciple, keeping her shut away from Frank and the outside world. Frank isn't really sure he still loves Nola: she's become so strange and distant, and so violent that he fears for Candice's safety whenever she goes to visit her mother (in some ways, *The Brood* is like a distorted-mirror image of *Kramer vs. Kramer*). Then, too, Raglan's theories are a bit scary. As his book *The Shape of Rage* explains, he has gone the primal scream one better. He teaches his patients to release their anger and anxiety by manifesting emotion in their bodies. And just as tension can give rise to ulcers, so Raglan's patients break out in welts and sores and weird boils: the symptoms — and, perhaps, the cure — of their mental anguish.

Psychoplasmics doesn't quite work as a nightmare version of popular post-Freudian therapies: if anything has superseded the ambition to "get your head together" recently, it's the ambition to "get your body together," and the unsightly lesions which infest Raglan's patients are not the sort of thing that would attract the modern inner explorer. Still, the "shape of rage" is an extraordinarily resonant metaphor for the modern impulse to shed repression at any cost, to free imprisoned feelings and loose them upon an ostensibly understanding world. Cronenberg sympathizes with the tormented souls seeking succor in his film — he makes Nola herself a warm, immensely attractive figure — but he is essentially a moral conservative (as the sexual disgust in *They Came from Within* and *Rabid* demonstrates), and he uses his command of terrifying imagery to deliver a stern warning to those who would toy with the subconscious. Rather early on, we meet an ex-patient of Raglan's who's intent on taking the doctor to court. "Raglan caused my body to turn against me," the poor wretch confides. "I've got a revolution on my hands, and I'm not putting it down successfully." Whereupon he pulls away the towel swathing his neck to reveal what looks like the fossilized remains of some tiny, prehistoric creature: a hard, toothy growth that hangs above his throat like an amulet. One horror follows another; even for those whose minds it eases, Raglan's therapy proves dangerous. Nola's anger is soothed, it's true, but by means she doesn't understand. And, as we soon discover, her case proves the doctor's theories with terrible certainty: she has been giving unnatural birth to a brood of hideous children — the children of her rage — who, unbeknownst to her, have been stealing away from the Somafree Institute to carry out the murderous commands of her subconscious.

As a horror premise, Nola's deadly brood is not entirely original. One recalls the monster from Walter Pidgeon's id, for instance, in *Forbidden Planet* (1956); indeed, the brood is no more than a variation of the old *Doppelgaenger* motif, the Jekyll-and-Hyde story, or the werewolf tale: legends about how secret, unappeasable desires come to life. In horror stories from time immemorial, the monster has served as a mirror to "normality," and one remembers, too, the myths of the Greeks and the Gnostics, who believed that creation proceeded from a god's thoughts or feelings, which were hypostatized, turned into living beings. What makes *The Brood* so powerful is the way Cronenberg grounds this venerable myth in a nightmare of the flesh, in images that are redolent of disease and dysfunction, of cancer and the fear of corporeal change; in his world, parenthood can be as frightening a metamorphosis as a man's transformation into a werewolf. Our bodies are the mysteries closest to us, and Cronenberg knows it. He plays along the eerie edges of the mind-body duality, cooking up a visceral terror from our squeamishness about blood and tissue, and from the imponderable physicality of death.

Ordinarily, this sort of thing would amount to little more than a gross-out, as it often does in Cronenberg's earlier, more jocular films. But even though he has not yet weaned himself from the dumb, drive-in-movie impulse to display a blood-soaked corpse every time the brood attacks, Cronenberg's purpose here is not to curdle our stomachs. For the most part, he shies away from gory horror effects (*The Brood* is scarier than *Invasion of the Body Snatchers* but not nearly as scary as *Alien*), the better to concentrate on his characters' emotional states. His is a domestic drama, a metaphor for the pain and confusion and distrust that accompany the break-up of any relationship. Through the accumulation of nuances, gestures, and terse, off-hand remarks, Cronenberg tells us everything we need to know about the lives of Frank and Nola, and we experience their hurt and heartache as a sort of counterpoint to the horror.

Nola, for instance, is an essentially isolated, otherworldly figure, but Cronenberg has invented a brilliant method of exposing her interior life: he lets us observe the psychodramas that are part of Raglan's therapy. These are small, beautifully staged scenes during which Oliver

Reed's Raglan acts out the roles of Nola's mother, father, husband, and daughter. In the process, he becomes a disturbing projection of their darkest emotions; he is himself like an angry "brood." What Cronenberg has done here is most unusual; he's turned a horror device into a remarkable dramatic device as well. Reversing the usual tendency in horror films to let the characters serve the horror metaphor—as victim, as creator, and so forth—Cronenberg lets the horror serve the characters. As a result, the cathartic rush we experience at the film's climax—a truly astonishing sequence in which Frank, Nola, Candice, and Raglan all meet in the presence of the brood—approaches the pity and terror evoked by tragedy.

Moreover, Cronenberg's intimacy with his characters gives him a compassion that's almost startling in this creepy context. There are no villains in *The Brood*—not even Raglan, who, like the "mad scientists" in Cronenberg's earlier films, wins our sympathy the moment we recognize that he's as much the victim as the perpetrator of his experiments. Nola, too, is a pitiable figure, the monstrous addict of a psychotherapy gone berserk. In *The Brood,* Cronenberg goes beyond the notion of the banality of evil and introduces an idea that might be dubbed "the innocence of evil," a conception peculiarly appropriate to an era that, until the appearance of the Ayatollah Khomeini, could no more identify its villains than its heroes. If Renoir's compassion for his characters comes from an understanding that disasters occur because "everyone has his reasons," Cronenberg's comes from the understanding that disasters occur for no reason at all. Raglan sincerely wants to help his patients; Nola sincerely wants to achieve sanity; Frank sincerely wishes his wife well and wants to protect his daughter. But Cronenberg's world is not a reasonable place; here, it is the quest for reason that can produce monsters.

None of this would come across with such force were Cronenberg not so fluent a storyteller. Shot in dark, deep colors, *The Brood* moves from barren Canadian snowscapes to the glamorously rustic summer-camp buildings of the Somafree Institute—I haven't seen so much redwood paneling since *Moment by Moment.* The plot hurtles along at an alarming pace, like something shooting through a tunnel. Then, quite suddenly, we'll emerge into some enormous, glistening vista of horror: the unearthly scene, for instance, in which two wizened brood-kids, in little snowsuits like the one worn by the murderous dwarf in *Don't Look Now,* abduct Candice from school; or the gorgeous shot of Candice walking along a snowy highway, flanked by two creatures who are exactly her height, but who walk with a gait that is, in some dreadful way, much more determined. Many of the effects leave a lot to be desired (particularly the evil children's make-up, which makes them look too much like ill-tempered midgets), and so does some of the acting. Oliver Reed, who frequently behaves as though he's on a steady diet of testosterone, overdoes the whispery menace, and Art Hindle, as Frank, hasn't enough range to reach the film's highest emotional pitch. But some of the supporting performances are marvelous (particularly Robert Silverman's, as the harried fellow with the organic amulet). Best of all is Samantha Eggar's Nola, who is at once ghastly and very touching indeed.

Perhaps that's because Cronenberg understands her in a special way. For if Frank is the onscreen reflection of the filmmaker as horrified witness and victim, Nola is the reflection of the filmmaker as artist. Her giving birth to the brood is the ultimate act of self-expression, a perfect metaphor for the way an artist wills his creation into being but cannot entirely control it. And it is a perfect metaphor, as well, for the way a man might take the rage and insecurity he feels over the death of his marriage and purge himself of it, transforming it into something strange and unexpected: a story as frightening as a monster and as innocent as a child.

Boston Phoenix, January 15, 1980

CARNIVAL OF SOULS

Terrence Rafferty

Directed by Herk Harvey. Written by John Clifford. Starring Candace Hilligoss, Frances Fiest, Sidney Berger, Art Ellison, and Herk Harvey. **VidAmerica.**

When people compare movies with dreams, they're usually talking about the terrifying, irrational power that projected images can have, or about the helplessness and solitude we sometimes feel as we're pulled along in the dark. The only way in which most of this summer's movies are like dreams is that it's so hard to remember them. We may, upon leaving the theatre, have a vague sense that something has been nibbling at our consciousness; but, whatever it was, it didn't linger. (If I were pressed to account for my whereabouts on a given date in August, 1989, I'd have to think twice before claiming I was at the movies watching *Cookie* or *Shirley Valentine* or *The Abyss* or *The Little Thief;* even hypnosis might not prove that I had actually seen any of them.) Among the movies in current release, one of the very few that stay in the mind is Herk Harvey's *Carnival of Souls*. This bleak, unnerving low-budget horror picture was made in 1961 and released (mostly to drive-ins, on a double bill with something called *The Devil's Messenger*) in 1962, and hasn't had a theatrical run in New York until now. It's one of those movies that turn up on television at two in the morning, for people who prefer to take their bad dreams in the form of lurid, cheesy shockers interrupted by commercials. In the twenty-seven years since it was first dumped into theatres, this picture has never quite gone away. Even when its only life was as flickering, jumpy images on a small screen, it wouldn't stay dead. It's a real hour-of-the-wolf movie: it wakes you up and keeps you up.

The movie begins with an accident: a car with three young people inside plunges off a bridge into a river in Kansas. The townspeople gather to search for the bodies, alive or dead. Long after they've given up hope of finding survivors, a blond woman, Mary Henry (Candace Hilligoss), emerges from the water; she can't remember how she got out of the car. Soon after that—it's apparently just a day or two later—we see her pounding away at an enormous pipe organ. Despite her trauma, she seems to want to get on with her life: she's due to begin work as a church organist in Utah, and she's determined to arrive on time. On the long drive to Utah, Mary starts seeing things: the face of a pale, unsmiling man appears at the window of her moving car; a bit later, he seems to be standing in the middle of the deserted highway. For the rest of the movie, this ghastly guy won't leave her alone: wherever she goes, he turns up, watching her. Adding to the spookiness is a huge abandoned building at the edge of the Great Salt Lake: without quite knowing why, the young woman finds herself drawn to this looming edifice, a failed resort with a cavernous ballroom. She's afraid she's going crazy. We suspect that what's going on is a good deal direr than that.

The supernatural answer proves to be the correct one—no surprise. But *Carnival of Souls* isn't a conventional ghost story. Although it's obvious that Mary Henry is sort of *different*—not fully engaged in life, let's say — the manner of her not-quite-being is unusual. She seems to flicker in and out of existence. In the movie's most original scenes, Harvey disengages his heroine from her surroundings for several minutes at a time. At one point, Mary goes into a cubicle in a department store to try on a dress, and when she comes out she can't hear anything — worse, no one (except the audience) can hear or see her. It's a terrifying sequence, an unbearably direct expression of the world's indifference. (Imagine *Topper* directed by Ingmar Bergman.) After a while, she snaps out of it, but her relationship to everyday life remains fragile, tentative. She's more alone than any other horror-movie heroine you've ever seen. Her living quarters, in a boarding house, are as drab and featureless as Janet Leigh's motel room in *Psycho*. She's a kind of existential transient: her life fades in and out, as if she were watching it on an old TV with unpredictable reception.

Carnival of Souls, which was made, in black and white, for about thirty thousand dollars, by a bunch of industrial filmmakers based in Lawrence, Kansas, uses its cheapness expressively. The performances are variable, the settings are stark, the sound recording is erratic, and somehow it all works. The movie keeps going dead and then coming back to life. Some of the picture's stiffness, especially in the dialogue scenes, is clearly not intentional, but some of it is: Harvey (who has never made another feature) pulls us through the movie by alternating scenes of everyday life with visions of death, and daring us to locate ourselves; in the flat, neither-here-nor-there landscape of *Carnival of Souls,* we're never entirely sure where we are. George Romero has claimed this picture as an inspiration for *Night of the Living Dead;* the shockingly avid ghouls of his movie are obviously descended from the dead who dance in the ruined ballroom at the climax of Harvey's film. And David Lynch must have seen it, too. Now that this inspired oddity has been resurrected with a brand-new 35-mm. print, we may regret not seeing it in the small hours, alone in front of the tube. But, no matter how many people are in the theatre or what time of day it is, *Carnival of Souls* has the power to detach you from your surroundings and put you in the middle of its own distinctive nowhere. For eighty-eight minutes, you're immersed in it; and when you come up, the world looks stranger.

The New Yorker, September 4, 1989

THE COMPANY OF WOLVES

J. Hoberman

Directed by Neil Jordan. Written by Jordan and Angela
Carter, from her stories. Starring Sarah Patterson and
Angela Lansbury. **Vestron Video.**

The Company of Wolves is being saturation-dumped as if it were just
another horror flick—but this entertaining, unclassifiable film is something more than a belated addition to the werewolf cycle of 1980–81. A
collaboration between Irish novelist turned filmmaker Neil Jordan and
English literary fabulist Angela Carter, *The Company of Wolves* is a
luridly convoluted Freudian fairy tale, pitched somewhere between Joe
Dante's *The Howling* and Jean Cocteau's *La Belle et la Bête*.

The most tangible evidence of the vaunted British film revival since
The Draughtsman's Contract (and the most sophisticated screamer since
Roman Polanski's *Fearless Vampire Killers*), *The Company of Wolves*
unpacks Carter's nine-page story of the same name, placing the action
inside the fevered dream of an adolescent girl. Carter's meditation on
"Little Red Riding Hood" hyped the tale's libido (and added some
frissons) through the infusion of werewolfiana as poetic as it was
rampant. ("That long-drawn, wavering howl has, for all its fearful
resonance, some inherent sadness in it, as if the beasts would love to be
less beastly if they only knew how and never cease to mourn their own
condition.") What's miraculous about Jordan's film is how it literalizes
Carter's conceits without making them any less lyrical.

Deep within her dream, wide-eyed Rosaleen (13-year-old Sarah
Patterson), pout moistened with big sister's lipstick even as she imagines herself in some ersatz Dark Age, is a rapt audience for the paranoid
old wives' tales of Angela Lansbury's deliciously clucking Granny.
Knitting the girl an eye-searing crimson cloak of virgin wool, Lansbury
tells the grisly story of the traveling man and his innocent bride, warns
her against men whose eyebrows meet or who are "hairy inside," and
explains that werewolves are the bastards fathered by priests and born
on Christmas Day. ("By *priests?*" little Rosaleen exclaims. "Why do you
think they call them Father?" is the tart reply.)

The film isn't dreamlike per se, but it revels in (and reveals) the dreamlike qualities of even the most domesticated fairy tale—the repeated injunction not to "stray from the path," the mirrors Rosaleen keeps finding (most spectacularly in an eagle's nest), the continual, show-stopping metamorphoses between human and lupine. Once it finds its rhythm, the film's interlocking, Chinese-box structure is quite pleasurable: as with Otar Iosseliani's ill-fated *Favorites of the Moon* or the films of Raul Ruiz (and as befits a project that reportedly had its genesis when Jordan and Carter met at an academic conference on Borges), there's no mistaking *The Company of Wolves* for anything but a fiction.

Jordan's first film, *Angel* (released here last year as *Danny Boy*), was a *Point Blank*–derived metaphysical thriller whose often stunning visuals strained and broke under the burden of religious allegory. *The Company of Wolves* is far more assured and, shot entirely in the studio, offers images as rich as compost. The film unfolds in an autumnal netherworld—a damp, fecund Oz of soft earth colors and rounded, dwarfish forms. Far more than Boorman's tinsel-tawdry *Excalibur* or even Matthew Robbins' fen-dank *Dragonslayer*, *The Company of Wolves* has the sense of a dimly remembered, prehistoric Europe.

The "real" Rosaleen lives in a big country house, but she dreams herself into some Celtic outpost where the villagers are a lot closer to the caves than to the stars, and their vulnerability is tangible. The wolf-haunted woods are themselves a primal thing—sometimes outrageously so, as pythons drape themselves from the trees or toads perch upon gigantic toadstools to observe Rosaleen out for a walk with an amorous bumpkin. The outside is always wanting in. The stray marmot that sneaks into Granny's house at midnight foretells the man-wolf who arrives later. Not even the church is a sanctuary; tarantulas drop through the nave during the priest's pious evocation of Isaiah (". . . and the wolf shall dwell with the lamb").

Despite an occasional stab at class consciousness (the gentry as ravenous you-know-whats), *The Company of Wolves* so insists on itself as a metaphor for Rosaleen's sexual awakening that, like Charles Perrault's moralizing "Little Red Riding Hood" (the conclusion of which is quoted with ironic gusto over the movie's end credits), it seems to reduce the fairy tale to a single, overemphatic reading. But this is to ignore the film's heady changes in tone—from farce to poetic horror, with special effects so yucky in their wit, you have to laugh with appreciation—as it purports to peel the onion of Rosaleen's unconscious. Although the girl's dream never ends, *The Company of Wolves* winds up with an image of shattered virginity as visceral as any in the movies. At the same time, Jordan and Carter are genuinely witty about sex. (Rosaleen receives sound advice from her comely, hard-working mum: "If there's a beast in men, it meets its match in women too.") Neither a solemn art film nor a brainless teen pic, this may well be the best dating movie in town.

"Children know something they can't tell," Djuna Barnes opined in *Nightwood*. "They like Red Riding Hood and the wolf in bed!" Barnes's overripe, phantasmagorical prose style is an obvious precursor of Carter's, and *The Company of Wolves* could well be subtitled *Nightwood* — so tangled and nocturnal is its narrative, so filled with blood and yearning its tale. A horror film as literate as it is visionary, it's great fun — and that's not a cheap thrill.

Village Voice, April 30, 1985

THE FURY

Kevin Thomas

Directed by Brian De Palma. Written by John Farris, from his novel. Starring Kirk Douglas, Andrew Stevens, John Cassavetes, and Amy Irving. **CBS/Fox Video.**

Brian De Palma's *The Fury* is so exciting — and such a triumph of style — that the less revealed about its plot the better.

It's probably saying too much merely to state that it involves a supersecret government intelligence agency, a man (Kirk Douglas) determined to locate his missing son (Andrew Stevens) and a girl (Amy Irving) with extraordinary psychic powers. Along the way there's all manner of action and adventure; something exciting or suspenseful is happening in every fast-moving sequence.

A comparison between *The Fury*, which John Farris adapted from his novel, and De Palma's last film, the tremendously popular *Carrie*, is inevitable because they both have young heroines who discover they can wreak havoc purely through mental telepathy. However, whereas *Carrie* was a dark comedy (which nevertheless reminded us of the thoughtless cruelty of youth) that ended up jolting us out of our seats, *The Fury* embraces more elements and has a wider scope. It moves from some light comic touches right after its jarring opening to a progressively somber tone, evoking finally the intense pathos of the classic horror pictures.

The satisfactions of *The Fury* are many (though it's not for the squeamish). For those of us who have followed Brian De Palma's career back to his brief but already promising *Murder à la Mod* in the mid '60s, it's gratifying to see him grow more assured with each film. Indeed, at any moment *The Fury* could lapse into the ludicrous, but De Palma's control is so taut and filled with bravura that he makes plausible the most bizarre — and bloody — psychic manifestations, not to mention much physical derring-do. Without indulging in the gratuitous, lingering displays that lead to morbidity, De Palma keeps you at seat's edge. He seems to be able to get away with everything.

In doing so, De Palma has made the best kind of movie, the kind that relies as much as possible on the camera to tell the story — to create a world of its own — and keeps the dialogue and exposition, especially, to an absolute minimum. In accomplishing this, the contributions of Farris, cinematographer Richard H. Kline, production designer Bill Malley, composer John Williams (who has come up with an appropriately fulsome score in the grand Bernard Herrmann manner) and any number of special effects technicians are substantial.

It's the people, as always, who must involve us. It's such a pleasure to watch an authentic star like Douglas run the gamut, leaping from buildings, taking on villains (and disguises), ranging in emotion from good-natured kidding, loving concern, and affectionate pride to grief-stricken rage.

John Cassavetes is a lethally manipulative, enigmatic agent, and Miss Irving and Stevens (the son of Stella) are likable young people, endangered by their unusual abilities. (The serious point that *The Fury* makes is that society tends to destroy those uniquely gifted individuals it is not prepared to assimilate.) In a welcome return to the screen, Carrie Snodgress is Douglas' lady, who works with conscientious parapsychologists Charles Durning, Carol Rossen and Fiona Lewis (who is placed in a position of conflicting loyalties). Joyce Easton is Miss Irving's brisk society mother, and William Finley is a singularly weird tracer of lost persons.

De Palma gets the best from these actors and many more. Eleanor Merriam, for example, has a terrific scene as a fearless elderly lady delighted to have a witty intruder terrify her tiresome son and daughter-in-law.

Except for a single sequence shot in Israel, *The Fury* was filmed entirely in Chicago and its environs, and it benefits from the relative unfamiliarity of a wide range of locales. *The Fury* is definitely not for impressionable youngsters or those turned off by Grand Guignol, but it's a treat for cineastes and for horror fans.

Los Angeles Times, March 15, 1978

HENRY: PORTRAIT OF A SERIAL KILLER

★

Peter Travers

Directed by John McNaughton. Written by McNaughton and Richard Fire. Starring Michael Rooker, Tom Towles, and Tracy Arnold. **MPI Home Video.**

It sounds like a bad TV movie or one of those grind-house rip-and-renders. Or at the very least like something you don't waste time reading or thinking about. Bear with me. *Henry: Portrait of a Serial Killer* is a stinging chiller with a provocative past and a potentially bright future.

It came from Chicago. First-time feature director John McNaughton started shooting this graphic tale of a mass murder back in 1985. He had a cast of talented unknowns—drawn mostly from Chicago's Organic Theater Company—a meager budget of $120,000 and four weeks to get the job done.

MPI, a local video firm run by the brothers Waleed and Malik Ali, financed the project. They wanted a horror film. McNaughton provided something more: a raw, transfixing character study that plumbs a twisted mind. At the Chicago International Film Festival in 1986, the film drew interest from distributors, but they were quickly scared off after the Motion Picture Association of America (MPAA) slapped *Henry* with an X rating. An X on a film means that major theater chains won't show it, most newspapers won't advertise it, and nobody makes a buck.

So *Henry* sat on the shelf until last year, when MPI's publicity director, Chuck Parello, persuaded Chicago's Music Box Theater to do a few midnight screenings. A similar arrangement was made later in New York. Those who didn't walk out — many did — were usually impressed. Documentarian Errol Morris (*The Thin Blue Line*) invited *Henry* to the 1989 Telluride Film Festival, in Colorado, where Morris served as guest director. Reaction was divided but not indifferent. *Henry* now has a real chance at finding an audience, though one roadblock remains. The MPAA refused to modify the X rating to a more salable R when the film was resubmitted uncut last May. Waleed Ali says the MPAA didn't even suggest changes. "They told us they wouldn't know where to cut," he says. "The film is too disturbing."

Rejecting the MPAA decision, MPI decided to release *Henry* without a rating on a city-by-city basis, starting in Boston late last month. It's a risky move and a significant one for American independent films. MPI is battling a system that, in effect, blocks the distribution of films that don't meet ill-defined moral standards. (Scenes in *Angel Heart* and *Scandal* were snipped to dodge the MPAA's kiss of death.) If this defiant, uncut *Henry* wins over theater owners and audiences, a blow may be struck for other challenging films that don't deserve to be censored or lumped with snuff flicks and pornography.

It's ironic that those drawn to *Henry: Portrait of a Serial Killer* by its title alone are likely to be the most disappointed. The movie doesn't shy away from gore: Bodies are kicked, punched, slashed, shot and dismembered. But half of the sixteen murders take place offscreen. There's more mayhem in any of the R-rated *Friday the 13th, Nightmare on Elm Street* and *Halloween* movies. Those films offer supernatural villains and cardboard victims; they're easy to shake. Not so *Henry*. The film is no masterpiece, but it is spare, intelligent and thought provoking.

McNaughton and coscreenwriter Richard Fire based their fictionalized script on Henry Lee Lucas, a convicted serial killer who confessed to murdering more than 300 people over two decades. Watching a segment about Lucas on TV's "20/20," McNaughton was struck by Lucas's low-key charm, a trait he felt explained how a killer could get close to his victims. The film's initial glimpse of Henry (Michael Rooker) shows him thanking a waitress. "Real nice smile you got there," he says, before hopping in his car to search for a victim.

McNaughton takes his time showing Henry in the act of murder. As in Joseph Ruben's *Stepfather,* Terrence Malick's *Badlands* and Hitchcock's classic *Shadow of a Doubt,* the intent is to demonstrate how madness can wear an ordinary, even pleasing face. At first we see only the aftermath of the crimes: corpses arranged in horrific tableaux while the soundtrack echoes with the victims' death throes. Rooker, who later acted in *Sea of Love, Eight Men Out* and *Music Box,* is extraordinary as Henry. Polite and soft-spoken, he uses only an occasional steely glint to betray the rage simmering beneath Henry's bland facade. It's a scary, resonant performance, and a great one.

Henry shares a drab Chicago apartment with a prison buddy named Otis, skillfully played by Tom Towles. The plot trigger is the arrival of Otis's sister Becky (Tracy Arnold), a topless dancer from the South who wants to find a respectable job and send for her daughter; her husband

Michael Rooker, who plays Henry in *Henry: Portrait of a Serial Killer,* shows more glee when clowning around with director John McNaughton (right) than he does as the movie's abrupt, affectless killer. (Photo copyright © 1990 by Maljack Productions, Inc. and Filmcat Incorporated. All rights reserved. Courtesy Greycat Films.)

is in jail on a murder rap. Otis treats his sister with barely concealed contempt and incestuous lust — though the gentlemanly Henry aims to see he doesn't follow through on the latter impulse.

As the three share meals and conversation, McNaughton crams in a heap of background. Becky was abused sexually by her father; Otis has a yen for a high-school boy to whom he sells marijuana; Henry, at fourteen, killed his mother, a hooker who dressed him as a girl and forced him to watch her in bed with johns. In less skilled hands, this psychobabble might sink the picture. But McNaughton wisely refuses to condescend to these stunted characters or reduce them to their dossiers. His tone is disengaged but not dispassionate. Arnold, in a heartfelt performance, makes Becky's need to connect palpable. Seeing nothing of Henry's current murderous proclivities, she sees him as a lifeline.

Otis wises up when Henry snaps the necks of two tarts they take parking. Shocked at first, he gleefully joins Henry on his killing spree, soon surpassing his mentor at conscienceless brutality. In the film's most terrifying scene, the one that prompts the walkouts, Henry and Otis attack a suburban family and videotape the deed. "Take her blouse off," Henry tells Otis, who is grabbing a struggling housewife. "Do it, Otis. You're a star." Cinematographer Charlie Lieberman, a find, turned a camcorder over to Rooker to shoot this scene as Henry would. The video footage — grainy, unfocused, crazily angled — makes the carnage joltingly immediate. It's a stomach churner. Later, Otis replays the murders at home in slow motion, savoring even the moment when he tried to have sex with the woman he just killed, only to be stopped by Henry. Some thread of morality still exists in Henry; none remains in Otis.

As the film builds to its shocking climax, McNaughton exposes a world stripped of standards. "I love you, Henry," says Becky as she drives off with him to what she hopes is a new life. But for Henry, love is a trap. He must remain affectless, impersonal. The film, to its credit, does not. *Henry* makes you squirm, a sane reaction to the sight of innocent people being slaughtered. The movie doesn't cop out by pretending Henry has no connection with us and our apathetic, debilitated society. Far from glorifying Henry's fury, McNaughton rubs it in our faces. Sure we recoil. That's the point.

Henry is hard to take, but its intensity is not something the MPAA needs to protect us from. McNaughton has made a film of clutching terror that's meant to heighten our awareness instead of dulling it. At the end, Henry is still out there among us. And he's no B-movie monster in a hockey mask. He could be the guy next door. This film gives off a dark chill that follows you all the way home.

Rolling Stone, March 8, 1990

NEAR DARK

Henry Sheehan

Directed by Kathryn Bigelow. Written by Bigelow and Eric Red. Starring Adrian Pasdar, Jenny Wright, and Lance Henriksen. **HBO Video.**

Well, the leaves might not be turning wondrous shades of red and gold, but there's one sure sign in Southern California that autumn is here: we're being swamped by a flood of horror pictures. They show up in a trickle beginning shortly after Labor Day, and steadily gather in force until, come Halloween, they make up a raging torrent. Formerly a time when low and moderately budgeted films could elbow their way into theaters amidst a seasonal downturn in major studio releases, fall has become an extra season for the majors — several of which are just big-time exploitation outfits anyway — to grab a piece of the horror pumpkin pie. Even though the majors have become extra players, however, they haven't managed to push their discount competitors out of the market. So now we're inundated with knife-wielding teens, goop from beyond, and Satan in all his myriad and banal forms.

Still, no matter how the slasher slices it, a lot of it is still baloney. The typical '80s horror film is, first of all, almost always a crude affair that substitutes special effects for any kind of real suspense, secondly, based on an umpteenth variation of some blatant, oversimplified Freudian shibboleth, and, thirdly, not scary. Of course, public and critical expectations seem at an all-time low, too, so one is faced with the bizarre sight of a second-rate piece of desperately gory claptrap like *Hellraiser* actually being praised as, of all things, "stylish." Not to mention the same encomiums bestowed on questionable talents like Tobe Hooper and Wes Craven. In fact, the only two talents to work in the horror genre with anything resembling consistent artistic accomplishment are George Romero and David Cronenberg.

Against this background of gobs of product unaccompanied by the most basic felicities of style comes Kathryn Bigelow's *Near Dark,* an emotionally complex, thematically resonant meditation on the horrors of love, loneliness and alienation. All this intelligence comes packaged in a story of vampirism that makes other efforts in the field — *The Lost Boys* comes rapidly to mind, but there are others — look pallid and timid. This is a movie that, while not as dishearteningly bleak as Romero's work or as stomach-wrenching as Cronenberg's, projects a truly upsetting image of revulsion and horror, and its scenes of blood-letting — especially a long spectacular set piece featuring the killing of the clientele of a lowlife tavern — are not merely gross, but genuinely disturbing.

Just as pervasively disturbing is Bigelow's imagery of the attraction between two lovers. Mae (Jenny Wright) is the mysterious, good-looking girl who, with a nonfatal bite, has caused the transformation of young Caleb into a vampire. Caleb (Adrian Pasdar), a fresh-faced farmboy, can't make the final transition, however. He desperately needs blood to survive, and normal food just serves to sicken him, but he can't bring himself to kill. After a truck ride in which Mae has had to bring down the prey for the both of them, she opens a vein in her arm — as she's done before — and allows Caleb to suck the freshly ingested blood from it. As he sucks thirstily from it, she has to push him away, fearful that he'll take it all and inadvertently destroy her. As he falls, he leans back rubbing his bloody lips, and laughs with a strange exhilaration, as if he has sated himself with something more than food.

Something more than food is what the film is about. It's about that something that nourishes social groups and keeps them together, and what feeds romantic relationships and tightens those bonds. For however unearthly their conditions, Caleb and Mae are really just a pair of young lovers, though more star-crossed than most. Caleb first sees Mae eating an ice cream cone on the deserted streets of his small Oklahoma home town. He offers her a lift, and as the dawn draws ever closer, his amorous teasing — which is clearly causing her some kind of inner struggle — causes her to make the fateful bite. As the rising sun nears the horizon, she bolts, leaving Caleb to stumble across plowed fields. As the sun burns off the morning damp, it seems to be affecting the stumbling youth until, within sight of his widowed father and little sister, a battered RV, its windows painted black, races across a field. An arm reaches out and pulls him aboard. He's been snatched by a traveling band of renegade vampires — an older couple, a hood, a young kid, and Mae. Now that Caleb has crossed a barrier, he has to travel with them as they make their way across the rural countryside, tearing up the landscape with their horrific version of a crime spree.

If the plot sounds familiar, it should. It's a more or less direct lift from Nicholas Ray's debut film, *They Live by Night*. Though the title makes it sound like it is a vampire movie, too, Ray's film is one of the greatest of young-love-on-the-run films, about a pair of kids (Farley Granger and Cathy O'Donnell) who, fugitives, end up with a motley pair of bank robbers during the Depression. Their ersatz family, at first their protectors, become their oppressors as their outlaw lifestyle eventually begins to put unbearable pressures on the lovers. They have to plan an escape from their escape.

There's nothing wrong with borrowing a plot if you can do it justice, and Bigelow certainly does. For one thing, she obliquely credits Ray by echoing the earlier film's famous opening shot — a helicopter shot of a car racing across a barren field — several times. Bigelow's bloodsucking bandits are caught in the same trap as Ray's more prosaic criminals. Having loosed the bonds of society, they now find that freedom is accompanied by danger, the threat that no one else is bound by convention any more than they are. Bigelow's brave new crosscountry raiders are now revealed to be deeply neurotic, driven by appetites that they have either repressed or are now venting with awful destructiveness.

Caleb's initial appearance tells us almost everything we need to know about him. Arriving outside a tavern with his pick-up truck, he lets the easy, wise-ass banter of a pair of friends almost goad him into an unnecessary fight. Clearly he has some deep-seated, hidden pressures that are about to blow. Mae's lure is an easy one, an immediate respite from his normal life. She holds open the promise not only of sex but also of change and escape.

But if Mae symbolizes the upside of rebellion, her traveling companions are vivid symbols of the downside. Led by a gravelly-voiced, scarred old soldier, Jesse (played by Lance Henriksen with menacing authority in the film's outstanding performance), who's been biting necks since he was in the Civil War, they include a saucy, hard-bitten dame, Diamondback (Jeanette Goldstein, the woman marine from

Aliens), a biker-type hood, Severin (Bill Paxton), and a dangerous 11-year-old, Homer (Joshua Miller). The obvious cracked mirror-image of a typical family does nothing to mitigate the menace they impart immediately, and Bigelow introduces them in a cacophony of dark quick shots, as they race their enshadowed vehicle across the burning daylight of the fields to a lonely utility garage and dark respite.

These are very modern vampires, and the periphery of society holds out an apparently eternal hiding place. Their dwellings are lonely garages and isolated motels; their prey are society's other marginals — crooks, night workers, wastrels. Bigelow's scenes of the feeding frenzies are practically brilliant. The pack, restless and angry that Caleb has refused to kill, and warning him that if he doesn't, he'll be destroyed, wander into a roadhouse one night. "Shitkicker heaven!" exclaims Severin as he parades through the place, trying to pick fights with the seedy, dangerous-looking customers. Bigelow plays out the destruction of the bar and its inhabitants in excruciating detail, then, with only a moment's pause, leads right into a shootout between the vampires and police, a shootout that's deadly because, despite their repeatedly demonstrated immunity to bullets, the creatures are threatened by the sun pouring in through bullet holes. If nothing else, with these two scenes, Bigelow has put to rest forever the notion that women can't direct action. These scenes are as well shot and edited as work by the best contemporary action directors — Walter Hill, John Carpenter, you name him.

However, it's the air of deep, neurotic melancholy that makes *Near Dark* work. The film's rhythm is set by lonely, nighttime vistas, incantatory shots of the sun setting and rising. The sun becomes a rich symbol of life and death in the film, for all of its movements spell the end for someone, either the vampire's victims or the vampires themselves. But it's the underpinnings of emotional reality that really set the tone. Both Caleb and Mae feel fatally marked, stuck with their situation, unable to reintegrate into society. Their deep sense of alienation, of being unable to trust anyone but each other, is an accurate deepening of feelings many unhappy young people feel. Bigelow does open a door for them, and they do manage to force a happy if violent ending, but somehow there's a certain lack of, if not conviction, then symmetry to it. More convincing is the fiery destruction of Jesse and Diamondback, the unregenerate killers and outsiders, who die with Diamondback's blessing of "Good times, baby."

The truth is that in life, these young notions of feeling out of place are not so much resolved as replaced with other problems, so any resolution of them is bound to feel arbitrary. Jesse and Diamondback, as blowsy, lined and haggard as they might be, embody youth in their actions, so their dissolution, vaporous and final, seems more real than the kids' resolution. However, that is more a source of tension than failure in *Near Dark*. The film's purgation of terror is as vital and energizing as can be. This is one hell of a movie.

L.A. Reader, October 9, 1987

PARENTS

Jonathan Rosenbaum

Directed by Bob Balaban. Written by Christopher Hawthorne. Starring Randy Quaid, Mary Beth Hurt, Bryan Madorsky, and Sandy Dennis. **Vestron Video.**

Having already opened and speedily closed in both Los Angeles and New York, *Parents* arrives in Chicago under a bit of a cloud. Brilliant but uneven, this ambitious feature doesn't have a script that's worthy of its high-powered direction, doesn't build as dramatically as it might have, and clearly bites off more than it can chew. But it is still the most interesting and exciting directorial debut that I have encountered in some time—a "failure" that makes most recent successes seem like cold mush. Choosing a movie to take with me to a desert island, I would opt without a second's hesitation for *Parents* over such relatively predictable Oscar-mongering exercises as *Rain Man, The Accidental Tourist,* or *Dangerous Liaisons,* because it's a movie that kept me fascinated, guessing, and curious—even when it irritated me.

Parents is the first feature directed by native Chicagoan Bob Balaban, whose previous directing credits include a short (*SPFX*), the pilot episode of the TV series "Tales From the Darkside," an *Amazing Stories* segment, and a Showtime special built around comic magicians Penn and Teller. He's also had wide exposure as an actor, even if few moviegoers seem to recall him by name. Onstage, he started out as Linus in *You're a Good Man, Charlie Brown,* and he most recently appeared in David Mamet's *Speed-the-Plow* on Broadway. His movie roles include the kid who propositions Jon Voight in a Times Square movie house in *Midnight Cowboy,* the prosecuting attorney in *Prince of the City,* scientists in at least three films (*Altered States, 2010,* and *Close Encounters of the Third Kind,* where his character was also the Francois Truffaut character's interpreter), a government investigator in *Absence of Malice,* and a parole officer in the current *Dead Bang.* His diary of the shooting of *Close Encounters,* brought out in paperback in 1978, makes for a good and intelligent read.

One of the clear benefits of this background is his deft handling of actors — not only professionals like Randy Quaid, Mary Beth Hurt, and Sandy Dennis, but the inexperienced Bryan Madorsky, who plays the movie's ten-year-old hero, Michael, and the only partially experienced Juno Mills-Cockell, who plays his best friend. The unexpected, lyrical freshness of Madorsky and Mills-Cockell is effectively set off by the mannerist caricatures of Quaid and Hurt, as the hero's parents, and by Dennis, who plays a neurotic but sympathetic grammar-school psychologist. Dennis's character exists halfway between the kids and the parents, sharing the shy awkwardness of the former and the age and size of the latter.

One thing that all these characters have in common is that Balaban presents them more as distilled essences than as fluid, changing personalities, much as a ten-year-old boy might perceive himself and others. In fact, much of what is most exciting about *Parents* stylistically is its expressionism, which focuses more on impressions, situations, and atmospheres than on unfolding events or plot twists; it is only when the film belatedly begins to follow conventional guidelines of genre and narrative that it finds itself in trouble.

Consider the movie's extended opening, which deftly establishes Balaban's unusual approach to atmosphere and narrative continuity. As the credits begin, set to the strains of that nauseating '50s pop instrumental, "Cherry Pink and Apple Blossom White," we see aerial shots of endless reaches of identical ranch-style houses, succeeded by a huge close-up of a moving blue '50s-era Oldsmobile; the film's title appears over the grille and then breaks apart, like taffy or chewing gum.

We cut to the car's interior, stuffed with a family and its possessions. Lily Laemle (Mary Beth Hurt), sitting in the front, is prattling on to her

Young Bryan Madorsky has doubts about the suburban façade erected by his mother and father, Mary Beth Hurt and Randy Quaid, in Bob Balaban's horror comedy, *Parents*. (Photo by David Whitaker, courtesy Vestron Video.)

son, Michael, in the back about how glad she is that they have moved, while her husband, Nick (Randy Quaid), drives. A subjective shot of the passing neighborhood (under Madorsky's credit) is followed by a frontal shot of tiny Michael, surrounded by luggage and looking out the windows on both sides with his liquid eyes, which establishes the film's overall vision as being very closely allied with his own. Three more shots are devoted to the utter unctuousness of a crossing guard, who draws the car to a halt so that schoolchildren can pass, and of Michael's parents, who wave back at him with petrified cheeriness.

Then the prologue continues with a long series of incidents — some consecutive, some spread out over an extended period of time. The overall effect is oddly eventless, because the unannounced temporal leaps and similar lengths of the shots make each incident seem equivalent to every other, regardless of whether they are narrative events or more general behavioral descriptions of the characters. In quick succession, we see Michael's new school as the Laemles drive past it, a static shot of their ugly new house, Lily and Nick (now fully settled in) essaying a mambo in their living room, Lily planting blotches of white icing on a hideous pink cake, Nick putting a golf ball across the living-room floor, Nick and Lily ritualistically attending to their outdoor barbecue, a close-up of the repulsive meat being delivered by Lily on a tray to husband and son at the dinner table, and finally — over Balaban's directorial credit and the last phrase of the instrumental — an exterior shot of their house at night.

This is followed, in turn, by a shot of Michael's profile in extreme foreground as he sits on the living-room floor, lost in thought, with his parents much farther back, in the dining room — a striking low-angle, deep-focus, wide-angle composition. In fact, throughout the latter part of this long introductory sequence, Balaban's use of low angles and distorting wide-angle lenses recalls some of the eerie spatial effects used by Stanley Kubrick and Raul Ruiz, as well as Kubrick's and Ruiz's main precursor, Orson Welles. (In particular, this profile shot is a dead ringer for many to be found in Ruiz's child-oriented films, such as *City of Pirates* and *Manoel on the Island of Wonders*.) Critic Manny Farber once wrote that Welles's "efforts with space" in *Touch of Evil* were "to make it prismatic and a quagmire at the same time," and this precisely describes Balaban's vision in *Parents* as it is structured around Michael's alienated viewpoint. This vision leads to the depiction of Nick, the father, as an overbearing gargoyle, the spread-out, long-skirted, flowery effect of the mother, Lily, and the cavernous reaches of the Laemles' house seen as both a performing arena and a confining trap.

The overblown tackiness of the film is more poetic and atmospheric than literal, and when the focus eventually shifts to Michael's nightmares (which involve blood, meat, and a confused notion of what his parents do together late at night), we can accept them as a logical extension of the overall vision. It's only when we are obliged to take his nightmares as the literal truth that the poetics start to come apart, and so does the film.

It's not difficult to accept Michael's parents as metaphorical cannibals whose appetites for food and sex are somehow intertwined. All the other adults in the community — apart from Millie Dew (Sandy Dennis), the school psychologist — including Michael's teacher and Nick and Lily's friends, are equally grotesque and sinister, as is the world that they inhabit and the culture they espouse. (Nick is a defoliant expert at a plant called Toxico.) But when Michael's nightmares prove to be real, and we're asked to accept Nick and Lily as literal cannibals (unlike their neighbors), the poetic metaphor no longer applies — the clanking machinery of formulaic horror movies takes over, complete with accompanying clichés. Even in a satirical context, the notions of secrecy and paranoia appear a bit displaced: in the late '50s, when the film is set, Nick's work as a defoliant expert would have been more secret than the movie makes it out to be; instead the movie's notion of secrecy is restricted to the home — to Nick and Lily's sexuality and cannibalism, which are treated as being related satirically (if not literally) to Nick's profession. The problem, in other words, is that the film's uses of satire and poetic metaphors, its plot and its "program," aren't always compatible.

It's hard to know whether to blame Christopher Hawthorne's script for this or some more general flaw in Balaban's conception. Perhaps the real problem isn't the filmmakers' deliberations at all but the cannibalistic demands of the commercial marketplace, which decree that *any* plot, no matter how silly or hackneyed, is preferable to no plot at all. It's possible, in other words, that Balaban and Hawthorne may have been obliged to degrade their overall conception simply in order to be able to make this movie.

Parents suffers as well as triumphs because of its opposition to certain cherished ideas. One of these received notions, adopted most commonly by spectators born in the '60s or later, is that the 1950s in this country were a kind of golden age, which we can now look back upon as a lost paradise. (A few years ago, when I was teaching film at the University of California in Santa Barbara, my course in Hollywood films of the '50s was especially popular for just this reason. When I asked students what made the '50s seem so attractive to them, they usually cited prosperity and the importance of traditional family values — the former based on their false impression that the U.S. economy was in better shape in the '50s than in the '60s.) Anyone who continues to believe that today is likely to experience *Parents* as a solid kick in the teeth, which is all to its credit.

The other received idea, even more widespread and ingrown, is that movies should be made exclusively in popular genres and with familiar stories. This movie, however, remains original and exciting only as long as it manages to *elude* conventional storytelling and goes straight down the tubes as soon as it capitulates to it.

The connection between these two ideas might be pointed up by a look at two of the films of David Lynch, whose style and vision provide a telling cross-reference to that of Balaban in *Parents,* and whom critics everywhere have been evoking in discussions of *Parents*. The brilliance of Lynch's first feature, *Eraserhead,* largely depends on its nonnarrative aspects, while the much greater popularity of his *Blue Velvet* depends on both its adoption of a more conventional story line and its ironic evocations of the '50s as a period of blissful and wholesome innocence—a notion the film somehow manages both to subscribe to and undermine without ever forcing the audience to deal directly with this contradiction.

Broadly speaking, in *Eraserhead* as well as in *Blue Velvet,* Lynch remains an "apolitical" filmmaker, which in the context of the '70s and '80s means a politically conservative one: resolutely nonanalytical, virtually Manichaean in his treatment of women (all of whom are either "good" girls or "bad"—i.e., sexy), a biological determinist in his view of sex and procreation, a voyeuristic puritan in relation to both sex and violence (which, in *Blue Velvet,* go together like ham and eggs), and a reactionary in his purely nostalgic relation to the past. The fact that he nonetheless appeals more to liberals than to conservatives can perhaps be explained by the kinkiness of his worldview, a kinkiness that is almost impossible to find in leftist artists.

Before it takes its nosedive into incoherence, *Parents* can't be accused of having any of these retrogressive traits—which makes it so incongruous that critics have been linking this movie so insistently to Lynch. (The film's poor commercial showing in both New York and Los Angeles also suggests that critics who have been linking it to Lynch aren't necessarily doing it any favors, either.) Far from being nostalgic about the '50s (i.e., the present) like *Blue Velvet, Parents* is corrosively analytical about the subject, and there's no real innocence to be found or celebrated here; even Michael has too much of a morbid streak to qualify as "pure" (like the Laura Dern character in *Blue Velvet*).

Ironically, Balaban's sense of the awfulness of the physical and spiritual decor of the '50s is much closer in some ways to that of John Waters, even if Balaban considers negative the same cultural detritus that Waters's camp sensibilities would define as a plus. Ultimately, the least fashionable aspect of *Parents* may finally be what's most important and interesting about it— that its aesthetic biases are not only related to its moral, social, and political biases, but interchangeable with them. This gives *Parents* a certain conceptual integrity even when it flounders, as satire or as a horror movie, and suggests that if Balaban manages to get ahold of better material in the future, we might be in for some genuine revelations.

Chicago Reader, April 7, 1989

THE STEPFATHER

★

David Edelstein

Directed by Joseph Ruben. Written by Donald E. Westlake.
Starring Terry O'Quinn, Jill Schoelen, and Shelley Hack.
Embassy Home Entertainment.

The Stepfather — the story of a man who marries into existing families
and then massacres them — is a classic TV movie. It's a pretty good
movie-movie, too, but on the small screen, side by side with Ward
Cleaver (Hugh Beaumont), Jim Anderson (Robert Young), and all those
twinkling TV dads, it's going to blaze up like a fever dream. When we
meet the Stepfather (Terry O'Quinn), he's surrounded by the freshly
butchered corpses of his latest family, the littlest still clutching her
teddy bear. Dad washes up, shaves off his beard, packs his things; before
he leaves, he shakes his head and puts a boat into the chest where it
belongs. Next time, he thinks, junior will remember to put his toys
away.

A year later, he's Jerry Blake, husband of homemaker Susan (Shelley
Hack) and stepfather to pretty, 16-year-old Stephanie (Jill Schoelen). In
Rosedale, Washington, Jerry sells houses and the American Dream. To
mommies and daddies, he explains that the family is a sacred thing, and
he believes it, too; he practices what he preaches with a vengeance. Jerry
has a sheepish grin and a sentimental tilt of the head; he buys a puppy
for his daughter and says, "Can we give this little guy a home?" He
potters around the house looking for ways to make himself useful, and
he's a whiz at building birdhouses and fixing screen doors. Jerry keeps a
full set of tools in the cellar, where he goes whenever a cloud appears on
his horizon — a youth on the front step kissing his daughter, a challenge
to his authority, a newspaper clipping of a past massacre. Then his
features freeze in confusion, he hurries down the stairs, and he smashes
his hammer repeatedly against his worktable, jabbering, "What we need
here is a little order. A little order here. Little order here. Little
order . . ."

Boyish, blue-eyed, blandly handsome, Terry O'Quinn seems vaguely
familiar but more vague than familiar; it's a shock to discover he's had
substantial parts in *Places in the Heart, Mrs. Soffel, Space Camp, All the*

Right Moves, Heaven's Gate, and a slew of TV movies. The guy doesn't register the way stars are supposed to, and since the stepfather is a man who can slay whole families and disappear without a trace, O'Quinn's anonymity makes him eerily spectral. Stephanie senses there's something off about her stepdad — he's all TV tics and homilies, he isn't *filled in.* O'Quinn's performance is cunningly cribbed from the tube. In one of his best scenes, he gazes at an episode of "Mr. Ed" with a look of utter rapture, and for a mad moment he and Alan Young (Wilbur) seem to trade places before our eyes.

The Stepfather isn't a psychological portrait; it's more like a psychositcom, and director Joseph Ruben (he did the exuberantly junky *Dreamscape*) has shot it with the kind of wry tenderness Hitchcock brought to *Shadow of a Doubt.* The film is magically clean, a dewy blur of suburban serenity, with smooth tracking shots over lawns that have an after-the-rainfall green. The blandness is a gag, and it makes the violence, which comes in spasmodic jolts, that much more horrifying. When Jerry splits a man's skull with a two-by-four, the board bisects the frame, and the vertical motion itself makes the audience jump, a sudden *fortissimo* crash in Ruben's surprise symphony. Jerry sends his victim's car over a cliff, and he strolls away, whistling "Camptown Races" (the carnage motif).

It's a one-joke movie, but the joke is wonderfully subversive, like Stephen King's in *The Shining.* (O'Quinn would have been perfect as the daddy in that.) It's not the culture's violence that drives people mad, the film implies, but its fake harmony — especially the sunny world of TV sitcoms, where every crisis is handily resolved (in 26 minutes), every family is a "bunch," and every father knows best. When you hear about a sitcom actor having a rough patch — when Robert Young, for example, admits to being a severe depressive — it's not really a surprise, because the folksy authority those people project is a form of lunacy. Ruben and writer Donald E. Westlake have drawn a clean line from "Father Knows Best" to *Friday the 13th.* No wonder Jerry Blake, the patriarch with dwindling power over his wife and daughter, goes mad — he's living in the wrong universe.

So, in a way, is our president, which is another reason *The Stepfather* has so much resonance. What's bloodcurdling about Ronald Reagan is not his politics (there are precedents, at least, for them) but the TV-dad manner he uses to articulate them — the way he can smile, nod his head, say "welp" and "gee," and go on to spew the lies of a delusional paranoid. Dad's had blood on his hands for years now. You can imagine Reagan at a press conference reeling off a speech from *Hellcats of the*

Pacific, stopping short, scratching his head, and asking—as Jerry Blake asks, before all hell breaks loose—"Who am I here?"

There are minor flaws in *The Stepfather*. The film has a clunky, red-herring subplot (but with a good punchline), and I wish Ruben hadn't thrown so many Hitchcock homages (heroine in shower, birds on phone wires) into the climax. The finale, although cathartic, doesn't quite transcend the stalking-killer-with-a-knife genre. Otherwise, this is a perfect little thriller. As a bonus, it offers a lovely performance by Jill Schoelen, who hugs herself like a child supplying a pair of fatherly arms; Schoelen has the gift of making her flirty self-consciousness seem the character's, not her own.

Audiences at *The Stepfather* are quiet. The movie gives them plenty of places to laugh, and they do; but most of the time, there's a chill in the air. We can joke about Ward wielding the cleaver, or a family spat becoming a family spatter. But a daddy who isn't a daddy—that's still the scariest thing in the world.

Village Voice, March 3, 1987

STRANGE INVADERS

★

Richard T. Jameson

Directed by Michael Laughlin. Written by Laughlin and William Condon. Starring Paul Le Mat, Diana Scarwid, Nancy Allen, and Louise Fletcher. **Vestron Video.**

Centerville, Illinois: A quiet little Midwest burg, of a kind always separated from the main highway by a banked railroad crossing that makes a tuning-fork sound as your car wheels roll over the rails. Diner, gas station, red-brick Protestant church, and an overgrown tourist-home rather than a hotel or motel. Narrow roads in and out, lined with great heavy-boughed trees, and cornfields stretching away under a sky that, it seems, could never be any color but that vivid yet easeful blue that marks summer's readiness to slide into autumn. Not precisely a

Norman Rockwell place, but definitely a place where the preferred item of periodical literature would be a *Saturday Evening Post* with a Norman Rockwell cover. A 1958 town intact in 1983, because 25 years ago the place was taken over by beings from outer space and, apart from displacing the original Middle American inhabitants, they haven't changed a thing.

Strange Invaders is the second film by the team of William Condon (co-writer) and Michael Laughlin (writer-director). Their first, *Strange Behavior* (unfortunately never shown here theatrically), also dealt with a small Midwest town that had come under a sinister influence, though mad-scientist rather than extraterrestrial in origin. There's something piercingly realistic yet eerily abstract about the milieux of both films, which may derive in part from the fact that their *echt*-American locations were actually found in Ontario and New Zealand, respectively. At a less subliminal level, Condon-Laughlin's movies also jolt our complacency about the familiar by filtering classical genre tales—horror in *Strange Behavior*, sci-fi in *Strange Invaders*—through a deadpan comic style.

Unimaginative reviewers have dismissed *Strange Invaders* as mere spoofery, sporadically amusing in its mild way but finally too dependent on the audience's ability to recognize the prototypes that are getting bent out of shape. Condon-Laughlin are not above in-jokery—Ken Tobey, the star of Howard Hawks' sci-fi classic *The Thing* (1951), plays one of Centerville's more prominent new residents (or "Newman," as his name would have it); a photograph of Steven Spielberg with speaker horn in front of his face turns up among some sketches of putative extraterrestrials. But for the most part the film's humor, and, well, *strange*ness spring from much subtler, and quite distinctive, sources.

The story-proper (after an elliptical pre-credit account of the take-over) begins in the present day and focuses on a thoroughly human Columbia University entomologist played by Paul Le Mat. His estranged wife (Diana Scarwid) shows up one day to deposit their daughter with him while she goes back to her "hometown," ostensibly for a funeral. Weeks pass and she doesn't call; moreover, the phone company is powerless to get through to the town ("Happens all the time"—no sweat at Ma Bell's). Le Mat drives to Centerville, finds no sign of Scarwid, has some decidedly weird experiences, and departs the scene after getting a good look at your proverbial bug-eyed monster standing alongside the road. No one is prepared to believe him, of course—not the government's ET specialist (Louise Fletcher), not the airhead (Nancy Allen) who writes the UFO pieces for a *National Enquirer*-type tabloid. The aliens, meanwhile, are also on the move: they very much want to claim Le Mat's daughter as one of their own, and they come to New York to get her. And so on.

Laughlin maintains a consistently droll tone through all of this (smiley-droll rather than hohoho), and does so on several stylistic levels. For one thing, there's the offbeat, hop-skip-and-a-jump trajectory his narrative describes. The thread of the story remains clear, but we are often surprised, and quietly discomfited, by the sense that Scene C has been inserted between Scenes A and B, or that more might have been milked — at least, more *would* have been milked, in a conventional film — from one situation before abandoning it for the next. The suggestive leaving-out of expected exposition, the oh-you-don't-really-have-to-be-shown-all-that,-do-you? directorial attitude, is something Laughlin shares with masters as exalted as Lubitsch and Ozu; and if there's scarcely evidence as yet that he belongs in their class — well, his method is still tantalizing, and a gratifying tribute to the viewer's cinematic intelligence.

What encourages the benefit of the doubt — that Laughlin is an artful, rather than simply a sloppy, storyteller — is that his spatial logic often rhymes with his narrative logic. He shoots in wide screen and delights in provocative separations and imbalances within his frame. And he throws away sinister comic details with a breeziness that verges on the insidious: When Scarwid shows up at Le Mat's apartment door with their daughter, an unidentified man wheels the child's bicycle in behind them. He's there in one shot, absent in the next and thereafter; and none of the characters sees fit to mention either his presence or his absence.

And there's that business of time-frame. *Strange Behavior* isn't so much of a spoof of '50s sci-fi formulae as it is a running commentary on styles of cultural awareness. One reviewer complained how odd it seemed that people in such a desperate hurry to make connections across a third of the continent didn't just climb on an airplane, but rather traveled by car or train. In perhaps the most sublimely daffy moment in the film, a contingent of Centerville's "strange invaders," decked out in '50s beehive hairdos and Robert Hall casualwear, debark in New York City from a charter *bus!* (Even the alien spacecraft seen at the film's beginning and end looks less like a *Close Encounters* Mothership than a fubsy cross between a zeppelin and a Greyhound.) Quite apart from being a flaw, such shenanigans strike me as essential to the movie's subversive textures: finally *Homo americanus* seems less comfortable in, and less appreciative of, the American heartland and its enchanted spaces than the imitation Americans from Planet X. It's Norman Rockwell–land that now looks like another planet to us, its horizons gently rustling with alien corn.

Seattle Weekly, November 2, 1983

OFF THE BEATEN LAUGH TRACK

T hroughout the '70s, Mel Brooks, Woody Allen, and Neil Simon dominated American movie comedy. In the '80s a new generation of comics and sketch artists came into their own, many influenced not just by Brooks and Allen but also by comedians from Mike Nichols and Elaine May to Richard Pryor. The '80s generation came to movies from stand-up acts and improvisational comedy companies such as Second City by way of late-night TV shows like "Saturday Night Live" and "SCTV." In their peak roles, such performers as Bill Murray, John Candy, Andrea Martin, and Robin Williams brought astonishing combinations of audience rapport and inventiveness to their characterizations—the best of vaudeville met the best of situation satire.

The Man with Two Brains was one of Steve Martin's most uproarious collaborations with director Carl Reiner. Rob Reiner's directorial debut, the rockumentary parody *This Is Spinal Tap*, starred a slew of inspired comics, including Harry Shearer, Christopher Guest, and Michael McKean. Albert Brooks, who received an early boost to his starring-writing-directing career when he made a series of short movies for

"Saturday Night Live," perfected his persona as the man you love to tolerate in his third film, *Lost in America*. And Robin Williams gave one of his sweetest, most rounded performances in the unheralded *The Best of Times*.

The rest of the selections in this group are more unusual. The late French-Canadian director Claude Jutra brought a sympathetic, pungent sensibility to the sex-role comedy *By Design,* in which a lesbian couple has a baby. And Jerry Lewis made a contemporary nervous-breakdown comedy, called *Cracking Up* on HBO and *Smorgasbord* in theaters. I once asked a French woman if she, like so many of her compatriots, actually liked Jerry Lewis movies. "Sometimes, when I see them for the first time, I don't think they're funny," she admitted. "But then, when I know what's coming, I just laugh and laugh." For those who don't intend to see *Smorgasbord* twice, J. Hoberman's explication provides a head start.

THE BEST OF TIMES

Michael Wilmington

Directed by Roger Spottiswoode. Written by Ron Shelton. Starring Robin Williams and Kurt Russell. **MCA Home Video.**

At the core of *The Best of Times* is a nearly irresistible premise: Suppose you could somehow wind the clock back past the moment that most embarrasses you, that worst of times when you choked, failed everybody and went down in disgrace. Could you, with added wisdom and perspective, redeem your fatal flop? Wipe it out? Or would you, as Marcel Proust suggested, prove we learn nothing from our mistakes, but that we are doomed to repeat them?

The Best of Times cannily plays it both ways: giving us a lip-smacking tale of all-American wish-fulfillment and a witty satire of its dangers. The dreamer is Jack Dundee (Robin Williams), obsessed with the time, a decade ago, when he dropped a 65-yard touchdown pass from star quarterback Reno Hightower (Kurt Russell), destroying Taft High School's chance to break an eternal losing streak against arch-rival Bakersfield. The movie follows Jack's try to exorcise his demons by fast-talking the Taft alumni into replaying the game, in the hope that fate will make sticky his fingers and fleet his feet if the long bomb comes his way again.

It's a story idea that seems dubious at first, but manages to flesh out wondrously — mostly because scenarist Ron Shelton has such a wick-edly tight grip on the absurdities and dynamics of small American cities. His Taft (the town near Bakersfield where USA for Africa's "Hands Across America" video was recently shot) is a barren, played-out-looking place, dotted with empty stores and oil wells that resemble huge, abandoned Tinker Toys . . . the dead end of the American Dream. This is a town with a cabaret where the lounge act "star" balances chairs with his teeth. In this post-McLuhan backwater, football has a ritualistic significance: The high school athletes are gladiators, carrying — for one brief shining burst — the town's honor. Their elders are has-beens (or, like Jack, a never-was) reduced to flabby spectator-ship, couch-potato junkies hooked on a weekly fix of "Monday Night Football."

The irony is that disgrace didn't ruin Jack. It may, in fact, have helped spur him on to his somewhat ridiculous success: marriage to the daughter (Holly Palance) of a Bakersfield booster-nabob (Donald Moffat) and vice presidency of the Taft branch bank. But his role is equivocal.

The town cozies up to him for loans and mortgages, but he's still "Iron Hands" Dundee, the klutz who dropped the ball, one more dorky symbol of Taft's century of futility. Jack's logic (in a way, he's right) is that, in towns like Taft, nothing really matters but The Game. It was his only real chance for heroism. Even worse, the genuine hero, Reno Hightower, was the real loser that day. His knee shattered on the play Jack blew, he's now a beer-bellied, unkempt mechanic and auto painter (he decorates vans with copies of "Starry Night" and signs them "Van Go!") whose ex–homecoming-queen wife (Pamela Reed) wants to ditch him for Los Angeles. Reno, like Jack, has a last pure shot at redemption with The Game. But, unlike Jack, he has no need. He knows he was good.

Shelton's script is so wonderful that you can forgive its excesses and flaws: the way it never quite convinces you of the budding buddyhood between Jack and Reno, the way it over-schematizes their marital wrangles. It's probably fitting that Shelton, like Kurt Russell, was once a semi-pro athlete (a baseball infielder). He has a trenchant slant. He doesn't give us that fairy-tale jock-schlock milieu Sylvester Stallone keeps sloshing around. (The *Rocky* movies are exactly what someone like Jack Dundee would dream up: Dundee, who wrote a prize-winning senior essay titled "God, My Friend.") Shelton's viewpoint is acid, but affectionate. Director Roger Spottiswoode (who made *Under Fire* with him) serves it up with nice economy, a crisp cool eye, wry speed.

Maybe the best thing about *The Best of Times* is its co-stars: Williams and Russell. The wives, Moffat, M. Emmet Walsh and the rest of the cast are good — but these two couldn't be better. As Reno, Russell really captures the essence of a small-town Golden Boy gone to seed: He not only convinces you that he once had all the moves, he makes you sorry he's lost them.

Williams, maybe the most brilliant comic actor around, makes Jack just pushy and obnoxious enough — enough of a genuine dork — to keep you off balance and guessing all the way through. Spazzy, snazzy Jack has a weird self-conscious slickness, and sometimes Williams carries him into mad inspiration: as in one fantastic bedroom strut, whirl and strip-tease pirouette for Mrs. Dundee, topped off with the clip-tongued lascivious chant: *"Got-ta, got-ta satisfy!"*

In the best of times, cinematically, *The Best of Times* would still look good. In what's closer to the worst, it looks even better. This is a movie that should make you laugh, with an ending that should moisten your eyes — if you ever played ball, or cheered for it, or sat in the bleachers on a cool fall day with the school band blasting under brown leaves, or got the tiniest twinge when you heard "Pomp and Circumstance." And, especially, if you've ever dropped a ball.

Los Angeles Times, January 30, 1986

BY DESIGN

★

Stephen Schiff

Directed by Claude Jutra. Written by Jutra, Joe Weisenfeld, and David Eames. Starring Patty Duke Astin, Sara Botsford, and Saul Rubinek. **HBO Video.**

You've probably never heard of the sunny new sex comedy *By Design*. It hasn't played in New York or Los Angeles or anywhere else in this country, because it's been sitting on a shelf since its completion more than a year ago, and its distributors don't know what to do with it. They've booked it into the Exeter Theater for a test run — and I'm afraid it'll die a quiet death there. Here, after all, is a movie whose big star is Patty Duke Astin — get your tickets early, folks — and whose title is as enticing as a dream date with Ron Hendren. Besides, the movie's Canadian — like back-bacon and certain odd forms of football — and if that weren't damnation enough, it's about lesbians. Name three successful films about lesbians. Hell, name one.

Finally, the kiss of death: *By Design* is understated. Directed and co-written by the Québecois director Claude Jutra (*Mon oncle Antoine, Kamouraska*), it has the sweet temper and wistful battiness one finds in a handful of recent comedies — all of them by French-speaking directors working in English. In movies like Jean-Claude Tramont's *All Night Long* and Louis Malle's *Atlantic City,* the French whimsy that, undiluted, can turn a movie all wet-nosed and cuddly is tempered by a raw, American flair for the outrageous. And the result is a brand of farce in which anything goes — but quietly, unemphatically, with a dash of elegance. A lot of Americans can't figure out this sort of comedy. The jokes may seem bland or obvious, because they're never shoved at you; they emerge naturally from the situations. Even the slapstick is modest: the camera doesn't linger to congratulate itself after the pratfalls. This modesty is a French style; it's part of what people found endearing in early Truffaut, whose films always seemed to be blushing at their own richest effects: the camera would cut away a beat too soon, as if refusing applause. *By Design* behaves the same way. Jutra, who worked exclusively in French from 1958 to 1975, gives the jokes and the drama exactly the same punch, and the entire film feels antic, fresh, and debonair. The characters, a pair of lesbian lovers who run a fashion-design business, never do what you expect, but everything they do fits. When they surprise you, it isn't that they've gone out of character; instead, you feel you're discovering who they are. Even when they're dastardly, they're likable; the movie's free-wheeling atmosphere forgives everything. Afterward, you may feel free-wheeling and forgiving, too. *By Design*'s way of looking at things is like a high, and you want to bask in it for hours.

The first half hour, though, is a little off-putting: the characters seem sitcomish and glib, and the sexual gags leer. They're supposed to, though — Jutra is cheerfully setting us up. *By Design* is a post-liberation sex comedy. Its characters have long since gnawed through the fetters of puritanism — in fact, they've become rather smug about their kinkiness. Helen (Astin) and her younger lover, Angie (Sara Botsford), let their fashion business insulate them from the world's calumnies. They are the compleat lesbians: cool, self-satisfied, and calmly dismissive of men. And their photographer, Terry (Saul Rubinek, from *Ticket to Heaven)*, is the compleat MCP, goosing the models in their dressing rooms and treating them like cattle during photo sessions — and then hightailing it out to the local fast-food emporium to seduce a teenybop-per or two. In quick, deft strokes, Jutra sketches a carnival of mores. A saturnine clothing tycoon named R.B. invites Helen and Angie to meet the latest pair of homosexual fashion designers to have benefited from his marketing, and we watch our heroines sniff haughtily at the way Paul and Henri design clothes — and the way men conduct a gay relationship. R.B., meanwhile, is married to a servile Japanese woman — in his bed, as in his business, he's a shogun.

Terry, meanwhile, turns out to have a sadistic streak. Jutra shows us his photo session with a beautiful 19-year-old model named Suzie (Sonia Zimmer); as she writhes under his camera, he mutters insults at her, and we can see that the anger she feels excites her — torturing Suzie, Terry is also seducing her. Which doesn't necessarily please him. Terry thinks of himself as an artist, and in a world where sex is endlessly, boringly available, his "art" sets out to de-eroticize it. His work in progress is a wall-sized matrix of photographed breasts — single breasts, not pairs: all staring out at his bed like fleshy voyeurs. "This is the essence of femininity," he tells his latest hot-to-trot conquest. "You forget about women. You forget about breasts. Rhythmic! It's a purely rhythmic pattern. Ba-boom. Ba-boom. Ba-boom ba-boom!" Then he offers the girl a robe, the way a doctor would, and tells her she'll be number 73. And 74.

In *By Design,* Jutra has set himself a formidable task: how do you make a sex comedy in the wake of the sexual revolution? Sex comedies are about people longing for forbidden fruit—Doris Day or Jayne Mansfield, Cary Grant or Marilyn Monroe. But *By Design* is set in a world where no fruit is forbidden. And Jutra's solution is ingenious; he's made a movie about forbidden procreation. Helen, you see, is intent on becoming a mother. And according to Canadian law, lesbian couples can't adopt. Since artificial insemination strikes Helen as, well, gross (a brief, hilarious scene obligingly demonstrates), that leaves only one choice: finding a man. Jutra turns the women's search for a suitable stud into feminist slapstick; Helen and Angie dress to the nines and march through the streets of Vancouver ogling men—and the men, who are less than adept at the feminine art of ignoring oglers, make idiots of themselves. When Helen and Angie bring a construction site to a dead halt, the hard hats brandish their phallic jackhammers the way Jayne Mansfield clutched twin milk bottles to her bosom in *The Girl Can't Help It;* it's a moment of giddy visual invention. In the end, though, the only acceptable stud is Terry. And Terry makes it easy. Helen is the only woman he can't have, so he's fallen madly in love with her.

What follows is the film's spectacular centerpiece, a lyrical, spinning roundelay that encompasses nearly every erotic variation imaginable, climaxing in a furiously funny orgy of homosexuality, heterosexuality, telephone sexuality, maternal sexuality, love, indifference, and rites of passage—not to mention a bizarre gambit wherein Helen and Terry achieve erotic union by panting over the same *Playboy* centerfold. This is the wildest sex scene a movie has given us in ages, but Jutra doesn't play it for guffaws—he brings out the tenderness in it. Like Bertrand Blier in *Get Out Your Handkerchiefs* and *Beau père,* Jutra wants to restore the mystery to sexuality. He wants to tell us that, as his title hints, sex makes its own rules; it never complies with our designs.

Shot by Jean Boffety, the movie is insistently bright and sparkly; its Vancouver setting is all water and sunshine and pellucid skies, woody houses with wonderful views. The yummy trendiness of it all would probably be annoying if the movie relied on its settings for texture, but it doesn't. The movie's textures are all narrative; they're in the way Jutra tells a story, chewing on it, meditating, letting us see flashes of something disturbing underneath, and then withdrawing slyly into a joke.

His is the comedy of indirection. Hints that Angie may still like men don't need amplification; they surface and disappear, and Jutra refuses to milk them. Neither does he need to stage hideous heterosexual encounters to demonstrate Helen's honest distaste for men. Instead, he brings us to a singles bar full of noise, steam, and throbbing red light and then whisks us to a lesbian night spot, where the light is cool and the music is in a sexy, jazzy style that accommodates any sort of dance. Here Helen and Angie sway together, and we can see how their love works: their gestures agree, and their gazes rhyme. And the difference in their bodies — Angie is nearly a foot taller than Helen — may take you by surprise. It's sexual.

In fact, Patty Duke Astin and Sara Botsford have a startling erotic chemistry together; they're a real movie couple. Jutra is so sure of this that he stylizes their relationship, builds tableaux around it, turns it into music. Sometimes he even has them speak a comic jazz poetry set to walking bass lines by Chico Hamilton (whose score is marvelous, except for the unspeakable song that plays under the opening credits); it's reminiscent of Ken Nordine's Word Jazz, only it's sharper and funnier. Jutra has been an actor (he's played in his own films, including *Mon oncle Antoine* and *A tout prendre*), and he knows how to squeeze juice from a stubborn performance. And stubborn is exactly what Patty Duke Astin is (some of the other actors aren't stubborn; they're plain awful). Astin looks blotchy and tired, and her TV work has harmed her: she mugs now and goes for cheap reactions. But Sara Botsford tones her down. A rangy, angular-looking, redheaded actress who's worked for years on the Canadian stage, Botsford gives the film its calm, knowing center. She steadies Astin and makes their performances chime. And she has her own thrumming, low-pitched sensuality.

By the way the script bucks and jolts, you can tell it's been through a lot of revisions (occasionally, you catch whiffs of something truly unsavory), and the leading roles were probably intended for women much more beautiful than Astin and Botsford. But then the movie is peculiarly cast throughout. Saul Rubinek isn't nearly attractive enough to play Terry, but he's a terrific actor: he knows how to make sarcasm generous and sadness jaunty, and his face is clownishly expressive in a way that can remind one of Chaplin. The eyes plead, but above them the eyebrows are excitable, throwing off punctuation — they're parentheses, question marks, exclamation points. And a performance like his can make up for a lot. *By Design* doesn't have the beautiful-people chic we're used to in Hollywood movies (Canadian movies really do feel

Canadian); it's a bit messy. There are flat jokes and choppy scenes and (as the film's only Canadian champion, the critic Martin Knelman, has noted) the fashions are atrocious. It's not going to be a hit, I'm afraid; it won't even be the hot topic at next week's cocktail parties. But it has its own freshness and its own triumphant, low-rent style. And when you see it, you may find yourself feeling something close to gratitude.

Boston Phoenix, October 19, 1982

LOST IN AMERICA

★

Dave Kehr

Directed by Albert Brooks. Written by Brooks and Monica Johnson. Starring Brooks, Julie Hagerty, Michael Greene, Tom Tarpey, and Garry Marshall. **Warner Home Video.**

On the short list of today's formally inventive American filmmakers, Albert Brooks belongs right at the top. There really isn't anyone else in the Hollywood end of the art who's conducting the same kinds of experiments with visual presentation and narrative structure, who's analyzing the received formulas with so much acuity and intelligence, and who's set for himself the goal of creating a genuinely new kind of comic rhetoric. Indeed, if Brooks could arrange to have *Lost in America* dubbed into German it would fit effortlessly into a retrospective of the most formally aggressive works of Jean-Marie Straub and Danielle Huillet — it's that radical. Watching *Lost in America,* I was reminded more than once of Straub-Huillet's last feature, an adaptation of Kafka's *Amerika* retitled *Class Relations* (because of a quarrel over the rights, the film hasn't yet been released in the U.S.). Not only is there a kinship of title and subject (both films are about uprooted naifs, trying to make their way across an alien landscape), but also a striking similarity in the design of the brutally stripped-down images and a shared taste for impossibly protracted long takes. It isn't likely that Brooks has ever seen a Straub-Huillet film — or an Akerman, a Bresson, or a Godard. Yet, working on his own (and from a very different set of premises), Brooks has arrived at much the same point they have: he's one of the leading modernist filmmakers.

Because Brooks is a comedian — and a very funny one — he'll never have the same kind of cultural cachet as the unmistakably "serious" Straub and Huillet. He belongs to another, almost antiart tradition, that of the comic filmmaker who, in pursuit of his particular vision, gradually leaves his audience behind as his obsessive explorations take him into ever more dangerous territory. The movies seem to produce one obsessive comic genius every 20 or 30 years: Buster Keaton in the '20s, Frank Tashlin in the '50s, Jacques Tati in the '60s. In the '80s, Brooks is well on his way to becoming the kind of vitally marginal figure that they were in their times: he doesn't draw the crowds or acclaim of a Woody Allen (just as Keaton was always overshadowed by Chaplin), yet, because he hasn't been crowned the official comic spokesman for his generation, he's free to explore darker, more personal themes in more formally sophisticated ways. Keaton needed Chaplin, just as Brooks needs Allen: the consensus comic draws off the audience's need for identification and reassurance, leaving the marginal comic free to follow his own lights.

The paradox is that Brooks has identified himself with his intended audience more closely than any other comic in the medium's history. The great comedians of the past have all been eccentrics, in one way or another; Brooks, on the other hand, strives for a perfect normalcy, a seamless unexceptionalness, tracking the progress of the baby-boom audience and presenting himself, with each succeeding film, as their exact statistical image at each film's point in time. In *Real Life* (1979), he was a young idealist, committed to improving the world through his creative efforts. In *Modern Romance* (1981), he was a big city single, feeling the approach of the marriage deadline but unable to make the final commitment that would propel him into the world of his parents. In *Lost in America* he is, of course, a yuppie: a successful creative director with a large advertising agency confidently looking forward to a fat promotion and a new Mercedes. His wife, Julie Hagerty, is a personnel director for a major department store; by pooling their resources, they've managed to buy a $450,000 Los Angeles home. As the movie opens, they're ready for the move: under the opening credits, the camera snakes around the midnight house, inspecting the mountains of packing boxes waiting for the moving men. But a light is burning in the bedroom: haunted by some vague dread, Albert can't sleep.

David (Albert Brooks), a Los Angeles advertising executive, and Linda (Julie Hagerty), a department store personnel director, fret about purchasing a $450,000 house at the start of Brooks's satirical yuppie comedy, *Lost in America*. (Photo © 1985 The Geffen Film Company. All rights reserved.)

Brooks's comic persona is brazenly average. Unlike other comics, he doesn't present himself as especially witty, charming, or graceful; with the way he exposes his cowardice, anxiety, and insensitivity, he shouldn't even be very likable. (And he's a big guy, too, with the bulk and square jaw of a football player—nothing could be further removed from the sympathetic frailty of the Chaplin-Allen "little fellow.") His line delivery is so dryly uninflected, so free of the comic's "punchy" rhythms, that when he makes one of his potboiling appearances in a more traditional comedy (in something like Howard Zieff's *Unfaithfully Yours*, for example) he's almost invisible—he doesn't seem to be doing anything at all when he's placed alongside a laugh-beggar like Dudley Moore. Brooks's overwhelming averageness means that we identify with him easily, yet at the same time his averageness pushes us away— he's too much like what we fear ourselves to be. Helped along by Brooks's distinctive editing patterns (he resists both close-ups and cross-cutting, the two time-honored ways of binding up an identification between character and spectator), it is this strange rhythm of identification and alienation, of attraction and repulsion, that defines the peculiar transaction between spectator and screen at an Albert Brooks movie. We find ourselves sympathizing with Brooks's all-too-recognizable (and always realistically rendered) anxieties and frustrations, yet at the same time the coolness and the distance of the visual style is forcing us back, to a point of view outside the situation. There is a constant circulation between identification and alienation, between subjectivity and objectivity, and it is in this circulation, this instability, that Brooks's humor is born. To suddenly see objectively what we have been experiencing subjectively is to open a gap between two equally valid but hopelessly incompatible worlds: what seems of immense importance in one sphere seems vain and trivial in the other; courage becomes foolhardiness, idealism becomes self-deception. The gap is huge, absurd, and Brooks's comedy leaps from it.

Like Keaton, Brooks is fundamentally a realist, a filmmaker with a profound respect for the physical world. It's an aesthetic that shouldn't be confused with naturalism, that timid concern for plausibility, continuity, and motivation: an important part of respecting the real world is knowing that it isn't always believable, or even comprehensible. The plot line of *Lost in America* is propelled by unlikelihoods. The expected promotion turns out to be a cross-country transfer to a more subservient position, and Albert angrily quits. (The scene in the boss's office, with Brooks's manic shifts from smiling servility to eye-popping outrage and back again, contains some of the most impressive acting I've seen this year.) Albert decides to take advantage of the situation by cashing in the family savings (some $200,000) and, inspired by *Easy Rider,* setting out on a journey across America to "find himself." ("We have to touch Indians," he tells Hagerty, shortly before hitting the highway in his shiny new Winnebago motor home as the chords of Steppenwolf's "Born to Be Wild" thunder on the sound track.) The couple makes it as far as Las Vegas, where Hagerty, finally self-destructing after years of enforced conformity, blows their entire nest egg on an all-night roulette game.

The loss of the money arrives like an A-bomb from a clear blue sky, and it's particularly astonishing because, in both of Brooks's other films, women have provided the one element of stability and rationality in Albert's up-and-down existence. The stroke is wholly arbitrary, yet Brooks is careful to follow its ramifications down to the tiniest emotional detail, a process that turns a screenwriter's trick into something horribly, inescapably real. Brooks does not broaden or falsify his characters' feelings: Albert must move through a complexly rendered chain of shock, anger, resentment, and resignation before he can forgive his wife, and Hagerty must cross a similarly authentic terrain before she can forgive her husband for his lack of understanding and compassion. Brooks is able to portray psychological nuances that go well beyond the range of most contemporary Hollywood dramas; his accuracy of observation seems all the more striking in a comedy, where depth of characterization has long been rendered out of place.

Brooks renders his characters' feelings with a remarkable clarity and precision: every fleeting emotion is cleanly presented and immediately legible. This same clarity of regard extends to his rendering of people, objects, and landscapes: Brooks purges every trace of aestheticism or editorial comment from his frames, leaving the object to stand on its own, as something sharp, hard, and absolutely immediate. (In this, he goes straight against the grain of such fashionable filmmakers as De Palma and Coppola, who clot their images with so many overtones that the objects lose all their integrity, turning into wispy metaphors.) Brooks's long takes reinforce this feeling of solidity: by resisting the temptation to cut (to enforce a rhythm, to punch up a joke, or simply to vary the visual field), Brooks gives his actors and settings the time they need to exist on the screen, to occupy a place in the film with a weight that goes beyond the immediate demands of the screenplay.

It is this extra sense of weight, of solidity, that makes Brooks a modernist filmmaker. He doesn't simply think up gags, and then run out and trick up a setting that can contain them. The humor emerges from the setting, from the physicality of the place and the actors who inhabit it. This is the same shift in emphasis that Rossellini made when he invented the modern cinema with *Voyage to Italy:* the filmmaker no longer seeks to stage a pre-scripted "truth," but to find the truth of the situation as it emerges from the interaction of these particular performers in this particular space. For Rossellini, it was above all an aesthetic of drama; in adapting it to comedy, Brooks alters the ends but not the means. He lets reality determine the humor, and in the process, reality becomes the joke. When Albert and his wife have their first violent fight as they pause for a look at Hoover Dam, the joke isn't in the dialogue (which is quite realistic), but in the juxtaposition of the dialogue and the place. The domestic squabble is played against the immensity, the overwhelming physicality, of the dam: the sheer size and scope of the spectacle make their argument seem absurd; at the same time, the importance of the argument to the characters makes the dam itself seem like a ridiculous intrusion. The wild leaps in scale, the preposterous disproportionateness of the two different frames of reference (physical and emotional) that Brooks offers simultaneously, are what make the scene hilariously funny; in any other setting, or filmed in a way that gave the dam less of an immediate presence, the scene would be merely pathetic or banal.

Brooks doesn't need the spectacle of the Hoover Dam to produce this effect: it goes the same with the small desert town where he and Hagerty try to set up house after they've lost their money, and it goes the same with the minor characters Brooks comes in contact with—his treacherous boss, a sympathetic casino manager, an unemployment counselor. Brooks doesn't treat these minor characters as straight men he can bounce jokes off of: no matter how little time they have on the screen, he allows them to establish complete personalities and presences of their own—you feel they'll still be there after the movie crew moves away. It's easy for a filmmaker to mock supporting characters of this kind (particularly if they're small-town or suburban types, as many of the characters in Brooks's film are), and Brooks himself wasn't above taking this kind of cheap shot in his first feature, *Real Life*. But in *Lost in America,* the minor figures are presented without a trace of caricature— they're just as smart and assured as the stars, more so in some cases— and the humor produced by Brooks's uncondescending attitude is at once more mature and more complex. They are authentic enough to impose their own point of view, their own reality, on the action, and again the humor comes from the gap the competing realities produce.

Brooks's comedy is above all a comedy of disappointment. His characters set out in a haze of lofty ideals (a belief in the drama of day-to-day existence in *Real Life,* a quest for an all-consuming, romantic love in *Modern Romance,* a search for authentic, grass-roots experience in *Lost in America*), yet always find themselves bumping up against the same old banality and boredom, the inescapable unsatisfactoriness of the real, stubbornly untranscendent world. Because most of those ideals are movie-induced (the filmmaker-hero of *Real Life* was inspired by *An American Family;* in *Lost in America,* Albert wants to turn his life into a road movie), it is necessary to invent a different kind of movie in order to strike them down. Which is exactly what Albert Brooks has done: the formal system he has found for his films is, almost literally, a system of disillusionment—a way of stripping the cinematic image of its gauziness and dreaminess, of tearing aside the layers of abstraction and self-containment it has acquired over the years, and returning to the material world, to the thing itself in all its lumpy prosaicness. For many filmmakers, this return would be a tragic one; that Brooks finds in it a source of humor and optimism (the hero of *Real Life* goes mad at the end, but Brooks's characters in *Modern Romance* and *Lost in America* are allowed to begin again, with healthily diminished expectations) is the mark of an honest, thoughtful, and unsentimental personality — of a truly modern comedian.

Chicago Reader, March 15, 1985

THE MAN WITH TWO BRAINS
★

Richard Schickel

Directed by Carl Reiner. Written by Reiner, Steve Martin, and George Gipe. Starring Martin and Kathleen Turner. **Warner Home Video.**

How sweet it is to find a movie in which the hero, having lusted after purely carnal pleasures for much of its length, finally falls in love with a woman's mind. That there is no body attached to it, that it is, in fact, a brain kept alive in a bottle by a half-mad scientist, might strike some people as a little funny. It will strike vaster numbers of them as very funny — especially after Steve Martin pastes plastic lips on the bottle so he can kiss his beloved.

Dr. Michael Hfuhruhurr (for a sample of this movie's longest-running gag, try pronouncing that name aloud) has been under a strain. A desperately randy brain surgeon ("I had the top of her head off, but that's as far as it went"), he marries one of his patients, only to discover that Dolores (well played by Kathleen Turner) is not as nice as she looks. After six weeks, she still refuses to consummate their union, although when someone has just undergone Hfuhruhurr's specialty, the cranial screw-top procedure, one tends to believe her when she

Steve Martin plays a premier brain surgeon who loves his work in *The Man with Two Brains*. (Photo © 1983 Warner Bros. Inc. All rights reserved.)

claims to have a headache. Still, that's the least of her meanness, and one is sympathetic, even relieved, when Martin makes a citizen's divorce (it consists of making an announcement and taking a hike) in order to sin in his mind, as it were.

This is the most assured and hilarious of the three Martin–Carl Reiner collaborations. There is something classically American about its monomaniacal pursuit of a gag every five seconds, characterization and redeeming social value be damned. The movie is rather like a

Henny Youngman monologue combined with a *National Lampoon* spread. And it offers reassuring proof that the spirit of arrested adolescence lives on, at least for one more summer.

Time, June 20, 1983

SMORGASBORD

★

J. Hoberman

Directed by Jerry Lewis. Written by Lewis and Bill Richmond. Starring Jerry Lewis. Warner Home Video.

Jerry Lewis doesn't just want to make you laugh, he wants you to think he's the greatest human being who ever lived, and "the total filmmaker" besides. If there's a needier, more tormentedly ambitious oddball in American pop culture, I'm not sure I want to know about him. Lewis may not have been the most demonic exponent of Borscht Belt hysteria ever to come tummling down Route 17 (cognoscenti claim the young Buddy Hackett), but he's the only one to entertain delusions of Chaplinesque grandeur.

As a filmmaker, Lewis's vulgar modernism garnered him even less respect than his vulgar clowning — his championing by Parisian intellectuals is regarded here as a national joke, the ultimate proof of French perversity. But there's more than one path to greatness, and pushing pathos past the breaking point, Lewis made himself the maestro of coercive sentimentality. Manic outbursts and all, the psychodrama of his annual telethon is a national ritual. Still, you can't guilt-trip patrons into the theaters — which is why Lewis's 1983 *Smorgasbord,* shown on HBO as *Cracking Up,* is having its theatrical premiere this weekend at the Thalia.

True to form, Lewis plays Warren Nefron, a nerd so neurotic and klutzy he requires a brand new Yiddish epithet to characterize his utter haplessness. Nefron isn't even permitted to end his own misery. In the first of several comically failed suicide attempts, he hangs himself and pulls down the ceiling. (As the credits have it: "Jerry Lewis — who else? —

is . . . CRACKING UP.") Actually, the weak ceiling is not an inept metaphor for the entire film. Employing the episodic gag structure he developed in 1960 for *The Bell Boy* (still his funniest, most likable movie), *Smorgasbord* soon collapses into as disconnectedly opportunistic a succession of vignettes as might ever cavort through the brain of Rupert Pupkin. Flashbacks to Nefron's 15th-century French ancestor give Jerry a chance to revel in pseudo-French babbling with occasional interpolations of mock Japanese. Other gags showcase the blowsy Vegas celebs — Milton Berle, Sammy Davis, Buddy Lester — whose presence Lewis considers axiomatic to movies and telethons alike.

More conceptual than funny, exhibiting Lewis's typically adroit use of off-screen sound, *Smorgasbord* has the ascetic, abstract quality one associates with auteurs in the moody twilight of their obsessions. Throughout the film, Lewis-as-Nefron keeps observing Lewis-as-other (a moronic bank robber who mugs for the surveillance camera, a cretinous guru down from the Himalayas, an idiotic state trooper who inadvertently blows up his car) as though looking for some misplaced part of his personality. In the end, he's cured by a hypnotic suggestion (his cue being the film's title) which turns him into a creature we might call Jer — Lewis's idea of himself as a happy, friendly, and normal guy. The cure is signified by Nefron's newfound ability to pick up some doll on Sunset Boulevard and take her to see *Smorgasbord*.

As this suggests, art is scarcely remote in Lewis's world. When fired upon, TV sets shoot back; when Nefron visits a museum, the art works attack him, pissing on his leg, even escaping from their frames. It may seem primitive compared to Woody Allen's *Purple Rose of Cairo,* but that's the point. You'll never find a moronically grinning Woody wearing flippers to keep him from slipping on a treacherously polished floor, then sticking two cigarettes in his nose and barking like a walrus in triumph merely because he's succeeded in traversing the room without falling on his face. Either you find Lewis's manic outbursts funny or you don't. I do.

Here, Lewis's best slapstick sequences exhibit a powerfully dreamlike helplessness. Given Nefron's death wish (underscored by a running cigarette gag), *Smorgasbord* is at least as dark and a lot funnier than *Hardly Working,* Lewis's 1979 unemployment comedy and only domestic hit since the '60s. In France, where it was released two years ago under the endearingly familiar title *T'es fou Jerry!*, the film's "tonic pessimism" was compared to Swift and De Quincey (Gérard Legrand, *Positif*). This may be excessive — but it's not, if one takes Lewis seriously, irrational. Lewis is the clown prince of arrested development. He sees infantilism as the human condition; as Serge Daney points out in a *Cahiers* review dourly named for a film by Jean-Marie Straub (*"Smorgasbord de Jerry Lewis: Non Reconciliés"*), Lewis is unlike Woody Allen in that he treats even psychoanalysis with total disrespect. "The shrink, for him, is something out of a Punch and Judy show."

Beneath Lewis's unctuous sentimentality (pace Sir Richard Attenborough, he's the most bombastic do-gooder in show biz), there's the terrifying nihilism of the guy who'll do anything for a laugh. Lewis knows this, and as a personality, his fascination — indeed, universality — comes from the grotesque, Elie Wiesel moral heaviness he uses to control those crazy impulses (as twisted as muscular dystrophy), which nevertheless persist. Perhaps someday we'll see *The Day the Clown Cried*, which Lewis made in 1971 and never released. The film is set in a Nazi concentration camp; Jer plays the clown who entertains children on their way to the gas chambers. The idea is so horrifying it might almost make Ronald Reagan (whose perception of his own job really isn't so different) stop and think.

Village Voice, May 21, 1985

THIS IS SPINAL TAP

★

Sheila Benson

Directed by Rob Reiner. Written by Reiner, Christopher Guest, Michael McKean, and Harry Shearer. Starring Reiner, McKean, Guest, and Shearer. **Embassy Home Entertainment/Nelson Entertainment.**

A fan calls Spinal Tap "the world's loudest and stupidest heavy-metal band." These four dim Brits who have played together 17 years, possibly 16 years too many, are also, hands down, music's most hilarious group. But don't rush off pell-mell to find their next concert: Spinal Tap exists only in the febrile brains of its creators, four inspired satiric actor/

writer/musicians. All we have is *This Is Spinal Tap,* a pseudodocumentary of their last, disaster-riddled American tour.

Our intimate backstage and onstage glimpses of this mythical group is a work of love for movie director Marty DiBergi (Rob Reiner, the film's co-writer and actual director), something of a dim bulb himself. To document his idols' first American tour in 6 years, DiBergi has passed up the chance to direct *Attack of the Full-Figured Gals* — as well as *On Golden Pond 3-D.* But he's prepared. He has his safari jacket and obligatory baseball cap (this one says *USS Coral Sea,* actually) and his crew is ready to record every intimate conversation or incipient breakdown. The twin worlds of documentary moviemaking and rock music will never be the same.

Trouble begins over "Smell the Glove," the album Spinal Tap has come to promote. The cover sexist!? That beautiful girl, sublimely naked on her hands and knees, a dog collar around her neck, sniffing an extended glove, *sexist!?* Their minds reel. And if you ever wanted to see reeling minds, try those of the Tap's lead guitarists and brothers-in-art, Nigel Tufnel (Christopher Guest) and David St. Hubbins (Michael McKean), the pride of London's Squatney district.

Next is their whirlwind tour, a juggernaut on three wheels. Ordered to bypass Boston, they accept the bland explanation that Boston "isn't a college town." In Cleveland they never make their way out of the bowels of the auditorium to reach the stage. It's in Memphis, as cancelled bookings force them to sing *a capella* at Elvis Presley's gravesite, that their collective brows begin to furrow.

This Is Spinal Tap is the blissful wonder that it is because it is smart as well as affectionate. Every detail is a zinger, from Bobbi Flekman, the head public relations woman for Polymer Records, to Spinal Tap's totally awesome production numbers, featuring a smoke-breathing Satan's head which occasionally even works, and musician-eating plastic clamshells which *never* do.

The film's four inventors and principal performers, Reiner, Guest, McKean and Harry Shearer, have created parody as perfect as the great mock newspaper issue, *Not the New York Times.* (Its co-author, not incidentally, is part of the large and accomplished cast. Tony Hendra plays Spinal Tap's beleaguered road manager, Ian Faith.) And they work with a rapier, not an entrenching tool.

Los Angeles Times, March 8, 1984

THEY SHOOT WESTERNS, DON'T THEY?

What new wine could be poured into the bottle of the western?" Pauline Kael asked in 1970. ". . . The myths of the Old West, with the heroic figures of authority and the coming of law and order, no longer touch off the right reverberations in an audience."

Talented directors, many of whom first fell in love with movies because of westerns, kept looking for that new wine. After Sam Peckinpah, in Kael's words, "exploded the bottle" in his 1969 hit *The Wild Bunch,* he continued to ferment his own blend of lyricism, cynicism, and idealism among the shards. Next he made the piercingly sweet *The Ballad of Cable Hogue,* in which Cable, cutting against the spirit of the counterculture, first reaches fulfillment when he raises the American flag over his waterhole. In *Cattle Annie and Little Britches,* Lamont Johnson celebrated two spunky females who serve as mascots and inspirations for an aging outlaw gang—roles that westerns usually reserved for young men. In *Barbarosa,* Fred Schepisi trained an anthropological eye on a Tex-Mex outlaw legend and came up with a movie that isn't only mythic, it's also about the creation of myth. And in

Burt Lancaster is Bill Doolin, the aging leader of the Doolin-Dalton gang, whose scruffy outlaw bunch gets recharged by the title characters in *Cattle Annie and Little Britches*. (Photo by, and courtesy of, Chris Johnson.)

Buffalo Bill and the Indians, a wormwood companion piece to *Annie Get Your Gun,* Robert Altman simultaneously revived and debunked the Wild West spectacle by depicting it as the root of all show biz.

But the studios didn't know how to label and market these directors' new wine — as Peter Rainer's case study of *Cattle Annie and Little Britches* illustrates.

THE BALLAD OF CABLE HOGUE

Richard Schickel

Directed by Sam Peckinpah. Written by John Crawford and
Edmund Penney. Starring Jason Robards, Stella Stevens,
and David Warner. **Warner Home Video.**

One great subject obsesses director Sam Peckinpah. It is the closing of
the American frontier around the turn of the century. He has made
other films about the West, but his best work is that in which he gives
free rein to his complex feelings about this historical event. Mostly he
seems to believe that we took more of our sense of identity, as individuals and as a nation, from the frontier than we realize (or perhaps are
willing to admit), and that we have been lost and drifting ever since it
ceased to offer us the potential of personal freedom radically and often
violently defined.

In *Ride the High Country,* almost a decade ago, he gave his most
balanced, most carefully controlled statement on this subject in a film
of surpassing beauty and subtlety, a film which, incidentally, gave
Randolph Scott and Joel McCrea the roles of their lives to close out
their careers as western heroes. Last year, in *The Wild Bunch,* which I
think was probably the best American film of the year, he presented a
more violent version of his vision, here and there flawed, but at the very
least a masterpiece of the action director's craft. Now, in *The Ballad of
Cable Hogue,* he takes up his great theme in a new mood — comic,
elegiac, leisurely and peaceable. I think it is less than his best work — but
a great deal better than about 90 percent of the stuff to which we are
ordinarily subjected at the movies.

Rambling and episodic in development, the film really does have the
improvisatory, folkish, legendary quality of a ballad (though the temptation to present such a piece as musical accompaniment to the picture is,
thank God, resisted). It recounts in deliberately simplified — almost
childlike — terms the title character's abandonment in the desert (without food, water or weapons) by his prospecting companions; his
discovery, when he is nearly dead of thirst, of a spring that both saves
and changes his life. For it is located on a state line and is the only water

Jason Robards plays the desert rat who finds "water where it wasn't" in Sam Peckinpah's lyrical fable *The Ballad of Cable Hogue*. (Photo © 1970 Phil Feldman Productions, Inc., and Warner Bros. Inc. All rights reserved.)

for a very long way. There he opens a modest hostelry and there, after years of profitless wandering in the wilderness, he prospers.

Much besides material prosperity comes to him as he waits by the side of the road — a fraudulent preacher (David Warner) whose relationship to the film's main line is ambiguous, but who is at least an interesting character; a good-hearted prostitute (Stella Stevens) with whom he shares a lovely idyll that seems to make the desert bloom; a chance at last to revenge himself on the men who left him to die out there in the first place. His final visitor, however, is the modern world, automobiles jouncing along the stage track, and with it comes death, as it always does in a Peckinpah movie. But the manner of its arrival — casual, humorous, surprising — and the manner of its greeting — graceful and even charming — is done with a sense of beauty and irony that was, for me, overwhelming.

I don't want to discuss in detail the last sequence of the film, since so much of its effectiveness depends on your being unprepared for it. This much, however, should be said — that it is so good and right that it entirely disarms the vagrant critical thoughts that had been gathering before its arrival. For one must admit that the humor implicit in some of the earlier scenes is not fully realized on screen and that some of that which is realized is disappointingly familiar, with archetypes too often dwindling into clichés. More than once Peckinpah and his film are saved simply by the fact that Jason Robards is present in the title role. His Cable Hogue, a man who talks frankly and openly to God, a man of sentiment, rough-hewn common sense and primitive capitalist shrewdness, is a wonderful character — a walking summary of the pioneer virtues as Peckinpah sees them. It is, in short, a dream role — the best Robards has ever had in the movies, and he is more than up to its demands; indeed, one suspects he was born to fulfill them. A lesser actor might have stomped and shouted his way through it, but he manages to shade the role with marvelous delicacy, in the process providing Peckinpah with the rock-solid foundation for a movie that is dangerously careless in some aspects of its carpentry, creaking and swaying as it shifts under the pressures he applies to it. Even so, it is a curiously compelling film. Like a child's playhouse, we come to love it not for its perfect symmetry but for the open way it expresses the feelings of its creator.

Life, March 27, 1970

BARBAROSA

Terrence Rafferty

Directed by Fred Schepisi. Written by William D. Witliff.
Starring Willie Nelson, Gary Busey, and Gilbert Roland.
Nova Home Video (Canada).

Fred Schepisi's *Barbarosa* looks like a Western, but at heart it's a ghost story. It opens with a magnificent desert landscape, a composition of rocks, mesas, sky, and open land that looks hard-edged and immutable — and then it begins to change. The light keeps shifting — the background darkens, then the foreground, the middle ground lights up like a radiant stripe across the screen, then it's all reversed, and a shadow seems to darken boulders one at a time, in abrupt, unpredictable jumps — changing in ways we can't quite follow, or fix into a pattern. This mysterious landscape is seen several times more in the course of the film, and the narrative never places the characters in it. But in *Barbarosa* the western landscape is a haunted house: we know the mythic characters are there, whether we see them or not. There's a moment early in the film when Barbarosa seems to pop up out of nowhere, as if he's ridden up out of the ground; and there's a moment later on when he seems to disappear into thin air as he's running through a forest. *Barbarosa* is full of wandering, of sudden departures and unexpected returns, movements that seem as capricious as the light on the desert — but all within a fixed frame, a sharply limited physical and psychological geography; the film is all repetitions, variations, echoes.

The fixed frame here is a story of exile, a story whose details emerge gradually, one small bit at a time. Barbarosa (Willie Nelson) has been a fugitive from his own family for thirty years, driven from the Zavala home on his wedding night by his father-in-law, Don Braulio (Gilbert Roland). He's condemned to circle around his own wife and daughter, darting through Braulio's defenses for two furtive visits a year, spending the rest of his time eluding and, reluctantly, killing the young Zavala men who are sent out to kill him. Karl (Gary Busey), the farm boy whom Barbarosa picks up along the way, is on the run from his in-laws, too: he killed his sister's husband in a fight. Karl, clearly, is an image of the young Barbarosa — he sees his future in the old outlaw, and Barbarosa sees his past in him. They tell their stories to each other as they ride through the ghostly landscapes, and as they sit by the fire at the camps they make in ruined adobe shells of abandoned homes.

Karl's story is a simple one, but Barbarosa's is complex, full of history — a story that's lost its innocence. When Braulio tells it to a room full of Zavala boys — boys whom he will some day send out, one by one, in search of Barbarosa — the legend comes out in one smooth piece, polished by years of telling and retelling, too perfect for us to trust it very much. And the children seem to know their responses by heart, like a litany: Braulio may tell them this story every night, sitting in his windowless, cavelike room spinning the image of a mythic Barbarosa out of thin air. But on the night we hear the story, the living Barbarosa is elsewhere in the house, visiting his wife, and Karl, his eventual successor, is watching and listening at Braulio's door.

This may be *Barbarosa*'s strangest scene: it's an important bit of exposition, but it comes halfway through the movie and its staging is stylized almost to the point of parody (the flickering light and cavernous decor; the hushed, automaton-like responses of the children; the squawking raven at Braulio's side). But it's a crucial scene, a graphic illustration of how superfluous the real Barbarosa has become. He's in the house, within Braulio's reach, but the old Don is unaware of his presence, totally possessed by the mythical Barbarosa that he's created. Barbarosa isn't onscreen at all while Braulio tells his story, yet he's present, defined completely by the elements of his myth: Braulio, its author; the Zavala boys, its audience; and Karl, its future incarnation. As the scene goes on, the bizarre ghost-story atmosphere seems more and more appropriate. The living man who's known as "Barbarosa" (we never do learn his real name) doesn't exist here, doesn't need to — he's been disembodied.

Barbarosa isn't the first of Schepisi's heroes to suffer this fate. The seminary teachers in his first film, *The Devil's Playground,* have spent their lives trying to forget their bodies — to "transcend" them — and some of them, a little horrified, realize that they've succeeded. Their aim is to become pure spirit, and that's what they're teaching their students, too: one seminarian boasts of being so alienated from his body that he no longer feels discomfort or pain, and in his attempt to prove it by swimming in a freezing creek, he dies — the ultimate transcendence. What's moving about *The Devil's Playground* is that its characters *know,* or are in the process of finding out, that their goal is a kind of death—a denial of their sexual urges makes them feel a little unreal to themselves, almost spectral.

The hero of *The Chant of Jimmie Blacksmith* feels unreal, too. As an aborigine in a white society, he's invisible to his masters. When, in frustration, he murders the white family that he can't be a part of, he *makes* himself visible, forces the society to acknowledge his existence. But his social existence is still just an image in the minds of his oppressors: he's now a legend, a symbol—the murderous, ungrateful black. And, of course, he's forfeited everything with his crime; from the moment he commits his first murder, he's a dead man. All of Schepisi's films are ghost stories: they're about people who exist for others only as spirits, myths, abstractions, people who have died to the world in advance of their physical deaths—and who continue to live in some strange, painful middle ground, homeless, neither here nor there.

Barbarosa, though, doesn't have the grim intensity of the earlier films. Barbarosa's the oldest of Schepisi's protagonists, the one who's lived with his situation the longest, and he's gone past anguish to a kind of resignation: even when night puts him in a melancholy, reflective mood, his words of wisdom are, "What can't be remedied must be endured." What Barbarosa has to endure is the living-out of the legend created by Braulio's obsession, a myth that he knows can't be changed or destroyed but only manipulated a bit, played with. The pain is there, but after thirty years Barbarosa isn't a tormented or an angry spirit— he's rather a wistful, prankish one. The tragic force of the earlier films is present only in Karl's story: he's younger, his wounds are fresher, and he's not at all used to being the object of another man's obsessive vengeance. When he arrives back home after months of wandering with Barbarosa and is forced to kill Herman Pahmeyer (the vengeful father of the man he killed), his violence isn't cathartic: Karl doesn't *want* to kill Pahmeyer, and the act doesn't change anything, anyway—Karl's father is already dead, and he loses his only sister not long after. Karl feels no triumph, and we share his feeling of emptiness. It's the way Barbarosa must have felt after killing his first Zavala: Karl shouts "No!" before shooting Pahmeyer—just as we've heard Barbarosa do before killing one of his would-be assassins. This is Schepisi's characteristic method, building his film with a gradual accumulation of details, repetitions, allusions, toward a climax which illuminates the film's concerns without fully resolving them.

Those details and allusions are more densely layered in *Barbarosa* than ever before—so densely, in fact, that it's just about impossible to sort out all the repetitions and variations in the film's visual and narrative motifs. They just merge into a single, omnipresent entity, a kind of persistent echo like the swelling chants of "Barbarosa" that occur at several points in the course of the film. The allusions are hypnotic, like a rhyme scheme, and they all have to do with death (a cantina that looks like a burial mound; Barbarosa rising from his grave as Karl is burying him; Barbarosa cauterizing a wound, smoke rising from his body as he applies the burning stick, a shot later recalled by an aerial view of his cremation) or with the gradual convergence of Karl's identity and Barbarosa's (the marks on the cheek that each receives in his first scene — Karl's from a thorn, Barbarosa's from a Zavala bullet; Karl's early chance encounter with Eduardo, ultimately Barbarosa's killer; the shouts of "No!" before killing). The first time Barbarosa and Karl appear in the same frame, they're bending over a dead Zavala.

The extraordinarily dense texture produces interesting effects, unexpected ones. One thing it *doesn't* produce is a symbolic structure: the repetitions and variations don't "work out" to a coherent statement about myth, or identity, or anything else. Schepisi and his screenwriter, William Witliff (who also wrote *Raggedy Man*), aren't even very interested in exploring the truth or falsity of the myth: Barbarosa's isn't a heroic myth, one that the man himself must be measured against and found worthy or unworthy; and by the end of the film we *still* don't have a full reliable account of the incident that caused the rift between Braulio and Barbarosa, the origin of the legend. Schepisi's real subject is less abstract, but more elusive, more mysterious. *Barbarosa* is about how it feels to live inside a myth, to be a character in someone else's story — how it *feels* to be turned into a ghost. The myth is always there, but only as the landscape the characters ride through, the fixed frame, the house they haunt. And the repetition of motifs is what creates this effect of enclosure: the narrative moves easily, loosely, from one incident to the next, ranging over a vast and various landscape, but it keeps coming back to the same themes, the same locations, wandering and then returning home. The landscape becomes *familiar*. By the last third of the film, the visual and narrative associations have piled up to such an extent that every scene is charged with a kind of inevitability; everything, by that point, feels to the viewer like remembered experience.

So we know before Karl does that he's going to assume Barbarosa's myth after the outlaw's death. We've already seen him become a part of the myth, the "gringo child" who rides with Barbarosa; we've seen him begin to fall in love with the outlaw's daughter; we've seen him shoot a gun exactly as Barbarosa's taught him; we've seen him grow a wispy, reddish beard; we've seen him lose his own home, his own family; we've seen him ride with Barbarosa through a desert so bright, so dazzling that both riders become, for a moment, transparent. We know, too, that Barbarosa the man has been dead to the Zavala family for thirty years: Karl's just another body to fill the myth, a slight shift in the light on the landscape. And Schepisi has created a vision of the West in which death and loss are the constant background, and memory's as tangible as the rocks — the ruined adobes, the half-buried bodies sticking up out of the sand. When Karl rides into Braulio's courtyard, whirls his horse around, and disappears back into the night, he's become the tangible memory of Barbarosa — just as Barbarosa, for better than half his life, had been the memory of himself.

And just as *Barbarosa* — unlike most Westerns, which reach back into the past or the history of the genre for their emotional resonance — creates its own past, its own memories within the viewer. *Barbarosa* is too original, too self-sufficient to be judged as a Western. It is, rather, the latest of Fred Schepisi's fables about the oppressions and losses that turn men into ghosts.

Film Quarterly, Winter 1982–83

BUFFALO BILL
AND THE INDIANS

Judith Crist

Directed by Robert Altman. Written by Altman and Alan Rudolph. Starring Paul Newman, Geraldine Chaplin, John Considine, Burt Lancaster, and Joel Grey. **Playhouse Video/Key Video (division of CBS/Fox Video).**

To each his Bicentennial offering and celebration. For movies, small doubt that the appropriate offering is Robert Altman's *Buffalo Bill and the*

Indians — a celebration of the show business, the stardom, the ethic, and the verities that have been embodied in American history and epitomized by Hollywood.

It is fitting also that Altman, whose *Nashville* last year gave us a clear and devastating perception of the contemporary state of the nation, should cast his creative eye on history with the clarity, humor, and affectionate cynicism that have been the hallmarks of his work. From his concept of the Strangelovian world of medical healers working amid the bloodletting and slaughter of war in *M*A*S*H* and the bird-world of 1970 in *Brewster McCloud*, the myth-shattering view of the frontier in *McCabe and Mrs. Miller* and of the private eye in *The Long Goodbye*, Altman turns to the creation of historic mythology, to the making of the legend, the emergence of hero and of star, the contradictions of contemporaries, the remnants of the past. And truth, he concludes, is whatever gets the most applause.

The Altman vision is a personal one, the story and screenplay developed in collaboration with Alan Rudolph; hardly a trace remains of the Arthur Kopit play *Indians*, which "suggested" it. Part fact, part fiction — what *does* get the most applause? — it offers us a huge encampment, "just east of the Rockies," where William F. Cody is ensconced as "the Lion of the Show Business before the show business was invented." In the tent community housing Buffalo Bill, his entourage, and his between-tours Wild West show, celebrities, hangers-on, performers, and the public come and go. The producer, Nate Salsbury, whips the show into shape; the publicist, Major Burke, gabs grandiloquently for the benefit of the press; and Buffalo Bill preserves his stardom between beakers of booze and bouts with his favorite female singer of the moment. In the saloon the legend-maker, Ned Buntline, tells all comers of his discovery and creation of the star (an old soldier has another version to tell awestruck kiddies outside); in the arena Annie Oakley practices her sharpshooting with minuscule targets held by her quivering husband, Frank The-World's-Most-Handsome-Living-Target Butler.

And then there is a burble of excitement through the camp, the arrival of a new act. The Major has the publicity line: "Foes in '75 — Friends in '86." Salsbury, who has been wondering whether "by enlarging our show we had possibly disimproved it," at Cody's request tries to get Buntline out of the way: "Nothing personal. We've just signed the most futurable act in our history and I don't want anything or anybody interfering with it." Nostalgia, he notes, "ain't what it used to be." The "futurable act" is Sitting Bull, brought to the Wild West show by the army — "to make a broad-assed fool out of him," Buntline notes, because "a rock ain't a rock once it's gravel." But Sitting Bull proves himself a rock, silent amid the "titanically momentous welcome" Salsbury offers, and amid assurances from Buffalo Bill that "after one season you will never be mistaken for a below-average, run-of-the-mill, forgettable Indian chief." Through an interpreter, Sitting Bull sets forth his demands; on his own he establishes himself, comes and goes as he chooses, defines his own performance. He has come to meet the Great White Father — and to everyone's surprise but his, the President of the United States does arrive, taking in the Wild West show as part of his honeymoon trip. But the difference between a President and a chief, Cody notes, "is that the President knows enough to retaliate before it's his turn."

Paul Newman's Buffalo Bill, a cold-eyed but haunted man who skirts buffoonery by keeping a tight rein on his mirror- and poster-image, is the ultimate star, nightmare-ridden but quick to turn each accident or twist of events to his own advantage, discarding each moment as it becomes the forgettable past, completely convinced of the burden of posterity. He is indeed a servant of his public, hoping his hair will grow as long as Custer's but wearing a wig in the meantime, immutable, determinedly a living statue, with hallucinated conviction that white endures, that the red skin is the red man's burden. "A hundred years from now, I'll still be Buffalo Bill — Star," he tells Sitting Bull's ghost, "and you'll just be the Indian. . . . I give 'em what they expect."

The producer — a tiny dynamo in Joel Grey's impersonation — malaprops his way through grandiose phrases to keep his star happy and his show together; Kevin McCarthy's Major, his speech as flowing as his hair, "wearily, wearily" serves the press; Cody's nephew, Harvey Keitel's innocent sycophant, rides herd on his uncle's interests, frankly noting that "there is no business like the show business."

The brave cowboys and fierce Indians and bucking broncs ride and fight and parade to the wonderfully brassy sassy melodies "for every momentous moment" created by Richard Baskin for Buffalo Bill's Cowboy Band, and in the show-biz atmosphere the bitter truths of fakery emerge. The film is aptly subtitled "Sitting Bull's History Lesson" — a lesson found in the confrontation between the fact and the fraud on the huge canvas. It is enriched by Geraldine Chaplin's Annie Oakley (and softened by her empathy for Sitting Bull); John Considine's foolish stage-husbandry as Butler; Bonnie Leaders's ample mezzo-contralto, displaced by Noelle Rogers's cool lyric-coloratura, rivaled by Evelyn Lear's independent lyric-soprano; Pat McCormick's Grover Cleveland with Shelley Duvall his ingenue bride and E. L. Doctorow his provider of aphorisms. And finally there is Burt Lancaster's Ned Buntline, saturated and at last surfeited with his own creation, facing its actuality and its durability, the realization thereof "damn near a religious awakening."

With moments of brilliant inspiration, and of pedestrian point-making, there is a surface simplicity in Altman's view—one that seems anticlimactic, as any post-*Nashville* work would seem. But it is the restatement of the obvious that counts here, an awareness of our false historic values, a recognition of the revisionism that marks one's maturity and growth. The final confidence in Buffalo Bill's eye is the warning: the great men die, the created legends endure, and history, according to Sitting Bull, is "nothing more than disrespect for the dead"—something worth remembering at Bicentennial moments.

Saturday Review, July 10, 1976

CATTLE ANNIE
AND LITTLE BRITCHES

★

Peter Rainer

Directed by Lamont Johnson. Written by David Eyre and
Robert Ward, from the novel by Ward. Starring Amanda
Plummer, Diane Lane, and Burt Lancaster.

Cattle Annie and Little Britches, a turn-of-the-century Western starring Burt Lancaster and directed by Lamont Johnson, has some of the most finely felt moments of any film I've seen all year.

Lancaster, playing Bill Doolin, the scruffy, noble leader of the infamous Doolin-Dalton gang, gives one of the best performances of his career. Amanda Plummer and Diane Lane, as Cattle Annie and

Diane Lane (left) and Amanda Plummer play the adolescent easterners who, inspired by Ned Buntline's dime westerns, go West and become Cattle Annie and Little Britches. (Photo by, and courtesy of, Chris Johnson.)

Little Britches — frontier waifs who at first tag along with the gang and ultimately become its inspiration — are a remarkable duo. Currently, there are no definite plans by its distributor, Universal Pictures, to release the film in Los Angeles. (I saw the film last week at a private screening for Lancaster.)

Most of the current movies are so dismal that, when a good film comes along, one might logically expect some fanfare. But, for the studios, a movie's marketability is far more important than its quality. *Cattle Annie,* which was completed over a year ago, has been deemed virtually unmarketable by its distributor. It opened sporadically in Miami and Georgia last spring, with no advance screenings and no catchy ads in the papers. It was dumped in New York on April 24 in a run-down Times Square movie palace that didn't even feature poster art for the movie on the sidewalk. Under such conditions, is it any wonder the film did badly? The good reviews the film received in these towns didn't help because, in most cases, the film had already left by the time they came out.

Cattle Annie was not an in-house project for Universal; it's an independently made movie that was picked up for distribution by the studio. In such a situation, the studio picks up a distribution fee no matter how much money it makes, and it incurs none of the risk or expense associated with production. If the film does not attract audiences immediately, the studio may pull the picture rather than "waste" any more money on advertising. There's no enthusiasm for attempting to build an audience slowly.

When a movie such as *Cattle Annie* performs badly, the studios often use its failure as proof that they were right about its unmarketability. But it doesn't take much to see how self-fulfilling those studio prophecies really are. It's almost impossible to launch a movie these days without a full-fledged, thought-out ad campaign, including TV spots. Without such a campaign, a movie doesn't have a chance of finding its audience because it's never around long enough for anybody to see it. Word-of-mouth has become a mystical catch phrase in the movie business; it's supposed to explain why some movies are hits and others miss. But a slip of the lip can't sink a ship that hasn't even been launched.

"If a movie doesn't come out and seize the audience by the throat, there's a general kind of apathy and indifference to the picture," says Lamont Johnson in reference to the studios' philosophy of distribution.

Cattle Annie doesn't collar you; its storyline meanders and it never clinches any central conflict. But it has qualities of feeling that the grab-'em movies can't approach. It doesn't help that it's a Western; Westerns have been in commercial disrepute for some time now, and *Heaven's Gate* may have killed off the genre. Still, I don't buy the unmarketability myth surrounding this film. Surely a campaign could be developed that would feature Burt Lancaster, Rod Steiger, Scott Glenn (the brutal cowpoke in *Urban Cowboy*), John Savage, and Diane Lane (who was pictured on the cover of *Time* magazine two years ago in connection with a story on young female stars that mentioned the "soon-to-be-released *Cattle Annie*"). If Universal had any feeling for what makes a star, it might even design an ad campaign around newcomer Amanda Plummer, whose talent shoots across the screen like an acetylene torch.

Cattle Annie was originally developed by Rupert Hitzig, of (Alan) King-Hitzig Productions, in 1977. (King-Hitzig's latest film is the upcoming *Wolfen,* starring Albert Finney.) Hitzig, a Western buff,

Amanda Plummer made her movie debut as the fire-breathing Cattle Annie in Lamont Johnson's *Cattle Annie and Little Britches*. (Photo by, and courtesy of, Chris Johnson.)

commissioned novelist Robert Ward to write a novel based on the real-life exploits of two frontier girls. Hitzig always intended to make a movie out of the material, but, as he tells it, "It's easier to sell a novel to the movies than a script. A novel has a hard cover on each end and it's written in prose."

After the novel was published by William Morrow, Ward wrote a script that, several drafts later, attracted the attention of John Wayne. King-Hitzig waited a year for Wayne, whose health finally prohibited him from making the picture. When Burt Lancaster entered the project, everything fell into place. Hemdale Film Group, based in England, and the United Artists Theater Chain, put up the majority of the $51 million budget. There were pre-sales to Home Box Office and CBS. During filming, at least one major distributor offered to pick up the film, but the production team decided to wait until they had a completed film and then accept the best offer.

"In retrospect," says Hitzig, "we probably should have accepted the offer." When *Cattle Annie* was screened for the major studios, as well as some independent distributors, the response was disheartening. According to Johnson, "The studios liked it but they didn't have the conviction to back it up. They thought the movie didn't fall into any readily classifiable group. The one question I kept hearing over and over again was 'What is it?' "

After Universal picked it up, the studio waited a year before finally releasing it in the South. During that time, neither Johnson, Hitzig-King, nor Salah Hassanein, the president of the United Artists Eastern Theaters, was consulted about how to market the picture. (UA Theaters is not affiliated with the United Artists Corp.) Lamont Johnson found out that the film opened in Florida from a friend at the *Ft. Lauderdale News*. In addition, Alan King, Burt Lancaster, and the other cast members have offered to appear on talk shows to plug the picture. No one has yet taken them up on their offer.

Why does a studio pick up a movie if it doesn't have any intention of promoting it properly? Officially, no one at Universal is talking. Bob Wilkinson, executive vice-president for domestic distribution, was unavailable for comment. His assistant, Ben Cammack, declined to talk about the picture at all. It's quite possible that *Cattle Annie* was picked up for purely political reasons, and that there was never any intention to promote it. Says one Universal executive, who asked not to be named, "We sometimes pick up movies to get in good with producers. It's possible *Cattle Annie* was picked up in order to make a connection with King-Hitzig. *All Night Long* (the Gene Hackman–Barbra Streisand comedy that Universal released, and promoted badly, last spring) was made to strike a connection with Sue Mengers (the super-agent wife of the movie's director, Jean-Claude Tramont)." If this is the way friends are made in Hollywood, how does one make enemies?

There's a phrase in the agency business that the movie studio advertising-publicity people would do well to adopt: "Sell it, don't smell it." If the Universal people don't like *Cattle Annie,* what can their opinion be of their latest Western release *The Legend of the Lone Ranger*, with its blow-dry cinematography and cotton-candy dramatics and *Gentleman's Quarterly* cowboys? But *Lone Ranger*, because it was an expensive film (more than three times the budget of *Cattle Annie*) and because the Lone Ranger logo had built-in marketing possibilities with young audiences, was given a big send-off. To no avail. *Cattle Annie* has nothing going for it except quality; the way movies are made and marketed today, apparently that's not enough.

Whenever a terrific "little" picture is dumped, there are always a few critics who, in support of the film, raise a stink; and sometimes, as a result, the studios are embarrassed enough to re-release the film. It happened with *Pretty Poison* and another terrific Lamont Johnson film called *The Last American Hero*. (Johnson must feel like he's been through the *Boor* Wars.) But the re-release is often just as half-hearted as the original release; the studio, still trying to prove it was right about dumping the movie, dumps it again.

Cattle Annie hasn't even been *released* in most areas, but the syndrome is the same. That's why the best rumor I've heard yet is that the UA Theater Chain may buy back the film from Universal and release it around Oscar nomination time. (*Reviewer's note:* The rumor, alas, was unfounded.) It'll probably get a few nominations.

Los Angeles Herald Examiner, June 21, 1981

SHADES OF NOIR

T he "existential," doom-tinged crime thrillers that thrived in the '40s and early '50s—movies the French dubbed *film noir*—probably appealed to audiences because of their brutal frankness in dealing with the three primal subjects: sex, death, and money. Describing the characters in *Double Indemnity,* James Agee wrote, "Among these somewhat representative Americans, money and sex and a readiness to murder are as inseparably interdependent as the Holy Trinity."

As a genre, *film noir* has always been hard to pin down. It encompassed James M. Cain's lust stories, Dashiell Hammett's and Raymond Chandler's hard-boiled detective fiction, and journalistic melodramas like *Kiss of Death.* The cynical, sometimes paranoid attitudes of the characters are what distinguished *film noir.* In the '40s and '50s, these movies offered a refreshing alternative to the yea-saying of mainstream American mass culture. As Agee once pointed out, they gave the most adventurous Hollywood directors a chance to smuggle meaning as well as meanness into their moviemaking.

When some of the greatest American directors—Arthur Penn,

Robert Altman, and Francis Ford Coppola, for example—set about redefining America in the '70s, they often came up with contemporary *noir* films. Penn's *Night Moves* and Altman's *The Long Goodbye* offer conservative and radical updates, respectively, of the Hammett-Chandler legacy, and Coppola's *The Conversation* tackles a different sort of detective—a surveillance expert. Altman also produced Robert Benton's *The Late Show,* another skewed look at the life of a private eye.

In *Cutter's Way,* expatriate Czech director Ivan Passer brings *noir's* pessimism into the sunshine of Santa Barbara, California. And in *Straight Time,* the blackest of them all, Dustin Hoffman gives what is arguably his best performance, as a paroled thief who can't reform.

Probably the lightest of these films is Robert Mandel's thriller *F/X,* but even this series of jolts and japes about a movie special effects wizard who gets used by shady government agents is relentlessly cynical about contemporary power games. It's like a pop version of De Palma's *Blow Out.* In *F/X,* as in all *noir* films, the disquieting darkness persists after the lights go up.

THE CONVERSATION

Joy Gould Boyum

Directed and written by Francis Ford Coppola. Starring Gene Hackman and John Cazale. **Paramount Home Video.**

Francis Ford Coppola's *The Conversation* is a horror film for our time. For while some of us may, like our ancestors, fear the supernatural and the fantastic—the devil, ghosts, monsters, and all things that go bump in the night—nearly all of us stand with fear and trembling before the black magic of contemporary technology. And it is precisely such technology that makes for menace in this effective and unnerving film.

The plot through which *The Conversation* works its terrors concerns a professional surveillance man named Harry Caul, "the best bugger on the West Coast," who at the time we encounter him is in the hire of a

Gene Hackman stars as a San Francisco surveillance expert with a passion for invisibility in Francis Ford Coppola's post-Watergate thriller, *The Conversation*. (Photo courtesy Paramount Home Video.)

powerful and nameless business executive apparently after evidence that his wife is an adultress. With astounding technical skill, Caul and his assistants manage to record the conversation of the young wife and her young male companion as the two circle through the noisy midday crowds of San Francisco's Union Square, a conversation which presumably reveals the two arranging for a rendezvous at a hotel. Running these tapes over and over again, studying the photographs his team has also supplied, re-seeing the couple in his mind's eye, Caul discovers that what he is involved in is not simply a case of adultery but may possibly be a case of murder. And part of our excitement in watching the film is that we experience with him this reevaluation of reality.

As a film which touches, then, on wiretapping, the invasion of privacy, and the unreliability of human perception, *The Conversation* comes to us trailing with it clouds of associations: most immediately, of course, the current events surrounding Watergate, but also Antonioni's film *Blow-Up* and Orwell's novel *1984*. And these associations work both to intensify our fascination and to extend our feelings of horror from the fiction projected before us to the reality of our actual lives.

But these associations can also mislead. For the film's chief concern is not with the terrors we may feel at the prospect of having our most intimate conversations and actions subject to surveillance; nor is it with our dreadful sense of helplessness before the increasingly massive and increasingly incomprehensible technological network in which our lives now seem enmeshed. The film is not even centrally involved with the elusiveness of reality or the fallibility of the human mind in assessing it.

As fascinating as these themes may be, *The Conversation*'s chief interest lies elsewhere. It is the *effect* of this technology on our personalities and traditional values that is its essential subject and that makes for its greatest horror — and not simply, as we might suspect, the effect of this technology on those who are under surveillance but the effect, above all, on the surveillance man himself.

Harry Caul, the supreme master of the art of surveillance, has become its supreme victim. For he has had to trade in for his mastery the most essential aspect of his humanity: human involvement is prohibited to him. As the perfect spy he must keep himself anonymous, which involves not only living in an impersonal environment — an apartment cleansed of all distinctive personal effects, all individualizing character — but also refusing all intimate relationships. He cannot afford the risk of friends and family — and even the woman he occasionally uses for sexual release cannot be privy to his address, his telephone number, the nature of his work, or the nature of his feelings. He cannot even risk feelings themselves. And the crisis of the film is in fact precipitated when he allows human sentiment to emerge.

He begins to care about the fate of the couple whose conversation he has recorded and in this way makes of himself a man to be watched by others. At the end of the film, it is Harry Caul who is threatened by the electronic enemy of invisible cameras and microphones and who, in his search for the hidden invaders, must reduce his monk-like apartment to rubble, first destroying its minimal furnishings, then baring its walls to their frames and stripping its floors to their beams.

The point is as unmistakable as it is terrifying: in a world where one's private self is always open to invasion, the only protection would seem to lie in destroying that private self—or, in Harry Caul's particular case, in doing away with even the most meager remnants of human personality.

And Harry's dehumanized quality, dramatized for us with impressive subtlety by Gene Hackman, is reflected in the texture of the film as a whole. The world that Francis Ford Coppola (who as director, scenarist, and producer of the film is unquestionably the author of all we survey here) has created for us is one of glass and chrome office buildings, of neutralized and uniform hotel rooms made distinct from one another only by their different numbers, of vast empty spaces, of deserted corridors, of transistorized gadgets, of locks and bolts and keys which only underscore, in their inadequacy, the vulnerability of privacy and in fact of human life. This is a world as well where people when they appear are almost always seen at a distance, and often from harsh angles, and where both actual and symbolic walls separate one human being from another. When Harry—whose name, let us not forget is "Caul," suggesting both his second sight and his protective covering—goes to visit his mistress, he never bothers to take off his plastic raincoat, not even when he's lying on her bed. And later, at the conclusion of several sequences worthy in their tension of Hitchcock, we will see a corpse who is also wrapped in plastic.

The mention of Hitchcock here is not gratuitous, for as a thriller alone, *The Conversation* would be worth our attention. But as a thriller which also expresses our actual and collective nightmares, it absolutely demands it.

The Wall Street Journal, April 14, 1974

CUTTER'S WAY

★

Kevin Thomas

Directed by Ivan Passer. Written by Jeffrey Alan Fiskin, from the novel by Newton Thornburg. Starring Jeff Bridges, John Heard, and Lisa Eichhorn. **MGM/UA Home Video.**

Right at the start, director Ivan Passer lets you know that *Cutter's Way* is going to be something special as the credits unroll in front of a parade in slow motion that gradually changes from black and white to color. The accompanying music is, by the way, not mariachi, which is what the paraders' Spanish costumes would suggest, but a mournful, foreboding whine created on a glass harmonica and a zither.

This opening creates a languorous, ominous mood that exemplifies the precarious lives of Passer's three Santa Barbara drifters — Cutter (John Heard), a brilliant, boozy vet who lost his left eye, left leg and most of his left arm in Vietnam; his best pal Bone (Jeff Bridges), a golden boy and compulsive womanizer who gets by hustling rich women, and Cutter's wife Maureen (Lisa Eichhorn), who drowns her sorrows over her husband's fate in vodka drunk straight from the bottle.

That Bone is briefly a suspect in a rape-murder and later believes he knows who the actual killer is provides *Cutter's Way* with a plot that allows it to evolve into one of the most devastating indictments yet filmed of the neglect of Vietnam veterans. At the same time, *Cutter's Way* is an elegant and suspenseful genre piece shot through with flashes of the darkest humor.

In adapting Newton Thornburg's novel *Cutter and Bone,* Passer and writer Jeffrey Alan Fiskin avoid almost all conventional exposition, which means that it takes about 45 minutes for the film to come into focus. Yet there is such a distinctive, compelling look and feel to the film that it continues to be as captivating as it was at the start. Most important, of course, its people engage you deeply — even before you get to know them fully. The key figure is Cutter, and it is Heard's signal achievement that he never makes you feel sorry for Cutter himself but rather allows you to perceive in him the whole tragic waste of Vietnam.

Cutter actually is a pretty outrageous guy. He'll introduce dumb-founded barroom pals as Rosencrantz and Guildenstern and Karl Marx and even bait some black pool players. He'll drunkenly wreck his neighbor's car — and then glibly talk his way out of it with the cops. But now, all of a sudden, there's a focus for his abundant rage: that suspect in the rape-murder. He's a self-made oilionaire (Stephen Elliot), one of those all-powerful figures in our society who never have to put themselves on the line but always put somebody else's life in jeopardy instead. For Cutter he's a warmonger who symbolically must be called to account for Vietnam. But is this man, in fact, really the rapist-killer? To his credit, Passer doesn't send us home still guessing.

From Joan Micklin Silver's *Between the Lines* to her *Head Over Heels* and beyond, John Heard always has been an idiosyncratic, persuasive actor and never has been more so than as this shaggy, furious wild man. Yet *Cutter's Way* accommodates another fully realized portrait in Bridges' Bone, a quintessential Santa Barbara type who lives off his looks and charm. A friend (Arthur Rosenberg) wants him to consider a career in boat sales, something he dabbles in. "You look great on the deck," says the friend, perhaps with a trace of envy, since he's fat and unhandsome himself. And in Eichhorn we experience the price that can be extracted from Vietnam veterans' wives.

Cinematographer Jordan Cronenweth makes a telling play of light and shadow, and the moods he creates are complemented perfectly by the venturesome score, the work of Jack Nitzsche. Ann Dusenberry is the dead girl's sister, a simple type whose conflicting emotions — greed, revenge, lust for Bridges — can easily, and sometimes comically, be read in her face. Nina Van Pallandt is a nakedly satisfied client of Bridges.

Cutter's Way seems in all aspects an impeccable film, yet in the grim wake of *Heaven's Gate,* United Artists pulled the film from circulation after it received a less-than-wonderful reception in Manhattan early this year. However, Nathaniel Kwit of United Artists Classics, that division of UA that ends up with all its so-called "difficult" films, has now given it another chance and is even considering launching an Oscar campaign for Heard. Above all, *Cutter's Way* is a triumph for Passer, a distinguished Czech emigre who, after a long struggle and many disappointments, has finally made his mark in American films.

Los Angeles Times, September 13, 1981

F/X

★

Bruce Williamson

Directed by Robert Mandel. Written by Robert T. Megginson and Gregory Fleeman. Starring Bryan Brown and Brian Dennehy. **HBO Video.**

Every movie season needs a nice electric shock before things really seem to get rolling. Last year, we had *Witness*. So far this year, *F/X* (Orion) is the knock-your-socks-off thriller the competition will have to beat. In moviemakers' jargon, F/X means special effects, and director Robert Mandel drops a load of cunning filmlore between the witty, wiseass lines of a screenplay by Robert T. Megginson and Gregory Fleeman. Australian Bryan Brown, with a breakthrough role to back his previous bids for stardom in *Breaker Morant* and TV's "The Thorn Birds," plays Rollie Tyler, a special-effects wizard recruited by some Justice Department plotters (Cliff DeYoung and Mason Adams) who want him to fake the public assassination of a Mafia chieftain (Jerry Orbach) about to turn state's witness. For a while, Rollie wants none of it; he's having too good a time dreaming up monstrous moments for such box-office epics as *Vermin from Venus* and *I Dismember Mama*. But he takes the job and soon finds himself so ensnared that he may *be* a murderer, in fact, and knows damned well he's at the top of *somebody's* hit list. To match Brown's gritty performance as a resourceful but inexperienced rigger of illusions suddenly thrust into a world where people shoot real bullets, there is Brian Dennehy — in top form, as always — playing the rule-bending New York detective who can smell a rat a mile away. Seeing how a crackerjack suspense drama is put together by movie magic and getting an adrenaline rush at the same time more than compensate for a few muddled or loosely wired twists in the screenplay. *F/X* delivers high-gear excitement from start to finish.

Playboy, May 1986

POSTSCRIPT: *F/X is a nice original thriller with a canny filmic angle that should have done better than it did. Both the movie company and the leading* *actor, Bryan Brown, have told me that they believe the title was the real problem. The reviews were fairly good, but the public never got the message; it sounded like weird science-fiction or something. The movie reportedly did very well, however, as a videotape, and a year or so later Brown (an old acquaintance) told me that they were planning a sequel. The sequel, F/X 2, starring Brown and Dennehy, started shooting April 30, 1990. —B.W.*

January 1990

THE LATE SHOW

David Denby

Directed and written by Robert Benton. Starring Art Carney and Lily Tomlin. **Warner Home Video.**

Ira Wells, the aging and decrepit Los Angeles private eye who is the hero of the nifty new detective thriller, *The Late Show,* lives alone in a cruddy furnished room and doesn't get around much anymore. Wells (Art Carney) has a gimpy leg, and a perforated ulcer occasionally doubles him over in pain; his eyesight is beginning to go and he wears a hearing aid. He's not eager to take chances these days, and no one really needs him anymore. He's so poor he doesn't even own a car—the ultimate indignity in Los Angeles. Having worked in a sordid business for over 30 years, Wells doesn't expect much from the human race: he calls women "dolls" or "chippies" and complains about the messiness of their lives; men he expects to be crooks or fools or both. In all, he has that peculiar acid impatience of intelligent, disappointed middle-aged men, but he's too proud to let himself go and take it out on the world. A melancholy loner, he's instinctively honest—as only people who have been tough on themselves for a long time can be.

Wells hates listening to people talk—most of what they say is bullshit anyway—and as for himself, he always comes immediately to the point. His opposite in every way is Margo (Lily Tomlin), a young Californian (maybe 35) who is hopelessly, obsessively garrulous, launching into sentences before she has any idea what she wants to say. Margo is one of those people who seem to do a little bit of everything (acting, pushing drugs, transporting stolen goods, running "errands" for people, etc.) without ever settling into a job or even a fixed identity. Adrift in a sea of "self-realization," she's been through so many kinds of therapy and has so much jargon banging around in her head that she can't utter three sentences without contradicting herself. She's the type of woman who spends more time analyzing her relationships than actually having them. And yet she has a gift that makes her almost wonderful, a gift of empathy: she knows what it is to be a human being. She falls in love with Wells, who's too tired and lonely to ditch her.

The Late Show's writer and director, Robert Benton, who with David Newman scripted *Bonnie and Clyde* and *Bad Company* (which he also directed), deserves our gratitude for having invented these eccentric yet utterly plausible characters and gotten Carney and Tomlin to play them. The film has severe structural problems that may baffle and annoy a lot of people, but it's a winner nonetheless, a fluky, smart little movie filled with miscellaneous pleasures — a line here, a scene there — that stay in the mind long after the formal problems have been forgotten.

From the beginning, the odd couple of Carney and Tomlin carries the film. Earlier in their careers, both these actors found a large audience by working in a broad, caricature style; in *The Late Show* the caricatures have disappeared yet the comedic energy is still there, refined and subtilized, flashing out at crucial moments. Heavier now and mysteriously sadder, Carney gives a marvelously exact, entirely unsentimental portrait of the physical limitations of middle age that will astonish anyone who remembers the bluster and noise of his Ed Norton days. Carney has achieved the stillness of a great movie actor. Through most of this picture, as in Paul Mazursky's *Harry and Tonto,* he does his most beautiful work while listening to the chatter around him; his characters now are distanced from us, often disgusted or merely bored, and the signs of their interest or disbelief flicker briefly and then recede from view. In *The Late Show,* most of the comedy comes from Carney's stolid resistance to Tomlin's nutbrain chatter. Locked together in a peculiar intrigue that neither of them understands (nor do we), they're like a bear and a wet hen sharing a cage and trying not to get in each other's way. Tomlin's long riffs have nothing to do with the thriller plot; all her talk has to stand on its own and interest us for its own sake (a terrible burden for any actor), and yet Tomlin almost never falls back on the tricks and mannerisms she knows we like. Keeping those gums well-covered, she makes saucer eyes at us only once or twice as she races through the nonsense with a reckless assurance that takes your breath away.

It seems that Margo has been transporting stolen goods for a certain friend but refusing to turn over some of the money she's received; when her friend steals her cat in retaliation and threatens to strangle it, Margo hires Wells's old partner, Harry (Howard Duff), to get the cat back. Harry promptly takes a .45 slug in the gut and dies, and then. . . . But we'll never get anywhere this way. Detective stories are often absurdly over-complicated, though the good ones finally make the complexity pay off. In a good detective story or movie, the initial intrigue – the corpse on the beach, the straying wife, the stolen necklace – leads the detective into an ever more entangled web of complicity and corruption until we ultimately confront not a lonely criminal or a few isolated acts of violence, but an entire society run by criminal violence and fraud. In its oblique, off-handed way, the detective genre has often criticized the values of our society with greater force and coherence than more ambitious forms of socially conscious literature and filmmaking. For an understanding of the nasty side of American life in the '30s and '40s, for instance, many of us would rather read Dashiell Hammett, Raymond Chandler and even James M. Cain than, say, John Steinbeck. From Hammett one gets a kind of violent comic metaphor for capitalist acquisitiveness; from Chandler a sense of spreading rot, a malaise oozing out of the pores of the rich; recently, Ross Macdonald's work has painted a rather powerful picture of the moral disruptions produced by the rootless culture of Southern California. The best detective movies, with their love of gleaming, repellent surfaces – corruption as *style* – have hit us in different ways but with equal force. In *Chinatown* the social meanings no longer lay buried: Jack Nicholson scratched the surface and found capitalists operating like criminals, controlling the fate of California at a crucial moment in its history.

Benton is not interested in penetrating the corruption at the center; his field of vision is much smaller, focusing on the petty grifters on the edge of the action. Unfortunately, he never makes the relationships among his characters clear enough for this vision to take hold. *The Late Show* is coy and cute and much too obscure when it most needs to be straightforward and comprehensible. As the movie goes on, fresh characters are introduced or referred to in passing, new corpses turn up, theories are propounded to explain it all, and yet the central events (all taking place off camera) are infuriatingly murky. At the end we sit there with knots in our stomach, frustrated in our simple desire to comprehend.

And there are other things that are perverse. If Benton has the sense to make Wells and Margo so recognizably human, why does he turn the chief villain, a big-time fence named Birdwell (Eugene Roche), into a silly, revue-skit heavy? Birdwell has a comic tic: he can't stop praising the goods that he's fencing. Here one senses the quirky, parodistic touch of Robert Altman, the film's producer. Birdwell is a mistake; a detective thriller needs a convincingly evil antagonist. Benton does much better with Charlie (played by *Maude's* Bill Macy), an out-of-work theatrical agent and hustler who brings Margo and Wells together. Charlie, a repressed, quiet little ferret with a pencil-line mustache, commits evil because he's too weak to resist an easy buck.

Benton has kept the atmosphere of his film rather modest. I would guess that he's purposefully avoided cinematic "poetry," shooting a slice of Los Angeles that doesn't look like much of anything: laundromats and bars and plastic apartment complexes. The mediocrity is part of what he's trying to convey, even if it isn't always exciting visually. At the beginning of the movie a slow pan around Wells's seedy room — pictures and mementos on the walls, the opening page of a never-to-be-completed novel lying in the typewriter — establishes with easy economy the feeling of a second-rate life that has just about run its course, and we know we're in sure hands. Since *Bad Company* (1972), Benton has picked up the tempo of his scenes dramatically. There isn't a dull moment in this film, and a few scenes are portentous in a juicy, Hitchcock style: the gore on the corridor walls that leads to murder, the punctured water bed spilling its blood-tinted contents under a doorway, over a balcony and onto the street below. Indeed, every time Margo and Wells enter a darkened room together, Benton tightens the mood like a winch winding in its line. The suspense of *The Late Show* is almost entirely pleasurable: we may not know what's going on half the time, but we care a great deal about these two people, and that makes up for an awful lot.

Boston Phoenix, March 8, 1977

THE LONG GOODBYE

Judith Crist

Directed by Robert Altman. Written by Leigh Brackett, from the novel by Raymond Chandler. Starring Elliott Gould, Nina Van Pallandt, Sterling Hayden, Mark Rydell, and Jim Bouton.

The buccaneers have been making the Hollywood headlines recently, what with the dismantling, absorption and swapping of studios, but it's the adventurers, the creative risk-takers and myth-breakers, who provide the life's blood of our movie experiences.

One of the most adventurous of moviemakers of the past several years is Robert Altman, who has shattered the Hollywood mold with each of his five films in as many years, from *M*A*S*H* to *Brewster McCloud* to *McCabe and Mrs. Miller* to *Images* and now with *The Long Goodbye*. Altman has dared again and may well catch the public unprepared. He has taken Raymond Chandler's Philip Marlowe, son of Sam Spade and godfather of Lew Archer, and seen him plain—just as his creator saw him in his commentaries on his own works. For Chandler saw his tough but idealistic and decent and ethical private eye as the figment of a romantic imagination, knowing with a realist's acceptance that it takes dirty men to thrive in a dirty business. Certainly, even in our films, we've come to recognize the cop as cop and not the heroic agent of righteousness of the Hollywood factory assembly line. Are we ready to cope with having one of our favorite dream figures of 'tec fiction and movies put in focus? After all, we're steeped in the tradition, with five earlier screen embodiments of Marlowe. Naturally and nostalgically we want more of the same, but it's twenty years later— exactly, in the case of *The Long Goodbye*.

It is into the 1973 world that Altman has thrust his Philip Marlowe and seen him, half in sorrow and half in laughter, as a man out of his time, clinging not only to the clothes, the unfiltered cigarettes, and even the car (a 1948 Continental convertible) but also, more importantly, to the ethic and morality of a time gone by. And, unfashionably at the moment but with remarkable success, he has embodied him in Elliott Gould, that capable actor over-exploited and misused after his initial success, who makes of Marlowe a loose man, a too rational and too caring man for now, a sotto voce commentary his bulwark, that foolish grin a facade for the devastating perception of where people are at. And when he puts his values on the line because he alone still cares about right and wrong and gets "You'll never learn — you're a born loser" in exchange, he does what the last righteous man has to do — in 1973. And down the road he goes, a shattered myth behind him and a surging swell of "Hurray for Hollywood" flooding the soundtrack.

With a lean tight screenplay by Leigh Brackett, whose credits include her coadapting *The Big Sleep* with William Faulkner, Altman has clung to the essence of the Chandler novel with the major elements of the book's several sub-plots retained and one character reversed, which may offend purists. But the result, with some offbeat and thereby excellent casting, with the lagniappe of satire, is a first-rate suspense melodrama. Beyond Vilmos Zsigmond's exquisitely muted cinematography to enhance the dream-like quality of the Los Angeles and Mexican locations, there's a grand joke in John Williams's score, via the title song, by Williams and Johnny Mercer.

The casting is adventurous, particularly with Nina Van Pallandt as the lady in distress; sportscaster Jim Bouton as the friend who involves Marlowe and comedian Henry Gibson as the unfunny sinister psychiatrist are very good, as are such pros as Sterling Hayden, as the alcoholic author, and Mark Rydell, as the sadistic bourgeois gangster. If you can not only take but also relish a bit of "now" (rather than future) shock and bear to have another movie myth shattered, in pure movie terms and high style, and with love as well as wit, *The Long Goodbye* is for you.

New York, October 29, 1973

NIGHT MOVES

Kevin Thomas

Directed by Arthur Penn. Written by Alan Sharp. Starring
Gene Hackman. **Warner Home Video.**

Night Moves is a stunning, stylish detective mystery in the classic
Raymond Chandler–Ross Macdonald mold. A tough yet vulnerable
private eye's investigation of a murder becomes a quest for his own
identity and a pursuit for the truth that cuts through many layers of
social strata. It all ends with a wry sense of irony over the eternal
treachery of human nature and of one's own illusions.

Lest this sound pretentious and therefore off-putting, let it hastily be
said that *Night Moves* is also a fast, often funny movie with lots of
compassionately observed people. This handsome Warners presentation is still another triumph for ever-busy, ever-versatile Gene Hackman, director Arthur Penn and writer Alan Sharp.

Precisely one hour into the film's succinct 99 minutes Hackman, an
ex–pro football star turned L.A. private eye, assumes he has his case
wrapped up. Hired by a onetime Hollywood starlet (Janet Ward) to find
her teen-age daughter (Melanie Griffith), missing for two weeks, he's
tracked the girl down in Florida where she has been living with her
stepfather (John Crawford) and brought her back home. But a short
time later, Hackman hears that Miss Griffith, while working as a stunt
girl, has been killed and begins to suspect it was not an accident.

While Hackman is on the case, he is also confronted with his own
rocky marriage to a sophisticated interior decorator (Susan Clark) who
wishes he would give up such boring, trivial work—and who has
drifted into an affair with another man (Harris Yulin). Hackman is only
too well aware of the sleazy side of his profession, yet he remains
obsessed with it—apparently because he had been driven to search out
his own father, who had long ago abandoned him.

Because Hackman is at odds with Miss Clark, he is especially
attracted to Crawford's Florida girlfriend (Jennifer Warren), a witty,
brisk outdoorsy type who's knocked around a lot.

Night Moves has been as beautifully articulated and carefully nuanced
as any of Arthur Penn's more obviously ambitious projects. From

respectfully treated, satisfyingly familiar ingredients Penn and Sharp, one of the finest younger writers in films, have evoked a fresh sense of recognition.

As always, Penn gets wonderful performances and works with the best craftsmen — for example, cameraman Bruce Surtees or editor Dede Allen (who, like Hackman, worked with Penn on *Bonnie and Clyde*). Along with those already mentioned, Edward Binns has the part of a lifetime as a veteran stuntman, a canny, good-natured Hollywood pro of the first order. For that matter, *Night Moves* itself is a tribute to the Hollywood genre movie at its reflective, revealing best.

Los Angeles Times, July 2, 1975

STRAIGHT TIME

David Ansen

Directed by Ulu Grosbard. Written by Alvin Sargent, Jeffrey Boam, and Edward Bunker, from a novel by Bunker. Starring Dustin Hoffman. **Warner Home Video.**

Straight Time sneaked into theaters like a thief in the night, a curious arrival for a movie starring Dustin Hoffman and one that seemed to imply cold feet on the part of Warner Brothers, the distributor. It should have arrived with fanfare. Though made up of familiar elements — an ex-con, bank robberies, lovers on the run — it is an unusual movie out of today's Hollywood and a very fine one. Small in scale, grittily realistic, charged with a fierce intelligence about how people live on the other side of the law, the film makes few concessions to an audience's expectations, but it has an edgy, lingering intensity.

The story, based on the novel *No Beast So Fierce* by ex-con Edward Bunker, starts very quietly. Max Dembo (Hoffman) is paroled from prison after serving six years for armed robbery. He comes to Los Angeles, finds a cheap room, has an uneasy encounter with his cynical parole officer (M. Emmet Walsh) and vows to find work and stay clean.

Dustin Hoffman plays a paroled thief who can't stay away from crime in *Straight Time*. (Photo © 1978 SweetWall Productions, Inc., the First Artists Production Company, Ltd., and Warner Bros. Inc. All rights reserved.)

Our sympathies are with him, though we suspect that the difficult terms of his parole could trigger his barely controlled rage at any moment.

The test comes soon enough when the cheerfully sadistic parole officer wrongly suspects him of shooting up in his room and throws him back in the can for observation. When Max emerges, and just when we are wondering how much more abuse he can take, he explodes — and so does the movie. In one dramatic act of revenge, he recommits himself to the outlaw life. *Straight Time* proceeds to show us just what that life is all about: the panics and highs of escalating burglaries; the loyalties and betrayals of friends; the scared but willing compliance of a pretty, aimless California girl who vows to stay with Max as long as she can stand it — and no longer.

We are fascinated by Max, but as Hoffman daringly and brilliantly plays him, we are never invited to love him. This is no charming con artist, but a ruthless, self-destructive man strung out on crime. Yet the movie is startlingly nonjudgmental. Though the heist scenes generate nerve-racking tension, it is not director Ulu Grosbard's intent to manipulate our sympathies for or against Max or to mount an indictment against society for its treatment of ex-cons. This tenacious, but never cold, objectivity is precisely what makes *Straight Time* such an anomaly today. What makes it so hypnotic is Grosbard's sharp behavioral eye, cinematographer Owen Roizman's superb evocation of Los Angeles's seedy underbelly and a cast that plays together with faultless naturalism. Walsh as the infuriating parole officer, Harry Dean Stanton as Max's partner in crime, Gary Busey as a dope-shooting, weak-willed confederate and Theresa Russell as the girlfriend all give supporting performances that put most of this year's Oscar nominees to shame. This modest-seeming movie takes big chances, and it just may be the sleeper of the year.

Newsweek, April 3, 1978

ALL SINGING! ALL DANCING! NO AUDIENCE!

Fans of old movies invariably ask why Hollywood doesn't make musicals anymore. Actually, it's a wonder that Hollywood kept making musicals as long as it did.

In the '50s and '60s, Hollywood's star-grooming, property-developing apparatus broke down. The studios no longer boasted the production teams who could build original movies around, say, Barbra Streisand the way they once did around Fred Astaire and Ginger Rogers. Hollywood filled the void with extravagant movie productions of Broadway blockbusters, from *Oklahoma!* (1955) to *Fiddler on the Roof* (1971), usually appearing years after the shows began their record-breaking theatrical runs. The time lag gave movie audiences the illusion that the Broadway musical was still thriving in the '60s and '70s. But when William Goldman chronicled the '67-'68 Broadway season in *The Season: A Candid Look at Broadway,* he already sensed the form's demise: "Musical comedy is in trouble today because the songwriters aren't there. The old ones are dead or dying, the young ones mostly dull." Eventually, Hollywood ran out of properties to convert or cannibalize.

In 1978, when Milos Forman set about filming the one smash hit musical of the '67-'68 season, *Hair,* he and Michael Weller completely rewrote and reshaped it. The most provocative movie musicals now derive their inspiration from sources other than Broadway. They come from the showmanship and mythmaking of rock stars like Prince (*Sign o' The Times, Under the Cherry Moon*). Or they come from writers and directors who absorbed the Old Hollywood song-and-dance numbers in their youth and put them to new expressive purposes, as screenwriter Dennis Potter does in *Pennies from Heaven,* the only MGM musical ever based on a BBC miniseries.

HAIR

Bruce Williamson

Directed by Milos Forman. Written by Michael Weller, from the stage musical by Gerome Ragni and James Rado, with music by Galt MacDermot. Starring Treat Williams, John Savage, Beverly D'Angelo, and Dorsey Wright. **MGM/ UA Home Video.**

Let me admit to being dead wrong in my expectations about *Hair,* for I stood with the skeptics who saw no way to make a 1979 movie musical from the definitive but outdated theatrical phenomenon that virtually begat the spirit of the late Sixties. The flower people and the antiwar protests are still part of it: *Hair* still opens with the burning of draft cards. And it *is* dated, in a sense, though transformed into a sad and funny and timeless fable about the way we were, or seemed to be, only a brief decade ago. One thing I should have remembered in anticipating too little too late is that Oscar-winning director Milos (*One Flew over the Cuckoo's Nest*) Forman, when he first splashed into international prominence on top of the Czech New Wave, made his mark with such lightsome young-in-heart human comedies as *Loves of a Blonde.* Everything about *Hair* brings out the very best in Forman. When he piles all his principal actors into an open convertible to speed across the wide, wind-swept desert singing *Good Morning Starshine,* it's not just a reprise of that long-familiar tune, it's a symbol of eternal flaming youth of any era. They are madcaps who make love, not war, but they only happen to be Sixties potheads and dissidents, high on life itself and a lot less angry than they used to be.

Time after time, the pure blazing exuberance of *Hair* simply carries you away. An occasional qualm may occur — lyrics blown off course in a monsoon of energy; inventive choreography by Twyla Tharp that often moves so fast that cameras seem unable to keep up with it. But what's a flaw or two in a film of a thousand delights? The bombardment of images by Czech-born cinematographer Miroslav Ondricek is almost nonstop, from an LSD wedding trip that takes place only in the hero's bedazzled brain to the hilarious *Black Boys–White Boys* number (sung by lusty gals and gay Army induction officers). Oh, yes, there's a middle-American hero in *Hair*'s simplified but effective new plot, underplayed eloquently by John Savage as Claude, the square Oklahoma kid who grabs a bus to New York for a couple of days before going into the Army. A funny thing happens to Claude on his way to the Statue of Liberty — he stumbles onto the Age of Aquarius in Central Park, which looks so much like Oz that even the mounted policemen's horses join the dance. Savage's fresh air of innocence in this role ultimately says more about love and peace than he managed to project as the pitiable paraplegic veteran in *The Deer Hunter*. No less terrific are Beverly D'Angelo as a society deb on the lam from Short Hills, New Jersey, Annie Golden as a hippie waif who's pregnant by someone or other and Dorsey Wright as Hud. But the big, big discovery of *Hair* is apt to be Treat Williams, as Berger the hirsute hippie. How he came to be called Treat is anybody's guess, but Williams struts through the memorable Ragni-Rado-MacDermot words and music as if the whole show had been invented yesterday. Reinvented by Forman with incandescent hindsight, *Hair* will be here tomorrow and the day after — no longer a nudity-as-novelty circus of freaks but an assured American classic.

Playboy, June 1979

POSTSCRIPT: *That* Hair *was not the huge success its admirers expected it to be was always amazing. In retrospect, I think 1979 was too early for '60s nostalgia to have an effect on the public. When I was teaching at St. John's University (a course in appreciating cinema) during the early 1980s, I would* *invariably arrange a screening of* Hair *for my students, who were invariably amazed. "Where has this movie* been?" *they asked. "Why haven't we ever heard of it?" Well, I suspect they hadn't heard of it because it had died an undeserved death. Looking back at it, always fondly (and because of teaching, for one thing, I have seen it a number of times), I always remember one glaring error or misstatement in my review: I encountered Treat Williams for the first time at an opening party for the film, and he said he'd been looking for me, to tell me that Treat is not a made-up actor's name, as I took for granted, but his very own — a common early American monicker. I stood and stand corrected.*

Interesting that the talented Forman has continued, with varying degrees of success, to make movies based on well-known books, from Ragtime *(nice, in my view) to* Valmont *(Liaisons Dangereuses lukewarmed over). But he never so improved on the original work as he had in adapting* Hair. *Maybe it is better to start with less brilliant material — sheer showbiz like* Hair. —B.W.

January 1990

PENNIES FROM HEAVEN

Pauline Kael

Directed by Herbert Ross. Written by Dennis Potter from his six-part BBC-TV miniseries. Starring Steve Martin and Bernadette Peters. **MGM/UA Home Video.**

Pennies from Heaven is the most emotional movie musical I've ever seen. It's a stylized mythology of the Depression which uses the popular songs of the period as expressions of people's deepest longings — for sex, for romance, for money, for a high good time. When the characters can't say how they feel, they evoke the songs: they open their mouths, and the voices on hit records of the thirties come out of them. And as they lip-sync the lyrics their obsessed eyes are burning bright. Their souls are in those voices, and they see themselves dancing just like the stars in movie musicals.

Visually, the film is a tarnished romance. The sets are stylized — not just the sets for the dance numbers but also the Chicago streets and stores, the movie houses, the diners and dives, which are designed in bold, formal compositions, for a heightened melancholy. This is our communal vision of the Depression, based on images handed down to us: motionless streets and buildings, with lonely figures in clear, cold light. The film actually re-creates paintings and photographs that are essences of America. There's a breathtaking re-creation of Edward Hopper's *Nighthawks* coffee shop, and it's held for just the right length of time. There's Hopper's interior of a movie house with a woman usher leaning against the wall, and there are bleary faces and purplish red-light-district scenes by Reginald Marsh, and thirties photographs of desolation, such as a dark flivver parked in front of a plain white clapboard house. These images blend in and breathe with the other shots. The whole movie seems a distillation of that forlorn, heavily shadowed period, while the songs express people's most fervent shallow hopes. When the hero, Arthur, a sheet-music salesman, a big talker just smart enough to get himself into trouble, goes on his selling trips, from Chicago to Galena, in 1934, the land is flat and deserted, with almost nothing moving but his little car chugging along the road.

As Arthur, Steve Martin has light-brown hair cut short, and when he calls up a song he has an expression of eagerness and awe that transforms him. You forget Steve Martin the TV entertainer, with his zany catch phrases and his disconnected nonchalance. Steve Martin seems to have forgotten him, too. He has a wild-eyed intensity here that draws you right into Arthur's desperation and his lies. Arthur believes the words of the songs, and he tries to get to the dream world they describe. At home in Chicago, he pleads with his wife for a little sex: he mimes a love song — "I'll Never Have to Dream Again" — and Connee Boswell's voice comes out of him. It's our first exposure to the film's device, and though we're meant to laugh or grin, Connee Boswell is saying something for Arthur that his petite and pie-faced wife, Joan (Jessica Harper), refuses to hear, and the mixture of comedy and poignancy is affecting in a somewhat delirious way. Joan cringes at Arthur's touch; she thinks his attempts to make love to her are evidence of a horrible, sullying perversion. Then, in the little town of Galena, when he's in a music store trying to get an order, a shy schoolteacher, Eileen (Bernadette Peters) walks in; Arthur mimes Bing Crosby singing "Did You Ever See a Dream Walking?" and Eileen dances to the music, and the two of them form romantic thirties-movie-star silhouettes in his mind. Eileen is pale and gentle, a brown-eyed blonde with soft curls — tendrils, really. She looks malleable, like the young Janet Gaynor. Eileen lives in a song world, too, and she's eager to believe Arthur's lie that he isn't married. She also has a spicy, wanton side; she turns into a Kewpie doll when she mimes Helen Kane's boop-boop-a-doops in "I Want to Be Bad." She has everything that Arthur wants, except money. As the story develops, it's so familiar it's archetypal; it's a manic-depressive libretto. Alfred Kazin has written about the passion of "a period — the thirties — that has had no rival since for widespread pain and sudden hope." That's what this black-humor musical, which Dennis Potter adapted from his six-segment BBC mini-series, is about.

The lip-syncing idea works wonderfully; it's in the dialogue interludes that the movie gets off on the wrong foot. Most of these scenes need to be played faster — to be snappier and more hyperbolic, with little curlicues of irony in the performances to point things up. For example, we see a gigantic billboard showing Carole Lombard with a huge black eye in Faith Baldwin's *Love Before Breakfast*. (It's the same billboard poster that appears in a famous photograph by Walker Evans, taken in Atlanta in 1936.) A little while later, with the Lombard poster looking on, a love-starved man grabs a blind girl, and when we next see her, dead, she has a black eye. The director, Herbert Ross, plays it straight, and so instead of being bizarrely, horribly funny it's peculiar. Black humor played too slow *is* peculiar; it may seem that the misery level is rising awfully high. Ross's deliberate pace makes the film's tone uncertain. Sometimes he doesn't go all the way with a shocking joke, or he muffles it, so the audience doesn't get the release of laughter. There's so little movement during the dialogue that the characters seem numbed out, and the audience's confidence in the film is strained — the discomfort of some of the viewers is palpable. I think our emotions get jammed up. Yet the scenes in themselves — even those that are awkwardly paced and almost static — still have a rapt, gripping quality. And even when a scene cries out for a spin, a further twist of artifice, the actors carry the day. Bernadette Peters has ironic curlicues built in, and her exaggerated Queens diction (which is certainly eccentric for an Illinois girl) gives her her own cheeping-chicky sound.

Besides Arthur and Joan and that heavenly angel cake Eileen, there are two other major characters. Vernel Bagneris (the director and star of the long-running show *One Mo' Time*) plays a homeless, stuttering street musician and beggar, the Accordion Man, whom Arthur picks up on the road, and it's Bagneris who mimes the title song. The version he lip-syncs isn't the happy-go-lucky Crosby version from the totally unrelated 1936 film that was also called *Pennies from Heaven;* it's that of Arthur Tracy, which is much darker and much more potent. The sorrow of the Depression and the hoping beyond hope are concentrated in this song and in the Accordion Man himself. Arthur Tracy's wrenching voice — it has tears and anguish in it — comes pouring out of the stuttering simpleton, and, as if the song had freed him, the Accordion Man dances, sensually, easily. With a photo-collage of the Depression behind him and a shower of shimmering gold raining down on him, he stretches and struts. I never thought I'd go around with the song "Pennies from Heaven" pulsating in my skull, but the combination of Arthur Tracy and Vernel Bagneris is voluptuously masochistic. Popular singers in the thirties brought out the meaning of a lyric as fully as possible, and the original recordings, which are used here, have the true sound of the period. (The bridges between these old arrangements and the dances — and the dance sequences themselves — are said to have been orchestrated "using antique recording equipment" to preserve the thirties sound; however it was accomplished, the result is worth the effort.) Where the movie misses is in the timing of the contrapuntal gags: after the Accordion Man has had his shimmering-gold epiphany, Arthur, feeling like a real sport, hands him a quarter. Ross somehow buries the connection, the shock. Everything in the material is double-edged; it's conceived in terms of extremes — the melodrama and the pathos on one side and the dream world on the other. Normal life is excluded. But the director keeps trying to sneak it back in; he treats the piled-on sentimental gloom tenderly, as if it were meant to be real life. (Would he be this afraid of the cruel jokes in *The Threepenny Opera?*)

The other major character — almost as much transformed as Steve Martin — is Christopher Walken, with dark, slicked-down hair. As Tom the pimp, who puts Eileen on the street, he has the patent-leather lounge-lizard look of a silent-movie wolf, and his scenes play like greasy magic. In his first movie musical, Walken, who used to dance on Broadway, has more heat and athletic energy than he has shown in his straight acting roles. He has never been quite all there on the screen; he has looked drained or packed in ice. (That's what made him so effective as the chief mercenary in *The Dogs of War* — that, and the tense way he walked in New York, like an animal pacing a cage.) Here, there's sensuality in his cartooned apathy, and when he first spots Eileen his eyeballs seem to pop out on springs. In a mock striptease in a saloon, he shows how powerfully built he is, and he's a real hoofer. He takes the screen in a way he never has before — by force, and with lewd amusement, particularly when he bares a grotesque valentine tattoo on his chest.

There hasn't been this much tap dancing in a movie musical in many years. Arthur does a derby-and-plaid-suit vaudeville routine with two other salesmen, who are played by Tommy Rall (best known to moviegoers as Ann Miller's partner in the 1953 *Kiss Me, Kate*) and spaghetti-legged Robert Fitch (best known to theatregoers as the original Rooster in *Annie*). It's a fast, showy number — to the Dorsey Brothers Orchestra's playing and the Boswell Sisters' singing "It's the Girl" — and the three men have wonderfully frilly gestures as they curve and sway to imitate femininity, and use their hands to model their dream girls' shapes in the air. Steve Martin doesn't slow his celebrated partners down; he's spectacular — he really is Steve (Happy Feet) Martin. In the film's most startling sequence, set inside the Hopper movie theatre with the weary blond usher, Arthur and Eileen sit watching *Follow the Fleet*. Arthur is transfixed, and as Astaire sings "Let's Face the Music and Dance" Arthur begins singing, too. He goes up on the stage, and Eileen joins him — two tiny, sharply edged figures in deep, rich color against the huge black-and-white screen images of Astaire and Rogers dancing, and they really seem to be there. They dance along with the stars on the screen, and then the two minuscule figures shift into black-and-white, and take over. Arthur is in tails, Eileen in a copy of Ginger's glittering gown with its loose fur cowl. And a chorus line of men in tails appears, tapping, like the men in *Top Hat*. It makes you gasp. Do Steve Martin and Bernadette Peters really dare to put themselves in Astaire and Rogers' place? Yet they carry it off. You may still be gasping when Arthur and Eileen leave the theatre (the exterior is a Reginald Marsh) and hear newsboys shouting the headlines. The police are looking for Arthur.

Herbert Ross has never shown much audacity in his other screen work, and when a director has been as successful as Ross has been with bland muck (*The Sunshine Boys, The Turning Point, The Goodbye Girl*), and has even been honored for it, it certainly takes something special to make him plunge in. Ross didn't go in far enough, but this is still quite a plunge. Dennis Potter's idea — obvious, yet strange, and with a pungency — provided the chance of a lifetime; Ross's collaborators must have felt it, too, and possibly they came up with ideas he couldn't resist. He had a superlative team. The production designer was Ken Adam, who designed the eight most imaginative James

Bond pictures and also *Dr. Strangelove, Barry Lyndon,* and *The Seven-Per-Cent Solution.* The film's greatest splendors are those re-created visions — particularly the coffee shop with Arthur and Eileen as nighthawks, and Jimmy's Diner, which has a sliding glass wall, so that the Accordion Man can slip out into the rain to dance. Among its more obvious splendors is an Art Deco Chicago bank in which Arthur, who has tried to get a loan to open his own music shop and been turned down, dreams that he's deluged with money: to the music of "Yes, Yes!" performed by Sam Browne and the Carlyle Cousins, he and the banker (the matchless Jay Garner) and a batch of chorines perform in a dance montage that suggests the harebrained variations of Busby Berkeley montages.

The choreographer, Danny Daniels, does each number in a different theatrical style, and he palpably loves the styles that he reworks, especially the lowdown, off-color ones, like Walken's "dirty" sandwich dance — he's wedged between two blowzy whores. With the exception of a few routines with chorus girls as Rockette-style automatons, Daniels' choreography isn't simply dance — it's gag comedy, in which each dancer has his own comic personality. The dances are funny, amazing, and beautiful all at once. There are no problems of pacing here (except that a few numbers are too short and feel truncated). Several of them are just about perfection. And with teasers — comedy bits that prick the imagination. Bernadette Peters has a big production number ("Love Is Good for Anything That Ails You") that's like a dance of deliverance. Her classroom is transformed into something palatial and white, with children tapping on the tops of miniature grand pianos, and with her in silver and white, shimmying down the center aisle. (All the costumes are by Bob Mackie.) And when Arthur dreams of himself as a happy man, settled down with both Joan and Eileen, the three of them mouth "Life Is Just a Bowl of Cherries," like a radio trio. It's an indication of the depth of Jessica Harper's performance as the little witch Joan, shrivelled by repression and hatred, that it takes a second to recognize her as the pretty brunette in the trio.

The cinematographer, Gordon Willis, provides the lighting to carry out Ken Adam's visual ideas, and it's different from anything that I can remember Willis's ever doing before. The movie is about ordinary experience in a blazing, heightened form, and Willis keeps the level of visual intensity phenomenally high. At times, the color recalls the vivid, saturated tones in the 1954 *A Star Is Born:* the images are lustrous, and are often focussed on the pinpoint of light in the dreamer-characters' eyes when they envisage the pleasures celebrated in the songs. Eileen's eyes switch on and off, and so do the Accordion Man's; Arthur is possessed by the dream — his eyes are always on. My eyes were always on, too: even when I wanted to close up the pauses between the actors' lines, there was never a second when I wasn't fascinated by what was happening on the screen.

Despite its use of Brechtian devices, *Pennies from Heaven* doesn't allow you to distance yourself. You're thrust into the characters' emotional extremes; you're right in front of the light that's shining from their eyes. And you see the hell they go through for sex and money. Arthur, the common man with an itch, will do just about anything. When he blurts out something about his wife to Eileen, he covers his traces blubbering about how horribly she died in an accident, and then uses the invented tragedy to soften up Eileen so he can hop on top of her. He's a bastard, but you're not alienated from him; the songs lead him by the nose. As it turns out, the one character whose dream comes true is the pinched and proper Joan, who has dreamed of taking revenge on Arthur for his sexual demands on her.

There are cruel, rude awakenings; maybe they should be more heartlessly tonic, more bracing. But they do give you a pang. When Eileen is happily dreaming away in her classroom, seeing it as a tap dancers' paradise, with the children tapping and playing musical instruments, the principal comes in, enraged by the noise that the kids are making, and he takes a ruler and smacks the hands of a fat boy — a boy who has been proudly blowing on a tuba in her dream. The injustice to the boy — the humiliation — is one of those wrongs that some people are singled out for. The boy is fat, Arthur is horny, Eileen is gullible, the Accordion Man is inarticulate. This double-edged movie supplies a simple, basic rationale for popular entertainment. It says that though dreamers may be punished for having been carried away, they've had some glorious dreams. But it also says that the emotions of the songs can't be realized in life.

There's something new going on — something thrilling — when the characters in a musical are archetypes yet are intensely alive. This is the first big musical that M-G-M has produced on its lot in over a decade. The star, Steve Martin, doesn't flatter the audience for being hip; he gives an almost incredibly controlled performance, and Bernadette Peters is mysteriously right in every nuance. Herbert Ross and Ken Adam and Danny Daniels and Gordon Willis and Bob Mackie and the whole cast worked at their highest capacities — perhaps were even inspired to exceed them. They all took chances. Do you remember what Wagner said to the audience after the première of *Götterdäm-merung?* "Now you have seen what we can do. Now want it! And if you do, we will achieve an art." I am not comparing *Pennies from Heaven* with *Götterdämmerung.* But this picture shows that the talent to make great movie musicals is out there, waiting.

The New Yorker, December 21, 1981

SIGN O' THE TIMES

Terrence Rafferty

Directed by Prince. Starring Prince and Sheila E. **MCA Home Video.**

This is by far the most entertaining of Prince's movies, because it's the simplest — just Prince and his wonderful band, in concert, playing a dozen or so numbers and dancing as dirty as they can. There's more than enough to look at and listen to: the stage set, a riotous neon cityscape, is always teeming with strange people (even when Prince is alone on it); the costumes range from bizarre to inconceivable; and the music is mercurial rock-jazz-funk-soul-folk, a roomful of styles all rubbing provocatively against each other. So we don't much mind that the direction (by Prince) is banal — lots of fast cutting and colored smoke — or that brief "allegorical" sequences occasionally deaden the spaces between the songs. Or even that the concert, filmed on Prince's 1987 European tour, ends with the heavy, messagey "The Cross," which puts a bit of a damper on the irresponsible fun of the previous eighty minutes. If the movie were less trashy and thrown together, if its taste were less erratic, it wouldn't represent its subject nearly so well. As an added attraction, the band includes percussionist Sheila E., who manages to look ravishing even surrounded by her massive drum kit; and when she steps out to the front of the stage, revealing her long, perfect legs . . . Well, she's a terrific musician, too. One number, "U Got the Look," while also part of Prince's live show, is actually a music video directed by David Hogan.

The New Yorker, December 7, 1987

UNDER THE CHERRY MOON

★

J. Hoberman

Directed by Prince. Written by Becky Johnston. Starring Prince, Jerome Benton, and Kristin Scott-Thomas. **Warner Home Video.**

There hasn't been a Hollywood comedy with an attitude like *Under the Cherry Moon*'s since *I'm No Angel,* and the bluenoses are already rising to the bait. The flaming creature who calls himself Prince may be the wittiest heterosexual clown since Mae West; black as well as campy, he's even more threatening.

Where *Purple Rain* was angst-ridden psychodrama, *Under the Cherry Moon* is revisionist Astaire-Rogers; it has the engraved titles and, thanks to cameraman Michael Ballhaus, the elegant black and white cinematography of a Woody Allen film. Prince and his crony Jerome Benton—Morris Day's sidekick in *Purple Rain*—play Christopher and Tricky, a pair of hustlers (from Miami, no less) living it up on the French Riviera, which Ballhaus succeeds in rendering as something like the world's largest outdoor disco.

In *Purple Rain,* Prince's off-stage persona was diffident and paranoid—the tormented Romantic genius as a postmodern James Brown. Here he's just a gigolo, primping and preening with outrageous self-regard, the supremely confident high priest of his personal Dionysian cult. The eye-batting, cheek-sucking gusto with which this pint-sized satyr revels in sleazoid stereotypes (pimp, dirtymouth, drag queen, lounge lizard) is almost *Cherry Moon*'s best running gag. The best one, though, is how seriously the naughty boy pretends to take himself. In

Prince followed his smash movie-star debut, *Purple Rain*, with his first film as a director, *Under the Cherry Moon*, and next made the sizzling concert movie, *Sign o' the Times*. (Photo © 1986 Warner Bros. Inc. All rights reserved.)

lieu of a business card Prince leaves one of his customers a note on her pillow, "Call me, Christopher," signed with a smile face. With deadpan bravura (somewhat undermined by a chorus of mildly discordant violins), Christopher declaims his poetry: "Life is a parade . . ."

Be that as it may, *Under the Cherry Moon* is a highly enjoyable circus of set-pieces. A Eurotrash garden party populated by old money-bags, depraved rich kids ("We have Porsche. We have cable. How about it, baby?"), and elephants isn't close to complete until Prince crashes it, wearing a bare-midriff, brocaded black bolero ensemble. The star took over the film's direction (from Mary Lambert, author of Madonna's *Material Girl* video) a week into the shooting and, all things considered, he did an extremely credible job. The script, by Becky Johnston (the first of the super-8 filmmakers associated with the old New Cinema on St. Marks Place to successfully go Hollywood), is as purposefully flimsy as *Flying Down to Rio* or *The Gay Divorcee* and no less surreal. "Once upon a time in the Bronx . . ." the film opens and bang-o, there's Prince in spangled turban, playing piano for some society dame, his eyes strafing her cleavage while Tricky passes him a series of wholly gratuitous handwritten instructions.

A gung ho second banana, Jerome Benton plays a streetsmart Edward Everett Horton to Prince's dissolute Fred Astaire. In keeping with the film's '30s ambience, Benton's broad clowning has startling intimations of Mantan Moreland or Eddie "Rochester" Anderson, but with a difference—you'd never catch Rochester leading a conga line of jetset swells. The happy-go-lucky Tricky is supposedly no less sexually irresistible than "sensitive" Christopher. (He leaves the garden party with his fists full of banknotes.) In some respects, Benton's is an even more cathartic performance than Prince's.

Christopher and Tricky (just the juxtaposition of the names cracks me up) are as de facto desecratory as the Marx Brothers in their *Monkey Business* prime. The whole film is predicated on the hilarious intrusion of their b-boy shenanigans into an environment of Marienbad-like gentility. The pair revel in black street jive (*Under the Cherry Moon* should make "wrecka stow" a household phrase) and flaunt the homoerotic subtext to their relationship—some of the film's funniest bits are predicated on their eye-rolling, lip-pursing, nostril-flaring confrontations. Once you get on Prince's wavelength, *Under the Cherry Moon* is disarmingly dopey. (If you show up wrecked for this film, you'll think you've dreamt it.)

Much of *Cherry Moon*'s giddy energy derives from its relentless goofing on the white Euro-world, including, of course, its females. Prince doesn't do himself any favors by rejecting an older black woman, but I suspect that critics who creamed over the chaste interracial romance in *Mona Lisa* will have a harder time here—regardless of the reasons they give. Steven Berkoff, the billionaire villain of the film, "is put off by seeing his lovely daughter in the arms of this peculiar young man, as what sane father would not be," Walter Goodman harangued the readers of the *New York Times,* ridiculously unaware that offensiveness to the Walter Goodmans of the world has much to do with the source of Prince's appeal. (Indeed, Prince seemed to throw Goodman into a fullscale heterosexual panic: "Asking the audience to believe [the film's women] would have anything to do with a self-caressing twerp of dubious provenance [like Prince] asks rather too much. More convincing is his affection for Jerome.")

I don't think I'd trust a revolution led by royalty (any more than a working-class hero they call "the Boss") but, as current pop goes, Prince is radically subversive. What Goodman snidely hints is unmanly is more exactly Prince's androgynous hedonism. He's the imp of the polymorphous perverse. Just as West scandalized the Hays Office by taking male sexual prerogatives for her own, Prince performs his own particular gender blur in eschewing the power associated with masculinity for feminine vanity and seductiveness. Yet, as with West, his campiness masks a pagan worship of sex. Anyone who doubts the serious heat of Prince's love scenes should study his hands in the clinch or, more to the point, watch what he does with his partner's hands.

Prince's fun is infectious, but, unfortunately, *Under the Cherry Moon* is weakest where one would logically expect it to be invincible. It's not just that, "Kiss" aside, the score isn't nearly as strong as *Purple Rain*'s. What's truly bizarre is that, given the film's evocation of the '30s musical, Prince restricts himself to two production numbers, one of them (a delirious vision of Christopher's ascension into heaven) thrown away under the final credits. This is virtually the only touch of restraint in the whole film; it's wild that so dogged a lover as Prince would so totally misjudge the libidinal economy of the movies. In that respect, *Cherry Moon* is a tease—all talk and no dancing. Perhaps Prince took *Purple Rain*'s reviews too seriously and wanted to show he could hold a film simply with the force of his personality. If so, he's won a pyrrhic victory.

In the end, Prince even goes so far as to equate Christopher with Christ—they're buddies, like Chris and Tricky. (According to my colleague Stanley Crouch, "dying and going to heaven" is a venerable Afro-American expression for making it with a white woman—thus the film's "tragic" climax may be less blissfully self-indulgent than it seems.) Prince is the complete narcissist. What makes his egomania bearable is his sense of humor, as well as his generosity toward other performers. He gave Morris Day the chance to walk off with *Purple Rain*, and he does the same with Jerome Benton here.

As Mary, the appropriately lovely object of his affections, British actress Kristin Scott-Thomas has ample opportunity to establish her comic credentials. It's Scott-Thomas's first movie and she makes an impressive debut, standing up to two of the most shameless scenerychewers of the season. (Three, if you count Berkoff.) But the bottom line is that when Christopher and Mary finally make love in some candlelit grotto, he appears to be naked while she keeps her clothes on. There's one way our auteur won't be upstaged. In *Under the Cherry Moon,* he's the prince *and* the showgirl.

Village Voice, July 15, 1986

ABOUT THE CONTRIBUTORS

David Ansen is a movie critic and senior writer at *Newsweek*. He is also the movie critic for AP Radio. He was formerly the movie critic at *The Real Paper*.

Jonathan Baumbach is a novelist and film critic. His tenth work of fiction, *Separate Hours,* was published in 1990.

Sheila Benson is the *Los Angeles Times* film critic.

Joy Gould Boyum currently reviews movies for *US* magazine. She has been the film critic for *The Wall Street Journal,* National Public Radio's "All Things Considered," and *Glamour* magazine. She teaches literature, film, and media at New York University, where she is a professor of Communication Arts. She is the author of *Double Exposure: Fiction into Film.*

Jay Carr is *The Boston Globe*'s film critic. He was previously the theater and music critic for the *Detroit News* and won the 1971–72 George Jean Nathan Award for Dramatic Criticism.

Charles Champlin is Arts Editor and Critic at Large columnist of the *Los Angeles Times*. He was also the paper's principal film critic from 1967 to 1980.

Judith Crist, an adjunct professor at Columbia University, began her career in film criticism at the *New York Herald Tribune* and has reviewed movies for a variety of publications and on television. She is the author of *The Private Eye, The Cowboy and the Very Naked Girl, Judith Crist's TV Guide to the Movies,* and *Take 22: Moviemakers on Moviemaking.*

David Denby is film critic of *New York* magazine and writes the "Rear Window" column for *Premiere.* His articles and reviews have also appeared in *The New Republic, The Atlantic,* and *The New York Review of Books.*

Roger Ebert is the syndicated film critic of the *Chicago Sun-Times* and co-host of the "Siskel & Ebert" television show. He is the author of *Roger Ebert's Movie Home Companion* and *Two Weeks in the Midday Sun: A Cannes Notebook.* He won the 1975 Pulitzer Prize for criticism.

David Edelstein is a film critic for the *New York Post.* He was for five years a film critic for the *Village Voice.* He also writes about beer.

Owen Gleiberman is the movie critic for *Entertainment Weekly.* He reviewed movies for *The Boston Phoenix* from 1981 to 1989. He has also written for *Premiere* and is heard on National Public Radio's "Fresh Air."

Hal Hinson is a film critic for *The Washington Post.*

J. Hoberman has reviewed movies for the *Village Voice* since 1978. He is a contributing writer to *Premiere* and has a regular column in *Artforum.* He is the co-author (with Jonathan Rosenbaum) of *Midnight Movies* and the author of *Between Two Worlds,* a history of the Yiddish-language cinema to be published by the Museum of Modern Art in 1991.

Richard T. Jameson is currently film critic for *Pacific Northwest* (Seattle). He edited the Seattle Film Society's journal, *Movietone News,* from 1971 to 1981, and became the editor of *Film Comment* in January 1990.

Pauline Kael began reviewing movies for *The New Yorker* in 1967. Since then, her work has been compiled in *Going Steady, Deeper into Movies* (National Book Award winner, 1973), *Reeling, When the Lights Go Down, 5001 Nights at the Movies, Taking It All In, State of the Art,* and *Hooked.* Her first two collections, *I Lost It at the Movies* and *Kiss Kiss Bang Bang,* include essays and reviews written for *Partisan Review, Sight and Sound, Film Quarterly,* and *The Atlantic,* as well as *The New Yorker. The Citizen Kane Book* contains her long essay "Raising Kane," and she also wrote the introduction to *Three Screen Comedies by Samson Raphaelson.*

Dave Kehr has been the movie critic of the *Chicago Tribune* since 1986. From 1975 to 1986, he was the movie critic of the *Chicago Reader.*

Terrence Rafferty reviews books and films for *The New Yorker*. His movie writing has also appeared in *The Nation, Sight and Sound, The Atlantic, The Threepenny Review,* and *Film Quarterly*.

Peter Rainer, the current chairman of the National Society of Film Critics, writes film criticism and commentary for the *Los Angeles Times* and writes regularly on film for *Connoisseur* magazine and *American Film*. From 1981 until its demise in 1989, he was film critic for the *Los Angeles Herald Examiner*. Rainer's writing has also appeared in *The New York Times Magazine, Vogue, GQ, Newsday, Premiere,* and *Mademoiselle,* where he was film critic from 1974 to 1984. Rainer has appeared as a film commentator on such television shows as "Nightline," "ABC World News Tonight," and "CBS Morning News." He has also taught film criticism at the USC Graduate Film School.

Carrie Rickey is a film critic for *The Philadelphia Inquirer*. She was previously the film critic for the *Boston Herald-American*. She is a contributing editor to *Fame* and has also written on art and movies for the *Village Voice*.

Jonathan Rosenbaum has written for over 50 periodicals, including the *Chicago Reader* (where he has been film critic since 1987), *Cahiers du Cinema, Elle, Film Comment, Sight and Sound,* and *Tikkun*. His books include *Moving Places: A Life at the Movies, Film: The Front Line 1983,* and, as editor, Orson Welles's *The Big Brass Ring* and *The Cradle Will Rock*.

Julie Salamon is the film critic for *The Wall Street Journal* and author of the novel *White Lies*.

Richard Schickel has reviewed movies for *Time* magazine since 1972; before that he was *Life*'s film critic. He is the author of many books, most notably *The Disney Version, His Picture in the Papers, D. W. Griffith: An American Life, Intimate Strangers: The Culture of Celebrity,* and *Schickel on Film*. He has just finished a study of Marlon Brando's film career, which will be published in 1990. He is also a producer-writer-director of television documentaries, the latest of which, *Gary Cooper: American Life, American Legend,* appeared last fall on TNT. He has held a Guggenheim Fellowship and has won the British Film Institute book prize.

Stephen Schiff is critic-at-large of *Vanity Fair* and a film critic on National Public Radio. A former correspondent on CBS-TV's "West 57th," and a Pulitzer Prize finalist in 1983, he has written film criticism for *The Atlantic*, the *Boston Phoenix*, *Film Comment*, *Glamour*, and *American Film*.

Henry Sheehan is the film critic for the *L.A. Reader*.

Michael Sragow has been the movie critic of the *San Francisco Examiner* since 1985. He was previously movie critic for the *Boston Phoenix*, the *Los Angeles Herald Examiner*, and *Rolling Stone* magazine. His book, television, and movie criticism has appeared in *Esquire*, *The Atlantic*, *Mother Jones*, *Harper's*, *The Nation*, *The New Republic*, *New York* magazine, *Film Comment*, *American Film*, and *Sight and Sound*.

Kevin Thomas has reviewed movies for the *Los Angeles Times* since 1962. A fourth-generation California newspaperman and native Angeleno, he was named a Chevalier in France's Order of Arts and Letters for his "contributions to French cinema."

Peter Travers is the film critic for *Rolling Stone* magazine.

Kenneth Turan writes on film and other topics for *Buzz* magazine. He has been a staff writer for *The Washington Post* and *TV Guide*, and film critic for GQ and National Public Radio's "All Things Considered." He is the co-author of *Call Me Anna: The Autobiography of Patty Duke*. He is on the board of directors of the National Yiddish Book Center.

Armond White is the film critic and arts editor of the Brooklyn-based weekly, the *City Sun*.

Bruce Williamson has been *Playboy*'s movie critic (and a contributing editor there) for more than two decades. He was movie critic at *Time* magazine from 1963 to 1967 and for a brief period was a movie-media critic for *Life*.

Michael Wilmington is a movie reviewer for the *Los Angeles Times*, contributing editor and movie reviewer for *Isthmus* (Madison, Wisconsin), and a contributing editor and video critic for *L.A. Style*. He was previously film critic of the *L.A. Weekly.* His criticism has also appeared in *Film Comment, Film Quarterly, Sight and Sound,* and *Movieline.* He is the co-author (with Joseph McBride) of *John Ford.* He has won four Milwaukee Press Club awards for reviews in *Isthmus.*

PERMISSIONS

Grateful acknowledgment is made to the following for permission to reprint copyrighted material:

David Ansen: for his review of *Hearts of the West* (*The Real Paper*, November 21, 1975).

The Boston Globe: for Jay Carr's reviews of *Heart Like a Wheel* (March 9, 1984); *Dreamchild* (January 31, 1986); and *The Dead* (January 15, 1988). Reprinted courtesy of The Boston Globe.

Boston Herald: for Carrie Rickey's review of *Repo Man* (July 6, 1984). Reprinted with permission of the *Boston Herald*.

Boston Phoenix: for David Denby's review of *The Late Show* (March 8, 1977); for Stephen Schiff's reviews of *The Brood* (January 15, 1980), *Best Boy* (April 29, 1980), *The Chant of Jimmie Blacksmith* (October 14, 1980), *Diner* (April 20, 1982), and *By Design* (October 19, 1982); for Michael Sragow's review of *Under Fire* (October 25, 1983); and for Owen Gleiberman's reviews of *The Lonely Passion of Judith Hearne* (January 29, 1988) and *The Last Temptation of Christ* (August 19, 1988).

Joy Gould Boyum: for her reviews of *The White Dawn* (July 29, 1974) and *The Conversation* (April 14, 1974), which originally appeared in *The Wall Street Journal*.

Chicago Reader: for Dave Kehr's reviews of *Love Streams* (September 28, 1984), *Lost in America* (March 15, 1985), and *After Hours* (October 11, 1985); and for Jonathan Rosenbaum's reviews of *Housekeeping* (January 22, 1988) and *Parents* (April 7, 1989).

Judith Crist: for her reviews of *The Long Goodbye* (*New York* magazine, October 29, 1973), *Buffalo Bill and the Indians* (*Saturday Review,* July 10, 1976), and *Bound for Glory* (*Playgirl,* February 1977).

The Philadelphia Inquirer: for Carrie Rickey's reviews of *I've Heard the Mermaids Singing* (October 7, 1987) and *High Tide* (July 8, 1988) from *The Philadelphia Inquirer.* Used by permission.

Playboy: for Bruce Williamson's reviews of *The Last American Hero* (October 1973), *Hair* (June 1979), and *F/X* (May 1986). Reprinted with permission.

Terrence Rafferty: for his *New Yorker* reviews of *Sign o' the Times* (December 7, 1987) and *Carnival of Souls* (September 4, 1989), and his essays from *The Atlantic* on *Comfort and Joy* (November 1984) and the animated art of the Brothers Quay ("Twin Cinema," June 1987).

Rolling Stone: for Michael Sragow's reviews of *All Night Long* (April 2, 1981), *Blow Out* (September 3, 1981), and *Southern Comfort* (October 29, 1981), all copyright © Straight Arrow Publishers, Inc., 1981, all rights reserved; and of *Personal Best* (April 1, 1982), copyright © Straight Arrow Publishers, Inc., 1982, all rights reserved; and for Peter Travers's review of *Henry: Portrait of a Serial Killer* (March 8, 1990), copyright © Straight Arrow Publishers, Inc., 1990, all rights reserved. Used by permission.

Julie Salamon: for her *Wall Street Journal* review of *Lodz Ghetto* (March 23, 1989).

Richard Schickel: for his review of *The Ballad of Cable Hogue,* which originally appeared in *Life* (March 27, 1970).

Henry Sheehan: for his *L.A. Reader* review of *Near Dark* (October 9, 1987).

Time: for Richard Schickel's reviews of *Go Tell the Spartans* (September 25, 1978), *Handle with Care* (November 7, 1977), *The Man with Two Brains* (June 20, 1983), and *Smash Palace* (May 17, 1982). Copyright 1978, 1977, 1983, and 1982, respectively, Time Inc. Reprinted by permission.

Kenneth Turan: for his *New West/California* magazine reviews of *The Stunt Man* (September 1980) and *Chilly Scenes of Winter* (November 1982).

University of California Press: for Terrence Rafferty's review of *Barbarosa*, from the Winter 1982 issue of *Film Quarterly*, Vol. 36, No. 2, copyright © 1982 by the Regents of the University of California.

Village Voice: for J. Hoberman's reviews of *The Company of Wolves* (April 30, 1985), *Smorgasbord* (May 21, 1985), and *Under the Cherry Moon* (July 15, 1986); and for David Edelstein's reviews of *The Stepfather* (March 3, 1987), *Weeds* (November 3, 1987), and *Thy Kingdom Come, Thy Will Be Done* (March 1, 1988).

The Washington Post: for Hal Hinson's reviews of *Hamburger Hill* (August 28, 1987), *The Good Mother* (November 4, 1988), *The Dressmaker* (February 10, 1989), and *The Adventures of Baron Munchausen* (March 24, 1989), copyright © *The Washington Post*.

Armond White: for his *City Sun* review of *Distant Voices, Still Lives* (August 30–September 5, 1989).

Michael Wilmington: for his *Los Angeles Times* reviews of *Danny Boy* (June 20, 1985), *The Best of Times* (January 30, 1986), and *Salvador* (April 10, 1986).

Thanks go to Capitol Entertainment; Island Pictures; Michael Finnegan of Warner Home Video and Judith Singer of Warner Bros.; Nancy Cushing-Jones's office at MCA Publishing; Fritz Friedman of RCA/Columbia Pictures Home Video; Jeff Lipsky of Skouras Pictures; Jean-Claude Tramont; Richard Rush; Mae Woods; Anne Talltree of the Screen Actors Guild; Lamont Johnson; Neil Hartley; Catherine Prager of Vestron Video; Alan Adelson; Jeff Diamond; Hollace Brown of Paramount Home Video; and Roxie Releasing for helping procure stills, or permission to reprint stills, or both, for this collection.

INDEX OF FILMS REVIEWED